Yone Noguchi
The Stream of Fate

Edward Marx

Volume Two
The Eastern Sea

2025

Yone Noguchi
The Stream of Fate
Volume Two
The Eastern Sea
By Edward Marx
First Edition
©2025 Botchan Books
www.botchanmedia.com
All rights reserved
ISBN: 978-1-939913-09-8 (Hardcover)
ISBN: 978-1-939913-10-4 (Paperback)
10 9 8 7 6 5 4 3

Contents

About the Text	xi
Kichō: Homecoming *1904–1905*	1
Glow of the Firefly *1905-1907*	51
Shadowy Roamers on the Holy Highway *1907-1910*	101
Imperial Japan *1910-1913*	143
Distinguished Lecturer *1913-1914*	177
Our Modern Minds *1914-1918*	234
Let the East Greet the West *1918-1921*	287
Illustrations	359

To the friends of Yone Noguchi
on his 150th birthday

About the Text

In this book Japanese names are given in English order (personal followed by family name), except for archaic names given in the traditional order, and bibliographical citations, which follow the order used in the publication. As in Japanese usage, writers and artists are sometimes referred to by their personal names. Long vowels in Japanese words are indicated by macrons (following modified Hepburn style) except where normally omitted in common English usage ("Tokyo" rather than "Tōkyō").

Non-standard English is generally retained in quotations, the use of "[*sic*]" being restricted to errors of typography, unintelligible text, and errors of fact.

Translations are my own unless otherwise indicated.

Illustration credits appear at the end of the volume. Acknowledgments appear at the end of Volume Three.

Abbreviations

The following are used for frequently-cited sources and names, in addition to standard abbreviations (such as UP for University Press and rpt. for "reprinted"):

ADA: [Yone Noguchi], *The American Diary of a Japanese Girl: An Annotated Edition*, ed. Edward Marx and Laura E. Franey (Philadelphia: Temple UP, 2007).

ASW: Isamu Noguchi, *A Sculptor's World* (New York: Harper & Row, 1968).

BP: Blanche Partington.

CEL: *Collected English Letters*, ed. Ikuko Atsumi (Tokyo: Yone Noguchi Society, 1975). Cited by letter number. Emended, where possible, after examination of the autograph materials.

CWS: Charles Warren Stoddard.

CWSP: Charles Warren Stoddard Papers, catalogued as *Collection of Charles Warren Stoddard Papers, 1867-1918*, BANC MSS C-H 53, Bancroft Library, U of California at Berkeley.

Dentō: *Dentō ni tsuite* [On Tradition] (Tokyo: Maki Shobō, 1943).

EE: *Early Essays*, ed. Edward Marx (Santa Barbara: Botchan, 2022).

Eibei: *Eibei no jūsan'nen* [Thirteen years in England and America] (Tokyo: Shunyōdō, 1905).

EMAP: Ethel Marie Armes Papers, Hoole Library, University of Alabama, Tuscaloosa.

FP: Frank Putnam.
FPL: Letters to Frank Putnam, catalogued as *Yoné Noguchi Letters and Ephemera, 1899-1921*, BANC MSS 82/130 z, Bancroft Library, U of California at Berkeley.
FSL: Letters to the Four Seas Company, catalogued as *Yone Noguchi letters, 1918-1923*, BANC MSS 78/125 z, Bancroft
FTES: *From the Eastern Sea* (London: Unicorn P, 1903).
Fūkei: *Watashi wa gendai fūkei o kiru* [I cut the modern scenery] (Tokyo: Shinchōsha, 1928).
HM: Huntington Library Manuscript Collection.
IN: Isamu Noguchi.
INF: Isamu Noguchi Foundation, New York, Research Collection.
JH: *Japanese Hokkus* (Boston: Four Seas, 1920).
JSL: Joaquin Miller and Yone Noguchi, *Japan of Sword and Love* (Tokyo: Kanao Bunyendo, 1905).
JT: *Japan Times*.
J&A: *Japan and America* (Tokyo: Keio UP; New York: Orientalia, 1921).
Kenkyū: Toyama Usaburō, ed., *Shijin Yone Noguchi Kenkyū*, 3 v. (Tokyo: Yone Noguchi Society, 1963-75).
Kichō: *Kichō no ki* [Homecoming chronicle] (Tokyo: Shunyōdō, 1904).
KM: Keio manuscripts, *Noguchi Yonejirō kankei shiryō*, Keio University Library Rare Book Room.
LG: Léonie Gilmour.
LG: Edward Marx, *Leonie Gilmour: When East Weds West* (Santa Barbara: Botchan, 2013).
LHJ: *Lafcadio Hearn in Japan* (London: E. Mathews, 1910).
LoC: Library of Congress.
NY: Noguchi Yonejirō.
Ōshū: *Ōshū bundan inshō ki* (Tokyo: Hakujitsusha, 1916).
Pilg.: *The Pilgrimage* (1909), 1 v. (Tokyo: Kyobunkwan P, 1912).
SC: *The Summer Cloud* (Tokyo: The Shunyodo, 1906).
SJA: *The Spirit of Japanese Art* (London: J. Murray, 1915).
SJP: *The Spirit of Japanese Poetry* (London: J. Murray, 1914).
S&U: *Seen and Unseen: Or, Monologues of a Homeless Snail* (San Francisco: Burgess & Garnett, 1897).
SS: *Short Stories*, ed. Edward Marx (Santa Barbara: Botchan, 2023).
SYN: *The Story of Yone Noguchi* (London: Chatto & Windus, 1914).
VV: *The Voice of the Valley*, Intro. Charles Warren Stoddard; ill. William Keith (San Francisco: Doxey, 1897).

TT: *Through the Torii* (London: E. Mathews, 1914).
YN: Yone Noguchi.
YNSoF1 *Yone Noguchi: The Stream of Fate, Volume 1: The Western Sea* (Santa Barbara: Botchan, 2019).
ZGP: Zona Gale Papers, State Historical Society of Wisconsin, Archives Division.

The Eastern Sea

Here in Japan we do not make an art of biography-writing; and I wish that such a modern fashion of the West may never invade our Japanese literature. And I think that English literature would be ten times better off without it too.

—"A Japanese Defence of Lafcadio Hearn"

1

Kichō: HOMECOMING

1904–1905

"It may be that I shall never see him again," Léonie Gilmour explained in a letter to her Bryn Mawr College friend, Catharine Bunnell. "I have a fancy as if he were a bird that flew through my room and is vanished." Léonie looked, at this stage, less like the Madonna of the Annunciation than the Madonna del Parto, Our Lady of Parturition. Though eight months pregnant with the child of Yone Noguchi, her relations with the Japanese poet had not thawed since their winter parting. After receiving his late August letter informing her of his departure for Japan, she had come to this new city of angels following her mother, both of them looking to make a new start. "I console myself—or try to—saying that I am more fortunate than other women who must see their lovers grow old, indifferent, and perhaps even commonplace, whereas mine will be ever young, and ever a poet."[1]

Léonie was unaware her poet was now betrothed to Ethel Armes in Birmingham, Alabama—as unaware as Ethel was of Léonie. In the house she shared with her mother and siblings on St. Charles Street, Ethel was busy managing Yone's literary affairs, typing his articles and sending them out to American periodicals, where they were now in considerable demand, as the Russo-Japanese War continued to dominate the news.

The surroundings of their house, at the base of Red Mountain, were picturesque. "Nowhere, perhaps, in the country is there a hill so marvelous and rich in color as this, for nowhere else is so much oxide of iron concentrated, this that gives the rare, strong tinges of violet and vermilion." The mining of the iron ore, which provided much of the city's livelihood, was, thankfully, hardly visible. "Every once in a while, a few dark straggling curls of smoke blow over the mountain's head like witches' hair. That is all that the world in the valley ever sees or knows of

1. LG to Catharine Bunnell, 30 Oct. 1904, in *LG* 107.

the wild little mining camp that crouches there on the red hills' crest like a thing lost, hiding behind the purple rocks in very sight and sound of the city, but silent, remote as a star."[2]

Ethel's explorations of her new hometown on horseback—which she rode cross-saddle, like a man—had sparked gossip, obliging her to educate readers of the *Birmingham Age-Herald*. "In other parts of the country," she explained, "this mode of riding horseback has been for several years past quite the conventional thing, and recognized as, by all odds, the safest and most beneficial way a woman can ride. Just exactly why its reception in this city has not been an enthusiastic one—excepting by the three or four young women who have adopted it—is because so few Birmingham girls ride, have any particular interest in horses or even the slightest knowledge of things equestrian."[3]

Ethel had planned to join Yone in Japan in the autumn, but had postponed her departure until March. She had befriended Annie Kendrick Walker at the *Birmingham Age-Herald*, where she had written a few sketches, and began writing for the *National Magazine*, edited by Yone's friend Frank Putnam: articles like "Aloha, Wela, Wela!"—a reminiscence of Charles Warren Stoddard's Hawaiian-themed Washington "Bungalow" where she had first met Yone in December 1900. In the December 1904 *National*, Ethel's article would follow "In the Bungalow with Charles Warren Stoddard: A Protest Against Modernism," Yone's own reminiscence written before leaving his East 26th Street apartment in late March.[4]

Stoddard, still convalescing in Harvard Zoologist William Woodworth's house, was happy to accommodate Putnam's request for pictures. "Today I shall send you by express seven (7) photos of the interior of the Bungalow to choose from," he replied on September 20, including, with the various rooms and an exterior view, photos of his former lover, "*Kenneth the Bungalow Kid*, and if you use the picture you might print that line under it," he instructed, and his French cook, Jule, "the Major Domo of the Bungalow."[5] Putnam used them all. Stoddard appeared to be gradually accepting the painful news of Yone and Ethel's engagement.

A Cricket in Nihonbashi

On Sunday, September 18, 1904, the *Manchuria* docked at the Yokohama port where a seventeen-year-old Yone had once cried as his brother disappeared into the crowd. Now, almost eleven years later, he was again dismayed to see no familiar faces in the welcoming crowd, though he had

2. Ethel Armes, "Pastels of Birmingham," *Birmingham Age-Herald*, 6 Dec. 1903, 7, 14 Dec. 1903, 8.
3. Annie Kendrick Walker, "The Introduction of the Cross Saddle in Birmingham," *Birmingham Age-Herald*, 29 Nov. 1903, 18.
4. Ethel Armes, "Aloha, Wela, Wela!," *National Magazine* 21:3 (Dec. 1904): 308-18; YN, "In the Bungalow with Charles Warren Stoddard," *National Magazine* 21:3 (Dec. 1904): 304-08; "A Protest Against Modernism," KM 32.
5. CWS to FP, 20 Sept. 1904, CWSP.

written home to announce his arrival. Eventually he made his way to the station and boarded a train for Tokyo. It was only after the train arrived at Shinbashi that he realized his brother Fujitarō, who had come to meet him at Yokohama station, had ridden the same train: they had failed to recognize each other. Noguchi only became aware of his mistake when his brother joined a party in which he recognized Madame Isonaga, "the lady who used to look after me with motherly care"—the party was in his honor. "I was no other than Rip Van Winkle," he thought sadly.[6]

1. Pier of Yokohama.

He was taken to Fujitarō's house in Tokyo's Nihonbashi district, as he wrote, "to wash off my foreign dust and slowly renew my old acquaintance with things Japanese."

> Oh, that memorable first night after thirteen years abroad! I spent it alone in the upstairs room where I was left to sleep. I did not fall asleep for many many hours as my back already began to ache from lying on the floor in the Japanese fashion; and my nostrils could not make themselves free from a strange Japanese smell, indeed the soy smell, which I thought was crawling from the kitchen. As I said, the rain dropped quite incessantly; the lamplight burned feebly; and I was alone. Listen! What was that I heard? Well, it was a cricket singing under the roof or behind the hanging at the *tokonoma*. I exclaimed then: "Was it possible to hear the cricket in the very centre of the metropolis?" My mind at once recalled the following *hokku* poem by Issa:
>
> > "Let me turn over,
> > Pray, go away,
> > Oh my cricket!"

He was reminded of Yeats's "Lake Isle of Innisfree," thinking of Issa, "the *hokku* poet at the mountainside of Shinshu, and his shabby hut 'of clay and Wattles made' where he indeed lived with the insects, practically sharing his house with them."[7]

6. "Latest Shipping," *Japan Mail*, 24 Sept. 1904, 353-4; *SYN* 169-70.
7. "What is a Hokku Poem," *Rhythm* 12 (Jan. 1913): 359, rpt. *TT* 136-37. Issa's haiku: "negaeri o suru zo soko noke kirigirisu."

2. Nihonbashi district, circa 1900.

Noguchi found himself a celebrity in Tokyo. On the day of his arrival, the front page of the *Yomiuri Shimbun*'s literary section, which had published several articles about his English poems, featured a long poem in his honor by Rohan Kōda, one of the leading writers of the day.[8] The *Yomiuri* filled several columns a few days later with Noguchi's random observations, and enjoined him to write a series of articles as he reacclimated himself to Japan.[9]

He found little war news to report. "Not a shout of victory in the streets of Tokio! Not a single cry of 'Banzai!' The only sound now, as it ever was, 'Koran-Koran,' the music of the wooden clogs." The best he could manage was a conversation with a complaining hotel clerk which he wrote up for the New Orleans *Times-Democrat*, where his friend Flora Field worked. "Any jinrikisha man used to make one yen and a half daily before," the clerk told him. "To-day he can scarcely make one yen." There was "no business whatever." The hotel's profits were down thirty percent. "And everything is rising in price." Some had benefitted from the war, notably "the lantern and flag makers (Japan can not express her joy without them), candle makers and music stores." But the celebrations, like the recent one for the victory at Liao Yang that went on for three days, were an added expense the overtaxed residents could little afford. "Our hotel was obliged to contribute a large amount of money—why yes, simply obliged to!," the hotel clerk complained. "Truly the poor people can not stand it. There is much dissatisfaction and complaint among them. But their voice is small and perhaps inaudible."[10]

8. "Noguchi Yonejirō shi ni yosu" (To Mr. Yonejirō Noguchi), *Yomiuri Shimbun*, 18 Sept. 1904, 1.
9. "Shijin Noguchi Yonejirō-shi no danpen" (Mr. Yonejirō Noguchi's fragments), *Yomiuri Shimbun*, 21-22 Sept. 1904, 1.
10. "'To Suffer Is Only Natural for the Japanese Poor,'" New Orleans *Times-Democrat*, 30 Oct 1904, rpt. *EE* 124-26.

3. "Mr. Yone Noguchi (From a photograph just taken in Tokio)."

Noguchi was asked to give a lecture at Keio, his old school, and chose Joaquin Miller as his topic.[11] He sent an English version to Ethel to type for Putnam's *National Magazine*, and wrote Frank a few days later apologetically. "Oh Frank did I write to you from Tokyo where I arrived just a week ago? I forget what I was doing for—oh, tremendously busy, you know! Really I do not know what I am going to do and what I will become—really. Here come and go so many people—six or seven people call on me every day and I got to pay my own visit myself. My hands are full of nonsense and social matters." Though flustered, he was "happy so far," having "met a good reception in Tokyo." "These Japanese take so much interest in my work, and asked me— D— such a nonsense. Dont ask me what— Dinners and dinners! And talk and talk. And nothing else. Isnt it awful? I must hurry back to America, and be lazy for a while. Here I cannot find myself—which I wish to do. I cannot read the books and perhaps cannot write even a line."[12]

The Hearn Inquiry

Noguchi needed to write many lines. To fund Ethel's travel to Japan and their future life together, he needed to expand his literary production and shift focus away from unprofitable poetry and unsuccessful fiction towards the more lucrative war journalism and Japanese cultural essays. It had been less than a year since Noguchi had placed his first proper essay,

11. The November 1 lecture appeared as "Shijin Mirā" (The poet Miller), *Keiō Gijuku Gakuhō* 83 (15 Nov. 1904): 8-13; 85 (15 Dec. 1904): 32-36.
12. YN to FP, [Sept. 1904], FPL 34.

on the death of kabuki actor Danjurō Ichikawa.[13] When the war vastly increased demand, he had quickly increased his productivity, churning out articles introducing American readers to Japanese art, fiction, newspapers, popular songs, theater, and humor. The increased demand would not last long. And he was still finding his footing as an essayist.

In "A Japanese View of the Books about Japan," Noguchi surveyed the field with a critical eye. Basil Hall Chamberlain's well-known *Things Japanese* might be, as Viscount Hayashi said, "the best ever written," but Noguchi found the writings of the "worthy professor with infinite learning in Japanese" to be "scholarly in exactitude, seldom expanded with a literary imagination," which was, he supposed, "the very reason why he will never command a greater audience."[14] He moreover considered Chamberlain's translation of Japanese classical poetry "a failure." But readers had little ability to judge. "Even the excellent translation by W.G. Aston (dear old gentleman now living snugly in East Devon, England), in his *History of Japanese Literature* did not succeed in making a proper impression, while Sir Edwin Arnold's version, with a plenty of occidental 'light and shadow' was welcomed." It was as "any Japanese store-keeper on Broadway or Fifth Avenue will tell you": there was "little appreciation of purely Japanese ware, and the things that they do buy could hardly be called Japanese." Nor did Anglophone Japanese writers offer anything better. Kinnosuke Adachi's prose writings "may be the best prose display on the part of a Japanese" were it not blemished by "superfluous jugglery with the vocabulary." Inazō Nitobe's *Bushido* was "a most admirable essay on the moral discipline under the feudal regime," but had been—until propelled to fame by the war—"somewhat slighted by American critics."

The writer whose achievement most impressed him was Lafcadio Hearn, who had managed to achieve popularity without anything worse than a tendency to over-idealize Japan through "a certain veil of mist." It saddened Noguchi that "even today his admirable work is hardly known in Japan." Japanese, reading his work in translation, had inquired, "Are we really such interesting people?"

Despite Noguchi's avowed admiration, Hearn's name came up only occasionally in his writings: in an article on Kōyō Ozaki, whom Hearn was "expected to have a paper on," and in another on "Buddhism in America," he would "not forget to mention Lafcadio Hearn in this connection . . . how many a thousand English readers got a glimpse of Buddhism, or Japanese Buddhism . . . from Hearn's 'Kokoro' or 'Glimpses of Unfamiliar Japan'?" he wondered.[15] "Mr. Hearn's gentlemanly volumes" were also recommended in Noguchi's unpublished story, "In Love Success

---

13. "Japan's Greatest Actor is Gone," New York *Morning Telegraph*, 1 Nov. 1903, rpt. EE 24-28.
14. "A Japanese View of the Books about Japan," EE 287-89.
15. "Koyo Ozaki," *Reader* 4:2 (July 1904), rpt. EE 106-7; "Buddhism in America," *Boston Evening Transcript*, 23 Mar. 1904, 17.

Street," as an antidote to Pierre Loti's *Madame Chrysanthème*.[16] And he had reviewed Hearn's *Kwaidan* after an April request by *The Bookman*, although this would not appear until October.[17]

The Greek-born, Irish-American Hearn had settled in Japan in 1890, married an impoverished former-samurai divorcée, and became a Japanese citizen, taking his wife's family name to become Yakumo Koizumi. Hearn had moved to Tokyo in 1896 to teach English literature at the Imperial University on the recommendation of Basil Hall Chamberlain, who had earlier helped him find teaching positions in Matsue and Kumamoto. When the university proposed to cut his hours and lower his salary in 1903, Hearn had angrily resigned and accepted an offer to teach at rival Waseda University. Increasingly reclusive, Hearn rarely saw anyone besides his students, and discouraged visitors at the Nishi Ōkubo house on the outskirts of Tokyo where he lived, as Yakumo Koizumi, with his wife Setsuko and their three children. Noguchi was well aware of Hearn's inaccessibility, but had promised to penetrate the mystery and send an article "to a certain magazine publisher in New York," intending to be the exception. "Since I know some people very well that the professor became acquainted with while wandering in America, and since I have some similar tastes, I didn't expect to be turned down." He had asked Sakusaburō Uchigasaki, a Waseda lecturer and former Hearn student, to present a copy of *From the Eastern Sea* with a letter, in hopes Hearn would agree to see him.[18]

4. Lafcadio Hearn, circa 1900.

Noguchi's chances of success were, in reality, slim. Hearn was so averse to visitors that he was reluctant to see even his own friends. Noguchi's list of literary acquaintances, though extensive, was unlikely to prove much of a calling card. Nor were his poems, in which Hearn, a firm believer in traditional poetic forms, would immediately have detected the

16. "In Love Success Street," SS 149.
17. "Lafcadio Hearn's 'Kwaidan,'" *Bookman* (N.Y.) 20 (Oct. 1904), rpt. *EE* 115-17.
18. "Hān-shi mibōjin to no danwa" (A Conversation with Mr. Hearn's Widow), *Jiji Shimpō*, 10 Oct. 1904, rpt. *Kichō* 127.

lamentable influence of Walt Whitman, whose poetry he considered "the work of a little child." "To Japanese students of English literature it is in the supreme degree dangerous and bad," Hearn had warned in his lectures; Whitman "should never be imitated in his sins against the laws of the English language."[19]

5. **Waseda University in 1909.**

Noguchi wrote several conflicting versions of what happened next. According to his first Japanese version, Noguchi was taken to see Waseda's founder, Shigenobu Ōkuma, on September 28th. Ōkuma was busy entertaining a foreign visitor, so Noguchi, rather than waiting, went off looking for Hearn, although he had not yet heard anything from Uchigasaki. When he asked if he might see the professor, he was told, to his great surprise, that Hearn had passed away.[20]

Noguchi sent a more imaginative English account of the "Death of Lafcadio Hearn" to Stoddard a few days later, which he afterward published in the New Orleans *Times-Democrat*.[21] He began by granting himself a proper invitation: "It was a piece of great luck, thank God, to hear from him that he will be glad to see me at his school on 28th of September. I promised myself that I will persuade him to take me to his home." Instead of the missed meeting with Ōkuma, he added a meeting in which Ōkuma, informed of Hearn's death, offers praise of the late writer:

> Soon after I was sitting with Count Okuma, the greatest statesman and the founder of the Waseda University, in his drawing room. He had not as yet been informed of Mr. Koizumi's sudden death. (By the way, it was from a heart failure.)
>
> "He was the spokesman of Japan in the real meaning," said Count Okuma. "He has done for our country more than two or three regiments in Manchuria. He has done, spiritually, as much as Togo's fleets at Port Arthur. Yes, sir; he did. Japan was understood in America through his work. What a fortune!
>
> "And what a flexibility of his mind! What a beauty in his imagination!

---

19. Lafcadio Hearn, *On Poets*, ed. R. Tanabe, T. Ochiai, I. Nishizaki (Tokyo: Hokuseido, 1838): 817, 825, 841.
20. "Hān-shi mibōjin to no danwa" 127.
21. "Death of Lafcadio Hearn," New Orleans *Times-Democrat*, 4 June 1905, 31, rpt. *EE* 232-33.

What a clearness in his style! He carried upon his shoulders the heavy task of the interpretation of our country. And he carried it bravely and successfully. Now one of the Japanese prides is gone," the count sighed. Mr. Takada, the chief secretary of the university, came in presently to inform the count formally of Mr. Koizumi's death.[22]

Among the many glaring improbabilities in this conversation, one might point to the unlikelihood of a politician like Ōkuma arguing that Hearn had "done for our country more than two or three regiments in Manchuria" and "as much as Togo's fleets at Port Arthur." It was Noguchi himself who thought he could serve his country better with the pen than the bayonet. But even if such a claim were justifiable, it would never have been made by a career politician like Ōkuma. And of course, if Noguchi had been in a position to record Ōkuma's comments on the subject, he would hardly have failed to mention it in his Japanese version as well. In any case, by the time Noguchi wrote up Hearn's funeral a week later, he had decided to take credit for the comparison himself, and refined it into something more memorable: "Surely we could lose two or three battleships at Port Arthur rather than Lafcadio Hearn."

By 1922, Noguchi was telling his Japanese readers an entirely different story of how he heard about Hearn's death.

> At the time of my return to Japan, I very much wanted to meet Yakumo. However, I also thought that if Yakumo disliked meeting people, I wouldn't insist. But the shock I felt upon hearing of Yakumo's death is something I can still easily imagine even today, eighteen years later. I heard of his death in the dining room of the Imperial Hotel. I was in the middle of eating a steak, dripping with blood, with a friend. At that moment, I felt it inappropriate to hear of his death in a Western-style building of the sort Yakumo hated. His death seemed to mock my own excessive Westernization, and I felt a deep sense of shame. At that moment, I certainly shouted, "It would have been better to lose two or three battleships if we could have kept him alive." At that time, it was during the climax of the Russo-Japanese War. There are probably people who know that these words of mine were quoted in Bisland's biography of Hearn. The Russo-Japanese War ended. Japan managed to avoid losing even a single battleship, but we lost Koizumi Yakumo. However, over the past eighteen years, who knows how many battleships have been decommissioned.[23]

The rewrite was evidently an attempt to bury the Ōkuma-Waseda story: Noguchi, as an avid recycler of his earlier writings, could hardly have forgotten his earlier account. The new story seems more reconstruction than recollection: Noguchi says he "can easily imagine" (*yōi ni sōzō suru koto ga dekiru*) the scene, not that he "can easily remember" it. The most glaring

22. YN to CWS, 10 Oct. 1904, HM37953; "Death of Lafcadio Hearn," mss., dated 30 Sep. 1904, HM; "Death of Lafcadio Hearn," New Orleans *Times-Democrat*, 4 June 1905, 31, rpt. *EE* 232-33.
23. "Koizumi Yakumo," *Kaizō* 3:10 (Oct. 1922), rpt. *Senkusha no kotoba* (Kaizōsha, 1924), 240-41.

misstatement must be the one about Japan not losing even a single battleship during the Russo-Japanese War. Even as poor a war correspondent as Noguchi could hardly have failed to hear something of the numerous Japanese naval vessels sunk during the war.[24]

6. Hearn's funeral procession.

"Death of Lafcadio Hearn" ends with Noguchi hurrying to Hearn's house to pay his respects but lacking the courage to enter: merely standing by the fence, he glimpses the candles at the household shrine, feeling deep sadness at the sound of a baby crying. Nothing, however, stopped him from attending Hearn's funeral two days later on September 30. It was a grand affair. For all his eccentricities, Hearn had been a beloved teacher, and the attendees—some forty professors, a hundred students, and three foreigners—included many figures of importance among the Tokyo literati. Noguchi's notoriety at this time was nevertheless such that his arrival at the ceremony was vividly remembered by one of the student attendees, the nineteen-year-old future astronomer Nojiri Hōei.[25] It was quite late and the funeral party was just breaking up when a "tall Japanese gentleman" placed his shoes at the *genkan*.[26] "It's Yone Noguchi!"

24. The lost ships, mostly sunk by Russian mines, included two proper battleships (the *Hatsuse*, which took down 496 crew members, and the *Yashima*), three gunboats, four cruisers, and a corvette. Noguchi attempted to hide the callousness of his comment by translating "lost" with the vague "*nakushite*" (lost, misplaced, disappeared) and mentioning decommissioned battleships, as battleships lost to old age were somehow relevant.
25. Hōei Nojiri, "Koizumi-sensei no omoide," *Herun* 29 (1992). Noguchi's letter describing the funeral was summarized in the *New York Times Book Review*, 19 Nov. 1904, 783.
26. At 5'3½" (See *LG* 83) Noguchi was slightly above the 5'2½" average height for Japanese males,

declared an older Waseda student, Gyofū Sōma. "Those were the days of Noguchi's return to Japan when articles that couldn't say enough about him were practically monopolizing the *Yomiuri*'s Sunday book page," Nojiri recalled. Some of the comments were envious and even malicious, even doubting that Noguchi actually existed. Yet there he was at the funeral—the new literary star that had suddenly appeared on the scene.

7. Hearn's funeral: jinrikisha men outside Hearn's house.

Hearn had left his mark on a number of future writers and scholars of note, some of whom would come to be closely associated with Noguchi in the following decades. There were the poets Bin Ueda and Bansui Tsuchii, future drama innovator Kaoru Osanai (who later shared with Noguchi his student notebooks from Hearn's class), future novelist Hakuchō Masamune, then a literary columnist for the *Yomiuri*. They were Japan's modernists in the making—the generation that would bring Japanese literature into the twentieth century. Some of Hearn's former students were already well aware of Noguchi: Hakuson Kuriyagawa, an English literary scholar of some note, had reviewed Noguchi's English poetry collection in three successive *Yomiuri* Sunday supplements a year earlier.[27]

Ten days after the funeral, when Noguchi wrote to Stoddard enclosing his "Death of Lafcadio Hearn" draft, he was also able to report that he

---

according to anthropologist Erwin Baelz, cited in Frank Brinkley, ed., *Japan*, v, 5 (Boston: Millet, 1902), 252.

27. Kuriyagawa Hakuson, "Noguchi Yonejirō no Ei-shishū" (Yonejirō Noguchi's English poetry collection), *Yomiuri Shimbun*, 29 Nov. 1903, 2, 6 Dec. 1903, 2.

had called on Mrs. Hearn and "had a delightful chat—in literary sense" and was "going to write it up immediately."[28] He did write it up in both Japanese and English, with some substantial differences between the versions. The Japanese version went to the *Jiji Shimpō* and was included in his book *Kichō no ki* in December.[29] The English version went to Ethel as "The Real Conversation with Mrs. Lafcadio Hearn," structured as a dramatic dialogue between himself and "Mrs. L.H." Ethel changed the somewhat pretentious dialogue form into an easier-to-read narrative, in which form it appeared in the *Japan Times* as "A Conversation with Mrs. Lafcadio Hearn."[30]

Noguchi had probably visited the Koizumi house on October 2 (as stated in his Japanese article) on his way to see Shōyō Tsubouchi, the famed novelist of the 1880s, now a respected dramatist and Waseda professor. And he probably did have a "real conversation" with Setsu Koizumi, Hearn's widow. But where his English article depicted a conversation between Setsu and himself, the Japanese version explained, "I had a talk about the professor with Mrs. Koizumi and Mr. Shigenori Minari (a relative of Dr. Ume who looks after all of the Koizumi business). The following is the conversation with Mrs. Hearn and Minari."[31]

Setsu's reminiscences have become an important part of Hearn's biography, but the circumstances of their compilation remain unclear. Some of the material was likely compiled later "complying with a request made by Elizabeth Bisland" for material for her edition of Hearn's *Life and Letters*, as Yoji Hasegawa suggests. But some was already being used by Noguchi in the weeks after Hearn's funeral. Minari may have begun compiling the notes partly to inform the absent Dr. Ume about the family's situation, partly out of curiosity, and partly out of a historian's habit, making use of conversations overheard before and after the funeral, as Setsu reminisced about her late husband with the many visitors who came to pay their respects. Noguchi evidently had access to Minari's complete version when he compiled a new "Mrs. Hearn's Reminiscence" in 1908.[32] Minari, according to Hasegawa, "personally discredited the authenticity of Noguchi's rendering." But the other published versions suffered from

28. YN to CWS, 10 Oct. 1904, HM 37953.
29. "Hān-shi mibōjin to no danwa," 127-40.
30. "The Real Conversation with Mrs. Lafcadio Hearn," KM 20; "A Conversation with Mrs. Lafcadio Hearn," JT, 21 Dec. 1904, 6, rpt. EE 155.
31. "Hān-shi mibōjin to no danwa," 131-2. Shigenori Minari and Kenjirō Ume were both distant relatives of Setsu from Matsue, and both held positions at the Imperial University. Ume, a law professor with a doctorate from the University of Lyon, had been asked by Hearn to look after his family in the event of his death, but was obliged to rely for day-to-day assistance, on Minori, whose position as a historical researcher was less demanding.
32. YN, "Mrs. Hearn's Reminiscence," *Taiyō* 14:16 (Dec. 1908): 16-23; 15:2 (Feb. 1909): 17-24; rpt. "Mrs. Lafcadio Hearn's Reminiscences," *Pacific Monthly* (Feb., Mar. 1910): 117-126, 250-60; rpt. LHJ 31-79.

omissions and errors as well.³³ As a result Noguchi's version proved useful when Hasegawa made a new English translation in 1988.

Noguchi sent an article about the funeral, dated October 5, to Ethel to be typed and sent to the *Boston Evening Transcript* and other papers.³⁴ It was a touching elegy, an evocative portrait of Hearn, not as an eccentric recluse but as a beloved writer, teacher and father. Although less detailed than Margaret Emerson's account in *The Critic*, Noguchi's was the only one to appear widely in the American press. He did, however, manage to get the date wrong.³⁵

Home At Last

After several weeks of endless dinners and receptions where he was obliged to report "something about America," leaving him little time to write, Noguchi told the *Yomiuri* on October 5 he was leaving to spend ten days or so in his hometown, and would then make a stop in the Kansai area to attend a welcome party in Osaka on the 20th.³⁶ On another page he provided more rambling comments about his return to Japan.³⁷

Heading homeward he stopped in Fujisawa to see his brother Yūshin, newly appointed head priest of Jōkōji temple. Together, they paid a visit to the great Buddha of nearby Kamakura, where the visitor, as Rudyard Kipling had written in 1892, "May feel the Soul of all the East." When they returned to the temple in Fujisawa "under the soft greyness of evening" to spend the night in "the Buddhistic quietness which bit my soul; it was the first experience of my life," he declared in his English "Kicho no Ki" (Homecoming Chronicle).³⁸

On October 8th, it was "*kichō* after eleven years": homecoming at last.³⁹ He awoke early with the temple bells, and took the early train for Nagoya. The train traveled along the same Tōkaidō route celebrated by Hiroshige in his famous series of *ukiyoe* prints, though at a more rapid

33. Yoji Hasegawa, *A Walk in Kumamoto* (Folkestone: Global Oriental, 1997), 210, 263-64, The official Japanese version of Setsu's story appeared as *Omoide no ki* in 1914 in the first Japanese translation of Hearn's collected writings, but with numerous expurgations probably attributable to Setsu's "concern and discretion." A 1918 English translation of this version by Paul Hisada, *Reminiscences of Lafcadio Hearn*, was "severely criticized" for inaccuracies and omissions.
34. "The Passing of Lafcadio Hearn," *Boston Evening Transcript*, 5 Nov. 1904, 20. The article subsequently appeared under various titles in the *Birmingham Age-Herald*, *Washington Post*, *Atlanta Constitution*, and *New York Times Book Review*.
35. Noguchi's article has Hearn "buried on the afternoon of the 29th with Buddhist rite," but both the *Japan Mail* and *Japan Chronicle* agree it was the afternoon of the 30th.
36. YN to FP, 10 Oct. 1904, FPL 35; "Yomiuri-sho," *Yomiuri Shimbun*, 6 Oct. 1904, 1; "Noguchi Yonejirō wa kyōri Owari ni omomaki jūsū-hiai daizai no yotei" (YN plans to proceed to Owari hometown for a stay of more than ten days), *Yomiuri Shimbun*, 6 Oct. 1904, 1.
37. "Noguchi Yonejirō kichō ato no kansō" (Yonejirō Noguchi's thoughts after returning home), *Yomiuri Shimbun*, 6 Oct. 1904, 5.
38. *Kichō* 166-67; "Kicho no Ki," SYN 166.
39. The word *kichō*, comprised of the characters for "return home" and "morning," refers specifically to a return to Japan from abroad.

pace. Disappointed not to find "Fuji-san's lotos-peak soaring through the morning ether," he was "in a measure comforted later at Suzukawa," when the great mountain "peeped out from the clouds." Noguchi had dedicated *From the Eastern Sea* "To the Spirits of Mount Fuji." Now, confronting the great mountain, he found "no word to express his majesty and grace"; he felt "as if I were happily running through a dreamlike garden." Not even the rising sun flags, emblems of wartime, marred the beauty of the scene for the poet in reverie. "My patriotism jumped high with the sight of the flag," he wrote.[40]

After changing trains, Noguchi arrived in his hometown of Tsushima, where, he wrote, "I frightened my old father at the station, who was actually trying to find me among some other people." His father, after recovering from the shock of his son's changed appearance, hustled him off to the Tsushima Shrine, saying, "We must make a thanking worship immediately to Tenno Sama; I have been praying for his protection for you all the time. It is, of course, through his divine favour we have you here making a safe return." Tennō-sama was Tsushima's local deity, Gōzu-Tennō, the ox-headed emperor, whose mysterious image resided in the shrine. At the long-anticipated reunion with his mother, both wept; Yone-ko almost looked like a *Seiyōjin* (a Western person) she told him; even his nose and eyes were "just like those of a Western-sea man."

Okuwa Noguchi was not the only person to regard her returning son with awe. As reports of his arrival spread through Nakajima-chō, friends and neighbors began to call: "they couldn't raise their heads from reverence and fear before me," Noguchi reported. "The president of the Tsushima Grammar School called on me at night, and wished me to make a speech before his students. The younger people of my street were all for giving a dinner in my honour. All the guests left my house at about ten o'clock. Before I went to bed, I was calmly rubbed by a shampooer."

"Here I am at my old home in the country town with my old mother and father who cried from joy," he wrote Putnam on October 10.[41] He enjoyed the comforts of home and reacquainted himself with neighbors like Ku-san, the carpenter's son with whom he had learned penmanship, and Hiko-san, for whom he had drawn pictures as a child, both now married, with children. As he reaccustomed himself to small town life he became aware of the effects the war was having upon it. One young man from his street had been wounded and was recovering in a Nagoya hospital; another was still at the front. "Although his mother-in-law patriotically submitted, saying, 'It is for our country's sake,'" Noguchi observed, "I could clearly espy her voiceless complaint; her daughter, the wife of her soldier son, is sick in bed while her two children cry." An official announcement arrived: "it was to bid us make our presence to

40. SYN 167.
41. YN to FP, 10 Oct. 1904, FPL 35.

see the soldiers off to the front." Another night, "we all lighted our front gate lanterns to express our joy over the Lio Yang victory." "We do not make any noise even in joy," Noguchi adds, "and are facing the war with such a silence which is only the voice of life and death." Gōzu Tennō's shrine was doing a brisk business: "The big wood fires will be burned right before the shrine all night; the daily worshippers, doubtless the relations of soldiers at the front, are said to be more than five hundred. A few *sen* will make you the happy possessor of an *omamori* or charm which will very likely protect your fighters from bad luck; and a special prayer will be given to you on your appeal." At the Tsushima Grammar School, visible from Yone's upstairs window, "even the girls must sing the war songs nowadays."[42]

Noguchi had not managed much English writing in the month since his return. Aside from his Hearn article, he had sent an article on Joaquin Miller to Ethel Armes, who forwarded it to Putnam to use in the *National*. Ethel took the opportunity to send along her own long, illustrated article about Stoddard, entitled "Aloha, Wela, Wela!," which would appear alongside Yone's Stoddard article in December. Frank had a favorable impression of Ethel and her writing, which came as a great relief to them.[43] Ethel, who was "running a syndicate of Yone's stories," was not entirely enamored of the *National*, but thought Frank Putnam "an angel of an editor." "The National will run a story of mine every month 'for life' Mr. Putnam says!" she informed Alice Wiggin. "Of course Alice please understand they are all but simple little sketches—so expect nothing big."[44]

"To see the beauty of a Japanese autumn, it is said, you must come to Kyoto." Having never had the opportunity for such an extravagant trip in his student days, Noguchi jumped at the invitation to visit an old Nagoya middle-school friend, Hirosaburō Taki, now managing the Kyoto branch of his father's trading company.[45] On October 28, he was "pleased to be in Kyoto with *andon* and candle-sticks," feeling as if he "had flown back to the sixteenth century—the dear age of slow life, half song and half sorrow."[46] Kyoto, home to Japan's imperial family from the end of the eighth century until the Meiji Restoration, was a great contrast to Tokyo and America; it was a "perfectly undisturbed oasis . . . where you can sing the oldest song, and let the world go by as it pleases." It was a city full of literary history. Noguchi had a hankering to see "the gracefully gracious shape of Higashi Yama, which, as some well-known poet wrote, looks a sleeping beauty

---

42. SYN 173.
43. YN to FP, 10 Oct. 1904, FPL 35.
44. Ethel Armes to Alice Wiggin, 10 Nov. 1904, EMAP.
45. Takisada Nagoya, a textile company, still in business as of this writing.
46. Andon are oil lamps of paper stretched around a frame. Such styles were already antiquated even in Kyoto, where unsightly electrical wires were strung across the great Sanjō bridge and throughout much of the city.

under a *futon* or quilt."⁴⁷ In the evening he walked toward the great eastern mountain, crossing the famous Kamogawa river. "I thought it quite lucky to see, as I stood on the bridge over Kamo Gawa, the same moon which was sung and sung by the thousand *uta* poets, those nobles and princesses of Japan's golden age—it is a long time ago now."

On the next day, Noguchi and Taki traveled to Arashiyama in western Kyoto, famous for its autumn scenery: "What a wonder—the most rare sight of the mountain and river through the tinted mists of *momiji* or maple leaves." They hired a boat with three men to push it up the river, turning back at Hotsugawa, where they gave a lift downstream to three brushwood-selling girls. In the evening, they traveled back to the eastern side of the city to dine at the secluded Hyōtei restaurant near Nanzenji. Later he wrote a poem about Kyoto:

> Mist-born Kyoto, the city of scent and prayer,
> Like a dream half-fading, she lingers on:
> The oldest song of a forgotten pagoda bell
> Is the Kamo River's twilight song.⁴⁸

While in Kyoto he also ran into young Arthur Ficke, who was touring the city with his family. In Tokyo, he had spent a pleasant afternoon with Ficke in Tokyo visiting the Hyakkaen flower garden in Mukojima, strolling around Asakusa, and enjoying hot sake at a soba shop. Now, he invited him for an evening visit to Taki's home on Takoyakushi-dori, a centuries-old machiya still lit by oil lamps, which fascinated Ficke.⁴⁹

On November 2, Noguchi left Kyoto for the last stop on his autumn *kenbutsu*: a day in Nara, "the capital of the eighth century, with its avenues of lichen-patched stone lanterns, and with a hundred temple bells echoing down the calm groves, an Olympus of *uta* poem and art in those lyric ages of Japan," where he regretted his failure to bring a copy of the *Manyōshū*, the famous poem anthology from the Nara age. "And I was making my presence in a *yōfuku* or foreign dress—such a modern informal sack coat!—I thought that *eboshi* and *shitatare* which were worn by the courtiers in those days were the proper outfit for such an old city of incense and dream." In vain he sought out a book of *uta* in a bookshop on Sanjō, and had to settle for a worn copy of Fitzgerald's *Rubáiyát*. "But I thought that the dear old man would not find this place entirely uncongenial; surely he could make a paradise with the help of a lady and *sake* out of this tired city."

He visited Nara's famous deer park and the nearby Kasuga Taisha, the eighth-century Shintō shrine established by the powerful Fujiwara clan to protect the new capital. At Tōdaiji he saw the great eighth-century

---

47. He was thinking of Ransetsu Hattori's haiku, "futon kite netaru sugata ya Higashiyama": "wrapped in a futon / a figure is sleeping: / Higashiyama."
48. "Kyoto," *Ayamegusa* (Tokyo: Jozandō 1906), rpt. *Pilg.* 57.
49. "Raichō seru Fikku kun" (Ficke is coming), *Yomiuri Shimbun* 8 Apr. 1917, 7.

Nara Daibutsu, older and larger than even the great Buddha of Kamakura. "I could not understand," he noted, "how the Japanese who made such an immense idol in the old days came to be considered clever only with small things."⁵⁰

Noguchi returned to his hometown of Tsushima the following day, and, the day after that, wrote a letter to Putnam, from whom he had received a note before his departure asking for an article on the late Lafcadio Hearn. Noguchi replied that he had written two or three articles on Hearn; the one he sent to Putnam, "Lafcadio Hearn, A Dreamer," was mainly the recollections of Sakusaburō Uchigasaki. Yone promised to attend to Putnam's request for an article on E.C. Stedman as well. He was enjoying Japan's fall weather. "Certainly the Nature is very good to Japan. I am grateful to be born as a Japanese, and still more, I am grateful that I have many good friends in America. I am like a sky-lark who lives in two worlds—sky and land. I am sure that America is the sky full of freedom, and Japan the land sweet and kind and mother-like." He was rather worried about the war. "Japan is having a terrible time now with Russia. Perhaps I will be called up to Army. If it was the case, I must hurry back to America. I cannot afford to be a soldier now. If I was five years younger, it will be a different thing—you understand it."⁵¹ Noguchi stayed another week in Tsushima enjoying the pleasures of home. On November 8, as the year was "showing her last beauty before her winter's sleep," he was contemplating the falling, golden leaves of the maple tree in the garden planted by his grandfather, and thinking again of the death of his sister Tsune. Now her place was filled by his niece Yoshi:

> With a fan, with the little joy of Japan,
>   Dance you O Yoshi San:
> Your dress, red and white, flashes on
> Like the falling leaves of dream.⁵²

Yoshi-san was the young daughter of his brother Hidenosuke, the eldest son who would inherit the family home according to Japanese custom.

A month had passed since Yone's return to Tsushima, and he would soon be leaving again. That night there was another welcome dinner given by the whole town of Tsushima: "there were more than two hundred people, among them the mayor of the town and the member of the House of Commons whom the town elected." Noguchi returned home to find his mother warming his night-robe over the fire box and planning a pudding in honor of his farewell. "I had so many callers next day as my departure was told among the people. Many of them brought me many letters to be delivered to their sons in San Francisco or in Chicago; doubtless they thought that America is just as small as Japan, where you

50. SYN 179.
51. YN to FP, [Nov. 1904], FPL 38.
52. "O Yoshi San," *Ayamegusa*, rpt. *Pilg.* 51.

can go in a day or two from one place to another. And some of them brought a little boy aged seven or eight hoping I might take him with me to 'wonderful Amerikey!'" In the evening, his mother prepared his kimono—he was determined to start for Tokyo "wearing a *kimono* and wooden clogs as a Japanese does"—and his father prepared the bath. "My niece came to me and said: '*Obarsama* said, Uncle, you shall wash yourself well as this is the last night at home.' 'Yoshi, tell her that I will save some dirt to come home again and wash it,' I replied."

After a brief return to Tokyo, Yone and his brother Tōtarō traveled to Fujisawa to attend their brother Yūshin's investiture ceremony at Jōkōji on November 12, an event he considered interesting enough to write up for the *Yomiuri*.[53] "We both thought how nice it would have been if our mother could have come today," Noguchi wrote, their mother being the family's serious Buddhist, who chided her children that they did "not even know how to recite the *nembutsu*." Their father, for his part, had commented that "if Yūshin were to become priest of a 17th- or 18th-rank temple, it would bring shame on his brothers, but since he was able to obtain an 11th- or 12th-rank temple, the children are now all settled." The "innocent parents" expected Yūshin to pave his unbelieving brothers' path to the Pure Land. Yone was not so sure, but taking in the resplendant ceremony and atmosphere, he understood why Hearn had loved visiting temples. "Those who possess a poet's nature love temples, and temples make poets still more poetical."

8. **Investiture of Yūshin (center); Yone and his brother standing to the right.**

53. "Yo ga ani no nyūinshiki" (My brother's investiture ceremony), *Yomiuri Shimbun*, 4 Dec. 1904, 1.

A week after his return to Tokyo, Noguchi took a few moments to apologize to Frank Putnam: he had been "terribly busy."[54] "I cannot work at all since I am everyday called up to the society and clubs. I am continually asked to give a certain lecture (which is almost impossible for me as you know) and so many people will come to see me. This is the D— place for one who wishes to be alone and wants to do any wonderful sort of things. And in Japan you got to make yourself agreeable as much as possible, and make a smiling face all the time." "Perhaps," he concluded, "I must run away again to America."

Noguchi lectured the following afternoon on "Literary Life" at Tokyo Imperial University, as part of a Saturday afternoon lecture program arranged by *Teikoku Bungaku*.[55] The lecture, sandwiched between lectures on Korean palace architecture and Korean mythology, had been announced in *Teikoku Bungaku*'s special "Koizumi Number" a week or two earlier, and Noguchi could expect to be carefully scrutinized by the former Hearn students from the funeral. For this bookish lot, Noguchi's embrace of the "literary life" might fulfill a fantasy of how one might live in literature rather than simply reading it. That was certainly the case for Sakutarō Fujioka, a young professor of literary history who attended. At thirty-four, Fujioka was already recognized as one of Japan's great literary historians, to which he added a second specialty in art history, but chronic asthma had limited his opportunities for travel. His impression of Noguchi was of a writer whose heedlessness of polite Japanese language, disparaged by some present, seemed only natural after more than ten years in a foreign land. "To breathe the air of freedom under vast, boundless skies; to reject the paradigms of history; and to proclaim the gospel of total equality—are these not, indeed, the author's literary aspirations? A person with such aspirations, one feels, gives deep meaning to even simple and naïve utterances."[56]

Lectures were typically followed by dinners, and dinners by drinking parties, and it may have been in such circumstances that the prospect was broached of Noguchi treating the English literary world to an English translation of the "Koizumi Number." Or he may have simply decided to do so, as he so often did, without permission. In any case, he set to work translating half a dozen articles by Hearn's students and colleagues, though, in his enthusiasm he may have overestimated the demand, as only three made it into print.[57]

54. YN to FP, [Nov. 1904], FPL 34.
55. Announcement for "Bungakuteki seikatsu" (literary life), "Teikoku Bungaku dai-yon-kai koenkai" (Imperial Literature's fourth lecture meeting), *Teikoku Bungaku* 10:11 (Nov. 1904).
56. Fujioka Sakutarō, "Noguchi Yonejirō-shi no Kichō no ki o yomu," *Yomiuri*, 22 Jan. 1905, 1, rpt. *Tōho Ikō*, v. 2, ed. Haga Yaichi and Fujii Otome (Tokyo: Ōkura Shoten, 1912), 427-28.
57. A reminiscence by Hearn's colleague and former student, Sakusaburō Uchigasaki's (KM 5, 1) was published with partial attribution as "Lafcadio Hearn, A Dreamer," *National Magazine* 22 (Apr. 1905): 60-64. Another by Tokyo University chair Tetsujirō Inoue (KM 19) was published

His Country's Battles

Noguchi found time to see the autumn exhibition of the *Hakuba-kai*, a group of painters led by Kiyoteru (Seiki) Kuroda, "who has exhibited with such success in the Paris salon," as he noted (Kuroda had received a silver medal at the Paris World Exposition in 1900). The painters of the Hakuba-kai were combining "European methods in expression and technique," with traditional Japanese subjects, much as Noguchi had been doing in his poetry for the past several years. Reflections of war were notably absent in the exhibition. Noguchi took this as "a strong protest against the possible turning to be only a war nation," for "after all, Japan does not forget that she is a nation of poetry and art." The editors at the *National* evidently had a harder time seeing a gallery of flower-contemplating kimono-clad beauties as "The Art of the Fighting Japan" (Noguchi's original title), and renamed the essay, "Japanese Artists Ignore the War."[58]

9. Takeji Fujishima, *Chō* (Butterflies), 1904.

Noguchi had been studiously ignoring the war himself. He certainly had no intention of trading his pen for a bayonet, as the San Francisco papers had half-seriously anticipated. He explained to Frank, "It's possible

without attribution as "The Late Lafcadio Hearn," New Orleans *Times-Democrat*, 28 May 1905, 35. And one by Hearn's Matsue student Masanobu Ōtani (KM 17, 26) was published under Otani's name as "Lafcadio Hearn," *The Gateway* [Detroit] 4:5 (June 1905): 15-17. Noguchi seems not to have published his translations of three other Ōtani articles (KM.8 / 17, 22, and 44 / 52), nor the reminiscences by Hearn's former students Bin Ueda (KM 21, 3) and Hakuson Kuriyagawa (KM 53), nor another manuscript, dated Jan. 4, 1905 (KM 54), mentioning magazines "full of the Late Lafcadio Hearn" and "the extra number of the Teikoku Bungaku," consisting mainly of a long biographical clipping and a letter from Hearn to Chamberlain.

58. "Japanese Artists Ignore the War," *National Magazine* 21 (Mar. 1905), rpt. *EE* 204-08; "The Art of the Fighting Japan," KM 50.

for me that I will be called up to army. The country need some more ten thousand soldiers immediately. If I will be here too long, I have no way to escape this duty. I am not coward, I am not afraid to be a soldier, but I know better how to serve the country."[59] He could continue, like the painters of the Hakuba-kai, to "express Beauty and Love in the purest sense . . . while people were talking of war and war."

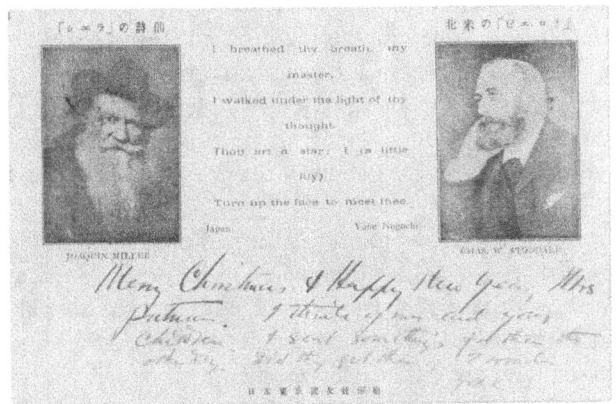

10. Noguchi's postcard to Mrs. Putnam (addressed to Frank Putnam), December 11, 1904.

His little homecoming chronicle book, *Kichō no ki*, a set of travel essays with ten new English poems for good measure, was another priority. The opening essay, "Crossing the Pacific," began by quoting the San Francisco *Bulletin*'s quip about Noguchi leaving San Francisco on the way to the front, but aside from a few bits of hometown war gossip, the book followed Noguchi's travels and reflections on his literary activities and associates, paying little heed to the ongoing war. It was, however, an attractive book, with a prefatory poem by a noted poet of Chinese verse, Neisai Noguchi, two photographs, and a colorful woodcut borrowed from Pamela Colman Smith's magazine, *The Green Sheaf*. Shun'yōdō, a respected literary publisher, had the book ready in December. Sakutarō Fujioka, reviewing it in the *Yomiuri*, appreciated the way Noguchi wrote Japanese prose "without the burdens of convention or the clutter of classical allusions . . . writing that flows freely from the heart . . . full of immediate poetic feeling, far more than the beautifully wrought works of traditional writers."[60]

For a writer who had supposedly returned to Japan to write stories about the war for American newspapers, Noguchi had made surprisingly little effort at investigative journalism. On the way back to his hometown, he noted national flags, groups of children shouting "Banzai! Banzai!" at his passing train, and the occasional "triumphal arch with which the people celebrated the Liao Yang victory." His had, however, managed to collect a fair number of war stories in "the little town of Tsushima,

59. YN to FP, 18 Nov. 1904, FPL 36.
60. Fujioka Sakutarō, "Noguchi Yonejirō-shi no Kichō no ki o Yomu," 428.

which, small as it is, gave 40 soldiers for Japan." At one nearby house a mother had shown him the last letter from her boy, a lieutenant fallen at Liao Yang; at the next, the family had told of their boy, wounded in the same battle, recovering at a Nagoya hospital. There had been stories of families making sacrifices: an old woman had had to sell her kitchen utensils to deliver a war summons to her traveling son, an old carpenter had finally given up drinking after sending thirteen of his apprentices to the war. At the Tennō shrine, where he saw "a hundred lanterns lighted and many a holy fire built, . . . mothers and sisters and wives of the men at the front gathered together praying for victory." He concluded that Japan's fighting capacity and burning patriotism was to be found in the country towns and villages; "few of the people of the city have such a pure samurai spirit."[61]

Noguchi's tourist activities in Kyoto and Nara had evidently turned up no noteworthy evidences of war, but there were plenty to be found at the chrysanthemum shows that opened mid-November in Tokyo—particularly the show at Dangozaka—where "scenes from Port Arthur and the battlefields of Manchuria are cleverly represented by the rarest chrysanthemums." One picture, formed from two thousand chrysanthemum roots, depicted Captain Hirose, "that valiant and brave officer—and his fellow Kesshitai (Determined to-die) comrades," their ship tossed upon a sea of flowers, their farewell song written below the flower waves. Other tableaus represented Russian Admiral Makaroff, standing on the bridge, sword in hand, going down with his ship—"a tribute to the enemy"—and a less complimentary depiction of "Russian Soldiers Assaulting Chinese Women."[62]

11. Sinking of the *Pallada*, December 8, 1904.

61. Yane [sic] Noguchi, "The Fighting Spirit in Japan Found in Rural Districts," *Brooklyn Eagle*, 18 Dec. 1904, rpt. *EE* 151-54.
62. "Monuments of Flowers are Built to the Dead," New Orleans *Times-Democrat*, 8 Jan. 1905, rpt. *EE* 183-87. Noguchi was evidently new to chrysanthemum shows, as he supposed Dangozaka the name of an exhibitor, a mistake he corrected in "The Chrysanthemum," *Taiyō* 13:13 (1 Oct. 1907): 16-20.

By December, Noguchi had settled down to churning out the war stories for which the American papers were clamoring. In contrast to Jack London, whose eagerness to get into the thick of things had led to his being sent back to California by the Japanese army, Noguchi sought maximum literary effect with minimal exertion. Readers had as yet developed few expectations with regard to journalistic integrity. Yet even with the low standards of the day it is surprising to find Noguchi disregarding such common concerns as truth, accuracy, objectivity, responsibility and integrity—disregard so flagrant that most of his war journalism would be better described as journalistic fiction.

Since the spring, Noguchi's preferred style of decadent journalism was the constructed interview. He had "interviewed" William Butler Yeats by adding a dining table, a knife, and a hand gesture to some translated sections of a pair of essays on the Irish writer's work. He had created an imaginary Japanese war correspondent, K.O. Fukui, who conducted interviews with naval officers in Sasebo and volunteer nurses in Tokyo. In November, he had "interviewed" Count Shigenobu Ōkuma, by repurposing material translated from Ōkuma's recent published lecture.[63]

12. Noguchi's portrait in *Kichō no ki*, December 1904.

From Count Ōkuma's drawing room Noguchi could travel in the blink of an eye to the battlefields of Port Arthur, which is where readers of several American papers found him reporting in mid-December.[64] "I rose early this morning," he wrote. "The air was sharp and cold, and mist wrapped the fighting regiments beyond me. The unceasing sound and thrill of cannon overhead reverberated through me. My servant brought me water—of a light gray color it was—some for me and a large bucket

63. "Okuma on Japan's Future," *Boston Evening Transcript*, 10 Dec. 1904, rpt. *EE* 146-50. Ōkuma Shigenobu, "Tōa no heiwa o ronzu" (On peace in East Asia), *Gaikō Jihō* (Revue diplomatique) 84 (Nov. 1904), 37-64.
64. "A Few Days at Port Arthur Before the Surrender," *KM* 15; "Under Port Arthur's Guns," *Boston Evening Transcript*, 13 Jan. 1905, 18; "Days at Port Arthur Before the Surrender," *New Orleans Times-Democrat*, 15 Jan. 1905, 31.

for the horses. Here at Port Arthur the horses are far more valuable than the soldiers." A typescript survives, with a deleted note explaining that Noguchi was one of "but three newspaper correspondents [who] succeeded in gaining access to Port Arthur." Noguchi, of course, was nowhere near Port Arthur. His stirring account of "Days at Port Arthur Before the Surrender," was presumably a translation of an account borrowed from a more adventurous Japanese reporter.

Often Noguchi could save himself even the trouble of translating by recycling articles he had created earlier in New York. At Christmas, he claimed to be visiting the soldier hospitals of Osaka in a story for his old nemesis, the *San Francisco Chronicle*. He described "the sharp odors of the medicine, the feeling of blood stain, the agony of suffering bodies—what an aftermath of battle!" and offered stirring accounts of the soldiers' exploits. He extolled the heroic qualities of Japanese soldiers telling stories like that of twenty-two-year-old gunner's assistant Koma Shinowara, who had requested to "leave his post for a few minutes" when a shell blew off his right hand, politely saluting with his left before going below. One of the wounded men had been on the *Fukui Maru* and witnessed the end of commander Takeo Hirose "whose name goes down in the stories of heroism forever, of our nation"; another told of the kindness of a Japanese sub-lieutenant giving water to a mortally wounded Russian officer. The only trouble was that the heroic stories supposedly heard in Osaka were taken from the "Little Stories of Brave Fighters" he had published in the *Boston Evening Transcript* and several other papers the previous July, before leaving New York. Ironically, the paper that had exposed Noguchi's plagiarized writing was now paying for it.[65]

13. Article in the *New York Tribune* Sunday Magazine, October 9, 1904.

65. "Christmastide in the Soldier Hospitals of Japan" *San Francisco Chronicle*, 22 Jan. 1905, 3. "Little Stories of Brave Fighters" appeared in the *Boston Evening Transcript* on 20 July 1904, and in the *Detroit Free Press* on 14 August; a shorter version appeared in the *San Francisco Call* under the title "Where Death Stalks," on July 28, 1904.

Patriotic women comprised another favorite subject for recycling. In "Women's Work for Japan," dated May 9, appearing in the New York *Globe* in June, K. O. Fukui observed "yesterday" a gathering of the Japanese Red Cross Society in Shibuya, where "150 ladies of the highest rank in Japan, all silently and deftly working" were gathered, making bandages for the army.⁶⁶ Noguchi could now miraculously observe, on November 6, the same event for the *Boston Evening Transcript* and New Orleans *Times Democrat*, with an encore performance on January 15 for the *San Francisco Chronicle*.⁶⁷

14. Marchioness Oyama.

A typescript for "The Russian Prisoners at Nagoya," dated January 15th, was published in the *Boston Evening Transcript*, the New Orleans *Times-Democrat*, and others. The article had Noguchi describing the prisoners, mostly "rough and boorish-looking young fellows," incarcerated at Nagoya's Higashi Honganji temple, "where the sun shines bright and the tinkle and melody of the bells sound even." The Japanese were "coming here from every province in Japan, traveling hastily as if to see some startling miracle: the giant Russians being guarded and cared for by the Japanese!" Noguchi, of course, would hardly have gone to so much trouble, despite Nagoya being on the way to Tsushima.⁶⁸

One would like to believe that Noguchi at least conducted the detailed

66. K. O. Fukui, "Women's Work for Japan," *Globe and Commercial Advertiser*, 16 June 1904, 9. A syndicated version of the article appeared as "Women's Part in War," Rock Island *Argus*, 28 May 1904, 9 and "Fair Toilers for Japan," *Palestine Daily Herald* (Texas), 1 July 1904, 3.
67. "Loyal Japanese Women," *Boston Evening Transcript*, 3 Dec. 1904, 12; "How the Women are Helping Japan," New Orleans *Times-Democrat*, 4 Dec. 1904, 31; "Japanese Women are at Work," *Minneapolis Journal*, 31 Dec. 1904, 12; "Royal Women of Japan Lead in Good Work for the Soldiers," *San Francisco Chronicle*, 12 Feb. 1905, 2.
68. "The Russian Prisoners at Nagoya," typescript, KM 16; the *Transcript* and *Times Democrat* articles were variously reprinted: "Thousands of Russians in One Japanese City," *Pensacola Journal*, 12 Feb. 1905, 10; "The Captive Russians," *Hartford Courant*, 2 June 1905, 17, among others.

interview with (or at least met) the Marchioness Oyama, Vassar-educated wife of Field Marshal Oyama, dated January 16th, that appeared in the New York *Sun*. Noguchi described visiting the Oyamas' American-style residence "situated in that rather picturesque part of Tokio known as Aoyama (Green Hill)," and offered a vivid account of how he was served afternoon tea by the Oyamas' charming daughter, toured the house, and discussed women's issues and the war with the Marchioness, one of the five Japanese girls sent to America in 1871 to be educated. "How I wish to visit there again!" she tells Noguchi.[69]

The nine dated manuscripts among the thirteen on war-related topics in the Keio collection all carry dates between December 13 and February 7.[70] Several carry personal notes to Ethel. "This is for the Globe and others. Don't send this to Los Angeles. Clover does'nt want this I am sure," he wrote on "Can Japan Stand Another Year?" dated December 13.[71] "This is clipped from the paper I do some work sometimes. Some English man is the editor and correct [sic] every writing I submit," Noguchi added in a postscript to "An Interview with Major-Gen. Nakamura" composed mainly of clippings (as were several other articles). Noguchi's claim of authorship was undermined by obvious differences in style, but it was all for a good cause: "Dearest, How is our business? I believe Everything is all right," he added. "When Will Peace Be Possible," dated January 30, ended with an especially encouraging postscript:

> Dearest:
> This article is for Frank. Are you well, sweetheart? Only love and kisses—that's all. Nothing to tell you. I want to kiss you and hold you just this minute. —Oh, how I wish to be with you! But— we got to work for our future's sake, have'nt we? Patience and courage, sweet heart. I will write you in a day or two, when I finish up one more article.[72]

69. "Marchioness Oyama, Japan's Social Leader," *New York Sun*, 19 Feb. 1905, 4.
70. "The Graphic Story of a Japanese Aid-De-Camp," dated ~~November~~ December 16th," "For publication Feb. 4th," pub. as "Won Fight By Nap," New York *Globe and Commercial Advertiser*, 20 Dec. 1904, KM 13; "Fool-hardiness of the Batto-Tai ('Drawn-Sword Company') at Port Arthur," dated "Tokyo Dec. 12th," "for the Globe and others," on back: "Globe / Transcript / ~~inter-ocean~~/ Globe-Democrat / Times," KM 28; "Can Japan stand another year?" dated "13th Dec. 1904 Tokyo," for "Globe / Transcript / Finances / Jan 25th," KM 7; "Little Stories from Port Arthur," undated (after Dec. 10), "for Frank's National," KM 29; "An Interview with Major-Gen. Nakamura," dated "Tokyo, Dec. 24th 1904," KM 11; "Japan Hears the Great Fall of Port Arthur," dated "Jan. 6th Tokyo," "for Globe and others," KM 27; "Japanese School Children and the Russia-Japan War" "for the National" (but not pub. there), KM 12; "In The Wake of the Surrender," "for Saturday Jan. 21st or Sunday Jan. 22nd," pub. as "In the Wake of the Russian Surrender," New Orleans *Times-Democrat*, 22 Jan. 1905, 31, KM 14A; "Incidents of Port Arthur," "for publication 21st," KM 14B; "The Russian Prisoners at Nagoya," dated "Nagoya, Jan. 15th," "for Saturday Age-Herald / Feb 5th," pub. as "Russian Prisoners at Nagoya Quartered in a Temple Garden," New Orleans *Times-Democrat*, 5 Feb. 1905, 31, KM 16; "When will Peace be Possible?" dated "Jan. [30th] 1905 Tokyo," KM 6; "A Few Days at Port Arthur Before the Surrender," "for publication Jan. 31st or Feb. 1st," pub. as "Under Port Arthur's Guns," *Boston Evening Transcript*, 13 Jan. 1905, 18, KM 15; "Japan's Diplomatic Success Against Russia," undated, [for] "Feb. 7th," KM 57.
71. "Can Japan Stand Another Year?" KM 7. Samuel Clover was editor of the *Los Angeles Express*.
72. "When Will Peace Be Possible," KM 6.

These few surviving comments to Ethel show Noguchi addressing her in a style considerably more romantic than his style to Léonie, but still with an eye to business.

A Fine Specimen

At Los Angeles County Hospital on November 17, Léonie, in a difficult delivery, gave birth to a boy; she was unconscious for nearly twenty-four hours, and the baby, too, was born unconscious. But they both pulled through, and Léonie, contemplating her new son, recalled the opening words of *The American Diary of a Japanese Girl*: "Kawaii Koto," meaning "how cute!"[73] Indeed, the nameless future sculptor was such a beautiful baby, and the mother so pleased with him, that a week later, when a woman reporter from the *Los Angeles Herald* got wind of the story and came to the hospital to see for herself, Léonie—though she protested that "as we have separated, this would not be a very pleasant time to announce a marriage"—relented when the reporter insisted, "I won't write about you, but just about the baby." With the swell of Japanophilia pushing against the growing anti-Japanese movement, it was hardly likely the reporter would keep her word.

15. *Shin Sekai* owner F. T. Kuranaga: "Wealthy Japanese Proud of His Fair American Spouse."

The *Herald* had been on a quest, finding not one but two babies born to white wives of Japanese men. The more prominent one was June Kuranaga, recently born to *Shin Sekai* owner F. T. Kuranaga, "the Japanese

73. "Yone Noguchi's Babe Pride of Hospital," *Los Angeles Herald*, 27 Nov. 1904, rpt. LG 112-13.

art importer, and his pretty American wife," who by an odd coincidence was named Leona. Kuranaga, the article explained, was "well able to live comfortably, having amassed quite a little fortune by his own efforts" and did "not allow his wife to soil her hands with housework," which was done by Japanese servants. He was quoted as saying in his "quaint English," "I am Japanese, my wife Iss American, my baby—noss anysing."[74]

Three pages later the future Isamu Noguchi, right hand clenched in a tiny fist, looked already determined to be something. "The young man gives promise of being in every way a fine specimen of the kind that is holding the attention of the whole civilized world." The reporter carefully scrutinized the specimen's racial characteristics. "In spite of the fact that baby was born under the flag of Uncle Sam and that his mother is an American woman, of the blue eyed type, he has not a single trace of anything but Japanese and the hair and eyes are as black as his father's ever were." (A standard tenet of white-supremacist racial pseudoscience was that the offspring of white and Mongolian intermixture of blood would always be Mongolian, just as Negro-white miscegenation would always produce a Negro. It was often claimed that these opposite races could not "amalgamate," and that the "mongrel" offspring, though apparently healthy, would become progressively enfeebled and eventually die out).

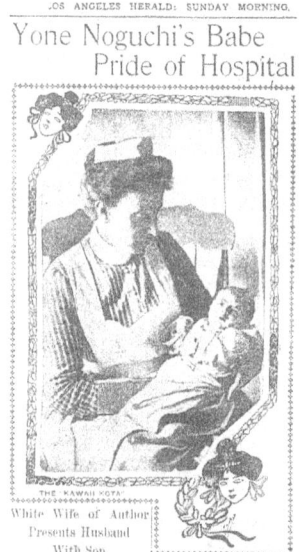

16. "Yone Noguchi's Babe Pride of Hospital."

The article gave an account of Noguchi's career, and of "the love which brought Laeonie Gilmore and Yone Noguchi together," ending with a melodramatic wartime separation. "In the meantime the son of an illustrious father lies in his cot in the hospital, and with his mother will wait for the day when peace shall again be restored and Noguchi will return to his adopted home." That day was not coming soon.

74. "Wealthy Japanese Proud of His Fair American Spouse," *Los Angeles Herald*, 27 Nov. 1905, 5.

Poetical Exaggeration

With all of Noguchi's invented meetings with famous people, it is a relief to find him actually listed by the *Japan Mail* among the prestigious attendees at the Tokyo English Speaking Society's annual dinner on January 28. The dinner was held at the Peers' Club (formerly the Rokumeikan—the luxurious but decaying "Deer-Cry Pavilion" that had housed the lavish dance parties and Western aspirations of Hirobumi Itō's first administration in the 1880s). Aside from Noguchi, the guests of honor came heavily fortified with titles and credentials: the trio of aged Harvard-educated barons Kanda, Kikuchi and Kikkawa, eminent zoologist Kakachi Mitsukuri who held doctorates from both Yale and Johns Hopkins, Keio sociologist Enoch Vickers, former Keio English professor Rev. Arthur Lloyd, and a Tokyo University professor of naval architecture. "All made highly entertaining and instructive post-prandial speeches," the *Daily Mail* reported.[75] None of this, evidently, met Noguchi's current standards for newsworthiness, for he did not bother to write about it.

17. The Peers' Club (former Rokumeikan).

Probably he sensed at the dinner that he himself was under scrutiny, especially by the professors associated with Keio. The Keio literature department had fallen on hard times, or rather, had never really risen from them. Founded in 1890 with William Liscomb as chair, it offered an assortment of courses—Rhetoric, History of British and American Literature, Chinese Literature, Psychology, and Ethics—with no specialized majors. Of the twenty students admitted in 1890, twelve had graduated (eight, including Noguchi, had left before completing the three-year course). Enrollments had dropped to the single digits after Anglican missionary Arthur Lloyd took over the department. Lloyd left in 1897 to become president of Rikkyō University, and the following year Fukuzawa brought in Thomas Sergeant Perry, whose Harvard credentials and name recognition—his great uncle was Commodore Matthew Perry—did little to slow the department's decline, and in May of

---

75. "Notes of Current Events," *Japan Mail*, 4 Feb. 1905, 118-19.

1901—Fukuzawa had died in February—it stopped operating completely, as no students were enrolled. It was only in 1904 that the department had been resurrected, following the passage of a law placing colleges under governmental oversight.[76]

Arthur Lloyd had taught a rhetoric course at Keio in 1903 after resigning his Rikkyō presidency; for the 1904 academic year he was moving up to Tokyo Imperial University to fill the vacancy left by Hearn. Hearn had been drawing an enormous salary of 450 yen a month before his departure, and Lloyd's substantial pay cut would allow the department to have a foreign professor in addition to several lecturers from the growing pool of talented graduates, starting with Sōseki Natsume and Bin Ueda, available at just 35 yen a month.[77]

Even private universities were in difficult financial straits under the heavy wartime taxation, and if Keio wanted to follow the usual method of staffing its literature department with its own graduates, Noguchi was a prime candidate. Even so, he could not have been eager to confront Rev. Lloyd, the professor whose courses he had fled as a student, nor Enoch Vickers, who now taught the course Noguchi vaguely recalled as "somebody's economy." He, or one of the numerous other Harvard graduates on hand, having perused the *Boston Evening Transcript*, might easily have raised some uncomfortable questions about Noguchi's impressions of Port Arthur, or some such topic, and spoiled Noguchi's hopes for a job at his alma mater. But the meeting was "very pleasant and successful," as the *Japan Mail* reported.[78] A week after, Noguchi wrote Putnam that he had been appointed to give lectures on American literature at Keio Gijuku, his old college, beginning in May.[79] "How long I will stay here in Japan is indefinite," he wrote. He needed Putnam's help to get books: "I cannot get here books, text books—in fact I cannot get any decent library book," he wrote. He gave Putnam a list of the ones he wanted: Stedman's *American Anthology* and two of Stedman's volumes of essays on poetry, William Archer's *Poets of the Younger Generation*, Carolyn Wells' *Nonsense Anthology*, Richard Le Gallienne's *How to Get the Best Out of Books*, and Harvard professor Barrett Wendell's *A Literary History of America*. "Dear Frank, Will you take the trouble to gather these books and mail them to me immediately? I want these books in the first week of April. Will you see about? They will cost some twenty dollars, I think. Will you pay this for me?—from the money for my stuff for your National. Or I will pay you from my pocket. I will do—Simply I want them quick. I need them for my lecture."

---

76. *Keiō Gijuku gojūnen-shi* (Tokyo: Keiō Gijuku, 1907), 231, 274-75.
77. On salaries see Yoji Hasegawa, *A Walk in Kumamoto*, 235, and Alisa Freedman, *Tokyo in Transit* (Palo Alto: Stanford UP, 2011), 86.
78. "Notes of Current Events," *Japan Daily Mail*, 4 Feb. 1905, 118-19.
79. YN to FP, 4 Feb. [1905], FPL 40.

With Japanese publishers eager to publish his books, Noguchi produced four during the course of 1905, each with a different publisher: *Japan of Sword and Love* (February 15), *The American Letters of a Japanese Parlor-Maid* (April 23), *Eibei no jūsan'nen* (Thirteen years in England and America, May 16), and *Hōbun Nihon shōjo no Beikoku nikki* (a Japanese translation of *The American Diary of a Japanese Girl*, November 1).[80]

Japan of Sword and Love, a collaboration with Joaquin Miller, was part of Noguchi's effort to make his mentor's work better known in Japan. According to Noguchi's account, during his brief stay in California the previous year Miller had been "so enthusiastic with Japan's victory. And he read to me many poems on Japan he had written; he was pleased when I suggested to him a book of collaboration under the title of *Japan of Sword and Love*."[81] "Many" was a slight exaggeration; Miller had written a total of three poems about Japan: "At Vespers in Tokio," a purported description of a Tokyo morning, published in *Sunset* in April 1903, "The Wee Brown Man," published in the *Harper's Weekly* of April 30, 1904, and "The Fisher of Nippon" in *The Century Magazine* for June 1904. He had also published an essay, "The Little Brown Men of Nippon," in *The Arena* in July. To these Noguchi added several tangentially-related poems: "To Russia," a poem from the 1880s criticizing Russian persecution of Jews, another early poem, "The Bravest Battle," which apostrophized the struggles of mothers during wartime, and "True Greatness," which made the case that true greatness belonged to the man who "loves, and lives content, complete, / With baby flowers at his feet." With these, Noguchi interspersed twenty-two of his own recent English poems and his *National Magazine* essay, "The Outcome of the War," and then added, to enhance Japanese readers' appreciation of his work, Rohan Kōda's poem written in honor of Noguchi's return to Japan.

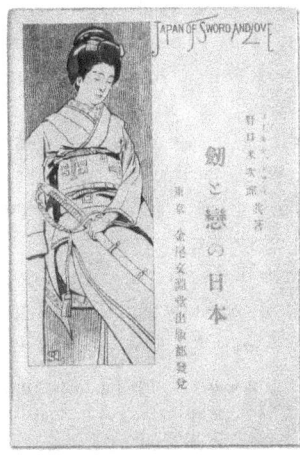

18. *Japan of Sword and Love*, 1905.

---

80. Published by Kanao Bunyendō, Shun'yōdō, Fuzanbō, and Tōadō Shobō, respectively.
81. SYN 79.

Japanese probably made up the majority of the book's small readership; Kanao Bunyendo, having little experience with overseas marketing and distribution, failed to capitalize on Miller's commercial appeal in Britain and America. Noguchi's journalistic connections secured a few notices about the "curious wedding of the East and West" (as the New York *Evening Post* called the little green paperback: "anything identified with Japan, and especially Japanese literature, commends itself to attention at present," the *Brooklyn Eagle* noted. The *Boston Evening Transcript* took a friendly interest in promoting the collaboration: "if intelligently read, this little collection of Japanese songs will give the reader much insight into the intellectual life of the East."[82]

But Miller's name was little known, and his Japonisme unconvincing, to Japanese readers. His stop in Japan in 1900, heading to China to cover the Boxer Rebellion for the *Examiner*, had been brief, and his odd descriptions of the country left serious doubts as to whether he had even set foot on shore. Noguchi sent off copies of the book to English papers, and evidently hoped for a favorable reception at the *Japan Chronicle* in Kobe, where Lafcadio Hearn had once worked. Robert Young, the paper's London-born Scottish editor, was "distinctly flattered by being regarded as a judge of Poetry" and, after four days' perusal, devoted a full page of his "Stray Notes" column to commenting, somewhat sarcastically, on Noguchi's "Fight, Fight, Fight!" and Miller's "Wee Brown Man."[83] A second full page (presumably by another editor) considering "English Verse by a Japanese" determined that "as examples of facility in the English language by a Japanese they are truly entitled to the term 'remarkable' and are worth treasuring as a curiosity; but this is a very different thing from giving them the rank of poetry."[84]

Young could not let matters rest there, however, and devoted another page-and-a-half the following week to Miller's outlandish comments on Japan.[85] The Japanese, according to Miller, were "the only entirely temperate people" he had ever known, their "wildest dissipation" being cold tea, which was to be found in great earthen jars "on almost every corner of the great thoroughfares in Japan." He had been delighted by the melody of the "sacred Gong-Gongs, bowls or drums" at Buddhist devotional services. Following the Japanese army to Peking in 1900, he had seen how the emperor responded to problems by telegraphing "Use the American hat" and "Use American bread." Such absurdities were "not worth serious consideration, and they would not receive notice from us were it not that Mr. Yone Noguchi, himself a Japanese, prints such an

---

82. "A Glimpse Toward Japan," *Brooklyn Daily Eagle*, 13 May 1905; "Books and Reading," New York *Evening Post*, 23 Mar. 1905, 6; "Books of the Day: Japanese Poetry," *Boston Evening Transcript*, 24 May, 1905, 20.
83. F.A.G. [Robert Young], "Stray Notes," *Japan Chronicle*, weekly ed., 13 Apr. 1905, 433.
84. "English Verse by a Japanese," *Japan Chronicle*, weekly ed., 13 Apr. 1905, 447-48.
85. "Poets on Politics," *Japan Chronicle*, weekly ed., 20 Apr. 1905, 460-62.

effusion and lets its absurdities go forth to the world without question." Noguchi "must be perfectly well aware that there is scarcely a sentence in the article which Mr. Miller has written which is not false either in actual statement or in implication, and yet he permits it to appear in a book published by himself as if Mr. Miller's phrensy were a sober statement of facts relating to Japan."

Noguchi sent two replies (both of which appeared in the following weekly edition): the first, on "Poetic Expression in an Alien Language," defensive, the second, on Miller, more contrite. "I acknowledge with you that his article appears to me as absurdity," he wrote. "Mr. Miller always exaggerates things. But his exaggeration is poetical . . . and his telling things is always interesting, however groundless."[86]

Noguchi pressed his case further the following week by sending a rather critical review of Arthur Lloyd's *Imperial Songs*, with the evident intention of illustrating that poetry was not simply a matter of native proficiency.[87] Young printed the review without comment. But a few weeks later he returned to the Noguchi-Miller theory of truth ("It may be unwise to exaggerate anything," says Mr. Noguchi, "but surely not a crime"), explaining that he had tried it out at his bank and at the law court with disappointing results.[88] Noguchi, however, thought he had acquitted himself well enough to include the exchange—minus the more contrite parts—in the Miller chapter of his autobiography.[89]

The Russo-Japanese War was entering its final stages. The Russian surrender of Port Arthur on January 2 had been the beginning of the end for the exhausted Russians, and the final land battle at Mukden (now Shenyang) took place in late February and early March. Japanese losses were heavy—71,000 Japanese died at Mukden—but spirits remained high.

On March 13, according to Noguchi's article for the *National*, "right after the successful occupation of Mukden, and when we were feverishly shouting 'Another great victory! Isn't it glorious,'" Noguchi was supposedly invited to lunch at the Ōiso seaside home of Marquis Hirobumi Itō, Japan's leading statesman. "We—the marquis and I alone—are at the luncheon table," Noguchi writes. "I had invaded his Oiso villa since morning." A one-on-one interview with the Marquis would have been an unprecedented journalistic coup for Noguchi, but as usual, there is reason to doubt the veracity of his account: substantial parts of his article were lifted from *The Review of Reviews*, which in January 1902, had published an Itō interview by Alfred Stead, who, as it happens, was also invited

86. YN, "Correspondence: Poetic Expression in an Alien Language," *Japan Chronicle*, weekly ed., 20 Apr. 1905, 480."Truth with a Capital T," *Japan Chronicle*, weekly ed. 20 Apr. 1905, 480-81.
87. YN, "A Translation of the Imperial Poems: Criticism by a Japanese," *Japan Chronicle*, weekly ed., 27 Apr. 1905, rpt. EE 215-17.
88. "Stray Notes," *Japan Chronicle*, weekly ed., 4 May 1905, 523.
89. YN, "Joaquin Miller," SYN 79-83; *Japan Chronicle*, weekly ed., 13 Apr. 1905 and 20 Apr. 1905; see also S. Tsushima, "Joaquin Miller and Japan," *Nation* 96 (29 May 1913): 544-5.

to lunch at Oiso. Noguchi most likely derived the Marquis' conversation—about the current political situation, among other topics—from other sources.⁹⁰

19. Mutsuhito, Emperor Meiji.

As the war was ending, Noguchi was completing another book of writings from his foreign experiences to be published in May. Entitled *Eibei no Jūsan'nen* (Thirteen years in England and America—adding a year was surely not a crime), it contained a curious assortment of published and unpublished articles in Japanese and English, along with a selection of letters received from famous writers.

Are You Not Wearing Love?

At the end of January 1905, Noguchi was still making plans for the arrival of Ethel Armes, who was set to leave San Francisco by steamer on March 18. Noguchi commanded Stoddard to give Ethel encouragement and a set of Stoddard's books to bring with her. "I will make your name known through whole Japan," Noguchi promised; then he would invite Stoddard himself to come and stay with them. "We cannot see even one thing—what things will turn up," he conceded, "but I will tell you definitely in these months when Ethel will be here."⁹¹

But something had, as his vague reference suggests, already turned up—an obstacle to the happy union, in the form of a certain *kawaii koto*. After its appearance in the *Los Angeles Herald* on November 27, the Japanese-American papers had picked up the story of the Anglophone poet's common-law wife, "Miss Gilmour" and her "lovely baby" at the Los Angeles County Hospital, anxiously awaiting the poet's return."⁹² By one means or another, the story made its way to Noguchi in Tokyo. What

---

90. "A Day With Marquis Ito," *National Magazine* 24 (April 1906), rpt. *EE* 264-72; Alfred Stead, "The Marquis Ito, Japan's Greatest Statesman," *Review of Reviews*, 25 (Jan. 1902): 22-27.
91. YN to CWS, 27 Jan. 1905, *CEL* 365.
92. So began the succinct summary of the story, reprinted from San Francisco's *Nichibei Shimbun*, in "Eibun shika no fujin to aiji" (Anglophone poet's wife and child), *Yamato Shimbun*, 8 Dec. 1904, 8.

is clear is that Noguchi wrote a (now missing) letter to Léonie about the situation on February 20. In it, "he asked her forgiveness, her consent to his marriage in Japan; asked about the baby, what she would him to do, that he must do, what she ought to do. He wished to God he could love her, but could not. [He] appreciated her kindness as kindness and deplored his 'temperament.'" Léonie's reply is also lost, but its contents may be surmised: she did not ask for reconciliation, but for the baby's sake she wished to have Noguchi acknowledge their marriage and his paternity; she could then legally obtain a divorce, and he would be free to marry whomever he liked. Noguchi, in an unusual act of conscientiousness, then wrote to Ethel on the eve of her departure to inform her about the situation.

Noguchi must have been aware of the likely effect of his confession to Ethel. Nevertheless, he did not give up hope. Still immersed in Miller's poetry, he took an old poem Miller had written to a benefactor of his youth, "Thomas of Tigre," which began:

> King of Tigre, comrade true!
> Where in all thine isles art thou?
> Sailing on Fonseca blue?
> Nearing Amapala now?
> King of Tigre, where art thou?[93]

Recasting its subject as "O Yuki San," a thinly-veiled Ethel in kimono, Noguchi transformed the poem into a love song, which appeared in the *Yomiuri Shimbun* on March 5.[94]

To O Yuki San

> Queen of love, My beloved,
> Where in all your isles are you?
> Sailing on the bluest sea?
> Nearing the Southern stars now?
> My love and beloved, where are you?
>
> Smiling toward Fuji Yama?
> Mirroring on the calmest sea?
> What have you in your hair?
> Is it a sweet marriage vow?
> My beloved and love, where are you?
>
> Queen of beauty, my beloved,

93. Joaquin Miller, "Thomas of Tigre," *Songs of the Sun-Lands* (London: Longmans, 1873), 211-12. Noguchi's poem inspired Stoddard to write a reminiscence about the subject of Miller's poem, "The King of Tigre," *National Magazine* 25 (Oct. 1906): 17-21. Miller usually referred to his benefactor as "The Prince," and identified him as "James Vaughn Thomas, of Leon, Nicaragua" in the dedication of *My Own Story* (Chicago: Belford-Clarke, 1890).

94. "To O Yuki San," *Yomiuri Shimbun*, 5 Mar. 1905, 2. The poem did not make it into the *National*, but did appear in the *Hilo Tribune*, 18 Apr. 1905, 2. It appears as a prose poem, "Queen of Love, My Beloved," in SC 121-22.

> Where in all your isles are you?
> Flying with the yellowest breeze?
> Singing the purple song today?
> My beauty and beloved, where are you?
>
> Walking by the pines, or underneath the cherry trees?
> Let me to you sing a song with a bird!
> What dress are you wearing today?
> Red or green? Yellow or grey?
> My beloved and beauty, are you not wearing Love?

On March 16, two days before Ethel's planned departure, he sent a copy to Frank Putnam, suggesting he might use it in the *National*. Although he made no direct reference to the situation, he alluded to it pessimistically: "I hope Ethel did'nt ask you money by my name. If she will come to Japan that will be another matter."[95]

Putnam, who had already been apprised of the situation by Ethel, dashed off a note to Stoddard:

> Yone writes me from Japan—I read between the lines his forshadowing of the fact his confession will prevent Ethel's coming to him—and a certain relief in that fact—or a very philosophic acceptance. The idea occurs to me that he may even have faked up the Los Angeles woman and child, as a byway out of his engagement—the oriental mind is subtle—too dam subtle—(pardon)—for me. For this thought, I have urged Ethel—who really seems heart-broken—against any steps to investigate the Los Angeles woman story. If she should learn the thing were a fake, that would give her a deeper hurt than what has gone before.[96]

Putnam refrained from printing the poem. By this time, Ethel was not "Sailing on the bluest sea," nor "Smiling toward Fuji Yama"; she was, perhaps, scowling towards California. Any speculation as to the color of her dress would have to favor black. She had already taken steps to investigate by asking a Los Angeles friend, Elizabeth Converse, to visit the alleged wife, enclosing a check to cover investigative expenses. Even as Putnam was writing Stoddard of his speculations that Yone had "faked up the Los Angeles woman and child, as a byway out of his engagement," Converse was dispatching the second of two letters in which she recounted to Ethel the results of her March 22 investigation. Ethel, in turn, showed the letters to Stoddard to solicit his opinion; with a writer's eye for a good story, he copied down their contents in full before returning them.[97]

Elizabeth Converse had first gone to the County Hospital where she found the official slip under the name of "Noguchi, Ella G.," age thirty; occupation, housewife; father, a native of Ireland; mother, a native of New York. "On the blank left for 'Married or Single' appears the initial

---

95. "To O Yuki San," YN to FP, 16 Mar. 1905, FPL.
96. FP to CWS, 23 Mar. 1905, CWSP.
97. CWS, copy of Elizabeth Converse to Ethel Armes, 22 and 23 March 1905, CWSP.

M," Converse noted: an inauspicious beginning. She was told at the hospital that the baby looked Japanese and that it was "beautiful and *Healthy* and bright," that a reporter from the *Herald* had written up the story, and that mother and baby had left the hospital on the first of December. Two hours later Converse had found the cottage—"a most poor one" she informed Ethel—where Léonie and her mother had moved a few weeks earlier, agreeing to cook breakfast and dinner for the two men who owned it in lieu of rent. The cottage was at the southwest corner of Evergreen cemetery in Boyle Heights, an inexpensive neighborhood in East Los Angeles, where readily available cheap parcels of land attracted an influx of new arrivals.

Converse was prepared for an ugly scene, but she found Léonie bafflingly cheerful. "Her attitude has simply swamped me," she confessed to Ethel. "I knew I could understand your agony and Yone's and expected to find the third dose of it, but not calm cheerfulness instead." Léonie herself was the supreme enigma. "In appearance Middle-West as they hang over the back fence. In manner as English [as] a queen." And "so very willing to talk." "I had expected frigidity or reticence as that is what I would have handed out to *anyone* and *everyone* who asked me questions under such circumstances." But Léonie was perfectly open and forthcoming, offering tea to the bewildered guest while she ate her own supper, apologizing that nursing the baby made her so hungry. Her mother, an old white-haired lady, held the baby, which Converse conceded was "a charming child, a glorious creature of vibrant body and sparkling eyes and sunshine of disposition." "A baby is worth twenty husbands," Léonie informed her.

When Converse had made clear the purpose of her visit, Léonie brought out the letter Yone had sent her on February 20 asking for her forgiveness and consent, and Converse read it eagerly. "Are you going to Japan?" she immediately wanted to know.

"Oh no!" was Léonie's response. "We have separated and will never live together." She did not want to stand in the way of Yone's happiness. She recounted the story of the relationship. She had known Yone now for five years, had revised all his manuscripts, and had a trunk full of them in her possession. Her marriage to Yone consisted of a document drawn up by him and signed that she thought had some legal value in New York.

Converse found this hard to swallow. "As an American girl," she asked, "why did you accept so flimsy a marriage ceremony—just a paper." Léonie did not answer at the time, although she later told Converse she believed implicitly in Yone's honour.

She and Yone had never lived together, Léonie continued; they were "too poor." She explained the circumstances of their four-month marriage, how the baby was the outcome of their last days together, how Yone had scoffed at her suspicion she was pregnant, how Yone had left New York in August, and a week later she had come to stay with her mother.

"She seems to accept as final that he doesn't love her, and can't love her, and there is not the slightest hint of a wail or a whine on account of it," Converse commented, adding: "I have indulged in a heap worse antics over a flirtation than she is doing over this." Léonie seemed perfectly content. "She is peace and happiness and courage and hope," Converse eulogized. "If she were the Mother of Jesus, she could not be more sure of herself or happier."

Léonie's main concern, she said, was to get a legal separation from Yone which would confirm the baby's legitimacy. She reiterated that she had no desire to stand in the way of Yone's remarriage; he had written twice asking her permission to remarry in Japan; Léonie had thought he meant to a Japanese girl, but was now coming to understand he meant Ethel. Converse asked if she would pity the girl Yone would marry; Léonie replied she would not; she believed in him. "She advises you to wait a while until she can get a *Legal Separation* in order to be sure her baby will be legitimatized." "Oh! I can't understand it," Converse commented. "She does not want help, or money, or anything; just her baby." There was only one explanation for such unconventional behavior: Léonie, she supposed, "must have been reading Walt Whitman."

What Ethel must have thought of this account is difficult to imagine. This Mother of Jesus, as "Middle-West as they hang over the back fence" (an inaccurate interpretation of Léonie's Greenwich Village bohemianism) who was "in manner as English [as] a queen," this Bryn Mawr graduate living in squalor with a white-haired mother and magnificent baby flaunting her unconventionality, this wronged woman, seduced and abandoned according to the conventions of the day, who could not even muster up a confrontational attitude toward the woman about to claim her still-beloved husband—if Elizabeth was "simply swamped" by her attitude, how much more incomprehensible it must have been for Ethel, who was to have been on the boat for Japan at the time.

But Ethel's main concern was Yone, not Léonie. Ethel herself was no slouch at playing the field, and her relationship with Yone had been a roller coaster ride. Yone had hoped his last-minute confession might be enough to keep the engagement from derailing. He had told Ethel that he had really not lived with Léonie, which was true, and that the newspaper story was full of lies, which was also true. But he had evidently not banked on Ethel's on-the-spot investigator digging up the whole sad tale of his relationship with Léonie. In the past Ethel had managed, through force of will, to make Yone fit her cherished image of ideal love, but that was out of the realm of possibility now. She had repeatedly told Alice how Yone adored and suffered for her, and how her love for him was built on this adoration. Now the foundation was shattered. The deep suffering Yone had endured in her imagination the previous December when they entered their final engagement was now replaced by the deep duplicity of those "three or four months" when Yone and Léonie were "living as man and wife," the meaning of which was clear. Then there was Yone's abandonment of a loving wife and baby to fend for themselves cooking for strange men in a shack. The credibility of the poet who had sworn to sacrifice his life for her was damaged beyond repair.

Although Ethel had broken off the engagement in March, Noguchi's spirits remained high through the month: the mail, though slow, had brought the requested parcel of books from Frank Putnam. Richard Le Gallienne's *How to Get the Best Out of Books*, a collection of introductory-level essays, was just what he wanted.[98]

In his latest poems he had imagined a future in which he and his O Yuki San "walked away from the city and noise, into the valley of Love and silence, thickly covered with mists and dreams."[99] Now, with the aid of Le Gallienne's essay on "How to Form a Library," he set himself to imagining his ideal study in an essay for *Gakutō* (the house magazine of the Maruzen book shop).[100] It would be "a tranquil place, not far from town yet near to heaven, only five or six blocks from the human world," where he might stretch out on a Turkish carpet on a summer afternoon beneath the pines, perusing the books in his library, beginning with Charles Lamb ("what delicate and graceful *Essays of Elia!*") surrounded by the numerous books he—or if the truth be known, Le Gallienne—treasured. Noguchi filled out his borrowed library with selections from the works of Japanese writer friends who had supported him ("I must not forget modern Japanese novelists: Rohan's *Five-Storied Pagoda*, Kōyō's *The Golden Demon*, and Dr. Tsubouchi's *Urashima*") as well as American and British writer friends: Stoddard's essays, young poets like Carman and Roberts, the elegant poet Miss Peabody and Miss Gale, and "the biography of Keats written by my dear and respected friend, Mr. Colvin." He did not miss the opportunity to discreetly plug his own work ("Where did I put *The Pillow Book*, I wonder? Ah, yes, I placed it on the shelf along with my own *American Diary of a Japanese Girl*.") And, while Le Gallienne was not identified as the source of much of Noguchi's book commentary, Noguchi did credit him for several lines of poetry.

The image of the ideal study remained with him for the rest of his life. But, sadly, it would not be the dreamy refuge where he and O Yuki San would make their own world together. "It was yesterday that I was driven out of the iron gate of Fate," he wrote in one of his new prose poems. "The voice said: 'you are not to return!' . . . And I hear a thousand voices echoing 'you are not to return!' Alas, I am to be fading like an idle song of emptiness."[101]

98. Richard Le Gallienne, *How to Get the Best Out of Books* (New York: Baker & Taylor, 1904).
99. "O Yuki San," *Shin Shōsetsu* (Apr. 1905), rpt. SC 14.
100. "Yo ga risōchū no shosai" (My ideal study), *Gakutō* 9:4 (Apr. 1905): 1-4.
101. "Out of the Iron Gate of Fate," SC 118.

Idle Song of Emptiness

Faced with this new reality, Noguchi's thoughts turned to "Dad." He wrote Stoddard on April 25 begging him to come to Japan. "I got a little Japanese house with a bit of garden. Come, Dad, be quick!," he pleaded. In a postscript, he asked, "Did Ethel write you about the Los Angeles woman?" "It is not so black with me as you may fancy," he added. "Don't trouble yourself with that matter, pray. I will settle it myself. And in fact it was all settled—a long time ago."

Stoddard, looking forward to some relaxation in California, could hardly be expected to jump at the chance of being cast as Ethel's replacement. He had foretold it all: "an early marriage, I fear you will live to sorely regret; and then if the Baby comes—that will ruin all," he had advised when Yone first consulted him back in 1902.[102] And so it had. He told Putnam, "I am likely to locate in some old Mission-Adobe village where I shall be unmolested; then I shall have my books, my siesta, my mass-wine, and no interruptions." Putnam sympathized but did not intercede, writing Stoddard on May 22, "Yone writes from Tokyo, very sorrowfully, 'I wish Dad were here this minute: he would understand!'" "Poor lad—," Putnam philosophized—"he has his uncomfortable hours to get through, same as Adam and Eve and the rest of us, but it will temper his blade and he'll be the better man for it in the long run, I guess."[103]

Whether or not Noguchi's uncomfortable hours were going to make him a better man in the long run, in the short term his American literary enterprises would be severely hobbled by the loss of his enthusiastic typist and agent. Publication efforts ground to a halt on the dozens of unpublished manuscripts and typescripts in Ethel's possession. Plans for Ethel to promote and market *The American Letters of a Japanese Parlor-Maid*, the long-awaited *American Diary* sequel published on April 23 by Fuzanbō, also had to be dropped.[104] Noguchi would have to be content with whatever sales the book could manage in Japan. To this end, the book carried Noguchi's preface in Japanese explaining how it had been based on his own hard American experiences, and a postscript by Waseda professor Shōyō Tsubouchi addressed to Miss Morning Glory, expressing his anticipation for the sequel to the *Diary* he had greatly admired. The book did notch favorable reviews in several prominent Japanese periodicals. A reviewer in *Kokoro no Hana* found Morning Glory "an extraordinary woman, rich in unique and sharp imaginative power, sincere, intelligent, and whimsically selfish. Unlike typical Japanese girls who daydream, she constantly observes everything around her. She quickly targets the vanity of Meriken ladies and assesses the character of gentlemen at a glance."

102. CWS to YN, 7 Nov. 1902, *CEL* 124.
103. CWS to FP, 31 May 1905, CWSP.
104. Miss Morning Glory (Yone Noguchi), *The American Letters of a Japanese Parlor-Maid* (Tokyo: Fuzanbō, 1905).

The reviewer found the writing "light and witty, though slightly difficult compared to that of Mr. Hearn. But this might be expected of such a brilliant woman."[105] A reviewer in the *Chūō Kōron* found the book's relative lack of poetic sentiment, compared to the *Diary*, compensated by its "sharp and practical observations."[106] But sales were dismal.

Although Ethel, fortunately for Yone, had no wish to publicize the scandal, it was impossible to contain completely. The effects were most dire among his woman journalist friends who knew of the engagement, namely, Zona Gale, Helen Bridgman, and Flora Field. Gale sent a letter, now lost, which "cast such a terrible accusation" over Noguchi that it remained in his drawer unanswered for several years, until he worked up the courage to beg for her forgiveness with the explanation, "I must have been a devil or something worse than devil."[107] He also lost touch with Helen Bridgman, who noted in *The Brooklyn Standard Union* "the engagement of marriage between Yone Noguchi, the Japanese poet and critic, whose residence of some years in America won him many friends, and Ethel Armes, of Birmingham, Ala., is broken."[108] Collateral damage included his productive relationship with the New Orleans *Times-Democrat*, Flora Field's paper—to which he had been contributing an article nearly every week since late October—which came to an end in June.[109] Among the pieces left in the care of Ethel presumably intended for the *Times-Democrat* were the series of reminiscences by the students and colleagues of Lafcadio Hearn, who had been literary editor of the paper from 1881 to 1887.

Noguchi had little time to worry about his dwindling American publications with his Keio lectures starting in mid-April.[110] Stoddard, with his many years of experience teaching at Notre Dame and the Catholic University, might have been a great help. But he would have to manage in his own.

Even with his dwindling American publications, May was far from a total loss: *Eibei no Jūsan'nen* (his bilingual assortment of essays documenting his experiences abroad) came out, and he had a substantial essay on "The Younger Poets of Present Japan" in the *Japan Times*, and another on "Royal Poets of Japan" in the *Boston Evening Transcript*.[111] June saw the last three *Times-Democrat* articles: the (unattributed) Tetsujirō Inoue reminiscences of Lafcadio Hearn, a biographical sketch of war hero

---

105. "Shinkan hihyō" (Criticism of new publications), *Kokoro no Hana* 9:7 (July 1905): 93-94.
106. "Shinkan hihyō" (Criticism of new publications), *Chūō Kōron* 20:7 (1 July 1905): 108.
107. YN to Gale, 25 Mar. 1909, ZGP.
108. [Helen Bartlett Bridgman], "Women's World," *Brooklyn Standard Union*, 7 Aug. 1905, 7.
109. "Climbing Dantai Mountain," New Orleans *Times-Democrat*, 2 Apr. 1905, rpt. SS 71-75; "What are the Horse-Thieves in Manchuria," New Orleans *Times-Democrat*, 9 Apr. 1905, 39; "On the Romanization of the Japanese Script," New Orleans *Times-Democrat*, 16 Apr. 1905, rpt. EE 209-14.
110. According to *The Keio Gijuku University* (Tokyo: Keio Gijuku, 1909), 40, the academic year was divided into three terms, April 16–July 15, Sept. 11–Dec. 25, and Jan. 11–Mar. 31.
111. "The Younger Poets of Present Japan," JT, 20 May 1905, 6; "Royal Poets of Japan," *Boston Evening Transcript*, 29 May 1905, 11.

Admiral Tōgō, and a piece on Japanese women's hair.[112] And for *Success* magazine, a profile of a Japanese gunpowder scientist.[113]

Three of his new English prose poems appeared in *Shirayuri*.[114] And in *Shin Shōsetsu*, his publisher Shunyōdō's literary monthly, where he had published his syrupy love poem, "To E.A.," the previous year, he now sang in poetic prose of his failing romance with "O Yuki San," the "Queen of my love" he had introduced in the *Yomiuri* in March. The romantic hopes "Did You Go to Marriage Shrine" ("O stars, come not, to-night, we have to make our own world, we two alone, O Yuki San and I!"), seemed fated to a sad, dreamy end in "Touch Me with thy Soft Hands": "the soft moon is rising, but never, never, never thy soft hands, thy soft hands again, O Yuki San!"[115]

The prose-poetry experiment had begun the previous December. Katsuichirō Andō, who graduated during Lafcadio Hearn's last year at Tokyo, had extolled the importance of prose poetry in an essay on the Decadent movement for *Teikoku Bungaku*.[116] In the 1890s, several Decadents put prose poems in their books. Oscar Wilde, in a privately-printed pamphlet, *Poems in Prose* (1894), Fiona Macleod (William Sharp) in *The Silence of Amor* (1896), and Ernest Dowson in *Decorations in Prose* (1899).

Of these, Fiona Macleod's *The Silence of Amor*, reprinted as a small, separate volume in 1902 by Thomas Mosher, drew Noguchi's special interest. Mosher, a benevolent pirate of the publishing world, reminded him of the romantic highwayman, Claude Duval, or the Japanese Nezumi Kozō. Mosher "rescued unfortunate, tear-soaked, pitiful writers, introducing them in beautifully-bound limited editions to aristocratic American reading circles."[117] Among these had been the pseudonymous Scottish writer Fiona Macleod. "Macleod's name was not particularly well-known until Mosher began reprinting his works. It is said that Sharp was deeply grateful to Mosher during his lifetime."

The Silence of Amor was the first English book consisting entirely of prose poems, although the subtitle "Prose Rhythms" declared the author's preferred term. "Prose is prose, and poetry is poetry," and "the two arts are distinct, though they may lie so close in method and achievement as to seem to differ only in degree."[118] Macleod had offered warm but qualified praise of *From the Eastern Sea* in 1903, saying, "what it lacks in form

---

112. "Death of Lafcadio Hearn," 4 June 1905, 39; "Admiral Togo: 'Demon Heihachiro,'" 11 June 1905, 35; "Soul of Japanese Woman is in Her Hair," 25 June 1905, 37.
113. "Dr. Gian Shimonose, Japan's Gunpowder Wizard," *Success* 8 (June 1905): 390.
114. "Sanbun eishi sansho" (Three English prose poems), *Shirayuri* 2:8 (1 Jun. 1905): 361: "Out of the Grey Forest," "By the Sea-Shore," and "The Song of [J]oy."
115. "Did you go to the Marriage Shrine," "Touch me with thy Soft Hands," *Shin Shōsetsu* 10:6 (1 June 1905).
116. Andō Katsuichirō, "Dekadan-ron" (On Decadence), *Teikoku Bungaku* 9:5 (May 1903).
117. "Moshā-ban no shoseki" (Mosher's books), *Gakutō* 21:18 (20 Sept. 1917), rpt. "Moshā," *Kaigai no kōyū* (Tokyo: Daiichi Shobō, 1926), 81.
118. Fiona Macleod [William Sharp], *The Silence of Amor* (Portland, Maine: Mosher, 1902).

(an inevitable lack, in the circumstances) it offers in essential poetry."[119] Macleod's even-more-formless productions could not be excused by the "circumstances" of writing "in a language so different," so instead of calling them "poems," he called them "prose-rhythms," explaining how the prose-rhythm employed rhythmic techniques such as monotony, repetition, inversion, and cadence, but distinguishing it from "the dubious 'prose-poem,' so apt to be merely ornate prose crested with metaphor or plumed with hyperbole." Noguchi liked them, whatever they were. "I had been reading your prose-poems, *The Silence of Amor*, and wished I could write such pieces myself. And here is the result!," he wrote, presenting Macleod with a copy of *The Summer Cloud*.[120]

The influence was more than formal. *The Silence of Amor* contained a poem entitled "Summer Clouds," inspiring Noguchi's book title. "Before the Rising of the Moon," one of the three new samples of prose-poetry that Noguchi sent to *Myōjō* for March, obviously came from Sharp's "At the Rising of the Moon." "At the rising of the moon I heard the falling echo of a song," Macleod had written. "Before the rising of the moon," Noguchi wrote, in a sort of prequel, "I hear the song echoing toward this way like a flowing tide,—the song I dreamed."[121] It did not matter if Macleod had dreamed it first. With the moon, "The air will turn to gold as with Love and kiss," he continued. Elsewhere in the poems there are echoes of Macleod's "Hy Brasil," a paean to the mythical Celtic island. "I heard the voice of the wind among the pines," Macleod wrote; "In dreams, now, I hear the cuckoos calling across a dim sea of light."[122] Noguchi heard the pines too—the California pines he had left, as well as the ones he had recently heard again outside his Tsushima bedroom window—and wrote:

> I hear you call, pine tree, I hear you upon the hill, by the silent pond where the lotos flowers bloom, I hear you call, pine tree.
>
> What is it you call, pine tree, when the rains fall, when the winds blow, and when the stars appear, what is it you call, pine tree?
>
> I hear you call, pine tree, but I am blind, and do not know how to reach you, pine tree. Who will take me to you, pine tree?[123]

The Younger Poets of Japan

Shirayuri (White lily) was a *Myōjō* offshoot formed two years earlier, largely by the eccentric firebrand poet-philosopher-critic-novelist Hōmei Iwano, who had become one of Noguchi's most important sources of connections

---

119. Macleod to YN, [1903], facsimile in *Eibei*, 39-40, text in Elizabeth Amelia Sharp, *William Sharp (Fiona Macleod): A Memoir Compiled by his Wife* (New York: Duffield, 1910): 409.
120. YN to Macleod, [Jan. 1906], in Elizabeth Amelia Sharp, *William Sharp (Fiona Macleod)*, 409. Sharp never saw the letter, having died on 14 Dec. 1905.
121. "Ei sanbun sanshō" (Three English prose poems), *Myōjō* (1 Apr. 1905): 40. The other two poems were "The Mirror of My Lady Beauty" and "The Twilight."
122. "Hy Brasil," Fiona McLeod [William Sharp], *The Silence of Amor*, 22.
123. "I Hear You Call, Pine Tree," *Gekkan Suketchi* (18 Apr. 1905), rpt. SC 82-83.

and stimulation during the past months. Iwano had arrived on the Tokyo literary scene in 1902. At the outset he "frequently published his poetry in the journal *Myōjō* and he participated actively in the *Myōjō*-group's poetry readings," but then decided he "could not satisfy his literary needs through the *Myōjō* group," and "therefore created a new literary group" in 1903 with two Waseda poets, thirty-nine-year-old Ringai Maeda, and twenty-year-old Gyofū Sōma, then still a precocious student.[124] *Shirayuri* began publication in November 1903, and soon emerged as an alternative to *Myōjō*, drawing contributions from many of Noguchi's friends and associates.[125] "We are extremely fortunate," Noguchi had written in his "Younger Poets of Present Japan" essay, "in having the new books" by the two *Shirayuri* leaders, Iwano's *Yujio* (the Evening Tide) and Ringai's *Natsubana otome* (the Summer Flowers and Young Girl).[126] "Homei Iwano is sincere," he wrote, "and his sincerity in thought as well as in expression often makes him appear too abrupt. He would appear artless like a naked tree in autumn. However, he is quite often strong and his sorrow is manly." Hōmei "makes an excursion into the land of dream and fantasy, but he does not reach the goal, and returns unsuccessful. And he is not rich in rhetoric like Ringai Mayeda." "Ringai's work is gorgeous like a brocade and less passionate naturally. . . . he is always after his own beautiful heavens. He is the poet of love and delight." Ringai's love and delight, however, were already in short supply. As Madoka Hori notes, "Hōmei, one of the founders of *Shirayuri*, had a falling out with Ringai and Gyofū at the beginning of 1905 and withdrew after publishing poems in the April, May, and June issues."[127] The following year Ringai and Gyofū became the main opposition to Noguchi's efforts to organize, with Hōmei's help, an international poetry society, the Ayame-kai, or Iris Club. Not surprisingly, Ringai is no longer to be found in Noguchi's revised 1914 "Poets of Present Japan."

The gifted though flawed Hōmei, however, remained a perpetual fascination. "We hear of a poet of promise with youthfulness and a certain amateurish fire, but never reaching to a state of maturity; such a poet is rarely guilty of falsehood or artificiality, but his want of the power of self-analysis is often wonderful," Noguchi wrote.[128] Iwano was "a born poet"; "the question with him is not how to sing, but how not to sing"; he was "the most versatile poet of the present day; and, naturally, he has unconsciously degenerated into every excess"; "his buoyancy and exaltation of imagination and swing" were impressive, though Hōmei had "yet to learn how to control his poetic impulse."

124. Yoichi Nagashima, *Objective Description of the Self: A Study of Iwano Hōmei's Literary Theory* (Aarhus, Denmark: Aarhus UP, 1997),
125. Among them, Shōyō Tsubouchi, Bin Ueda, Bansui Tsuchii, Takuboku Ishikawa, Sakusaburō Uchigasaki, Hakuson Kuriyagawa, Gekkō Takayasu, and Kyūkin Susukida.
126. "The Younger Poets of Present Japan," *JT*, 20 May 1905, rpt. *EE* 218-24.
127. Hori Madoka, *"Nijūkokuseki" shijin Noguchi Yonejirō* (Nagoya: U of Nagoya P, 2012), 115.
128. *SJP* 105-10.

20. Hōmei Iwano.

Noguchi later recalled how he was "dragged around by Hōmei as guide, after returning to Japan." On one occasion Hōmei brought him to a house near Shinjuku surrounded by twisted trees and sprawling weeds, where Keigetsu Ōmachi lived. The house of the poet-critic struck him as rather slovenly, but the casual way Keigetsu stood up after preparing *edamame* for his guests, urinated off the edge of the veranda, returned to his seat at the dining table, and began peeling potatoes, rather impressed him. Noguchi was "pleased to live in Japan where this unrestricted life is natural" and "determined to forget about the West."[129]

In contrast, he was frustrated in his attempts to break through Bin Ueda's protective veil of cigarette smoke.[130] It was only after Ueda's death, a decade later, that Noguchi confessed his disappointment that "our friendship never truly deepened beyond the initial meeting when we sat drinking tea and smoking in a building beside the pond on the grounds of the Imperial University. No matter how much I tried to draw closer to you, I always had the impression that you kept a 'haze of fragrant smoke' between us." It was, he thought, partly Ueda's character, which resembled that of Tokyo shopkeepers, "generous in understanding but comparatively lacking in sympathy . . . inhabitants of a neutral emotional realm," and partly that "both of us had reached the age—approaching thirty—where the desire to make new friends had faded, and our characters had hardened." Ueda was then teaching in Kanda.

> At the time you were employed at the Higher Normal School, and since my home was nearby, you would occasionally stop by on your way back from school. Even when you came to my house, unlike Iwano or Kambara, you would always sit quietly and properly. Somehow, I felt reluctant to open up to you, and I still remember thinking that perhaps you had come not for friendly talk, but to observe and study my room or my manner.
>
> Around the time of my returning, I had brought back with me mistaken

---

129. "Kensoku no nai seikatsu" (Unrestrained living), *Myōjō* 3:1 (Jan. 1923): 124.
130. "Ueda Bin-kun," *Jiji Shimpō*, 22, 25, 26 July 1916, 5.

or confused ideas about Japanese food, clothing, and shelter. Thinking back now on my nonchalantly ridiculous behavior makes me break into a cold sweat. I remember you once saw that I had placed four or five small Turkish-style soup bowls irregularly on the veranda facing the garden of my room, and you said, 'Interesting; this is an interesting way of doing things.'

Ueda's powers of perception were not, Noguchi thought, particularly sharp, but he was a remarkably perceptive reader, a virtual encyclopedia of foreign literary names whose "remarkable memory could instantly recall who wrote which passage and where it had been published." Frustratingly, his reticence extended to literary topics as well. "You always seemed to be wearing armor, and would not engage in topics like English or English poetry or literature. It seemed as though you made an effort to avoid speaking. Even in conversation, you were refined in your word choice (though at times you would launch sharp little sarcastic darts), always perfectly polite, the very image of a refined gentleman."

The Old Sires Alone

Noguchi's status as conquering hero of English letters remained tenuous. His literary success in America and Britain might inspire respect, even awe, or jealousy or suspicion, from his Japanese peers. But to really establish his claim to the privileged position he had staked out, he needed to visibly demonstrate the literary powers he had ostensibly acquired. There was perhaps no better way than to show that he could go head-to-head against older, more established writers in a familiar field such as poetry translation. A first provocation came from Arthur Lloyd's new *Imperial Songs; Poems by the Emperor and Empress of Jāpan and other Imperial and Distinguished Personages*, reviewed in the *Japan Weekly Mail* on March 25.[131] Tanka translation, the reviewer granted, was "an almost hopeless task. No one has ever thoroughly succeeded." And there were "very few foreigners in Japan to whom would have been officially allowed the privilege of translating and publishing poems written by the Emperor and Empress." Happily, Mr. Lloyd possessed the exceptional qualifications, being an erudite, widely respected scholar, and "a poet of no mean ability." The *Mail*'s reviewer admitted that it was presumptuous to say that Lloyd "had accomplished the feat as well as it is accomplishable. Some exceptional genius may discover a happier method one of these days. But in the meantime, we are content to admit Mr. Lloyd's claim almost to supremacy." The Anglican missionary who had presided over the gradual downfall of the Keio English department, and then left it for the more prestigious Imperial university, made for a fairly easy target. Still, Noguchi could not at first bring himself to do the deed, at least before first plagiarizing Lloyd and the *Mail*, as he did in his *Japan Chronicle* review, and another, entitled "Royal Poets

---

131. Arthur Lloyd, *Imperial Songs* (Tokyo: Kinkodo, 1905); "The Bookshelf," *Japan Mail*, weekly ed., 4 Mar. 1905, 319.

of Japan," which he sent on May 5 to the *Boston Evening Transcript* and *New York Globe*.¹³² But a few weeks after finding Lloyd's work fit for American consumption, he declared it unsatisfactory in a Japanese article for the *Chūō Kōron*. The critical turn had come about after the appearance of a second translator, Kenchō Suematsu, a Cambridge-educated baron married to a daughter of Hirobumi Itō, an excellent writer of English but an unimpressive translator of poetry.¹³³

Noguchi showed no fear in charging Lloyd with excessive wordiness and explanation, and Suematsu with a list of offenses, including the use of common adjectives, ineffective verbs, unnecessary and poorly chosen words, and forced rhymes, though he politely ended with praise for one Suematsu translation and several phrases.¹³⁴ The analysis was methodical and even-handed—he found praiseworthy points in both translations— and on point. The criticisms were justified. Lloyd had rendered one of the emperor's most famous compositions:

> They're at the front
> Our brave young men, and now the middle-aged
> Are shouldering their arms, and in the fields
> Old men are gathering the abundant rice
> Low bending o'er the sheaves. All ages vie
> In cheerful self-devotion to the Land.

The *Japan Mail* article had offered a shortened version, but Noguchi wanted to go shorter still:

> All the sons are gone to the battle-field, and
> the old sires alone keep the mountain and field.

Noguchi then addressed Baron Suematsu's translation:

> I suppose all sons to the front are gone,
> To do their duty all under arms,
> And their old sire at home alone
> Guards and watches their lonely farms.

The phrase "I suppose" was gratuitous and weak, the translation further weakened by Suematsu's redundancies (why "at home," "alone," and "lonely"?) and poor word choices. Noguchi did reserve some praise for a translation by his Tokyo University professor friend Kenzō Wadagaki:

---

132. "A Translation of the Imperial Poems," *Japan Chronicle*, 27 April, op. cit.; "Royal Poets of Japan," *Boston Evening Transcript*, 29 May 1905, 11. Borrowing liberally from *Imperial Songs*, Noguchi did identify Lloyd as the translator of the poems, but failed to acknowledge that the remainder of the article was lifted from Lloyd's introduction and the *Japan Mail*'s review.
133. "Gyosei no Eiyaku hiyō" (A criticism of the making of English translations), *Chūō Kōron* 20:7 (1 Jul. 1905): 41-46.
134. Baron Suyematsu, "The Heart of the Mikado," *Nineteenth Century and After* 57 (Apr. 1905): 566-72. Suematsu Kenchō, "Gyosei no eiyaku" (English translation of the Imperial poems), *Chūō Kōron* 20:6 (1 June 1905): 35-41.

> The sons all, ere this fall,
> At the country's call
> To the front are gone,
> Leaving farm and field and all
> In the hands of the sires alone.

Perhaps fearful he had gone too far, Noguchi tempered his criticism by praising phrases he liked in the work of each of the translators, and ended by politely expressing his gratitude for all of the translators' work.

The Baron, then in Paris, did not take the attack lying down, but countered in the next issue with sharpened pen. "I must say, with all due respect, I was surprised at Mr. Noguchi's apparent lack of sufficient knowledge of Japanese."[135] In his knowledgeable and dismissive rebuttal he explained the rationale for the choices Noguchi had questioned. It was not "mountains and fields" the old sires were looking after, but mountain fields, as he had tried to suggest by the more poetic phrase, "lonely farms." And surely one could be alone and not at home, or vice-versa, so the charge of redundancy was overstated. Elsewhere, he noted Noguchi's apparently poor understanding of the poems, explaining the nuances of the archaic poetic verb endings "nari," "keri" and "ran." He acknowledged that he was "not a person who writes poetry," as Noguchi had unkindly observed, but "if I were inclined to accept the role of a poet, I believe it would not be particularly difficult for me to be recognized as one of the foremost poets of the day." As a sort of demonstration, he translated his translations back into Japanese, but in a different form, to show that the meaning remained intact.

Given a chance for a counter-rebuttal in the same issue, Noguchi initially wavered, "thinking that not taking up the pen again in response would be an act of magnanimity," but then made the most of the opportunity.[136] On reading Suematsu's reply he had, he confessed, "burst into loud laughter." "I had not expected the doctor to be so narrow-minded and incapable of understanding matters." "In terms of Japanese scholarly ability, I am not as deficient as the doctor has rashly concluded," he asserted, before returning to the offensive. The emperor's poems used sincere, simple words understood by millions of Japanese people, enabling the poems to shine with brilliance and inspirational power. But the excellence of English prose and poetry depended on the choice of adjectives and verbs, which could, together, create a sense of beautiful, lively movement. Suematsu's choices "lacked sufficient attention or skill," which left him "more than a little dissatisfied." Turning the "ran" auxiliary into "I suppose" was a good example: if it really needed to be translated, a

---

135. Suematsu Kenchō, "Gyosei eiyaku ni tsuite Noguchi-shi ni kotau" (Answering Mr. Noguchi on the English Translation of the Imperial Poems), *Chūō Kōron* 20:10 (1 Nov. 1905): 50-53.

136. "Kasanete Suematsu hakushi ni tadasu tokoro ari" (Questions again for Dr. Suematsu), *Chūō Kōron* 20:11 (1 Nov. 1905): 65-68.

well-placed "would" was sufficient. Suematsu's defense of the combined "alone," "lonely" and "at home" seemed to miss the nuance of the word "hitori," which to Noguchi meant the solitary appearance of the old men, not their loneliness. Nor could he understand why Suematsu had used "to the front" for battlefield, and then felt obliged to add, as explanation, "To do their duty all under arms." "Poetry is not to be buried under layers of explanation," Noguchi explained.

Though it was no rout, Noguchi had acquitted himself well, inflicting a fair amount of damage on his old-guard opponents, taking only a few token hits in return. He afterward made amends to Suematsu by penning an admiring review of Suematsu's *A Fantasy of Far Japan*. "In the general matter of Japan, it is the best Japanese book that has yet appeared," Noguchi declared.[137] "It would be almost beyond imagination how far and deep his book has impressed itself on the mind of foreigners." Noguchi did make an effort to translate the famed *Hyakunin Isshu* tanka anthology in 1907, but never really warmed to the genre, complaining of its lack of intensity and artificial execution. And yet, three decades later, he was still telling of his plan to make his own book of translations of the Meiji Emperor's tanka.[138]

Brides of the Night

Stoddard saved a fragment of a letter Ethel wrote him soon after the emergence of the facts.[139] She was still distraught—"I haven't been able literally to write a sane line since it all happened," she admitted. She approved of Stoddard going to see Léonie and the baby personally. (He was contemplating a trip down the California coast). But it would make no difference in regard to the crux of the matter, as Ethel saw it.

> She says—you know—Yone lived with her the year—all that year he was writing to me & we were engaged—she says he was married to her all that time. I heard from him a few weeks ago & he says he lived with her one week only & that she lies. I do not think she lies. You can give me your impressions at least & find out if that is a lie. But—it makes no difference—nothing can—there is the child—his treatment of that woman—[It is] plain written that he never loved me yet & I do not think ever could love me.

She continued,

> It is strange—I used to dream he really cared for me & that was why I loved him so—because I thought he cared so much—but—you see—he never loved me once & never cared at all.

137. Baron Suyematsu, *A Fantasy of Far Japan or Summer Dream Dialogues* (London: Constable, 1905); YN, "Through a Japanese Screen," *JT*, 12 Jan. 1907, 6.
138. "'Waka' Poems of Late Emperor Meiji Are Being Translated into English," *JT*, weekly ed., 27 Oct. 1938, 10.
139. Ethel Armes to CWS, undated fragment, [1905], CWSP.

> I am not unhappy at all—Do not think I am feeling more than I do. I feel nothing whatever. I am very well now—though my strength is not back yet. I am however becoming interested in work again—in writing—if—if I could learn to write—
>
> That will come maybe some day.

Ethel's writing project was a little book she had started the previous year revolving around the village of Center Sandwich, New Hampshire, Alice's father's birthplace, where Ethel had spent part of a summer a few years earlier, before the Yone entanglement. Entitled *Midsummer in Whittier's Country*, it was written in achingly beautiful—if not always explanatory—prose, and illustrated with Ethel's own sketches ("reproduced they arent so dreadful" she assured Alice). The book offered local color and glimpses into former resident John Greenleaf Whittier's poems about the region and its native inhabitants, but the real subject was Ethel's enduring love for Alice, whose ancestral homeland had supplied the charmed setting of their summer rambles. "So we drove and we drove, Alice and I. We followed the roads as the flowers did, we embraced them, we adored them,—and we did not blame a single little aster! It was dark when we turned homeward, . . . Then we watched the stars come out. With half-closed eyes we watched the mystic fairness of the hills—those brides of the night—clouds and the stars—adorning themselves for their sweet bridegrooms."[140]

"My MAN," she wrote Alice on June 12, "Keep me always—star of your heart—Now you are in Center Sandwich and in the dreams. But your Indian bride will require you to be practical for the space of two or three weeks."[141] The book was to be out in a week, and she greatly desired Alice's assistance with local publicity. "Soon," she promised, "I will write and tell you everything. It is quite over and done with. I broke our engagement in March."

Four weeks later, with the book still not ready ("There was more work than I thought," she explained, but "I've seen it DONE actually so now it ought not to be long") she made good on her promise.[142]

> I send the letters that tell you it all. It is quite over now and strange to say I am not at all unhappy any longer. I do not feel anything at all. After the first wrenching out of everything—I breathed—freer—I believe. I was on the point of going when his letter of confession came and then—fortunately I had a friend on the spot who could serve me.
>
> Be sure to guard—as you will—secretly and return the letters.

Alice was likely the last to read Yone's declarations of love before Ethel consigned them to the fire.

---

140. Armes, *Midsummer*, 55-57.
141. Ethel Armes to Alice Wiggin, 12 June [1905], EMAP.
142. Ethel Armes to Alice Wiggin, 8 July [1905], EMAP.

Glow of the Firefly

1905-1907

As a junior faculty member at Keio, still on trial, Noguchi was encouraged to contribute to the university's monthly journal, the *Keiō Gijuku Gakuhō*. His lecture on Miller had appeared the previous year, but that essay had been primarily a personal reminiscence.[1] Professors were supposed to write literary studies of a more analytic sort, so, as summer approached, he set to work. "Novelists of Today," his essay for the June issue, displayed a wide familiarity with the field, offering brief comments on dozens of contemporary American and British writers (he neglected to mention that most were simply translated from Richard Le Gallienne's "The Novel and Novelists of To-day"), to which he added critiques of the relative backwardness of contemporary Japanese fiction.[2] For his July essay on the poet Shelley, he made a more serious effort, consulting several biographical treatments of the poet's final days, and making insightful comments about Shelley's engagement with the sea, a topic he had begun contemplating during his voyage home to Japan.[3] As Noguchi approached his thirtieth birthday, he could not help but measure himself against the great Romantic poet. "When Shelley died, he was only thirty years old. To die at thirty—wasn't that far too early? And yet, he left behind such magnificent works that he will remain forever a great figure in history." Noguchi did not seem to be aiming for permanent greatness himself with his next essay, "Russian Literary Master

1. "Shijin Mirā" (The poet Miller), *Keiō Gijuku Gakuhō* 83 (15 Nov. 1904): 8-13; 85 (15 Dec. 1904): 32-36.
2. "Genkon no shōsetsuka" (Novelists of today), *Keiō Gijuku Gakuhō* 91 (June 1905): 27-32. Richard Le Gallienne, "The Novel and Novelists of To-day," *How to Get the Best Out of Books* (New York: Baker & Taylor, 1904), 137-67.
3. "Umi to kumo to shijin Sherē" (The sea, the clouds and the poet Shelley), *Keiō Gijuku Gakuhō* 92 (July 1905): 40-47.

Gorky," cribbed from a recent essay in *Poet Lore*, but the essay was timely enough, with the Russo-Japanese War ending.[4] The ostentatious display of intellectual versatility would suffice for the moment. His next contribution to the journal, in October, would be a more casual chat about his thoughts a year after returning to Japan.

As the Russo-Japanese War entered its final stages, Noguchi took a few last stabs at war journalism. In a *Boston Evening Transcript* letter dated June 20 he offered a fairly accurate account of prevailing Japanese opposition to Roosevelt's peace proposals, Japan's expected list of demands, and an overview of the public debate. Noguchi was unsurprised at government efforts to quell public discussion of settlement terms, "lest a premature disclosure . . . should be the cause of excited discussion in the newspapers, tending to inflame the minds of the people and arouse popular excitement."[5]

As late as the end of April, Noguchi had no fixed address—Stoddard could write him, he said, at "Post Office, Tokyo, Japan."[6] But with the start of the school year came the need for a proper residence. He rented a house in a neighborhood near Tokyo University called Hisakata-machi, hired a couple of servants, and settled into his new professorial life, about which he would have almost nothing to say over the course of the next four decades.

Eventually summer came around, and after returning from a two-week trip to Kyoto and Osaka, he strung up a hammock in the garden to contemplate Japanese poetry. "First I'll call on / the pasania tree: / a summer grove" was a good Bashō hokku, he thought, as he began considering "A Global Perspective on Matsuo Bashō" for the September *Chūō Kōron*.[7] W.G. Aston's low evaluation of the poetic genre in his *History of Japanese Literature*—"it would be absurd to put forward any serious claim on behalf of Haikai to an important position in literature," Aston had written[8]—was, Noguchi thought, perfectly natural. Even the great Bashō had written very few poems, and as many as seventy or eighty percent of those, he believed, were not worth the trouble of translating. That was, he thought, the result of Bashō's having "placed more weight on the poetic life than on the actual written work." Bashō could be understood as "a minor great author" like the French symbolist poet Stepháne Mallarmé.

4. "Rokoku Bungō Gorugī (Russian literary master Gorky), *Keiō Gijuku Gakuhō* 93 (Aug. 1905): 19-27, based on Albert Phelps, "Maxim the Bitter," *Poet Lore* 15 (Autumn 1904): 53-69.
5. "Divisions Among Japanese," *Boston Evening Transcript*, 19 July 1905, 14. The piece was excerpted as "Peace Conference Difficulties," *Washington Post*, 24 July 1905, 6.
6. YN to CWS, 25 Apr. 1905, CEL 367.
7. "Sekai-gan ni eijitaru Matsuō Bashō" (A global perspective on Matsuo Bashō), *Chūō Kōron* 20:9 (1 Sept. 1905): 41-45. The hokku, "mazu tanomu shii no ki mo ari natsukodachi," was, as Toru Kiuchi observes in "Yone Noguchi's Invention of English-language Haiku," *American Haiku: New Readings* (Lanham, MD: Lexington Books, 2018), 8, the one Noguchi had translated "To wait with / There is also the live-oak / In summer time stands."
8. W.G. Aston, *A History of Japanese Literature* (London: Heinemann, 1899), 294.

Noguchi's sudden interest in Mallarmé was no doubt due to Bin Ueda's article about the French poet in the June *Myōjō*. Arthur Symons, the leading English promoter of Mallarmé's work through his *Symbolist Movement in Literature* (1899), had once compared Noguchi's own verse to Mallarmé's, and Noguchi, now painfully aware that his friendship with Joaquin Miller was more a liability rather than a credit, was keen to capitalize on his connection with Symons. Regrettably, he had failed to meet Symons in London, but now, in the sultry heat of Tokyo summer, he attempted to remedy the situation by applying his mind to imagining a meeting with Symons in London's Maida Vale. At this imagined meeting, Symons had spoken eloquently about trends in French literature, telling Noguchi about Mallarmé's famous Tuesday salons: "The poems we talked about in his house were an argument for a poetry full of life. It was not something to be published in a book. It was like looking at art, or a religion. It was a debate of live literature, blood flowing inside and breathing. He would say to himself, 'Oh, what a poetic life!,' sometimes smiling and sometimes preparing a cigar. Oh, those unforgettable Tuesdays! They are there no longer!" It was a fairly convincing simulation. Noguchi did have a point to make in the article: "If Bashō had been born in Paris, he would have been like Mallarmé, and vice versa." Both poets had published relatively little during their lives, being more concerned with living poetic lives than the actual writing of poetry. As a result, they had to be regarded as minor great poets rather than truly great poets.

Adventures of Léonie and Yo

In the summer of 1905, Léonie decided it was time to set up a proper home. "I suppose every easterner who comes to California comes hugging a dream of home," begins Léonie's tale. Not home "under the blighting eye of the landlord," but "home without any third party, no landlord, no 'other families' in the house or peering in your back windows; home with the dear sense of ownership encompassing it." Real estate advertisements offering lots for sale at $10 or $25 down and $10 a month, were everywhere. "So after a year of hesitation we struck out for 'Home.'"[9]

The lot Léonie and her mother chose was on Marietta Street a few blocks south of their current Boyle Heights address. (Léonie rarely gave out the address because the surrounding streets had not been cut through, due to a steep ravine, so the postman only delivered to a communal letter box on Stephenson Avenue). The spot secured, they acquired what they supposed to be "a striped tent in good order, fourteen by sixteen feet" (though it proved somewhat smaller). The tent represented the entry-level home in turn-of-the-century Los Angeles, to be succeeded by "the 'shack' with chicken yard in back and some bright flowers in front," and finally "the neat 'bungalow' with levelled lawn and trees of your own

9. "Founding a Tent-Home in California," *National Magazine* 23 (Feb. 1906), rpt. in *LG* 125-32.

planting." Installing a floor cost $12 for lumber and $2.50 a day for the two days of labor.

Moving day came after a two-day delay: Léonie "sat up in front of the express wagon beside a black man," her mother in the back, and Baby or "Yo" in his carriage "strapped securely on top of the load." After unloading their household possessions into the tent that now seemed ridiculously small, Léonie left the baby with her mother and started off to her afternoon job downtown, the rain soon falling in a steady downpour, immersing her in the sticky "dobe" of unpaved roads.

In the evening, Léonie returned to find the tent less waterproof than expected. "The only one dry thing in that room was little Yo (my baby) swathed in blankets in spite of his protesting kicks." A fly—"a sort of cloth roof, stretched over a center beam" would have to be added, bringing the price of the tent up to $25; then there was the water connection and piping, adding $12 or $13. And of course the monthly payments of $10 on the lot. But in three years it would all be paid for.

They passed a rough night, but in the morning, "warm sunshine flooded the tent, from above, from the sides. We needed no window. How glorious the life in a tent! Yo clapped his hands. Happy, happy boy!" Léonie worked Saturday, and Sunday they finished putting the tent in order. In the afternoon they were joined by Japanese student Matsuo Miyake, who brought a pair of ducks shot by his employer, which they fried in olive oil, and ate ravenously.

21. A Los Angeles tent house, circa 1900.

Although Miyake was still nineteen, he spoke English and French enthusiastically, though not always grammatically. He and Léonie had quickly developed an intimate friendship, the nature of which remained ambiguous, with Miyake adopting roles varying from the siblingesque to the potentially erotic: at times admiring student, younger brother, and surrogate husband. He was shortly to return to Japan, and Léonie, whatever she may have told Elizabeth Converse, had not completely ruled out a voyage to her sometime husband's country herself. The enthusiastic Miyake encouraged the idea, sending frequent notes on Japanese postcards depicting "rustic Japanese under cherry blossoms" and other appealing scenes through the summer of 1905 until his departure in August.

As the only member of Noguchi's inner circle with any practical understanding of conventional matrimony, it fell to Frank Putnam to point the way to the inevitable outcome of the crisis that had thus far eluded everyone else: Yone and Léonie would have to face their responsibilities and reunite. Putnam was a believer in family values, but the beauty of his plan happily required no embrace of social norms from Yone and Léonie, only their acknowledgment that they needed each other in a practical sense, which seemed evident enough. A preliminary truce was reached by summer, as Putnam reported to Stoddard on July 26:

> Yone writes saying his Los Angeles woman—dam'd little rascal, I could break him in two for that phrase—will market his American copy for her benefit and the baby's, hereafter, so I'm to use several of his articles during the next year. He says he doesn't care to sell anything in America, now that he is able to earn his own living in Japan, but thinks it may be better if he thus contributes somewhat to the support of his wife and babe. If I had only know[n] what was in his mind when he was with me, I think I should have given less time to poetry and more to ethics of civilization, in my talks and walks with the lad. But he is all right as God made him—and I like him that way.[10]

Stoddard, now in California, had not heard from Yone in an age, he wrote Putnam on August 1.[11] As for Yone and the "Los Angeles woman," he could only shake his head sadly: "what a pity he should have become entangled when he seems never to have really cared for her." But he was sufficiently curious to consider taking up Ethel's suggestion that he visit Léonie himself, telling Putnam of his hope to "see her and the child, anon, in Los Angeles." A few weeks later he reiterated his intention to "go to see her, and dandle the Kid," though the plan came to nothing. "I guess Ethel will come out all right," he added. "The bloodless tragedy has probably done them both good."[12]

The Poetic Life

With the end of summer approaching, Noguchi made an effort to reestablish his working relationship with Léonie, sending her an attractive postcard with the lines, "Mr. Murphy of 127, 5th Ave. New York will send you the Sada Yacco pictures, and you keep them. I will send you my article which will go with them."[13] The article on the famous geisha-turned-actress Sadayakko Kawakami was ostensibly an interview

---

10. FP to CWS, 26 July 1905, CWS Papers, Bancroft.
11. CWS to FP, 1 Aug. 1905, CWS Papers, Bancroft.
12. CWS to FP, 20 Aug. 1905, CWS Papers, Bancroft.
13. YN to LG, 1 Sept. 1905, CEL 369.

conducted at her seaside home in Chigasaki.¹⁴ Noguchi had been out of San Francisco in 1899 when Sadayakko, her actor-husband Otojirō and his troupe, had begun their rise to overseas fame. Back in Japan after a second tour under the wing of Loïe Fuller, Sadayakko was full of stories of her foreign experience. Like Noguchi, the Kawakami troupe had taken the hard road, arriving in San Francisco with little money and the vaguest of plans. Otojirō had thought his "new style drama"—political melodramas about Japanese exploits in the Far East—would appeal to American audiences, but in the end, it was his charming wife who saved the show. Audiences were thrilled with her dances and dramatic harakiri scenes, staged in the hastily restructured Kabuki plays the troupe began offering (to the dismay of Japanese purists). They had played before the Prince of Wales and the president of France, and befriended the great actors Henry Irving and Sarah Bernhardt.

MME. SADA YACCO IN THE MAD SCENE IN "HAMLET"
"She is like the music of a Japanese spring rain which is sad and sweet."

22. **Sadayakko Kawakami as Oriye (Ophelia).**

Now their plan was to reform the Japanese drama. Noguchi had already written in *The Critic* of the "immense sensation" created by their groundbreaking *Hamlet* and *Othello* productions, Japan's first.¹⁵ Otojirō's modernized staging of Shunsho Doi and Kayo Yamagishi's adapted translation reimagined *Hamuretto* in a contemporary Japanese setting. Young Hamura, a student at the new Kyoto Imperial University, made his intrance, in some productions, by bicycle. After encountering his father's ghost (played by Otojirō) he is sent by his uncle to Manchuria and Siberia, though he naturally escapes. Sadayakko played the part of

14. "Sada Yacco," *New York Dramatic Mirror*, 17 Feb. 1906, rpt. *EE* 258-63; YN to LG, 1 Sept. 1905, CEL 369.
15. "Shakespeare in Japan," *Critic* 46 (Mar. 1905), rpt. *EE* 200.

Oriye (Ophelia) with the right blend of sweetness and pathos; Noguchi found her "superbly gifted," particularly in the mad scene, where her sad song evoked tears.

Sadayakko was also charming and fascinating in American dress, playing the part of Tomoe (Desdemona) in *Othello*, a play which offered even more exotic foreign trappings, including a phonograph—the story itself taking place in Formosa (Taiwan). There, Tomoe, daughter of the treasury minister, falls in love with Murō (Othello), the Japanese commander-in-chief—a man of dubious birth. Noguchi found Otojirō's performance in the title role lacking in subtlety, and was disappointed that the character of Iya Goza (Iago) had been reduced to that of a mere stage villain. Admittedly, there were "immense gaps" in the translations, and in a few years, more faithful ones by Waseda University professor Shōyō Tsubouchi would appear. Tsubouchi would go down in the history books as the father of Japanese Shakespeare, while the groundbreaking Kawakami productions would be swept under the carpet. Even at the height of her fame, the geisha-turned-actress was frequently attacked in the Japanese press. But American audiences were eager for any sort of news about their Japanese idol, and Léonie was able to place Noguchi's interview in the *New York Dramatic Mirror*.

In a Japanese article on "My Thoughts One Year After Returning to Japan" written for a Keio publication, Noguchi tried to sum up his experience as a returning exile, seeing Tokyo as if from a foreigner's viewpoint.[16] "It was full of dark and unhealthy colors but I could see a different kind of beauty there, and it felt strange. It was like being captured by a devil. I could see ladies walking with high *geta* and men walking with very short steps; for a while I couldn't think that they were my brethren. When I saw the shopkeepers sitting at the front of their shops, I thought for a moment they were physically handicapped, with no legs." Now, however, he felt nothing strange walking down the street at Nihonbashi, and had, he claimed, "no special feelings about Japanese women." "Immediately after my return to Japan," he elaborated, "I was disappointed with Japanese women, famous in the West for their beauty." In America, the word *musume* had become a synonym for love and beauty, but to the returning Noguchi, Japanese women looked like *otafuku*, the comical, fat-cheeked women depicted on Japanese folk-masks. Gradually, however, he had become re-sensitized to Japanese beauty. "I was invited to a party one night," he recalled, "and saw a certain lady who had stayed in the States for six years, but seeing how she had spoiled the beauty of Japanese womanhood, I despised her. Japanese women must absolutely remain Japanese," he concluded; "only thus can they fully develop their beauty and love." He was harshly critical of the growing materialism. "I have always been proud that Japan was a country of art, filled with

16. "Kichō ichinen ato no kanshō," *Keiō Gijuku Gakuhō* 95 (15 Oct. 1905): 22-28.

literary imagination," he wrote, "but where," he asked "can you find the artistic and literary works resulting from this imagination?" Japanese society was becoming more and more materialistic. "Without enhancing the spiritual activities of valuing, loving, and longing for the Unseen," he declared, "Japan will be ruled by materialism."

His assessment of the war was similarly pessimistic. He had "witnessed the great drama Japan was performing on the vast stage of East Asia," to the astonishment of the West, but thought the West had overestimated Japan's motives. "The West praises Japan, saying, 'Japan fought Russia for the sake of the world, concluded a magnanimous peace for the sake of the world, and condemned the sin but not the sinner, thereby showing great benevolence.' Ah, but did Japan truly go to war based on such principles? Did it truly have magnanimity and, as foreign countries say, conclude peace under such a treaty with generosity of spirit?" This was a surprising question in light of Noguchi's persistent journalistic efforts to show Japan to Americans in exactly this idealized light. "Even Japan, as a nation, is fundamentally self-interested. When it fights another country, it does so for its own sake. If it agrees to an unfavorable peace, perhaps it is because it thinks it is for the greater good. Japan, both socially and politically, is a country that has been completely misunderstood by the world—or, in some strange way, overestimated."

Noguchi's pessimistic assessment of the present state of Japan was confirmed in September by the dysfunctional national response to the Treaty of Portsmouth ending the Russo-Japanese War, which he described for the *Boston Evening Transcript* in "Japan's Rage Over Peace," a day-by-day account of the country's descent into chaos.[17] The developments were not wholly unexpected. Japan's negotiators, Komura and Takehira, had left for the U.S.-brokered peace conference in July, and since "the public was fearful of the diplomatic result, since the Government's diplomacy is usually weak," the government had "been attempting to suppress the people's speech against herself ever since." Marquis Ito, a member of the Privy Council, had warned of the difficulties Japan faced in gaining the sympathy of the Powers, whose approval was essential to the success of the negotiations, explaining that Japan "should not base her terms solely upon her own self-interest, for if her reputation was to be maintained her demands must be such as would be regarded by the Powers as legitimate." Nevertheless, the announcement of the proposed terms, Noguchi wrote on September 1, had been greeted by cries of "Inglorious concession! Shame!" The "semi-official" newspaper, the *Kokumin*, had responded that "Our object in the present war was to drive Russia out of Manchuria and secure the stability of Korea, these objects being indispensable to our national safety. As a result of our victories, we have been successful in negotiating these objects." And more: "we have obtained the lease of Port

17. "Japan's Rage Over Peace," *Boston Evening Transcript*, 7 Oct. 1905, 3:2.

Arthur and Talien, the unconditional surrender of the Chinese Eastern Railway, the annexation of a moiety of Sakhalin and fishery rights in the Littorals." "Some say the peace is an ignominious one, because we have failed to carry our demands about an indemnity and the cession of the whole of Sakhalin," but these were only "visions conjured up by our extraordinary victories on land and sea." But the news had been received by the general population "with the utmost resentment." "We are all of the same opinion that the peace just agreed upon cannot be of a permanent nature. And we dare say that such terms are humiliating to Japan." "Not only the politicians who had been denouncing the Government, the general public and the ordinary 'man in the street' (even the jinrikisha men and coolies) express freely their indignation, the most sincere indignation." On the 5th, "Public indignation grows every hour," Noguchi reported. On the 7th, he wrote, "The police have no power to keep order. Darkness is over Tokio. Bloodshed, fire and fighting everywhere! . . . And the Government is stupidly attempting with every effort to stifle the nation's voice of resentment. The Government has been abusing the police power to its own advantage. Tokio was captured by anarchy and Hooliganism for the first time in the history of the Meiji era." "And another terrible spectacle was the attack on the official residence of the Home Minister." "Then the people separated into several parties and began to burn the police boxes one by one. There were more than 100 boxes in the city, and all of them were burned up or smashed, and it lasted for thirty hours." "Five hundred people were arrested, and 100 were pounded and killed. All Tokio was the saddest and most bloody scene."

After the chaos subsided, the economic shock and despair remained.[18] "We are told by the government organ, Kokumin, that it was known to be impossible to get a cent indemnity from Russia long before Baron Komura left Yokohama for America, but what a disappointment for the nation!"

A History Filled with Tears

"Here again I welcome Autumn—such a glorious Autumn with yellow leaves everywhere, and with golden Sun, and with such a pure sky," Noguchi wrote Stoddard in October.[19]

> However, I am sad sometimes with many things I miss here. And again I am lonely for America and for you. You are such a sweet old soul, and when can I see you again? Have you any hope to come to Japan? . . . My house is not noisy, being a mile far the city-center. We have here a thousand trees and flowers. I keep two servants, and everything is quite comfortable. Will you come over? I will treat you like a Lord. If you have enough money for the ticket, that will be sufficient. No money is necessary after your arrival in Japan. I make money enough for myself, and beside for somebody else.

18. "The Japanese Burden," New Orleans *Times-Democrat*, 12 Oct. 1905, 1.
19. YN to CWS, 20 Oct. 1905, *CEL* 370.

And Stoddard could be another Hearn, he suggested. "Dear Dad, I love you,—you know that."

Ethel was moving on. "Are you wondering where I am?" she inquired of Alice Wiggin on October 3. "I have been out on the open road again—hither and thither and yon! And now I'm on my way to Boston town!"[20] Alice taught in the high school of the Boston suburb of Franklin.[21] Ethel spent several weeks in Boston: spent time with Alice, "had a dream of a day" with Josephine Peabody, and went to the opera with a friend. She also met Frank Putnam. "Ethel has just gone home after spending some weeks in this vicinity," Putnam wrote Stoddard in November. "I believe her affections are healing rapidly—a charming, inconsequent child."[22]

Ethel had been a skilled actress in her schooldays, and could play a charming, inconsequent child easily enough. Her close friend Anne Kendrick Walker, however, was skeptical of Ethel's protestations of nonchalance over the Yone affair. "I never saw Ethel happy again," she wrote in a posthumous memoir. "That was a blow that she could not ever recover from."

Whatever the state of her emotions, Ethel needed a new focus. "The idea of *The Story of Coal and Iron in Alabama* came to me the second day after arriving in Birmingham during the late fall of 1905 [*sic*] when I saw Red Mountain and my first mines," she later explained. "The mining world was a new world. Something of its drama and romance had stirred me when in Chicago two years before . . . Not being able to find any book giving me the information upon the Alabama mines which I sought, I decided to write one, feeling that at last I had come across a subject absolutely new and a region unexplored, historically." Mining was Birmingham's main industry and the foundation of its economy. It is hard to imagine Ethel had not seen the Sloss company mines on Red Mountain, named for its rust-colored rock and seams of red iron ore. She must have learned something about the local mining business when she worked as a typist for a "mining man" the previous year. But returning to Birmingham after her Boston trip, she was perhaps seeing the mines for the first time as the lifeblood of her adopted city. Undertaking to write an Alabama mining history was her way of coming to terms with her new reality, putting to rest her dreams of escape.

If Ethel wanted hard toil to take her mind off her disastrous romance, she certainly found it. She naively thought she could write the book in three months, and after lengthy negotiations, succeeded in persuading the Birmingham Chamber of Commerce to fund the project for six. But the work ended up taking four years, so the compensation proved grossly inadequate. She later wrote that "insufficient food, lack of daily

20. FP to CWS, [Nov. 1905], CWSP.
21. EA to Alice Wiggin, 3 Oct. 1905, EMAP.
22. FP to CWS, [Nov. 1905], CWSP.

necessities, an illness of typhoid fever, continual money worry with the humiliation attendant upon it, false promises, deferred hopes and no sincere cooperation from the Chamber of Commerce marked three years of daily and nightly work on the book." When it finally appeared in 1910, sales barely recovered the printing costs. But it did establish her reputation as an independent historian. As James R. Bennett, the editor of the 2011 reprint (and incidentally, Alabama's Secretary of State) notes, it "remains the most referenced book on iron manufacture in Alabama." Today she is revered as a pioneering woman historian, while the name of Frank Putnam, who thought her a "charming, inconsequent child," is all but forgotten.[23]

MISS ETHEL ARMES

23. Ethel Armes, circa 1910.

Noguchi was not averse to making literary use of his love troubles, but he tended to do so in a somewhat veiled manner.[24] He published a philosophical reflection on love in symbolist form in the literary magazine *Shirayuri* in November. For Japanese readers still mystified by Western concepts of romantic love, Yone's overseas investigations, happy or tragic, were as exotically fascinating as Pierre Loti's Eastern affairs were to Westerners. But Yone preferred to convey his findings as a series of philosophical observations explained allegorically. Wisdom and silliness intermingled in the whimsical spirit of a Miss Morning Glory experiment. The kingdom of love, Yone explained, was a great realm where

23. James R. Bennett, preface to Ethel Armes, *The Story of Coal and Iron* (Tuscaloosa: U of Alabama P, 2011), xv-xxvi. Armes' later works included *The Washington Manor House: England's Gift to the World* (New York: Sulgrave, 1922), *Nancy Shippen: Her Journal Book, The International Romance of a Young Lady of Fashion of Colonial Philadelphia* (Philadelphia: Lippincott, 1935) and *Stratford Hall: The Great House of the Lees* (Richmond, VA: Garrett & Massie, 1936), which was introduced by Franklin D. Roosevelt.

24. "Ai-ren!" (Love!) *Shirayuri* 3:1 (1 Nov. 1905): 12-14. The title is a reversal of *"renai,"* a Meiji-era word used to describe erotic love on the Western model, compounded of the Chinese characters for "passion" and "love."

time seems endless, protected by a cruel, ogre-like gate-keeper. "Whoever wishes to enter must bring jewels of truth and smiles wrapped in a cloth of tears and present them to the king." He wanted, he said, to clip the wings of the bird called Love and fly with it to the highest peak. Love had taught him the vastness of his soul, immortality and eternity, made him a god. He described the allegorical House of Love. He had never felt more victorious than when he fell in love. "To love many kinds of people and many kinds of things is not wrong, but romantic love teaches the noble and profound joy of loving one heart and one body." This, however, "requires great resolve." Just as "Dante was guided to his destination by the radiance of the beautiful Beatrice, I too will follow the next torchlight," he declared. "To be victorious in Love is life's greatest challenge." Love could slip into the secret crevices of the heart to draw out hidden jewels. "The most unfortunate are those who cannot even fall in love." "It is not wise to be madly in love, but you gain more from loving madly than from loving wisely. What do you gain? A history filled with tears!" "I am," he explained, "a slave to Love in order to obtain a history." He and his beloved were together creating a society, even a universe. They were, in other words, gods.

24. *The Summer Cloud*, 1906.

There were more than a few tears in *The Summer Cloud*, Noguchi's new collection of prose poems, published by Shunyōdō in December. Most were shed by O Yuki San, the Japanized Ethel character. This "Japanese girl of tears and Love" appears in four poems: the erotic, hopeful "Did You Go to Marriage Shrine," the determined "O Yuki San" ("O stars, come not, to-night, we have to make our own world, we two alone, O Yuki San and I!"), the plaintive poem Noguchi sent to Putnam in March, now in prose as "Queen of Love, My Beloved," and finally, the dreamy, sad "Touch Me with thy Soft Hands."[25]

25. "Did you go to the Marriage Shrine," "Touch me with thy Soft Hands," *Shin Shōsetsu* 10:6 (1 June 1905), rpt. SC 37, 8.

> Touch me with thy soft hands, O Yuki San! They are soft as soft moonbeams on the singing sands, O Yuki San! They are soft as soft kisses of the eve, thy soft hands, they are soft as soft rivulets over the Spring lands, O Yuki San!
>
> Oh touch me again with thy soft hands, O Yuki San! I feel the passion and Truth of forgotten ages in their touches, O Yuki San! I feel the songs and incense in their touches, O Yuki San!
>
> Here by the sea I sit from dawn till the dusk, O Yuki San! I dream of thy soft hands, soft as soft foams on the laughing shore, O Yuki San! The sun is gone and the soft moon is rising, but never, never, never thy soft hands, thy soft hands again, O Yuki San![26]

By the time the book appeared, the *Age-Herald* staff (presumably Ethel and her friend Anne Kendrick Walker) were ready to enjoy a hearty chuckle at the poet's predicament.[27] "Doubtless if we knew the truth," reads the unsigned note—entitled "Oh, Mushi," in an apparently intentional conflation of the Japanese word for "insect" and the English word "mush"—"Yuki San's reply would read something like this":

> "Thou canst not make a touch today, O Soft Head. Thy words are as soothing as soft mush, but I am wise and can tell the difference between straight goods and hot air.
>
> "I am sorry that you sit by the laughing sea from dawn till dusk, O Sappy Head, for I fear me that you will contract a severe case of cold feet.
>
> "[M]y soft hands have other fish to fry than tickling you under the chin, O Pumpkin Pate. You ought to take something for it, and I would suggest that you try soft soap."

But no amount of "soft soap," the popular cleaning agent that was also a euphemism for flattery, could clean up the pumpkin-pated poet's mess at this late stage.

As for the success of Noguchi's prose poetry experiment as a whole, critics were divided. Some—Edwin Markham, Edith Thomas, and Alvin Langdon Coburn among them—found the prose form appealing. Arthur Ransome was among those who disagreed. Ransome saw plainly enough that many of the poems had been "altered to prose simply by the plan of their printing," and these made him realize that "the irregular, broken lines in which his poems were originally published had a real power over the effect the words produced."[28]

Noguchi also had limited success with his first attempt at selling a Japan-published book overseas—a practice he continued (with various modifications and occasional exceptions) through the remainder of his career. Publication in Japan allowed the book to be beautifully and inexpensively printed—with a full color woodblock print as the frontispiece,

---

26. "Pretty, Soft Hands," *Washington Post*, 30 Sept. 1906, ES4, rpt. SC 8-9.
27. "Oh, Mushi," *Birmingham Age-Herald*, 18 Oct. 1906, 4.
28. Arthur Ransome, "The Poetry of Yone Noguchi," *Fortnightly Review* 94 (Sept. 1910): 527-33.

and full-color flower ornaments on each page—but the lack of good English editors and proofreaders showed in the many uncorrected grammatical and typographical errors. An arrangement to have Brentano's in New York sell the book, and another twenty-five copies sent to Léonie, represented the greater part of the American distribution. Some copies were also sent to England, where a review in the *Academy* praised the "dainty, ethereal effects" made possible by the poet's courage to use English words "as if they were coloured scraps of mosaic fresh put into his hand."[29]

Meanwhile, in Boston, Frank Putnam continued to support the Noguchi entourage by accepting Léonie's lengthy "George Meredith—A Study"—presumably a remnant of her college days—for the *National*.[30] In January he sent Stoddard $50 for a Joaquin Miller article, for which he would use pictures given him by Yone, as well as a new portrait of Yone.[31] "Why don't you go to visit the boy in Japan?" he inquired of Stoddard. "What letters you would write from that beach! Gad, I believe it would give you twenty years more lease of youth—and it would be good for Yone to have your guidance for a time in the new paths he is treading." Surely Stoddard could find a steamship company willing pay his passage.

"I hope to see Yone in his own home one of these days," replied Stoddard, who was evidently warming to the idea. "The trouble is I have promised the 'Sunset' Maga[zine] a series of six articles and I shall not be free to go anywhere until these are off my hands . . . I believe if I went to Japan I could do a vol[ume] of Japanese Idyls. Perhaps I can secure a pass for an article."[32] But after completing the first of his "Old Mission Idyls," he had taken refuge at the San Jose Sanatorium under the care of "a score of white-winged sisters."

Noguchi continued his consideration of poetics in an unusually erudite Japanese essay on "English Poetry and Hokku," in which he attempted to explain and support his views on what constituted poetry.[33] Poetry, he said, involved description, and description had to address reality, but because poets worshipped at the shrine of beauty, the unbeautiful had to be rejected. Much, therefore, had to be excluded: including anything rustic, outrageous, barbarous, disgusting, dry, commonplace, ridiculous, silly, dull, mean, mechanical, profit concerns, and manners and customs. Noguchi also wished to argue that short poems were superior to long ones. Epic poetry would never be able to fully achieve the ideal of beauty. He found that a number of English poets shared this view, and offered examples of what he considered to be successful short poems in English. But there were

---

29. "Yone Noguchi," *Academy* 70 (24 Mar. 1906): 282.
30. "Leonie Gilman [sic], "George Meredith—A Study," *National Magazine* 23 (Dec. 1905): 272-77.
31. FP to CWS, 9 Jan. 1906, CWSP.
32. CWS to FP, 15 Jan. 1906, CWSP.
33. "Eishi to hokku" (English poetry and hokku), *Taiyō* 11:16 (1 Dec. 1905): 140-44.

limits to the influence Japanese short forms could have on English poetry. "If short poetry based on hokku was composed with the ideas of English poetry, it would be more valuable than Japanese hokku and its rhythm wouldn't be so quick. However, I think it would be unfortunate to change English poetry to the art of experts in the tea ceremony. In my opinion, I want Japanese hokku to develop more and at the same time, I do not want English poetry to be as short as hokku." Noguchi would remain committed to this belief in a hybridized approach to English hokku over the years. But in the following decade he would have to radically rethink his definitions of what should be included or excluded from poetry when modernism began to shatter the traditional conceptions.

Noguchi was back in the *Chūō Kōron* in January 1906 with a provocative call to "Come Out, National Poets who Represent Japan."[34] "Britain has become fully self-aware of its identity as a great empire, and with the arrival of Kipling has for the first time embraced poetry that testifies to its vitality," he wrote. In the United States, "Whitman sought to revitalize American poetry with great self-confidence and hope, and succeeded. He transformed the American poetic tradition from the beautifully delicate verse of Longfellow and Lowell into something vigorous: unprecedented free verse. Treated at first as a literary renegade, by the time of his death he had gained the respect of the world, and his powerful influence has not diminished." In contrast, in Japan, "haiku masters and tanka poets are mere relics," while the new-style poets, "struggling to align themselves with the rhythms and progress of the Western poetic world," did not yet represent the living spirit of the Japanese people, which was their inevitable responsibility. Japanese poetry, especially in the new style, but more generally as well, was aristocratic, incomprehensible to the general public and even those outside the poet's own circle. "I have never up to now encountered a poem or song in the entire history of Japanese literature that truly expressed the voice of the people. Japanese poetry has been nothing more than a plaything for well-educated gentlemen and refined ladies," he complained. "Japanese poetry is not united with the hopes that the Japanese nation now holds. Japan of the twentieth century must have a poetry suited to the twentieth century. Japan which has achieved real and vast expansion must have poetry fitting that reality. Therefore, I cannot help but cry out for a great revolution in the world of poetry. Let Japanese poetry become popular in spirit! Let it become open and inclusive! Only then will Japanese poetry truly become the voice and the living spirit of today's Japan." Perhaps it was, as Shunsuke Kamei argues, a "shallow argument," but it waged "a strong protest against the majority of Japanese poets who sang their private, petty feelings in flowery words and conventional forms."[35] Bin Ueda was among the skeptics.

34. "Nihon o daihyō-suru kokumin-shijin ideyo," *Chūō Kōron* 21:1 (Jan. 1906): 22-28.
35. Shunsuke Kamei, *Yone Noguchi, An English Poet of Japan* (Tokyo: Yone Noguchi Society, 1965), 70.

"[Noguchi's] political theories are not, of course, to be taken seriously, but going so far as to advise Japanese poets to set aside 'singing of stars, singing of the moon, singing of love, singing of violets,' is unacceptable, especially as he is himself a man who achieved fame precisely by singing often of stars, the moon, and love."[36]

A Very Important Letter

At the beginning of the new year, Noguchi took an opportunity to travel to Shanghai. A letter to Putnam from Shanghai's Astor House Hotel, dated January 8, 1906, says only: "Here I am in Shanghai for a week. I will write you from Tokyo soon." Another, sent on January 29, notes his return a few days earlier to Tokyo from Shanghai, "the maddest town of the Far East, the Chinese Chicago." Two months later he sent Léonie "my article about China being the print of my journey," asking her to forward it to Frank. "Frank will like the Chinese article, I am sure," he added. Frank didn't; he returned it to Noguchi with what Léonie referred to as "valuable suggestions." "I realize very well that his political essays are not what you might call the impartial judgement of the historian," she wrote Putnam. "He looks for the picturesque, and for effect. Also his style lacks the crispness, the terseness, the array of facts to set off his theories, which are considered proper to such journalistic work."

Noguchi did publish a Japanese article in a Keio university publication about his visit to Shanghai.[37] He had found it a sad and unpleasant place. The Chinese, who swarmed the ship when it arrived, only to be repeatedly and violently thrown off, seemed to have lost any sense of human dignity. "All of the countries are fighting like rats for the rotten meat which is China." The Japanese, of course, were among them. But there was something to be said for the fact that in Shanghai, in contrast to San Francisco, they were able to compete on equal, or even favorable, terms with Western nations.

Back in November, Noguchi had had a curious visit from a Japanese youth who introduced himself as Matsuo Miyake and delivered two letters from Léonie. Miyake had returned from his foreign travels two months earlier, and was staying at his uncle's house in Akasaka. "Autumn of Nippon (Yamato) is sweet and pensive," he had informed Léonie, inquiring, in his customary playfully-possessive manner, about "our dear Baby." She had replied, enclosing a letter to deliver to Yone and a letter of introduction. "I thank you with all my heart for your first sistery voices across the Pacific Ocean," Miyake had written back on November 12. "I will soon see Otō-San. I also thank you for your introducing note." Léonie had discussed with Miyake her idea to come to Japan and settle

---

36. Ueda Bin, "Kyōei-roku ichi" (Mirror reflection record I), in *Ueda Bin zenshū*, v. 5 (Tokyo: Kaizōsha, 1928), 522.
37. "Shanhai" (Shanghai), *Keiō Gijuku Gakuhō* 100 (15 Feb. 1906): 48-52.

in Kyoto, far from Yone, and Miyake wrote her again on November 16, promising to look into the question of schools there for the still-unnamed baby. But much still depended on Yone. On November 30 Miyake was able to tell Léonie that he had delivered the letter. "Having talked with Mr. Noguchi," he added, "I wonder what he is going to do upon you." Miyake soon found a job in Osaka as a journalist for the region's major newspaper, the *Mainichi Shimbun*. "After couple of days I will be a youth in the city of Osaka, near *our* Kioto," he wrote Léonie on January 25.[38]

Over the winter, Leonie and her mother, having clung to their tent "till it was threadbare, and longer," built a modest California-style pioneer shack—a redwood "box house" with a gable roof, "a one-room affair, twelve by twelve in size, the walls eight feet in height. . . . very warm and cosy."[39] "Our tent still stands—next door," she noted, "grey and weather-worn as an ancient sail. . . like an ancient fairy or a bearded witch." There, she could "go to sit among the cobwebs and dream—of a ship that sails on the high seas."

Yone had been making more convincing proposals, and between his invitations and Matsuo's, Léonie had arrived at a decision. "I am going to take Baby for a little trip across the Pacific Ocean about Feb. 1st," she wrote Catharine on January 20.[40] "Yes, we are really going to Japan, which is a fact that I can hardly realise though the time is so near. Yone is making all kinds of promises and I have been offered a position to teach in Tokyo, so that I shall be 'on my own hook,' and can make tracks if I don't like it." She had "had enough of California for awhile," and would "enjoy the misty-moist beauty of Japan by way of contrast."

In early February 1906, Léonie received a letter from Yone, dated January 28. "Dear Léonie," it began.[41] "You must be wondering why I did not write you—I was in China as I told you, and had been at Shanghai. Alas me!," he apologized, "I did not take my address book and unfortunately I forgot your address." He had written a letter from Shanghai, he explained, but could not mail it, and returned to find her letter with a check for 39 yen, for which he was grateful. He had been doing some soul-searching.

> Léonie, this is a very important letter, and so you must consider carefully, and answer me. Some time ago I suggested you of your coming to Japan. And again I am thinking of it. And I believe it would be better for you and our baby of course. Why? Because I can help in bringing up the baby, and he can escape from being a fatherless child. And it is an important thing I believe. And also I believe it would be easier for you to make living here in Japan. You must be a school teacher and work at a company. School

---

38. Matsuo Miyake to LG, 5 Sept., 12 Nov., 16 Nov., 30 Nov. 1905, 25 Jan. 1906, INF.
39. Leonie Gilmour, "A Little California House," *The West-Coast Magazine*, Dec. 1906, in *LG* 136.
40. LG to Bunnell, 20 Jan. 1906, in *LG* 141.
41. YN to LG, 28 Jan. 1906, in *LG* 143-45.

business is not hard here, and we respect a foreigner unduely to my thinking, and it is one advantage for you. Japan pays to a foreign teacher more than any Japanese teacher, and I think if you don't mind to teach, say, using your beforenoons and it will be sufficient for your living. Don't you want to do that? The main thing to consider is about *our* baby. I wish he will grow brightly and happily. I was wrong in past, and I repent greatly, and I wish to do for him. Will you bring him over to Japan? And I will get a job in school or company for you,—oh, well, we will talk the matter over when you will come to Japan. You consider this thing carefully, and let me know. I have some influence among the school, and it will be easy enough to get such a job for you. Remember, the main thing to consider is about the *Baby*. I am making money enough to support myself and a little house, but not enough to send money to you and keep the child in America. I am thinking that it would be better to bring up our child together. I think it would be wise to decide to come to Japan. Suppose you be in America? I think no good fortune will smile on you, and perhaps you are to live from hand to mouth, and—having the child as extra. Frank Putnam wrote me and said a bitter thinking of my turning out such a trifle newspaper stuff, and commanded that I will stop to do such a hack business. And I know that a writer's living is the most terrible thing—no matter to be a magazine writer or a book writer. I like to stop it—I must make money somewhere else. But it is not to say that I will stop to write anything, but I like to return to a poet, and to live in poetry. So you can not expect me to send you many articles hereafter, and naturally I will be far away from helping the child in a due form. If you come to Japan and don't mind to work four or five hours a day, we can solve our problem quite easily I think. We will work our salvation together. What do you think of it. I suffered enough, Léonie!

As for transportation, Léonie might come any time she was ready, but next autumn would be best; an intermediate class steamer ticket would cost around one hundred dollars; she could get some money from the *National* in exchange for his articles.

The tone of the letter was friendly but businesslike. He was not offering reawakened affections, only a newly-awakened sense of responsibility. His unspoken motivations may have been stronger. Isamu, when asked about his parents' relationship, would say: "It was almost like a business relationship. She was an excellent editor for him. When he got back to Japan, he didn't have the services of a severe editor that she no doubt was."[42] To that prospect were added the encouragements of Frank Putnam, and Matsuo Miyake's offer—or, as it must have seemed to Yone, threat—to give Léonie and "our dear baby" a home in the Kansai area.

The day after writing to Léonie, Noguchi wrote to "ever-hopeful Frank," who had written him a brief but inspiring letter in early December.[43] "Surely your letter makes me a better man." Frank was "sane" and

---

42. Yoshinobu Hakutani, "Father and Son: A Conversation With Isamu Noguchi," *Journal of Modern Literature* 17:1 (Summer 1990): 32.
43. YN to FP, 29 Jan. 1906, FPL. Putnam's letter is lost.

"courageous," and Noguchi trusted in his opinion. "I am weak sometimes, and must have your brotherly blessing and advise," he admitted. Frank had taught him "many wisdom and a lesson of humanity." He continued, "I was greatly mistaken in past. I am full of repentance nowaday. What you wrote about Mrs Noguchi is right to bottom. I must obey to what you think right, and I must follow gladly after which I must do according to Humanity. I was young, Frank! you forgive me, will you? I am afraid that you might think me worthless. That's another thing! If you think so, let it go! I am wiser and truer today." He outlined his plan, emphasizing his repentance: "I want Mrs Noguchi come to Japan. I had been thinking about the matter for a long time. I must do something for the child to begin with. Mrs Noguchi must have suffering—perhaps more than she can bear. Yes, I know she is the best and true. I am beginning to appreciate her, and Frank, I was blind. In one word I was young, Frank." He explained the practical difficulties of the situation and his thought that Léonie "must work four or five hours a day till I will build myself solidly in Japan, and make money enough"; he thought that, "as today she is working hard (in fact she was a hard worker in past) she will not mind to do that also in Tokyo." He enlisted Frank's support for the plan and asked him to "be a go-between for my own sake." He thought that "Mrs Noguchi might say 'No', if I write her to join me abruptly, and so I wish you will tell her my own thought and determination." "Mrs Noguchi is a sweet woman," he explained, "but she does not like any crooked action. I cannot force on her, and must respect her thought." Putnam was "the best man to break such a new[s] for my sake," and he was sure Frank would endorse his decision. "Only if such a decision did come earlier!," he lamented. "You believe me—I suffered enough from my own action and nightmare. I like to be on the right road." He intimated that he had informed his family of the situation: "my family don't speak English except myself, but have no objection," he wrote. "And on the contrary my brothers say that I must do what is right since I was a man in public. They hate shame."

Even Stoddard, in his letters to Putnam, was inclining toward reconciliation. On February 26, he wrote Putnam from San Jose, "I hope that Yone calls in his own out of the open. They should be with him, as perhaps the Crown Prince will save the throne from toppling."[44]

But Léonie did not respond to Yone's letter as anticipated. There were a number of reasons, not the least being the interesting job she had recently landed as assistant to the editor of *The Raven*, a new literary magazine housed on the top floor of Pasadena's newest four-story office building. Others were her growing fondness for California, and worries about leaving her mother. But the most likely was Yone's letter itself. She wrote back on February 24, explaining her thoughts:

44. CWS to FP, 26 Feb. 1906, CWSP.

My dear Yone:

I have read your letter—yes, several times. Of course you understand that I want to do the *very best* for baby, and as for wanting to keep him all to myself, why that is nonsense. I am only happy to share him with you. But whether it were wise to leave California at present and to go over to Japan—that is a question—I am *very doubtful* about it.

Listen: America is a good country, California in particular. Baby is well. He is happy. Though we be poor, he does not suffer from it. Maybe our way of living is not quite civilised—we live in a tent, where rains and wind come in at will—Baby has no shoes on his feet. He runs free as a squirrel on the hill side. Does it matter, our way of life? Roses are glowing on his cheeks. We built a little California house of one room beside the tent. There my Mother lives. And there I took Baby in on the day it was finished. He was like a caged bird lazily looking to door and windows for a way to escape. He does not like house: nor shoes.

He is growing like a flower under the sky. Shall I take him out of this beautiful green country to put in an ill-smelling city like Tokyo, where rains are incessant and winters are harsh? Wouldn't he turn into just a pale little Japanese boy? No, no, if I come to Japan, it must be to *Kioto* or some southern part of Japan. Such a change would not be too sudden. And education. Education is free here. I do not think much of "school" myself:

I could myself teach him everything he would learn in school. I dare say the schools in Japan are not much better than those here. But there is an education *outside of school;* that I understand. As far as the aesthetic side of life is concerned, I suppose Japan may be far superior to here. For the moral training and character?

I do not know. I believe there is much that is rarely lovely and precious in Japanese character (I have read "Bushido")—also some defects. No doubt you could help me to guide him aright. You will understand him. He is more like you than me.

Many a time I have thought, "Some day I will go over to Japan when Baby is five or six years old. Then I will have a little money, and better able to shape our life." I would like to put him to an Art school somewhere, where he will have eye and hand trained to express his idea—No matter if he become artist or not. I would like, if he shows ability, to train him as actor—something he must do different from our life. And still—all those things he could perhaps have here. What will my mother do if he goes away? She has become greatly attached to him. It would be the hardest thing to part now. And you talk of "social position" and "money". Let me tell you at once that everyone here is glad to make much of your son. And I can earn an existence wherever I be, I suppose, though it is different always to get a footing in a new place. Better in Japan? Oh, I don't know. And it is a minor question.

And you Yone! You like to return to be a poet, and to live in poetry. Very well! You will stop writing articles. Very well! And you must find some other business and then you will attend strictly to business, and be good man and citizen and father. And of course you will be happy(?) being so very good. Of course it is more important to be good than happy. But how about your poetry? Where will you find it? In business? In the crowding cares and responsibilities? In the companionship of a wife you *do not love*? Why? Because Frank Putnam thinks you should? Because of awakened thought of responsibility toward your boy? Maybe you think you will make amends for the past. Past is past, you cannot *amend* it. Maybe you think we, Baby and I, need you, we do not. Therefore I think it better we live apart. If I have chance to have work in Southern Japan someday I will come. And you can see Baby all you like. And we will have a proper separation when you get ready—and you will remarry according to your better and riper judgement. Baby and I have each other to love. Yes, that's better.

(I am learning to be editor now. I'd like to start a magazine of my own when I come to Japan. That is more interesting than school.)

Facing imminent departure and Yone's letter, Léonie had come down with a serious case of cold feet. Her list of objections was long, but the strongest, apparently, was the famous love poet's inability to even mention the word "love."

When she alluded to Yone's "bitter coldness," Frank Putnam was skeptical. In her reply, she granted that she had been "drawing on [her] imagination a little."[45] "If I believed what you say," she wrote, "I would go right over to Japan and shake Yone good and *make* him love me." She did love Yone, she said, but "simply I wish to do what is the very best thing and for once in my life I believe I have decided wisely." Yone had never been anything but charming to her, she said, "though I must have tried his patience by dissolving in tears every time he spoke to me for the last few weeks of our acquaintance." ("I couldn't help it and I suppose my condition had something to do with it," she explained, alluding to her pregnancy). She thought Yone "would try to be nice as possible and to make the best of a bad bargain," but she wanted him "to have something better in his life than that," and she herself was "too proud," and even "too much in love with him to undertake his 'reclamation.'" Putnam had himself expressed a concern that Ethel continued to have a hold over Noguchi, and Léonie too had wondered whether Ethel—toward whom she remained sympathetic—might come to forgive him. Putnam had also expressed some concern that Noguchi would marry a Japanese woman, perhaps thinking this concern would encourage Léonie to act quickly, but it did not. "You think he will eventually marry some Japanese woman—maybe that would be best," she wrote. "I should feel terribly for a little while," she supposed, "but I guess baby can comfort me for anything."

Léonie had just received a letter from Charles Warren Stoddard, she told Putnam. Yone had asked Stoddard to write her, and he had happily obliged, although he was not sure she wished to hear from him.[46] He

---

45. LG to FP, 14 Mar. 1906, FPL, in LG 154-55.
46. CWS to LG, 12 Mar. 1906, LG 152-53.

could not remember if they had met during the New York days he now barely recalled as a "horrible dream," but hoped to see and know her and "the little one" when he visited Los Angeles. Yone's last letter to him had been "very sweet and sad," he told her. "The tender spirit of fatherhood seems to have descended upon him and he writes as if he were lonely and regretful of much that has happened in the past. So are we all, I suppose, or so we should be," he added, thoughtfully. "You know Yone and I were very close to one another," he told her. "He was my 'Kid,' my 'Poet-child.' He called me 'Dad'—and does so still. He says in this letter: 'Since you are my father you must be a grandfather to my baby.'" Stoddard would be glad to do so. He wondered about her thoughts of joining Yone in Japan, told her he hoped to go himself the next year, and begged for a photograph of herself and the little one. "How I should love to have one! What is his name?"

Love of the Japanese Girl

Léonie's answer to Yone's "very important letter" of January 28 was, for some reason, not delivered until the end of March, and in the meantime he grew restless. He was undoubtedly intrigued by the ideal of the traditional, submissive Japanese wife like the one in "The Address of a Woman to her Husband," published in April 1906, who is made to utter thoughts such as the following:

> Thou art, O great lord, like a sea
> Stretching the bosom vast for forgiveness:
> Into thy bosom I peep with fear that is a woman's joy.[47]

If he was contemplating such a wife, he made no mention of the fact to Léonie, and continued to press her for an answer. "How did you decide?" he asked in another letter.[48] "Come to Japan? Or stay in California? Did Frank write you about my plan regarding to the baby and yourself?" He reiterated his "conclusion that we will build home together in Japan," and noted that Keio would be increasing his hours, and therefore salary, in April with the beginning of the new school year.

Her reply when it arrived, had been negative. "You may be wise," he wrote back on April 2, though he wondered if her decision was "firm like a rock."[49] Still, he was "not ready to say anything just now concerning to your letter," saying he would write again soon, but on April 22, when he wrote again, he deferred it again. News of the great earthquake in San Francisco had arrived, and he wondered if she and his other California friends were safe.

After five weeks of contemplation and some new advice from Frank,

---

47. *Shirayuri* 3:6 (Apr. 1906): 298-300, rpt. *Pilg.* 36-40.
48. YN to LG, [Mar. 1906], in *LG* 147-48.
49. YN to LG, 22 Apr. 1906, in *LG* 160.

Yone took up the question again in a letter to Léonie on May 5.[50] "I considered carefully over the matter which we have been talking lately," he began. "Frank Putnam wrote me that I must give you up. Really I do not know what I will answer to you." Putnam had evidently passed on Léonie's concerns about Ethel. "One thing is sure—" Noguchi wrote, "—I do not love Miss Armes today. She has been rather careless or mean to me for some time. . . . She has no interest in me, and also I have not. Everything is done, and over." As for Léonie coming to Japan, he conceded that "if you can build yourself up nicely, and be happy in California it would be useless and unwise to come over to Japan." The financial situation was still difficult, and he saw little hope of Léonie realizing her plans to start a magazine in Japan. "We have no English paper in Tokyo, except one Japan Times. And two or three English papers in Yokohama," he told her. Their circulation was small—around a thousand—and "the articles which were written for them are not paid." If she did not like to be a school-teacher, "it would be a hard case to solve." So, he continued, "I think, Léonie, it would be wise to wait—when we are doubtful. In due time, we may solve, I think, our problem better. Today I have no definite idea. I cannot ask you to come to Japan, when you are doubtful, and I am not positive in offering many opportunities and happiness. Wait! Only wait, when we are not sure to do things right. 'Wait', as Miller used to say. We may come soon to a better wisdom. Meanwhile, we will love Baby, and try to do our best." Now that the two were on friendly and business-like terms again, Noguchi could recognize the value of having Léonie remain in the States. "And I think just now it would be wiser to keep up things as before," he continued. "I will send you articles which are salable and good. You will place them as I tell you, and get some money. The arrangement between you and me would be same as before. You keep some portion of the money we make, and send me the rest." So Noguchi clearly felt that he had done his best to bring Léonie to Japan, and had made some practical gain in the restoration of Léonie's status as his agent and editor.

It was presumably around this time that Noguchi became romantically involved with Matsuko Takeda. Little is known about Matsuko's background (even her age); Ikuko Atsumi describes her as performing "domestic chores at his house," so she was probably one of the two "servants" referred to in Noguchi's October letter to Stoddard.[51] According to the chronology made by Usaburō Toyama, Noguchi married Matsuko Takeda in January, 1906. The date seems unlikely, not so much because Noguchi was incapable of marrying one woman while persuading another to come and live with him, but because he was in Shanghai for the better part of the month. It is easier, and certainly kinder, to

50. YN to LG, 5 May 1906, in *LG* 162-3.
51. Ikuko Atsumi, "Introduction," *CEL* 12.

suppose the relationship began in the spring, after Yone had accepted Léonie's declaration that she would not come to Japan. Matsuko's first child was born sometime in 1907, but the exact date is uncertain—the birth was recorded, according to the usual custom, on January 1, 1908. Yone neglected to inform Léonie of the change in his domestic affairs.[52]

How the relationship with Matsuko developed must be left to the imagination; however, Noguchi did publish a poem entitled "The Japanese Girl" in December 1906 which may offer some clues:

> O the oldest yet youngest love of the Japanese girl,
> O her fading yet lingering scent of heart!
> Let me kiss her ivory cheeks and let me die,—
> In the kiss I taste the youngest soul out of the ages old,
> I taste a rose out of the oldest brown earth.
> Her smile is the mist rising to the morning sun,
> Her cry is the evening bell dying into the dusk.
> She is a creation of sadness and love,—
> A Spring lantern floating in the song.[53]

Noguchi was willing to explain his ambivalent views on gender relations in greater detail if asked, as the *Chūō Kōron* had earlier that year, inviting him to contribute to a group of articles on the topic.[54] He began by sketching a favorable view of the United States as "the country where relations between men and women have developed most fully, without showing harmful effects," a country where "equality runs through everything: in thought, in education, and even physical training, to the point where the old sense of superiority and inferiority between the sexes has nearly vanished." In contrast, "Orientals—Chinese and Persians of course, but also Japanese—have long regarded women as slaves." This came from passion and jealousy being the dominant features of love. The French were similar to Orientals in this regard. The case of the Japanese laborers on the Pacific Coast was interesting: "busy with making a living and earning money, few concern themselves with women or indulge in sentiment. Yet when these Japanese return home, eight or nine out of ten at once fall into dissipation . . . when they first return to Japan, they treat women in the American fashion, but after one or two years, they abandon this and revert to the Japanese way. That is, they come to think of women as beings to be loved and petted rather than respected." Japanese women were also resistant to change, having become "creatures of emotion without intellectual activity, who

---

52. Toyama's chronology, *Kenkyū* 1:326, gives Hifumi's birthdate as January 1, 1908, but births were customarily recorded at the new year. Masayo Duus, *The Life of Isamu Noguchi*, tr. Peter Duus (Princeton: Princeton U P) 53, gives December 1907 as Hifumi's birthdate, but expresses some uncertainty and does not name a source.
53. "The Japanese Girl," *Tōyōhatagumo*, 126, rpt. *Pilg.* 126.
54. "Danjo kōsai ron" (On male-female social relations), *Chūō Kōron* 21:6 (1 Jun. 1906): 14-21.

for two thousand years have dwelt content in such circumstances." Japanese debates on the relations between the sexes were all very good, but adults would never overcome their upbringing: what was needed, in his view, was for children of both sexes to be raised together from childhood. The emotional character of Japanese, particularly women, would change slowly, if at all. And whether, and to what extent, such a change was even desirable, was debatable. He inclined to agree with those who feared that Japanese women would lose their charm if transformed from crystallizations of emotion into embodiments of intellect. Sexual difference did have a purpose. "Relations between men and women are part of the great natural way, so it would be best simply to leave them to unfold freely. Mere emotionalism will not do, but neither will a purely intellectual approach, which leaves women without charm. . . . As for myself, I would like to see the present generation of men and women offered up as a trial, and observe the results." Of course, Noguchi made a fine test subject himself, but he had little interest in offering up his own personal life for public scrutiny.

It is tempting to read the wild winter passion and devil-may-care attitude of Noguchi's poem "The Fantastic Snow-Flakes" (published in June 1906) in relation to the new romance. But Noguchi was the last person to get mixed up in a love suicide, a still-popular escape for lovers more concerned than Noguchi was about social expectations.

> Suppose we die together, eh,
> With the snow dying upon a pond?
> What a fantastic end, ha! ha! ha!
> What a fantastic end to die
> In the dying music of ancient love!
> Behold the snow and music die!
> What a coward, ha! ha! ha!
> Are you afraid to die, eh?
> Still you love a little caprice of world?
> What fantastic snow-flakes, ha! ha! ha!
> To leave no sorrow and to die!
> Such a coward, you my beloved!

Such sentiments (with ashes for snow-flakes) might have been appropriate in San Francisco, devastated by an earthquake on April 18, 1906. Noguchi was inspired to write a tribute to the city for the *Keiō Gijuku Gakuhō* in July—inspired (though he did not say so) by William Marion Reedy's elegiac "Frisco the Fallen" in the July *Philistine*, which described the city's wild post-quake atmosphere: "Life had been pleasure. Ruin was fun. Death—well, to have died in the fall of 'Frisco was something like coming home from battle against the Spartan shields."[55]

55. "San Furanshisuko" (San Francisco), *Keiō Gijuku Gakuhō* 106 (15 July 1906): 42-48; William Marion Reedy, "'Frisco the Fallen," *Philistine* 23 (July 1906): 55-64.

Stoddard had been in nearby San Jose continuing his rest cure on the morning that began with an undulation of the earth in a manner familiar to Californians, "a flowing motion, not in itself disagreeable, though it is apt to arouse one's suspicion and put one on one's guard. Then came the wave, a sudden impulse, instantly followed by a succession of overwhelming billows that threatened every moment to submerge us." Stoddard had resolved to remain in bed until the shock was over, but as the quaking continued and increased in violence, he sought protection under a doorway while "the whole chamber reeled as if it were a house of cards caught in the vortex of a whirlwind."[56]

In Oakland, Joaquin Miller was also in bed in his little chapel house with the door open, and heard the cattle lowing before the quake hit and recalled "a bump and a thump" as if he were "in a small boat bumping against a wharf." "I felt about four of these bumps and got up and went to my chapel door, and saw one of my Japanese boys at my right hand, and one at my left. I said 'Earthquake?' and they answered 'earthquake,' and we went back to bed. The cats went out and everything seemed satisfactory." Miller had breakfast and went out as usual to work in his garden with its spectacular view of San Francisco across the bay. "Then the smoke began to curl up, and it curled up high and strong." The fire went on for three days, destroying most of the wooden buildings in the city left standing by the quake. For Noguchi, who wished he had been with Miller upon the Heights ("tragedy is the highest poetry" he explained) it was an opportunity to reflect on his days in a now-vanished city: the palatial house at Van Ness and Sacramento streets where he had first lived as a schoolboy, the tall *Chronicle* building on the top floor of which he had gleaned material to translate for the Japanese papers, the library at City Hall where he used to read, the third balconies of theaters where he occasionally saw a play for fifty or seventy-five cents. Many saw the quake as a divine cleansing of a city grown too grand and sinful. Noguchi, too, was hopeful that "San Francisco will become a land full of studious and patient laborers once again, with no more speculation and vanity."[57]

The Iris Club

Noguchi was continuing to write English poetry: he had, in fact, sent William Michael Rossetti a manuscript for an early version of *The Pilgrimage* in February.[58] Rossetti sent back a preface for Noguchi to use if he wished. "I find that he has progressed very considerably in the use of the English language, approximately as an Englishman or an

---

56. CWS, "In the Teeth of a Temblor," *National* 24 (July 1906): 353-59.
57. Joaquin Miller in the *Oakland Tribune*, 6 May 1906, rpt. *Museum of the City of San Francisco* website <http://www.sfmuseum.net/1906/ew5.html>.
58. W.M. Rossetti to YN, 4 Apr. 1906, CEL 376.

American would use it," he wrote.⁵⁹ He did advise in his letter that Noguchi change, in "O Aki San," the phrase "My flesh grew in her presence." "I don't perhaps catch the *exact* sense which you attach to this phrase; but I am afraid that some English & American readers would attach to it a sense not particularly decent, & I would recommend you to omit the line." Noguchi had already printed the poem in *Kichō no ki* and ignored the suggestion. But he decided the book was not ready for publication, and ended up putting it aside for what would be another three years. As for his plan to stop writing articles, he had for the most part followed through on it, or nearly so, with the exception of the ones he still sent Putnam for the *National*.

Noguchi had been rediscovering the Japanese language as a medium for writing essays and criticism, if not yet poetry. Moreover, he was establishing a place for himself within Japanese letters, forming a wide circle of literary associates, and demonstrating his willingness and ability to compete and even lead. Now he was ready to test his status and abilities in the field. With a group of his poetic associates he determined in early 1906 to start a quarterly poetry magazine that would include both Japanese and English-language poetry. The magazine would be called *Ayamegusa* in Japanese, *The Iris* in English, and it was to be "a garden where poetic flowers of the East and the West compete in their fragrances"—a meeting-place for a new group of poets to be called the *Ayame-kai* or Iris Club.⁶⁰ The word "compete" was probably deliberate—from the outset, the Ayame-kai proved to be a hotbed of rivalry and controversy for its eight Japanese members and interested observers.

The Japanese members were mostly, like Noguchi, in their early thirties and acutely interested in current Western poetry trends. Five of them—Bin Ueda, Hōmei Iwano, Ariake Kanbara, Kaoru Osanai, and Kyūkin Susukida—would be remembered among the major figures of early twentieth-century Japanese literature. Ueda was the group's scholarly translator-poet, Iwano the eccentric poet-philosopher, Kanbara a talented poetic innovator fusing Western and Japanese styles. Osanai was sowing his poetic oats before embarking on a career as a modernizer of the Japanese theatre and early cinema, while Susukida, one of the first Japanese poets to embrace Symbolism, would later become chief literary editor of the Osaka *Mainichi Shimbun*, and a well-known essayist. Two poets of somewhat lesser talent rounded out the group: another young *Myōjō* poet named Hakusei Hiraki, and a forty-two-year-old Waseda graduate called Ringai Maeda, who edited (together with young Waseda poet Gyofū Sōma) the literary magazine *Shirayuri* (The White Lily), to which Noguchi had contributed several articles and poems.

59. The preface appears in some printings of *Pilg.*, as well as the 1923 Ars bilingual edition.
60. Kamei, *Yone Noguchi*, 69.

25. Bin Ueda, 1911.

Bin Ueda (1874-1916) was already a devotee of English and French Romantic poetry when he became a pupil, in 1896, of Tokyo University's newly-hired English professor, Lafcadio Hearn. He read widely in European literature, becoming a proficient translator of English, French, Italian, and German verse, and writing articles that introduced the Japanese literary world to the latest developments in European poetry, such as his 1896 article on the death of Paul Verlaine, his 1898 essay on new voices in French poetry, and his 1905 study of Mallarmé. His 1905 anthology of translations from European poetry, *Kaichōon* (The Sound of the Tide), provided, according to Tekkan Yosano, "the same nourishment to Meiji and Taishō poetry that Po Chü-i's *Works* had afforded Heian literature." "Probably no other work of modern poetry," writes Donald Keene, "with the possible exception of Tōson's poems, has enjoyed such popularity, but its chief importance was as an inspiration to the next generation of poets." Ueda had read far more extensively than Noguchi and had an excellent grasp of contemporary literary movements, but unlike Noguchi he had never met any of the poets he admired.

He was well aware that contemporary English poets lagged behind the French, but admired Rossetti, and his interest in Yeats, the Irish poet Hearn had highly recommended to his students, led to his publication of the first Japanese bibliography of Yeats's work shortly before Noguchi published his first Yeats article in 1903. Ueda was also very interested in Arthur Symons, the Welsh poet-critic whose groundbreaking study, *The Symbolist Movement in Literature* (1899) had introduced the English-speaking world to the newer French poetry.[61]

Noguchi had boldly established his Yeats connection with a bogus dinner story and plagiarized scholarship, so it was natural that he should do the same with Symons. In an article on Bashō Matsuo published in the *Chūō Kōron* in September of 1905, Noguchi went so far as to invent a visit to Symons's home in Maida Vale, complete with a lengthy discussion

---

61. Donald Keene, *Dawn to the West* (New York: Holt, 1984), 4:228.

of Mallarmé which formed the basis of Noguchi's contention that Mallarmé was a kind of French Bashō. Now, in June of 1906, having included several of Symons's poems in *The Iris*, he wrote Symons an importunate letter: "It is my greatest regret that I could not see you three years ago, when I happened to be in London. And you do not know how you are admired and loved in our younger writers of Japan. A month or so ago we were discussing the symbolism, and how I wish I had a copy of your book!"[62] Though he had included Symons's poems without permission, he could "sense" that Symons would not be offended, as the intention was "to show the specimens of best work of the younger English poets." "How your name glorifies the magazine!" he added. He asked Symons to send a picture and copies of some recent poems.

Fortunately, Symons delivered, not only sending his *Symbolist Movement*, a book of poems, and a picture, but also a poem entitled "Japan" dedicated "To Yone Noguchi" in manuscript:

> The butterfly,
> The frailest of things,
> Has colours that dye
> With jewels its wings.
> It is a flower,
> A mist, a breath;
> Its life of an hour
> Rejoices in death.
> There went forth a word,
> And the winged bright Japan
> Had the heart of a sword
> With the soul of a fan.

The arrival of the manuscript poem with Symons's letter and photo at the end of August came as an enormous relief. "Dear Mr Symons," he wrote back,

> Your most kind letter (with one poem), your picture and also your book of Twenty Songs are here yesterday. What a joy! They came to me like a lightening—yes, indeed! I thank you again for them. (And now your Symbolic Movement [*sic*] came from the publisher today.) Last night I and Professor Uyeda (he is a Japanese Arthur Symons) read your book of poems, and I agreed with him that the second piece called "To a Sea-Gull" is the best one. In fact we liked them all. By the way Mr Uyeda, one of professor at the Imperial University, is a symbolist and new leader of poetry, and he stands as you are in English literature. He says he likes to translate your work if you don't mind.[63]

Another member of the Ayame-kai, Ariake Kanbara (1876-1952), had also received inspiration from Lafcadio Hearn, albeit indirectly.

62. YN to Arthur Symons, [June 1906], Northwestern University Library Special Collections.
63. YN to Arthur Symons, 31 Aug. 1906, Northwestern University Library Special Collections.

Kanbara had fallen for English Romantic poetry after encountering an early anthology of translations, and subsequently studied at an English-language academy. He was "most deeply affected by the poetry of Dante Gabriel Rossetti, whom he learned about from the notes of a friend who had attended Hearn's lectures on English poetry at Tokyo University in 1899," and developed an "unconditional worship" of Rossetti that led to his being styled "the Japanese Rossetti."[64] Afterwards, Verlaine and Mallarmé became his poetic traveling companions. He had not yet found himself, but was "still wandering in the labyrinth of experiment, . . . In one word, he is a phenomenon, but not an achievement."[65] Though "a splendid poet in his own way," even a genius, Noguchi thought Kanbara's poetical atmosphere "too close and shut up": he was "not a free bird who sings to a star" but "a caged nightingale who is obliged to sing." He was "a minor poet in the best sense," valued because "his poetical mood is often sophisticated," but "too careful of himself—too timid like a shy bird."

Timidity was not a problem for the outgoing and eccentric Hōmei Iwano (1873-1920). Now remembered primarily as a novelist, he began publishing poetry in 1893. Like Kanbara, his poetry was influenced by Dante Gabriel Rossetti, particularly in his 1905 *Hiren hika* (Tragic Love, Tragic Songs). In 1906 he was publishing his most celebrated work of criticism, the "dogmatic and illogical" *Shimpiteki hanjū-shugi* (Mystical Semi-Bestialism), which even the unflappable Donald Keene calls "extremely difficult to understand."[66] Influenced by Western writers including Emerson, Swedenborg, Maeterlinck, Nietzsche, and Schopenhauer, the treatise promoted a view of man as instinctive and non-rational. Iwano "saw each individual human being as the sole center of the universe, striving to live fully and intensely at every moment and to make his life a symbol of total reality." The influence of French decadence was discernible, and more so in his 1908 *Shin shizen-shugi* (New Naturalism) where he argued for a "naturalistic symbolism" borrowing from Baudelaire, Verlaine, and Rimbaud. Noguchi admired his youthful passion and called him "the most versatile poet of the day," but found his frank confessional style lacking in suggestiveness and restraint, and his poetic talent immature and unrealized.[67] "It is not seldom we hear of the poet of promise, with youthfulness and a certain amateurish ardour, but never reaching to maturity in art. Such a poet is rarely guilty of artificialness and falsehood, but his lack of the faculty of self-analysis is often extraordinary."[68] Still, Iwano was "a born poet, and might be called a genius," and "can be trusted in his genuineness."

64. Keene, *Dawn to the West*, 4:229-30.
65. "The Poetry of Ariake Kanbara," *JT*, 20 Oct. 1907, 6.
66. SJP 106; Keene, *Dawn to the West*, 4:290.
67. SJP 106.
68. "Through a Japanese Screen," *JT*, 19 Jan. 1907, 6; see also NY, "Homei Iwano," *Shin Shichō* 3 (Dec. 1907): 53-58.

Filling out the roster of Japanese contributors to the first number of *The Iris* in June 1906 were three poets of lesser note: socialist poet Kagai Kodama, whose last book had been banned, Hakusei Hiraki, a *Myōjō* poet known for his nationalistic and iconoclastic verse, and Waseda poet and *Shirayuri* editor, Ringai Maeda. They faced off against English poems by Noguchi, Symons, Joaquin Miller, Josephine Peabody, W. B. Yeats, and John B. Tabb.

The Japanese side of *Ayamegusa* began with a "Foreword" presenting the magazine from a predominantly Japanese perspective. Though signed by Noguchi it was actually written by Iwano.[69] "Now that our country has achieved powerful and far-reaching development, the spirit of our literary world too has grown; its works increasingly express our unique character and are beginning to stand in opposition to those of other nations. At such a time, for small factions to form alliances, for minor groups to quarrel, to recklessly flood the world with a chaotic array of magazines, and to engage in trivial battles—what benefit can such behavior bring to the deeper life of the spirit? Should we not, like the small Greek states that united to face the mighty Persian army, put aside our narrow self-interest and confront foreign literature with poetic sincerity and dignity?"[70] Initial responses from the Japanese press were favorable, with the *Yomiuri Shimbun* running a series of "Readings of Nine Iris Club Poets" beginning in late June.[71]

But as work progressed on the second volume, controversy erupted. Noguchi had made a half-dozen substantial contributions to *Shirayuri*, which Hōmei Iwano and Ringai Maeda had co-founded with Waseda student Gyofū Soma in 1903. But in mid-1905, "Iwano withdrew from the Shirayuri group . . . partly because he was dissatisfied with the romantic turning *Shirayuri* had taken and partly because he could not accept Sōma Gyofū's leading position in the daily work on the journal."[72] Noguchi had continued contributing to *Shirayuri* after Iwano's departure, and invited Ringai Maeda to join the Iris Club, so could hardly have expected to open *Shirayuri*'s August number to find an anonymous hatchet job aimed at *The Iris*.[73] He responded with a letter expressing his profound disappointment that Ringai had published the anonymous and undignified criticism, calling it impudent and disgraceful.[74] While acknowledging that the piece contained some valid criticism, he lamented the erosion of literary decorum and urged Ringai, as editor-in-chief, to uphold the dignity and moral responsibility of literature.

69. Maeda Ringai, "Ayame-kai naijō" (Conditions in the Iris Club), *Shirayuri* 3:12 (1 Oct. 1906): 578; Hori Madoka, *"Nijūkokuseki" shijin Noguchi Yonejirō*, 113.
70. NY, "Hakkan no ji" (foreword), *Ayamegusa* 1 (June 1906), 1.
71. [Kōkōkakyaku Kakuda], "Ayamegusa o yonde kyū shijin ni atau," *Yomiuri*, 24 June 1906, 1.
72. Yoichi Nagashima, *Objective Description of the Self*, 31.
73. "Ayamegusa o yomu" (Reading *The Iris*), *Shirayuri* 3:10 (Aug. 1906): 523-26.
74. NY, "Maeda Ringai-kun ni atau" (To Ringai Maeda), *Shirayuri* 3:11 (Sept. 1906): 527.

His appeal fell on deaf ears. Maeda doubled down on his decision to publish the critique, defending the practice of anonymous criticism and the validity of the reviewer's complaints.[75] "Insults are not necessarily evil; the issue is whether the insult itself has value or not," he asserted, working himself into such a frenzy over the course of five pages that a full page had to be redacted.

Noguchi did not reply again to *Shirayuri*, but did write a letter to the *Yomiuri* explaining the history of the project and how it had run into publication problems due to slow sales. This had not been his fault, he insisted, but rather "the failure of Japanese new-style poets" and "the cold indifference of the Japanese poetry-reading public." Now his attempts to move the magazine to a new publisher were creating further difficulties.[76]

Shirayuri's October issue added fuel to the fire. The anonymous reviewer stepped forward, revealing himself to be (no great surprise) none other than Gyofū Sōma (now twenty-three and a university graduate).[77] In a mockingly polite tone Sōma offered Noguchi a five-page explanation, with further criticisms, of his pseudonymous critique, and of the evolution of his distaste for Noguchi. "When I first read your work and heard of your reputation in Britain and America, I admired your talent, courage, and ambition," Sōma wrote. He traced the decline of his esteem to one of Noguchi's self-promoting writings in the *Yorozu Chōhō* newspaper, "little more than self-glorifying boasts of your own inflated reputation." Then, when news of Noguchi's return to Japan had spread and he had been "welcomed as a curious and precious guest in our literary world," Noguchi had tried his hand at giving a lecture. "Ah, that lecture!" Sōma recalled: "Never have I felt so displeased as I did with your talk at the Imperial Literary Society." Sōma had been especially offended by Noguchi's disrespectful references to British and American poets, as 'that guy so-and-so.'" Noguchi had said he, as an anonymous reviewer, was "a fool without the right to enter the literary world," but it was Noguchi who "truly lacks the proper character to enter our sacred literary world. Our literary world must indeed expel those with frivolous views like yours," he declared. "Why? Because you do not place importance on the Japanese literary world, and yet you are a disruptive presence within it. You are a Yankee worshipper who constantly thinks of America in every matter. What have you to say for yourself?" Readers who made it through this screed were then treated to Maeda's five-page exposé of "Conditions in the Iris Club."[78] Maeda raised and sometimes tried to answer questions about Noguchi's

---

75. Maeda Ringai, "Noguchi Yonejirō-kun ni kotau" (Answering Yonejirō Noguchi), *Shirayuri* 3:11 (3 Sept. 1906): 528-33.
76. NY, "Ayame Kai tai Jozandō funsō" (Iris Club vs Jozando conflict), *Yomiuri*, 1, 2, 3 Sept. 1906, 5.
77. Sōma Gyofū, "Noguchi Yonejirō kun ni atau," *Shirayuri* 3:12 (1 Oct. 1906): 571-75.
78. Maeda Ringai, "Ayame-kai naijō" (Conditions in the Iris Club), *Shirayuri* 3:12 (1 Oct. 1906): 576-81.

questionable handling of finances, the reasons for the change in publisher and postponement of the second number, the non-participation of the foreign members, Maeda's public accusations and expulsion from the society, his alleged responsibility for a scurrilous *Yorozu Chōhō* article, the inaccuracy of reports of the quarrel's settlement and issuance of apologies, and, for good measure, concerning "a sensational article describing the relationship between Yonejirō Noguchi and the wife of a certain notable figure" in a certain magazine.

Though delayed for three months, *The Iris; No. 2* appeared on December 19 bearing the date "September 1906" and the Japanese title *Toyohata-gumo* (A Bank of Clouds). Most of the former Japanese members contributed, excepting Maeda and Susukida; Gekkō Takayasu and two others joined. For the English section, Noguchi culled from an even wider garden of Western poets, adding, from England, Alfred Austin, Laurence Binyon, Thomas Hardy, Laurence Housman, Alice Meynell, Lewis Morris, the Duchess of Sutherland, and from America, Bliss Carman, Madison Cawein, Mary Fenollosa, Louise Imogene Guiney, Joaquin Miller, Josephine Preston Peabody, Frank Putnam, Charles Warren Stoddard, and Edith Thomas. His prize, of course, was the poem "Japan (To Yone Noguchi)" contributed by the highly-revered introducer of Symbolism, Arthur Symons. Noguchi printed the poem in manuscript, along with the manuscript of "Occident and Orient" sent by Edith Thomas. By doing so, he effectively showed that the Iris Club was not "a so-called literary 'fraud society,'" even if, as Maeda had charged, "not a single foreigner actually submitted a contribution for the first volume."[79] But the demonstration had little force at this stage when so little remained of the hopeful spirit that had animated the Club's formation.

Thinking back on the Iris Club a decade later, around the time of Bin Ueda's funeral, Noguchi recalled how "an absurd quarrel broke out among our comrades—so ridiculous that now I'm ashamed even to talk about it—and I became the main target of their harsh attacks. At that time," he remembered, "Ueda defended me alongside Iwano and Kambara."[80] But "after the quarrel had settled down and we decided to have dinner together at some restaurant, I just couldn't bring myself to invite Ueda along with Iwano and Kambara. I couldn't converse openly with Ueda the way I could with the other two; I couldn't have an uninhibited, frank relationship with him. I felt that inviting Ueda would somehow stiffen the carefree and joyful atmosphere of our group and make it less enjoyable."

After sending off copies to his foreign friends, and paying off his year-end debts, Noguchi put his editorial misadventure to rest and prepared to face the new year.

79. Maeda Ringai, "Ayame-kai naijō," 578.
80. "Ueda Bin-kun (3)," *Jiji Shimpō*, 26 July 1916, 5.

The National Temperament

Since all of the voluntary and involuntary contributors to the *Iris* volumes were apparently friends of Noguchi, it is interesting to note among them Mary McNeill Fenollosa, the poet-novelist wife of former Tokyo University professor, art scholar, and Nō aficionado Ernest Fenollosa. As a teacher of political science, philosophy, and economics at Tokyo University from 1878 to 1890, Ernest Fenollosa's combination of Spencerian evolution and Japanese cultural nationalism had been a powerful stimulus for the "New Generation" intellectuals who had been Noguchi's mentors in his college days: Shigetaka Shiga's associate Setsurei Miyake had been one of Fenollosa's most devoted students. Noguchi was certainly aware of Fenollosa, if not the exact spelling of his name, before returning to Japan in 1904; he had noted in his review of Hearn's *Kwaidan*: "We are often told by foreigners that we do not know the true value of our own things. We were taught to prize Hokusai and Hiroshige, in art for example, by Professor Fennellosa [sic] and others. How often we were told that we should remain Japanese!"[81]

Fenollosa and his wife had returned to the United States in 1901. Noguchi might have had some opportunity to meet them there, and Stoddard, who often spent his summers in Tuckernuck with Fenollosa's close friend, and fellow Japanophile, William Sturgis Bigelow, might also have encountered him. But Fenollosa had not yet published anything significant, and his intimate familiarity with Japanese culture had not served him much better in the United States than Noguchi's, for Fenollosa had few opportunities to do more than serve as consultant to wealthy Oriental art collectors like the Detroit industrialist Charles Langdon Freer, who was busy amassing the artifacts that became the cornerstone of the Smithsonian's Asian art collection. In Japan, however, Fenollosa was "*daijin sensei*," the teacher of great men, and Noguchi had fallen in among his influential former students, notably Shōyō Tsubouchi and Kenzō Wadagaki, who both contributed prefaces for Noguchi's books.

The first indication of Noguchi's interest in the work of Mary Fenollosa—Fenollosa's second wife and former secretary (his divorce and remarriage in 1895 had provoked a minor scandal in Boston)—is an enthusiastic and well-informed February 1906 review of her two books of Japan-inspired poetry, in which he called her the most truthful and graceful poet among all the poets who came to Japan from the West.[82] And yet the source of the biographical information in the article is unclear: it might have been Fenollosa's former student, Kenzō Wadagaki, now a Tokyo University professor of law, economics, and literature, or, Tokuboku Hirata, Fenollosa's former junior colleague and Nō translator.

81. "Lafcadio Hearn's 'Kwaidan,'" *Bookman* (New York) 20 (Oct. 1904): 159-60.
82. "Nihon utaeru beikoku no onna shijin" (An American woman poet who sings Japan), *Taiyō* 12:2 (1 Feb. 1906): 115-119; "Fenorosa-fu" (Mrs. Fenollosa), *Shūmi* 2:4 (1 Apr. 1907): 53-59..

Fenollosa had become an increasingly avid student of Nō, and on his last trip to Japan, in 1900-1901, Hirata, his junior colleague at the Higher Middle School where they both worked, had served as his assistant, at the suggestion of Jigorō Kanō, the school's director, and Fenollosa's former student. Fenollosa put Hirata to work translating the texts of the Nō plays he was studying under Minoru Umewaka, a leading actor of the Umewaka school. The formerly daimyō-sponsored Nō schools had fallen on hard times, but were undergoing a revival with the awakening of cultural nationalism.

26. Kenzō Wadagaki.

Wadagaki and Hirata likely also played a role in interesting Noguchi in the traditional drama of Nō and kyōgen. "I cannot forget the impression carved on my mind which was then roughened, stiffened by the toss of Western life of quite many years, when I first entered Hosho's *No house*," Noguchi recalled a few years later. It had been October of 1905, and Noguchi had been taken to the performance by a friend who was "a great appreciator," perhaps Wadagaki, who headed off his list of recreations with "Utai (Japanese classical songs)" in his entry for *Who's Who in Japan*.[83] Noguchi had smiled seeing "the 'honorable names' of those occupants, lords or barons or what not, written on the wooden tablets stuck on each box; I think I must have felt even uncomfortable," he confessed, "on seeing myself among the select few." Noguchi had met Wadagaki, at Hearn's funeral.[84] The "portly gentleman" was warm and genuine, lived near him, and shared his passion for translation and transplanting Japanese literature into foreign lands. "From that very first meeting I went along with him straightaway to visit his home," and he was also a frequent visitor at Noguchi's, according to Hironobu.

83. The date is given as October "six years ago" in "The No Plays," *Taiyō* 18:1 (Jan. 1912): 19 and "some ten years ago" in the 1914 *SJP* (56). Kenzō Wadagaki (1860-1919) entered Tokyo University in 1878, and after graduating in literature and economics with honors in 1880, spent some years studying in London, Cambridge, and Berlin before being appointed to the College of Law in 1886.
84. "Ko Wadagaki hakushi" (The late Dr. Wadagaki), *Jiji Shimpō*, 20 July 1919.

In his earlier writing on Japanese drama Noguchi had written almost exclusively of kabuki, which remained a highly popular form, paying little attention to the arcane and aristocratic Nō. But Fenollosa had been dismissive of the kabuki, a "vulgar drama," he explained, "quite like ours . . . an amusement designed by the common people for themselves, and . . . written and acted by them."[85] Noguchi did not entirely dismiss kabuki but was critical of the current state of the Japanese theater, as he wrote in the *Jiji Shimpō*.[86] It was incoherent, overlong, and antiquated, there were no capable playwrights or actors, and the plays had little sense of unity. On the other hand, proposals to Westernize the theater came up against traditional features such as the revolving stage, the hanamichi walkway, and long-established audience habits, without which the Japanese drama would lose its distinctive qualities.

The Nō, on the other hand, was, in Fenollosa's view, "a form of drama, as primitive, as intense, and almost as beautiful as the ancient Greek drama at Athens." It was also nearly as difficult to understand as the ancient Greek drama, full of arcane references to classical Japanese and Chinese poetry and legends, and there was as yet no scholarly literature available to serve as a guide. Noguchi was not yet ready to try his hand at translating it. The kyōgen, however—Nō's comical cousin—offered an easier opportunity. Noguchi had in fact already translated one kyōgen as early as 1904, while still in New York: "The Melon Thief," published in March of that year in Boston's *Poet-Lore* magazine. The kyōgen, he explained there in his brief introduction, "may be regarded as a comic outburst of the national temperament."[87]

Now in the summer of 1906, Noguchi began translating a number of the short comedies, publishing five more in September and October, in *Poet-Lore*, the *Taiyō*, and *Waseda Bungaku*. The following summer, he collected these and several more in a bilingual volume called *Ten Kiogen in English*, published in Tokyo and sold under the imprint of the Tozaisha, a small Japanese import-export company with a shop in San Francisco's new Japantown, and also by Kegan Paul in London. It was not entirely unnoticed: French Japanologist Noël Péri gave it a careful and respectful review, and it was listed in the bibliography of Arthur Waley's anthology of Nō plays. But few copies sold.[88]

Noguchi also had an ongoing interest in possible English uses for Japanese zoku kyoku (popular songs), particularly the hauta, which he

---

85. Ezra Pound and Ernest Fenollosa, *"Noh" or Accomplishment: A Study of the Classical Stage of Japan* (London: Macmillan, 1916), 86.
86. "Engeki kairyō" (Theatrical reform), *Jiji Shimpō*, 15 July 1906, rpt. *Kabuki* 77 (Sept. 1906), 122.
87. Pound and Fenollosa, *"Noh" or Accomplishment*, 59, 61; YN, "The Melon Thief," *Poet Lore* 15 (Mar. 1904): 40-42.
88. N. Peri, *Bulletin Ecole français d'extrême orient* 9:1 (Jan.-Mar. 1909): 175-7. Waley in *The Nō Plays of Japan* (New York: Knopf, 1922), 260, misidentifies Noguchi's book as *"Twelve Kyōgen* (text and translation), 1911."

described in his 1904 essay on "Popular Songs of Japan" as "a form of popular song ... with much more subtility in expression" compared with other forms such as the dodoitsu.[89] In that essay he had transliterated and translated four examples. But since 1903 he had been experimenting with his own English imitations of Japanese songs, combining earlier Japanese lyrics with his own inventions. In several magazines he published "Hauta," "Zoku Kyoku," and "Cradle Songs," and his 1909 book, *The Pilgrimage*, collected three "Cradle Songs" and six "Hauta." Often, these were revisions of preexisting songs. There was, for example, a song that began, "tsuyu wa obana to neta to iu" which can be roughly translated:

> The dew says it slept with the pampas grass;
> The pampas grass denies that it slept with the dew.
> Which is it: they slept or they didn't sleep?
> The ears of the pampas grass were seen to emerge.

The song is based on wordplay impossible, and perhaps too risqué, to translate: obana, literally "tail-grass," is so-called for its resemblance to an animal's tail, while "ears" in the final line is a homonym for "cheeks" suggesting the embarrassment of the pampas grass. The song had already spawned some variations such as "tsuki wa shimizu to nete iu" ("the moon says it slept with the clear water"). Noguchi's version replaces the pampas grass with a firefly:

> The dew says she slept with the firefly;
> The firefly says he never slept with the dew.
> She says yes, he says no,
> He says no, she says yes.
>
> Ha, ha, ha, the glow of the firefly betrays
> The secret of his heart, yoiya sa, ha, ha, ha![90]

Noguchi's adaptation of the song made it easily comprehensible to English readers, but sacrificed some of the original's natural symbolism and wordplay.

Despite Noguchi's aversion to rhyme and meter, he was apparently quite proud of the hauta he had written collaboratively with Zona Gale, particularly the one beginning "Beneath the cherry blossoms sleeping," which he reprinted half a dozen times over a two-year period, and later translated into Japanese.[91] But any prospect of having the songs set to music and sung would have been rendered futile by Western audiences' aversion to traditional Japanese singing styles. When even a musicological Japanophile like Blanche Partington could scarcely endure the

89. "Popular Songs of Japan," *Poet Lore* 15 (Apr. 1904), rpt. *EE* 74-76.
90. "Hauta: VI," *Pilg.* 136.
91. In "Tokyo by Night" (1903), *Kichō* (1904), *Myōjō* (Jan. 1905), *Broadway Magazine* (Nov. 1904), *National Magazine* (Mar. 1905), *Eibei* (1905), and in Japanese in *Nihon kokumin tokuhon* (1933) and *Teihon shishū*, v. 2 (1947).

singing of a member of the Kawakami troupe, there could be little hope for Japanese songs in English. But as Noguchi wrote, "it is our latest literary movement that we take up the Zoku Kyoku (or vulgar song, including Dodoitsu, Hauta and others) seriously, and put a proper value on it, and some of our younger poets are trying to make a new Zoku Kyoku on the old ground." He was interested, he said, in the "experimental productions" of Kyūkin Susukida and others, and had praise even for his nemesis Ringai Maeda's forthcoming folk song anthology: "although it has many faults, doubtless, it should be respected and welcomed as a harbinger in such a line of literature."[92]

Fuji Sunrise

As Noguchi occupied himself with explorations of Japan's national culture, one inescapable national symbol loomed above him: the cone-shaped silhouette of Fujisan. With the arrival of summer, Noguchi, joining the exodus of sweltering, well-to-do Tokyoites, headed to Fujisawa, home of his priest brother, Yūshin, who was to join him in realizing a longstanding travel dream: the ascent of the sacred Mount Fuji.

On July 20, after the rains ended, the two brothers boarded the train at Fujisawa, arriving at 10 a.m. at Gotemba, where they took a horse car toward Subashiri, "the Eastern Gate," "one of the three places," Noguchi explained, "where the holy climb may properly begin," and supposedly the easiest.[93] "We left the place on horseback, accompanied by a mountain guide or *goriki*, who carried on his back plenty of food and water and some blankets and clothing. We wore large bamboo mushroom hats, on which the words, 'We two shadowy pilgrims of the holy highway' were written; and our shoulders bore, according to the fashion, wide straw rain-coats. We sang a song that was not of a city's rise or fall, but of a wind or flower, for we were glad that our ascent of Fuji mountain had started well."[94] Noguchi published a report of the trip in the *Keiō Gijuku Gakuhō* soon after his return, but his English version acquired some embellishments by the time it saw publication in 1913. The Keio version said only that they wore *manjūkasa*—knitted-straw rain-hats shaped like *manjū* (bean-paste dumplings). The hats were evidently meant for the Buddhist pilgrimage in Shikoku, in which the pilgrim (*ohenro*) visits eighty-eight temples connected with the Buddhist sage Kōbō Daishi.[95] The song of the "shadowy roamers of the holy highway" would become the "Proem" of his

---

92. "Japanese Popular Songs," *JT*, 21 July 1907, 6. Maeda's collection would be titled *Nihon minyō zenshū* (Complete works of Japanese folk songs) (Tokyo: Hongo Shoin, 1907), not, as Noguchi states, *Zoku kyoku shishū* (popular song poems).
93. "Pilgrims of the Holy Highway," *Graphic* 84 (27 Sept. 1913): 576. *A Handbook For Travellers In Japan* (London: Murray, 1903), 167-69, lists six routes up the mountain.
94. "Fuji tozan" (Climbing Fuji), *Keiō Gijuku Gakuhō* 103 (15 May 1906): 36-41.
95. "Dōgyō ninin" (two persons going one road), refers to the guiding presence of the Heian-era priest's spirit. Noguchi also uses the Shikoku pilgrimage term for his wooden staff "Kongotsuye."

1909 book *The Pilgrimage*.

Many Fuji pilgrims were affiliated with one of the Shugendō (mountain worship) sects. Though directly descended from Buddhist sects (the Murayama sect, founded in the 12th century by Buddhist ascetic Shōnin Matsudai, and the Fujiko or Fujidō sects, founded by Kakugyō Hasegawa in the late sixteenth century) they had evolved into a branch of "pure" Shintō, obliged by the Meiji government's religious reforms to formally renounce a millennium of Buddhist influence. The main branch, renamed Jikkō, had cultivated a strong nationalism. "According to the teachings of our sect," explained the Jikkō high priest representing Shintō at the 1893 World's Parliament of Religions, "we ought to reverence the famous mountain Fuji, assuming it to be the sacred abode of the divine Lord, and as the brain of the whole globe."[96]

There are compelling reasons to think Yone was more than a little attracted to the religion. A foundational doctrine of Fujidō was the revelation Kakugyō received during an ascetic practice in which he stood tiptoe on a wooden post, fasting, and going without sleep in a cave on the mountain, when the deity Fuji Sengen Dainichi disclosed to him that Fuji and the deity were "the source of the entire universe and all life; indeed, this deity and Fuji, as well as Kakugyō and his wooden post, all constitute the cosmic pillar of the universe."[97] Noguchi seems to have used this revelation for one of his early poems, "To an Unknown Poet" (later entitled "Lines"):

> When I am lost in the deep body of the mist on the hill,
> The world seems built with me as its pillar!
> Am I the god upon the face of the deep, deepless deepness in the
>   Beginning?[98]

Another Fujidō-reminiscent moment was, of course, the scene in Sturge-Moore's London drawing room, where Hokusai's Fuji print spoke: "Look askance at the western people, and manifest the poet's glory! You must neither fear nor tremble! Take courage, I command you!" In later years, Noguchi would continue to write about Fuji, notably in his essay "With Fuji Mountain It Begins and Ends."[99]

Yūshin, as a Buddhist priest, would not have had much use for Jikkō—perhaps that was why they had brought Buddhist pilgrimage gear and avoided the main approach at Murayama used by the majority of Jikkō sect pilgrims.

"The mists did not disappear even when we reached Umagayeshi,

---

96. Reuchi Shibata, "Shintoism," in *The World's Parliament of Religions*, ed. J. H. Barrows (Chicago: Parliament, 1893), 453.
97. H. Byron Earhart, "Mount Fuji and Shugendo," *Japanese Journal of Religious Studies* 16:2-3 (Dec. 1988): 218, 220.
98. "To an Unknown Poet" *S&U*, IX; "Lines," *FTES* 6.
99. "With Fuji Mountain It Begins and Ends," *Adelphi* (Ser. 2) 9:6 (Mar. 1935), rpt. *LE* 29-38.

or 'The Place to Bid Your Horse Adieu,'" Noguchi wrote. Despite the name they continued on horseback until the temple at Ichinomiya "where we were told that we must now walk." On the steep pathway they felt "like holy pilgrims with the song of prayer for 'Rokkon Shojo' (the six vital parts, the eyes, nose, ears, tongue, body and heart)"—the standard purification chant for Fuji climbers and one undoubtedly of Buddhist derivation. They "were obliged to stop at the place called Ochujiki, or 'Honourable Lunch Place,' although evening had not yet fallen," as descending pilgrims said the mountain-hut at the Second Station was not yet open."[100] "We rose early next morning,"—at 4 a.m. according to the Keio account—"and again the mists troubled our ascent. Suddenly the great sunlight burst forth upon Mount Fuji right before us." This seemed a good stopping point to the editor of the syndicate that published the story in dozens of small-town American papers; readers were probably unaware that Ochūjiki—less honorifically, Chūjiki-ba, or "food-stop place" in Murray's *Handbook*, was still 8 *chō*—half a mile—from the First Station, with another nine stations above.[101]

27. **Pilgrims at the foot of Mount Fuji, circa 1900.**

As they got underway the mountain was again nowhere to be seen, "only the dark-red lava which had been once thrown out from her top in her active days." The travelogue skips the long morning walk, barely pausing at the Sixth Station where they "did not see, in truth, anything at all . . . except the clouds, white or grey" dwelling briefly on "the most

---

100. As Noguchi explained, "the whole mountain is divided into ten stations, each with a stone hut, or Muro, where one can sleep." But stations might be closed or substandard; on the Subashiri route, according to the 1903 *Handbook*, "the best stations are 2, 6, and the top."

101. "Mountain of Fuji: Description of Visit to Holy Mount of Japan" appeared, unsigned, in *Chicago Daily Herald*, 7 Nov. 1913, 6 and numerous other papers; Chamberlain and Mason, *A Handbook for Travellers in Japan* (1903), 168-9.

dangerous part of the ascent . . . between the eighth and ninth stations, commonly called the 'Munetsuki Hatcho,' meaning the breast-high thousand yards." Here, Noguchi notes, "my companion sought rest, as his somewhat fat physique did not allow him to climb farther," while Noguchi continued on with the guide "to do 'Ohachi Mawari,' or 'The Circular Tour of the Mountain Top,' where are situated two holy springs." "After two hours," he writes, "I returned to the place whence I had started. I found my brother priest lazily walking amid the stone idols of Jizo and other holy worthies who, it is said, protect the dead children at a certain riverside of Hades." Yone's "imaginative eyes could see clearly that many children were here playing under the protection of the gods, nearer to the sun and stars, in the paradise of silence and rest."

28. On the Summit of Fuji, 1907.

The descent of the mountain was "almost miraculously easy," but the brothers decided to spend the night at the Sixth Station, for the sake of the sunrise. Awakened by the hut-keeper's *"Goraiko"* (the honorable coming of the light), the brothers jumped out of bed. "There in the east was the red large ball swinging up like a mighty king whose golden shafts of light dazzled the universe. The clouds changed from gray-white to white-silver, and from white-silver to pearl-rose." After a small breakfast they began their descent back to Gotemba.

Glad or Sorry?

Though Léonie had been working at *The Raven* since February, by May she had still received no paycheck. She enjoyed working for Theo Lowe, and would have been content to go on waiting, but one of her coworkers, displeased with Lowe's lavish lifestyle, went to the police and had him arrested on May 23.[102] Police and reporters soon discovered a series of similar complaints that had chased Lowe and *The Raven* from Oakland

---

102. On Lowe, see LG 165-67, 411.

to San Francisco to Pasadena, including allegations of fraud and embezzlement that had led to two warrants for his arrest in 1903 and threats from angry, unpaid former employees. Whether Lowe was a clever scam artist or an unfortunate "victim of the game of business chance," as his supporters contended, was never fully resolved. "Whether he is guilty or not I do not know," Léonie wrote Putnam on May 26. "Poor Mr. L—Even if he is a liar I really hope that he will wriggle out." It was a blow for Léonie's pride and finances, but she did not take it to heart. "Little Yo will have to go without strawberries for a while—I am selling the sweet peas out of my garden to make a little money."[103] The $60 Lowe owed her would have paid half the cost of their Japan passage, but she still had "a certain scheme" in mind to bring Ethel and Yone together. She was doing some typewriting for a Greek playwright and "codgelling my brains for thoughts upon the subject of 'Engaged Girls' in answer to a most polite request from 'Good Housekeeping,'" which had issued a call for articles on the subject from "the 'brightest and most wide awake' among their contributors." Putnam could perhaps appreciate the irony.

Exactly what changed Léonie's mind about going to Japan is difficult to determine, but it was no doubt a combination of many factors, including disappointment over the *Raven* fiasco, Frank Putnam's encouragement, Yone's continuing, if not always convincing, efforts at persuasion, Matsuo Miyake's enticing postcards, and her own curiosity. Then there was the situation in California. The earthquake had decimated the state's economy. Amid the chaos in San Francisco, racial tensions had erupted, and the resulting anti-Asian debates had spread to other cities. Racial tensions had been already on the rise: on March 21, 1905, even as Léonie was explaining to Elizabeth Converse her hope to have her marriage with Yone more formally recognized, the California legislature had amended the 1872 anti-miscegenation statute that invalidated "all marriages of white persons with negroes or mulattoes"; now Section 60 of the California Civil Code declared "All marriages of white persons with Negroes, Mongolians, and mulattoes are illegal and void."[104] Stories of police harassment were beginning to circulate. In San Francisco, Japanese immigrants with white spouses were placed under investigation, and

---

103. LG to FP, 26 May 1906, FPL.

104. The 1905 amendment followed a 1901 bill to add Mongolians to the anti-miscegenation statute that had been struck down as unconstitutional. Since the *issuance* of marriage licenses for "a white person with a negro, mulatto, or Mongolian" was already banned under Statute 69, the 1901 and 1905 amendments specifically targeted out-of-state interracial marriages. There had been questions of whether Japanese were Mongolians, but a U.S. Senate immigration commission report found that in California "Japanese are regarded as Mongolians" and "in fact, the amendment of the law in 1905 was meant to relate specifically to marriages between them and white persons." See Megumi D. Osumi, "Asians and California's Anti-Miscegenation Laws," in *Asian and Pacific American Experiences: Women's Perspectives*, ed. Nobuya Tsuchida (Minneapolis: Asian/Pacific American Learning Resource Center and General College, U of Minnesota, 1982): 13; *Reports of the Immigration Commission: Immigrants in Industries*, Part 25, vol. 1 (Washington, DC: Government Printing Office, 1911), 162, note b.

in Mill Valley, a Japanese youth had been arrested for writing a love note to a white schoolmate.

29. Isamu, Léonie, and Albiana at their newly-built house, late 1906.

Noguchi, being "well acquainted with the existence of an anti-Japanese expression in the Pacific slope" explained in a letter to the *Boston Evening Transcript* that "when the recent San Francisco affair was first reported, I positively disinclined to take any serious notice of it."[105] He had even contributed a letter to one of the Tokyo papers "explaining that such a tendency always appeared to form a part of the local labor politics in California, and it would soon become a thing of the past. But I was unfortunate to find soon that it had grown into a regular movement of a demagogic nature, with no little element of social violence, and with the support not only of the clergy, but a large section of the local public. The exclusion of Japanese children was reported. Then my denial to attach any significance to the matter was mistaken, and I regretted very keenly the trend of events in San Francisco." "However, the San Francisco affair may be settled," he concluded, "one thing is true, we are not increasing, but decreasing, our respect and faith in America, that hitherto were greater than that for any other country in the world."

The little redwood "box house" and tent could offer little protection against California racism for a half-Japanese child and his doubtfully-married mother, as even the ever-cheerful Léonie must have sensed. And

105. "As the Japanese See It," *Boston Evening Transcript*, 16 Feb 1907, 2.

finally, as she had confessed to Putnam back in March, there was the fact that she still loved Yone. Whatever her reasons, Léonie must have conveyed her new determination in a (now missing) letter in July, for on August 6, Yone casually mentioned to Putnam that "lately Léonie wrote me that she will come over to Japan." He added that he thought she was acting wisely and that he, too, would do his best.[106]

30. Léonie and Isamu in Los Angeles.

Yone had had more than his share of shocks that week, for Putnam had informed him, without much explanation, that he had left the *National* and was in the hospital. (According to a note later added to a subsequent letter, "Mr. Putnam was just recovering from a hernia operation.") Why he had left the *National* was not made clear, but apparently there had been some intimation of a problem as Noguchi noted that Putnam's departure had not surprised him. It came as a blow, however, as the magazine had provided a reliable venue for his articles, not to mention those of Stoddard, Léonie, and Ethel. Over the next few months Joe Chapple, the editor-in-chief, ran Noguchi's articles already accepted by Putnam, but there would be no new ones after that, and lacking Putnam's pro-Japanese influence, the magazine soon added Japan to its list of racial enemies, printing in February 1907 articles on "The Japanese Question from a California Viewpoint" and "The Menace of the Yellow Empire."

Even before the loss of the *National* Putnam had urged him to stop "turning out such a trifle newspaper stuff," and by this time Noguchi's writing for American periodicals had dwindled considerably, as he had warned back in February when he told Léonie, "you can not expect me to send you many articles hereafter." By April, suffering from financial problems, he had changed his mind: "I like to get some money every month from America, if possible, and so I will send you my article pretty regularly, I think." But the articles had been few and far between: besides

106. YN to FP, 6 Aug. 1906, FPL 49.

the *National* contributions, "Marquis Ito in Korea" and "The Making of Gods" (in the *Los Angeles Times*) and "Actors' Wives in Japan" (in the *New York Sun*) appeared between May and September.[107]

He had given up on Japanese newspapers as well, for reasons that were partly explained by a November article on "Newspaper Making in Japan."[108] "The story of American journalism and journalists"—bad as it was—"would make Japanese gape from wonder and unapproachableness." Japanese newspapers were slow, they were "terribly poor," they were dependent on the government for news, they lacked business managers, and there was "nobody more miserably paid than the Japanese newspaper man." Only editorial writers were well paid; for the rest, "it would be the most extraordinary thing if you were paid for your contribution." Many journalists were dedicated, and it was "perfectly admirable to see them working with a smile under such hard conditions." But they were young and inexperienced, often just out of school, and were "making journalism a stepping stone for a better job." Noguchi had found all this out the hard way. "Since I returned home in the autumn of 1904 I frequently contributed articles and they were printed promptly. After some months one of the publishers dropped into my place and left a Japanese fan with greeting. Yes that was all."

Noguchi's reflections on the sad state of Japanese journalism may have been inspired by the opportunity presented to him that Fall to write a weekly "Literary Criticism" column for the *Japan Times*. Noguchi had contributed a couple of important articles for the paper—his "Conversation with Mrs. Lafcadio Hearn" and "The Younger Poets of Present Japan," but this was his first shot at a regular weekly column.

The *Japan Times* had been founded in 1897 by Motosada Zumoto—a former translator for the Yokohama-based *Japan Mail* who had also served as Hirobumi Itō's secretary—and Zumoto's hometown friend, Sueharu Yamada, former director of Japan's leading shipping firm, the Nippon Yūsen Kaisha. As the first serious attempt at a competitive, Japanese-run English newspaper, it was designed to be a corrective to the multitude of foreign-owned English newspapers with their sometimes hostile and often misguided views of Japan. Yamada and Zumoto sought advice from Yukichi Fukuzawa. Yamada was a nephew of Fukuzawa's wife and had studied at Keio, and Fukuzawa enthusiastically supported his plan. Japanese politicians and business leaders, for whom the foreign papers were a constant thorn in the side, were equally pleased with the idea. "Mr. Fukuzawa persuaded the late Baron Yatarō Iwasaki, then Governor of the Bank of Japan, to make the Mitsui and Mitsubishi interests,

107. "Marquis Ito in Korea," *Los Angeles Times*, 13 May 1906, VI:15, and *Boston Evening Transcript*, 16 May 1906, 19; "The Making of Gods," *Los Angeles Times*, 24 Jun. 1906, VI:18; "Actors' Wives in Japan," *New York Sun*, 16 Sept. 1906, rpt. *EE* 282-86.
108. "Newspaper Making in Japan," *New York Sun*, 4 Nov. 1906, 5.

the Bank of Japan, the Yokohama Specie Bank and the Nippon Yūsen Kaisha finance Mr. Zumoto's paper."[109] Hirobumi Itō helpfully funded Zumoto's overseas trip to investigate the foreign newspaper world, a trip that "convinced him in the belief that an English-language paper was badly needed to remedy the general ignorance abroad about Japan." Japan's foreign press viewed the new entrant with skepticism and fear: extraterritoriality in the treaty ports would soon be abolished, and "since the Japanese Press Law recognises Japanese subjects alone in the capacity of newspaper proprietors," the *Japan Mail* wrote, "there is a possibility that foreign subjects or citizens may see themselves debarred."[110] Such concerns turned out to be overblown, and the *Japan Times*, downplaying its propagandizing in hopes of gaining the trust of its target readership, found its niche in the new century as the foreign community, obliged to leave the security of the treaty ports, learned to accept the law of the land.

31. Kazutomo Takahashi in 1909.

The *Japan Times* catered mainly to the expatriate community and, though solid in its news reporting and business coverage, lagged in its cultural and literary departments, which consisted of reports of sparsely-attended literary society meetings and dubiously-informed impressions and reports of Japanese cultural events. In 1906 the paper had been left in the hands of its assistant editors when Zumoto went off to Seoul to serve as secretary to Hirobumi Itō, the new Resident-General of Korea, and manage the *Seoul Press*. These included Tarō Yamada, the Yale-educated son of the paper's cofounder, and Kazutomo Takahashi, a University of Michigan graduate who had run the paper during one of Zumoto's earlier absences. In addition to his work at the paper, Takahashi also taught English at Keio, and it was likely he who approached Yone with the invitation to write a weekly column for the Saturday or Sunday edition.[111]

Noguchi's first fifteen columns ran under the title "Literary Criticism:

109. *Short History of the Japan Times in Commemoration of the 15,000th Issue of the Daily and Revision of Its Title* (Tokyo: Japan Times Ltd., 1941), 7.
110. "The New English Paper in Tokyo," *Japan Weekly Mail*, 27 Feb. 1897, 194-95.
111. *Keiō Gijuku shusshin meiryū retsuden* (Keiō Gijuku graduate biographies) (Tokyo: Keiō Gijuku, 1909), 351-52; *Short History of the Japan Times*, 53.

Through a Japanese Screen," and were somewhat rambling in focus. "You may act and appear fantastic without making much disturbance of public morality," began his first column on November 10, a quirky but forceful effort to grapple with the question of exoticism:

> Doubtless, to be exotic is not a crime. And it rises quite often to be of real value and invites our admiration. Again, exoticism on the surface does not mean exoticism of spirit. We are different—we are glad of it, I admit—from others. We think and act differently. We live and die, perhaps, in some different way. Know that we are frequently exotic and fantastic, not only in face and appearance, but also in our mental processes. But gold is gold everywhere. And Truth—big capital-lettered Truth—is Truth in any country.[112]

Since the "we" who are different were the exotic Japanese, Noguchi was very much attempting to accommodate a Western frame of reference. "We are much misrepresented on the foreign dramatic stage and in books; especially in so-called Japanese stories," he went on to argue, taking up the usual offenders: Loti, Long, Watanna. "It is not too much to say that their books are nothing but a mess of misinformation and misspelled Japanese words." Meanwhile "the good Japanese books"—he offered a list including Chamberlain, Aston, Hearn, and a long list of art-book authors—"are usually unread occupying a little corner of the library." Nearly all of Noguchi's approved authors turn out to be British; even the stodgy Edwin Arnold "is ten times better than any Japanese novelist so-called in America." Safely back in Japan, Noguchi was finally able to lash out at American literary institutions: "Not only are their Japanese novels, but American novels in general are poor. There is no other country which produces so much literary trash as America, sorry as I am to say it." The second half of the article mainly focused on a somewhat-too-appreciative analysis of anti-realist Japanese theatrical scenery-painting by Australian-British artist Sir Mortimer Menpes included in a recent anthology, *Japan as Seen and Described by Famous Writers*. Menpes, a follower of Whistler who had visited Japan, had addressed questions of theatrical regeneration in general and stage realism in particular, topics current in both Japan and the West which would preoccupy Noguchi and others a great deal in the coming years. In contrast to the Western theatre with its obsessive "craving for realism," the Japanese, in the view of Menpes, were "not led away by this struggle to be realistic," and this was "one of the chief reasons why the stage of Japan is so far ahead of our stage."

Noguchi was evidently given free rein to write whatever struck his fancy, and the results, if predictably uneven, were often interesting. Subsequent columns that year focused on the uta poetry of the late Naobumi Ochiai, Mary Fenollosa's novel, *The Dragon Painter*, Horace Traubel's

---

112. "Through a Japanese Screen," *JT*, 10 Nov. 1906, 6.

book on Whitman, Sōseki Natsume's recently-published first novel, *I Am a Cat* (which earned Noguchi's rare commendation as a true work of genius), a Pierre Loti story about Istanbul, and a travel book in Japanese by journalist Sohō Tokutomi, all interspersed with Noguchi's random musings. It was an ideal opportunity for Noguchi to explore and develop his talents as an essayist, and a record of his changing impressions of Japan. "To be a dreamer in this age is becoming a luxury," he wrote in one column. "There was a time in the East when Life was a dream, and a dream was a phase of life, but to-day the uncomfortable sound of the street cars drives away the gossamer and nightingale . . . One likes even to curse modern Tokyo and many other places."[113]

Noguchi also recognized the value of the column as an international political podium. He used one column for a letter addressed "To the Mayor of San Francisco," expressing his concerns about the chaotic situation in the city. Noguchi had known the new mayor, Edward Robeson Taylor, during his California days. Taylor had assumed the thankless task of bringing order to the lawless city when Charles Boxton, a thirty-seven-year-old dentist appointed by the Board of Supervisors to replace convicted extortionist Eugene Schmitz, resigned after a week in office. Taylor, a sixty-nine-year-old physician and poet, married to ex-governor Leland Stanford's niece, seemed to offer some hope of stability, but only a glimmer, since the sixteen members of the Board of Supervisors who had appointed him were also under indictment on bribery charges. Nevertheless, Noguchi expressed his confidence that the poetic mayor would bring order to the city and be a protector of the Japanese, who were being subjected to escalating attacks amid the general violence of a strike by the streetcar union. A number of incidents against Japanese individuals and businesses had already become the subject of federal inquiries at the request of the Japanese government. "Thousands of our brothers are trying to make an honest living under California skies. Your American poets used to teach me to believe in the future and humanity; I confess that I had been losing my faith from the so-called San Francisco affair during many months past. But now I feel inclined to sing again, seeing you upon the *dais* of light and peace." He remembered that Taylor had bid him farewell when he left California three years earlier at the time of the Russo-Japanese War, and had been "so enthusiastic in praising Japan and her action in defending Righteousness," and he quoted some of Taylor's idealistic poetry to further justify his optimism, and to fulfill the literary obligations of his column.[114]

Frank Putnam had also returned to the journalistic world after recovering from his illness. Taking his family west, he had taken a job as an editor on the Houston *Chronicle*. His many distractions prevented him

113. "Through a Japanese Screen," *JT*, 16 Feb 1907, 6.
114. "To the Mayor of San Francisco," *JT*, 28 July 1907, 6.

from maintaining much interest in the affairs of Noguchi and his women, and the correspondence became infrequent. On December 6, Léonie was reduced to writing to Stoddard, complaining, "One thing I regret is the nice long scolding elder-brotherly letters I used to receive from Mr. Frank Putnam in the days when he thought me an incorigible. Since I decided to do what he would call the proper thing he doesn't write a word. It is funny that one's friends always take more interest when one is a sinner and a rebel."[115]

Léonie had warmed to Stoddard's proposal of a visit after reading his "delightful fantastical bit of nonsense" in the *National*. "Sometimes I have thought you too frivolous. Really, Mr. Stoddard, I have had my doubts about you sometimes." She supposed he had heard from Yone San that she and the boy would be going over to Japan fairly soon, "that is, if poor Yone can ever scrape up the price of half a ticket via the way of the steerage people."[116] "Nothing could please me more than to see you and Yone and the wee one all together in Japan," Stoddard reiterated in his reply. "This Baby Boy is to be like no other Baby Boy in all the world. Mark my words and heed me!"[117]

Léonie wrote Frank Putnam on January 23, 1907: "What has become of Frank Putnam? Yone is asking, and I am wondering." The Japan trip was settled. "I am going to start pretty soon," she wrote. "In the meantime I am pegging away at my typewriter, gathering up the precious pennies just to throw them into the sea again for a bit ticket to cross that same." "Am I glad or sorry?," she wondered philosophically. "Really, I don't know. Call no man happy until he is dead." That ancient Greek proverb was an appropriate thought for one embarking on her own odyssey. "I can't tell you if I like it till I get there," she continued. "Yone's letters are ominous, to say the least. He warns me not to bring any 'dreams' with me."[118] This was certainly sound advice. The Ethel fiasco had not brought Noguchi to any realization that honesty might be the best policy, and he once again evaded disclosing any unseemly facts about the state of his romantic entanglements. Léonie had nothing to go on except his "ominous" tone. But she was resigned to fate. "Oh, well, I am tired of trying to do anything with him," she concluded. "I guess Baby Boy and I will take care of each other." And there was always Matsuo Miyake. "At present I may be able to assist you of your getting some situation in a school or college," he had written to her the previous August, evidently not informed of her plan to reunite with Yone. "Will it not be delightful to live in a Nippon no Iye, a Japanese residing house, together, you and I?!" He was writing the ending to his Japanese novel (never, apparently, published in

---

115. LG to CWS, 6 Dec. 1906, in *LG* 178.
116. LG to CWS, 9 Dec. 12 1906, in *LG* 178.
117. LG to CWS, 12 Sept. 1906, in *LG* 174.
118. LG to FP, 23 Jan. 1907, in *LG* 179.

book form), a sad romance between a Japanese girl, Tsuyu-ko, and her American lover, the final scene portraying the farewell of the two lovers at Tsuyu-ko's departure for Japan, "setting forth to sail to the Southern Ocean for seeking the ever-spring Islands, where they might live and [die] in love, an eternal love."[119]

---

119. Matsuo Miyake to LG, 31 Aug. 1906, in LG 173.

SHADOWY ROAMERS ON THE HOLY HIGHWAY

1907-1910

Noguchi was "heartily pleased to have the New Year's Day and January, in this modernized Tokyo with electric lights and telephones, again drowned in the old glory and tradition. The customary 'gate-pines' or *kadomatsu* are set before the doors, and the people all smiles and an excusable blush from *toso* or *saké* go to and fro distributing their happy greetings and profound bows. And within doors mothers and girls are merry, playing their *Karuta* cards with the *Hyakunin Isshu* poems."[1] Noguchi would soon be publishing his own translation of the popular thirteenth-century anthology—the first to appear in English. "The first Japanese literature, the classical uta of thirty-one syllables," had been "born in the twilight within the golden screens of the palace." That had been in the Nara Period, "the lyric age of Japan, having as the great light the uta poet Hitomaro." After Nara, Kyoto became "the centre of culture and song," "and when the Court left Kyoto for this Tokyo, some forty years ago, poetry and culture were also transplanted," and "the muddy moat of feudal age appeared in a new dress, making itself even a subject for a poem." Here, on the 18th of January the Emperor and Empress had presided over the "time-honoured impressive feast of the 'Reading of Poems'": the best of the twenty-thousand submitted on the year's announced subject—the "New Year's Pine."

But reading *The Life and Letters of Lafcadio Hearn* the following month, Noguchi understood why Hearn had "cursed Modern Japan and Tokyo."[2] In "this detestable Tokyo," Hearn wrote, "there are no Japanese

---

1. "Through a Japanese Screen," *JT*, 2 Feb. 1907, 6.
2. "Lafcadio Hearn's Despair in Tokyo," *JT*, 2 Mar. 1907, 6.

impressions to be had except at rare intervals. . . . To think of art or time or eternity in the dead waste and muddle of this mess is difficult."³ "To be a dreamer in this age is becoming a luxury," Noguchi wrote. "To be a poet even in Japan,—the 'desired of artists, poets and lovers,'—would be a great achievement. There was a time in the East when Life was a dream, and a dream was a phase of life, but to-day the uncomfortable sound of the street cars drives away the gossamer and nightingales."⁴

Far-Beyond Street

"The arrival of my two-year-old boy, Isamu, from America was anticipated, as it is said here, with crane-neck-long longing."⁵ The cynical biographer must throw some cold water on the enjoyment of Noguchi's account of "Isamu's Arrival." The lighthearted and amusing piece was not, as it appears, a spontaneous chronicle of paternal hopes written soon after the boy's arrival, but, rather, an obligatory declaration of marriage and paternal responsibility published at the time of the unsuccessfully-reunited family's final dissolution. The first-person pronouns were all Yone's, even if the story was mostly Léonie's. It was a good story, and no one who read the article in *Sunset*, the London *Nation*, Frank Putnam's *Southwestern Farmer*, or *The Story of Yone Noguchi*, would have been left in any doubt of Yone's acceptance of marriage and paternity. That no one could read it in Japan was a matter of no great consequence.

"This Mr. Courageous landed in Yokohama on a certain Sunday afternoon of early March": March 4, 1907. Isamu was, at least initially, an object of fascination to his father, who tried to imagine "a baby's first impression of Japan, many-coloured and ghostly." Léonie had attempted to save Yone from "a sort of mortification" by telling him how Isamu "used to sing and clap his hands for 'papa to come' every evening." But confronted with the actuality, Isamu was less enthusiastic. When Léonie, saying, "See papa," tried to make Isamu's face turn toward his father, "he shut his eyes immediately without looking at me, as if he were born with no thought of a father."

With Isamu packed into his beloved carriage, in which he had even slept on the steamer, the newly united family headed to the train station; there, however, Isamu expressed displeasure at being separated from his faithful vehicle, which was not permitted to accompany them inside the car. Arriving at Shinbashi station in Tokyo, he and the carriage were reunited again, and in opulent Ginza, the three had their first Japanese

3. Elisabeth Bisland, *The Life and Letters of Lafcadio Hearn*, 2 v. (Boston: Houghton Mifflin, 1906), 2: 332-34.
4. "Through a Japanese Screen," *JT*, 16 Feb 1907, 6.
5. "Isamu's Arrival," *LG* 181-88, from "Isamu and Others," *Sunset* 25 (Nov. 1910): 534-39; "Isamu's Arrival in Japan," *Nation* 8:20 (11 Feb. 1911): 798-800, rpt. *SYN* 185-99, and "Isamu Comes Home," *Southwestern Farmer*, 15 March 1911, 14-15. "Kakushu" (or "tsuru-kubi"), literally "crane-neck," means "anticipation," as in "kakushu shite matsu": "to wait craning one's neck."

supper, but Isamu, who "had been sea-sick, and had eaten almost nothing" during the voyage, was now "pale and thin," and "could hardly finish one glass of milk."[6]

32. **Ginza from Shinbashi, circa 1910.**

The name of the section of Koishikawa where Noguchi's home stood—Hisakata-machi, "Far-beyond Street," in his translation—may have been poetic, but this was little consolation as they dragged the heavy baby carriage, wrapped in a large *furoshiki*, or all-purpose cloth wrapper, through two city train lines, pushing it the last mile in the darkness up the hilly road still in bad shape after a recent snow. The forlorn trio "must have appeared to people's eyes quite unusual." "I think that it was not altogether unreasonable for Baby to keep crying all the time," the article has Noguchi admitting; "I was rather suspicious, looking at Léonie, that her heart also wanted a heartful cry from the heavy, exotic oppression, whose novelty had passed some time ago." But when Isamu did not stop crying "even after his safe arrival at this Hisakata home," Noguchi concedes, "it tried my patience very much, and I did not know really what to do with him." Isamu "cried on seeing the new faces of the Japanese servant girls, and cried more when he was spoken to by them."[7] It was not an auspicious beginning.

The arrival of a single white female passenger carrying a baby had not gone unnoticed by reporters on hand to cover the liner's arrival. No one knew much about what had compelled the woman to "travel the

6. "Isamu's Arrival," *LG* 182.
7. *LG* 183.

eternity of the great salt road without even a servant girl to call on," but the reporter from the *Yorozu Chōhō* heard she was called "Lionie Birma" and had been asking many of the Japanese passengers if they knew an English-language poet named Yone Noguchi.[8] The *Tokyo Nichi-Nichi* also heard from passengers that the woman (unnamed) had freely conversed with them about whether Japan was such a lovely country and whether they had heard of a poet named Yone Noguchi, a question that, as the rumor spread, seemed to be of more than literary interest.[9] Reporters from the *Yomiuri* and *Asahi* papers heard similar stories.[10]

By the end of the day the reporters had pieced together more of the story. The *Yorozu Chōhō* dug deepest, beginning by interviewing Noguchi's Keio literature department colleague, Kochō Baba, who knew something about Noguchi's affairs, but not the details. "I myself previously heard that Noguchi would soon greet his wife from America," he told them, "and I also heard that the fiancée has a child, but I don't yet quite understand which woman it is that is supposed to be coming this time."[11] A *Yorozu* reporter then went to Noguchi's house and reportedly received a full explanation directly from the poet. The lady, "Lionie Birma," age thirty-one (she was actually thirty-four) had been born in New York, and went to "Pru-Mawr" University at about the same time as Umeko Tsuda (the well-known Japanese educationalist). The reporter understood that Noguchi had employed her as a woman-reporter in 1900 when he was publishing a literary magazine, and had developed a secret admiration for her because "she has a style and manner not like an American lady, extremely plain like a Japanese woman." "Then, one summer night, for some strange reason, I wrote Lionie a marriage promise and went off to visit Washington. Returning to New York in November of 1902, Birma and I were together." All of which was close to the truth, if slightly garbled. Nor was Noguchi at all misleading in his succinct account of his relationship with Ethel Armes. "But when I developed a relationship with another woman who played music," he continued, "Birma and I finally discussed separation. And going off to the newly-available mistress I concealed what happened with Birma. After I returned home in 1904, however, the mistress, discovering the Biruma affair, became horribly angry and broke off her relationship with me."

The Monday papers told the story: "English Poet's Love Tale: American Woman Arrives, Yearning, Bringing Child," ran the headline in the *Yorozu*. The *Yomiuri*'s article was entitled "Journey of Passion: Pining

8. "Eishijin no enbun" (English poet's love tale), *Yorozu Chōhō*, 5 Mar. 1907, tr. LG 189-90.
9. "Eishijin no enpuku" (English poet's luck with the ladies), *Tokyo Nichi-Nichi Shimbun*, 5 Mar. 1907, tr. in LG 192-93.
10. "Koi no tabiji" (Journey of passion), *Yomiuri Shimbun*, 5 Mar. 1907, tr. in LG 191; "Beikoku fujin no koi" (American woman's love), *Asahi Shimbun*, 5 Mar. 1907, 6
11. "Eishijin no enbun" (English poet's love tale), *Yorozu*.

for Poet, American Woman Comes to Japan," while the *Tokyo Nichi-Nichi* chose "English Poet's Luck with the Ladies: Yone Noguchi and the American Woman," and the *Asahi* went with "American Woman's Love (Comes Admiring Japanese English-language Poet)." Overall, amusement at Noguchi's overseas romantic conquests was stronger than criticism of his moral profligacy. "Poet prodigies, living for beauty, living for passion, have always everywhere been subject to slander for their immorality and dissipation," the *Nichi-Nichi* observed. The *Nichi-Nichi* seemed to be on to something more than it was prepared to say directly, noting that the unnamed woman was "a bit dark-haired" and wondering, "had this woman, being shown the lines of Yone Noguchi's beautiful poetry, fallen even knowing that the brilliant poet was not sincere?" And "someday won't a blonde beauty's shape turn up at the little brushwood fence near Otsuka of some 'high-collar' Yokohama writer?"[12] The story Noguchi had given the reporters placed him in the role of a Japanese Don Juan resigned to welcoming his lovelorn, estranged American lover.

The story would have played out differently if Noguchi had mentioned—or the reporters had discovered—that Noguchi now maintained a second household with a pregnant Japanese wife. "Matsuko first learned about Yonejirō's American wife and child the day before they arrived in Yokohama," according to Masayo Duus. "She left the house in Hisakata-cho, taking one of the maids with her. Afterward Yonejirō spent most of the week in Kamakura, but when he came up to teach at Keiō he stayed at Matsuko's house in Yanaka Negishi."[13] That story would likely have elicited some public condemnation, for the papers were clearly sympathetic to Léonie's plight.[14]

Isamu's continuing crying likely provided an appropriate soundtrack to Yone's reading of the Monday papers. "When two or three days had passed, he stopped crying." He had taken a sudden interest in the workings of the paper *shojis*. His interest in his new home proved limited, however, and on the fifth day, "he earnestly begged his mother to go home," as he missed his grandmother. When Léonie tried to appease him by telling him to "go and see papa," he slowly stole toward Yone's room and slightly opened the *shoji*. When his father looked at him, Isamu banged the door shut and ran away crying, "No, no!" Returning to his mother, he reported that his father was not there. Yone "must have appeared to his eye as some curiosity, to look at once in a while, but never to come close to." Unsure how to address this curious being, he began to imitate the servants, responding "hai!" to Yone's clapping summons as they did, and attempting to call his father "Danna Sama" (Mr. Lord) as they did.[15]

12. Otsuka station is about a mile north of Koishikawa.
13. Duus, *The Life of Isamu Noguchi*, 54.
14. See *LG* 189-92.
15. "Isamu's Arrival," *LG* 185.

Léonie accepted, whether or not she believed, the story of Yone's school-night sleepovers and long absences; but did not nurture many hopes of marital bliss. On May 19, she confessed as much in her first letter from Japan to Frank Putnam—now in Houston, where he had taken a job on the Houston *Chronicle*. "Yone and I don't fight," she wrote. "But as for Happiness with a capital 'H' why I fear we are both too selfish, as you say." Yone had "changed so much I would hardly have known him," she added, "—especially in the shape of his nose and the acquisition of a moustache."[16]

33. **Isamu with two maids.**

Léonie also reported that "Yone seems to like the Boy tho he doesn't approve of his manners, which have suddenly flowered into a sort of wild Indian savagery amazing and dismaying." The Isamu article noted that "Isamu hates anything which does not move, or makes no noise." "When he has nothing new to play with, he will begin to open and shut the *shojis*, when he tires of that, he will try to go around the house and hunt after the clocks which I hid, as they lost the right track of the time since he came. And presently I send him away with a servant to the Botanical Garden to look at and feed the 'kwakwa,' as he calls the ducks."[17]

As might be expected, adjusting to Japan proved easier for the young Isamu than for Léonie. Evidently comfortable with his status as object of fascination to the local children, "Baby-san," as they called him, would proudly present himself for inspection at their request and was soon taking part in their games and picking up Japanese words. For Mamma-san, as Léonie was known to the neighborhood, it was "rather lonesome . . . because everyone speaks a strange language which I fear I shall never

16. LG to FP, 19 May 1907, FPL 53, in *LG* 193.
17. The Koishikawa Shokubutsuen (Botanical Garden) has been operated by Tokyo University since 1877.

learn. The mazy city streets (which are only dirt-roads) are all tangled up and I don't know which way is which." There were a few bright spots. Léonie the nature-lover found "green things growing everywhere." And they had been to the exposition then in progress in Ueno Park.[18]

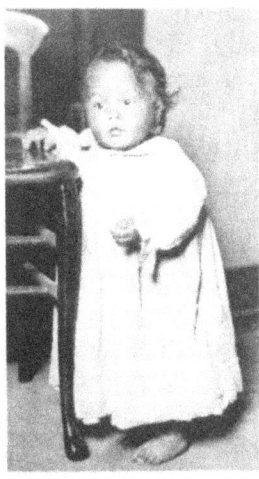

34. Isamu, circa 1907.

In addition to the regular servants, there was also a young student "houseboy," such as Yone himself had once been. Hironobu Noguchi, a student of Yone's priest-brother Yūshin at the Jōkōji temple, came to live in the Hisakata-machi house in 1907 when he enrolled at Shiba Junior High School. Hironobu's daily chores consisted of familiar tasks he had done for Yūshin at the temple—cleaning the entrance, living room, toilet, and lamps (Noguchi used gas rather than electric lamps and had two oil lamps in his study)—and new responsibilities like shining shoes, caring for umbrellas, and polishing furniture.

The house was in a quiet neighborhood about twenty or thirty minutes on foot from the station, Hironobu recalled. There was a jinrikisha stable in the neighborhood, and Noguchi had a regular driver. He kept late hours, reading and writing on an oval shaped desk in his study after everyone else was asleep, until two or three in the morning.[19]

Yone began to spend more time away from home in Kamakura, a two-hour train journey from Tokyo.[20] There, he stayed in a Buddhist temple called Zōroku-an, or Tortoise Temple, a smaller temple surrounded by trees near the entrance of the great Zen temple-compound of Engakuji, founded in the thirteenth century. "Life here is very quiet, grey in tone, and sweet in atmosphere," Noguchi reported to Putnam in a letter also dated May 19. "I found finally my ideal place in the Kamakura; and I will

18. LG to FP, 19 May 1907, in *LG* 193.
19. Noguchi Hironobu, "Noguchi Yonejirō sensei no omoide," *Kenkyū* 1:311.
20. "Kamakura is reached from Yokohama in 50 min. by the Tokaido Railway" and "the journey from Yokohama to Tokyo occupies 50 min." according to Chamberlain and Mason, *A Handbook for Travellers in Japan* (1903), 109, 101.

stay here as long as possible, and work."²¹

He was really working, according to Raichō Hiratsuka, a 22-year-old graduate of the new Japan Women's College who took refuge at the temple in 1908 to escape the scandal of her failed love-suicide with a married teacher. As she recalled, "The poet [Yone Noguchi] was also living on the temple grounds. Our paths crossed now and then, but according to the woman who served Noguchi his meals, he was a recluse. His only visitor was his American wife, who came once in a while but never stayed long. The woman also said he was eccentric and irritable, spent the whole day at his desk, and shouted at anyone who made a noise."²²

Kamakura was, of course, ideal not only as a writing environment, but also as a convenient explanation of where he was heading when he ventured out of the Koishikawa house, luggage in hand. On the other side of Ueno Park was his other house in Negishi where Matsuko waited. The homes of the two women perfectly embodied the traditional division between Tokyo's Yamanote and Shitamachi, or High and Low City, in Edward Seidensticker's rendering. "From the beginnings of its existence as the shogun's capital, Edo was divided into two broad regions, the hilly Yamanote or High City, describing a semicircle generally to the west of the shogun's castle, now the emperor's palace, and the flat Low City, the Shitamachi, completing the circle on the east. Plebeian enclaves could be found in the High City, but mostly it was a place of temples and shrines and aristocratic dwellings. The Low City had its aristocratic dwellings, and there were a great many temples, but it was very much the plebeian half of the city. . . . The vigor of Edo was in its Low City."²³ Many years later Noguchi recalled the Negishi neighborhood as the "only one spot in Tokyo where some fragmental reminiscence of a fool's paradise or golden dream under the old feudal age was still discovered, as if a broken spider's web among the trees; I used to take an afternoon walk to satisfy my mind longing for a better day, and often peeped into a curio-shop there."²⁴

Yone arranged some English teaching work for Léonie. Her favorite pupil was the young Lieutenant Iwamura, son of a certain Baron Iwamura, a heroic figure from the time of the Meiji restoration, she was told. "The old Baron sits in his big house overlooking the city, crippled with paralysis, a devotee of iris culture and morning glory culture—he plants a thousand varieties of the latter every year," she told her friend Catherine Bunnell. The son was tall, handsome, athletic, and versed in poetry, and he plied her with gifts. "If I mention morning glory seed, they are forthcoming. Singing insects? Here is a cage. Goldfishes? He

---

21. YN to FP, 19 May 1907, FPL 52.
22. Hiratsuka Raichō, *In the Beginning, Woman was the Sun* (Columbia UP, 2010), 122.
23. Edward Seidensticker, *Low City, High City: Tokyo from Edo to the Earthquake, 1867–1923* (New York: Knopf, 1983), 8.
24. *Sharaku* (Tokyo: Seibundo, 1932), 24.

will bring his sleeves full of them tomorrow. With such arts he wins my indulgence toward his frequent remissness in the matter of getting his lesson." Her other pupils included a professor of Electrical Engineering and a banker, and she had agreed to teach two mornings a week in a Girls' school beginning September.[25]

Léonie's lonesomeness, however, did not improve. She stopped writing to Matsuo Miyake. "I have been imagining that there must have been around you something very, very happy things or some troublesome ones," he wrote her in October 1907. "And it must be reason you do not write me these day. And I made up my mind not to disturb you with writing when you are in a very happy condition and not to make you to tell me and increase your uneasiness if you are in the other state." She was very likely in "the other state." It cannot have been improved by Matsuo's letter of two weeks later, in which he pressed her again to join him for an autumn visit to Kyoto, told her something about his work translating for the *Mainichi*, and then casually mentioned how happy his mother was living with him and his wife. "I have not told you before about my marriage," he confessed. "I will write you sometime of my venturing in my love affaire."[26]

At the Theatres

In his first year as the literary critic of the *Japan Times*, Noguchi had produced more literary criticism than he had in his whole previous life, and his command of the genre had developed considerably over the course of the year. After the rambling experiments of the first few issues, the pieces became more focused. Noguchi drew widely on the miscellany of subjects that typically interested him, though with a local emphasis. In January, Noguchi reviewed a book on Byron by popular novelist Hallie Erminie Rives (who was then in Tokyo as the wife of American diplomat Post Wheeler), *A Fantasy of Far Japan* by Baron Kenchō Suematsu, a book of impressions by a French-born American priest, Charles Wagner, Elizabeth Bisland's collection of Lafcadio Hearn's letters, and a Japanese poetry collection by his friend Hōmei Iwano. In February, when separate titles began to replace the generic title "Through a Japanese Screen," there were articles on the simple life and on poetry in the imperial court, and reviews of a British book on Korea and a Palestine travelogue by Sohō Tokutomi. During the spring and summer Noguchi continued to follow his interests, introducing readers to lesser-known Japanese writers like poetess-educator Utako Shimoda (1854-1936), supernatural short-story master Akinari Ueda (1734-1809), *Ayame-kai* poet Ariake Kanbara, reviewing new Japanese-English books like Kakuzō Okakura's *Book of Tea* and Shigenobu Ōkuma's *Fifty Years of New Japan*, exploring the work

25. LG to Catherine Bunnell, July 1907, in LG 194.
26. Matsuo Miyake to LG, 2 Oct. 1907 and 16 Oct. 1907, INF.

of British literary acquaintances like W.M. Rossetti and W.B. Yeats, reviewing the latest Tokyo art exhibition, exploring the cultural significance of the Japanese morning-glory, and considering the future of the Japanese theatre.

While still in New York, Noguchi had written an article about the Japanese theatre, describing the lively theatre-going experience of kabuki. Shortly after returning to Japan, however, he had been taken by a friend to see a Nō performance, and was won over to the medieval form, and its comical cousin, the kyōgen. He had translated one kyōgen, *The Melon Thief,* while still in New York, and undertook a series of them in 1906, producing a bilingual collection of *Ten Kiogen in English* in May 1907. But Noguchi had also become friendly with Kaoru Osanai and Shōyō Tsubouchi, leaders of the Shingeki (New Theatre) movement, which was then absorbed in adaptations of Shakespeare and Ibsen, among other European influences, and had written up an interview with geisha-actress Sadayakko Kawakami. He also frequented the yose or vaudeville theatres. In sum, his knowledge of the theatre was considerable, although he was by no means an authority on any particular genre. In August 1907, he devoted one of his columns to "The Japanese Theatre," comparing the new school (shimpa) "whose main idea is set upon the realism which we see in the West" with the old school (kyūha) that he admitted was "mightily waning." Turning Westernism against itself, he pointed to Western denunciations of the contemporary Western theatre, and turned again to Mortimer Menpes' effusive comments about traditional Japanese drama, noting that the old drama "always finds such admirers in the West."

Noguchi neglected to mention that the old Japanese drama also found many non-admirers in the West who complained of its tedium and incomprehensibility, its occasional silliness and auditory torments. But the admirers certainly existed—most famously Ernest Fenollosa, who had studied Nō in the 1880s and 90s with the famous actor Minoru Umewaka and translated a number of the plays with the help of a junior colleague, Tokuboku Hirata. Fenollosa had found in it the survival of a pure dramatic form comparable in intensity to the ancient Greek theatre. William Archer, the leading English drama critic, was fascinated by the similarities between the Nō theatre and the Elizabethan theatre. "I learnt more about the Elizabethan stage in Japan than I ever did from the performances of the Elizabethan Stage Society" he would write at the end of his two-month visit to Japan in 1908.[27]

But who was the mysterious foreign "critic of art and life" whose visit to the Nō theatre Noguchi described in his October 27, 1907 column, "With a Foreign Critic at a No Performance"? Together, according to the article, they had gone off to attend a Nō performance at the Hōshō

---

27. On William Archer's visit to Japan, see Peter Whitebrook, *William Archer: A Biography* (London: Methuen, 1993): 291-93.

one Sunday morning, the foreigner chatting cheerfully about how he was quite certain he was in Japan this time, "no mistake about it—Japan with poetry at heart," as they arrived hearing the sad music of the flutes and tsuzumi. The performance impressed him with its splendid costumes, theatrical decorum, and dramatic simplicity. The question of the identity of the foreign critic is of more than usual interest, for during the course of his conversation with Noguchi, he happened to observe that "the Nō . . . might be compared with the Greek play or the modern Irish plays of Yeats and others."[28] It was probably the first time the Nō had been linked with the name of W. B. Yeats, and the connection seems to have provided the basis for Noguchi's seminal article the following week, "Mr. Yeats and the Nō." But many of the foreign critic's comments—aside from the comparison to the plays of Yeats—were in fact derived from American artist John La Farge's description of his 1886 visit to a Nō performance with Henry Adams and William Sturgis Bigelow in *An Artist's Letters from Japan*. The foreign critic was a fictional construct, or at best, a composite.[29]

Noguchi was beginning to identify what he would call his "Japanese Celticism." In a column on "Yeats and the Irish Revival" published in April, he agreed with William Archer "in not making so much of the influence of race upon literature, which has been discussed extensively since the Irish literary revival has begun to make a somewhat strong impression."[30] Archer had been interested in the parallels between the plays of Yeats and Maeterlinck, "men of two races which it is the fashion to regard as diametrically antagonistic to each other in the structure of their souls." Noguchi and several of his fellow Japanese poets felt a similar affinity with the ideals of the Celtic movement. While Yeats "stands opposed to the encroachments of a uniform civilisation that is destructive [of] national and provincial variations of every kind," his work was also "the product of an exacting artistic conscience, and everywhere wrought with the utmost care." In the past, Yeats had been "abused mightily on the ground of his obscurity," Noguchi observed, noting that "hitherto, it is the fact that he has had only a small audience, however choice it may be." But he also noted signs that Yeats was "undergoing some change of literary ambition and scope; he is attempting to appeal to a greater mass but not in the same style with Kipling."

Léonie, whose father hailed from northern Ireland, probably contributed a good deal to Noguchi's appreciation of Irish drama. In Los Angeles, before her departure, she commended Yeats's *Plays for an Irish Theatre* to a former colleague at the Irish Catholic school where she had

---

28. "With a Foreign Critic at a No Performance," *JT*, 27 Oct. 1907, 6.
29. Edward Marx, "No Dancing—Yone Noguchi in Yeats's Japan," *Influence and Confluence* (Yeats Annual 17), ed. Warwick Gould (London: Macmillan, 2007), 56-57.
30. "Yeats and the Irish Revival," *JT*, 28 Apr. 1907, 6.

worked in New Jersey. A few months later she told her friend Catharine Bunnell that "The only interesting book she had read lately was "Lady Gregory's book of stories and translations of Dr. Hyde's plays— which last are *splendid*."[31]

In the new edition of Yeats's *Poetical Works* the volume devoted to Yeats's *Dramatical Poems* included a new preface in which Yeats endeavored to explain his views on playwriting. "A writer of drama must observe the [dramatical] form as carefully as if it were a sonnet," Yeats explained, "but he must always deny that there is any subject-matter which is in itself dramatic—any especial round of emotion fitted to the stage, or that a play has no need to await its audience or to create the interest it lives by."[32] Noguchi knew Yeats was too proud to ever make concessions to his audience. "I quite agree with Mr. William Butler Yeats that a drama has not to wait on its audience; and it would be a poor thing which has not the dignity of independence," he wrote in an attempt to paraphrase Yeats's argument, adding, for good measure: "the drama is first, the audience has to follow." Unfortunately, Noguchi misread Yeats's argument. Yeats was constantly vacillating between the opposing demands of audience interest and artistic independence and here he was again "attempting to appeal to a greater mass" as Noguchi had noted in his earlier Yeats essay.[33]

The misreading was a little embarrassing, and may have been one reason neither Noguchi nor Yeats ever mentioned the groundbreaking essay, "Mr. Yeats and the No," that appeared in the *Japan Times* on November 3, 1907. It could hardly have been the only reason. A decade later, when Yeats produced his first Nō-inspired plays, he acknowledged a debt only to Ezra Pound's editions of Ernest Fenollosa's Nō translations. "With the help of these plays, 'translated by Ernest Fenollosa and finished by Ezra Pound' I have invented a form of drama, distinguished, indirect and symbolic, and having no need of mob or press to pay its way—an aristocratic form."[34] Literary scholars have been somewhat baffled at Yeats's initial interest in the Nō, finding it "difficult to believe that Yeats could have developed his interest in, and understanding of the Nō from the translated texts alone."[35] Based on the assumption that "his information was limited to what he had gleaned from Ernest Fenollosa's translations of Noh plays and from meeting a few Japanese amateur singers of Noh plays and a Japanese dancer, Michio Itoh," and that, therefore, "Yeats had no direct knowledge of the underlying philosophy

---

31. LG to Sister Rose de Lima, 5 Nov.1905, in *LG* 134; LG to Catherine Bunnell, 20 Jan. 1906, in *LG* 141.
32. W.B. Yeats, *Dramatical Poems*, v. 2 of *The Poetical Works of William Butler Yeats* (New York: Macmillan, 1907), v-vi.
33. "Mr. Yeats and the No," *JT*, 3 Nov. 1907, 6.
34. W.B. Yeats, "Introduction," in Ezra Pound, ed., *Certain Noble Plays of Japan*, tr. Ernest Fenollosa, (Churchtown, Dundrum: Cuala P, 1916), ii.
35. Richard Taylor, *The Drama of W.B. Yeats: Irish Myth and the Japanese Nō* (New Haven: Yale UP, 1976), 53.

of the Noh drama," they have tended to overstate the originality of Yeats's Nō-inspired work.[36]

Noguchi's article offered no broad introduction to the philosophy of the Nō, to be sure, but it did lead Yeats point by point through features of the Japanese drama selected to appeal to his ongoing theatrical concerns. The Nō model could offer Yeats a small interested audience, a decorous theatrical atmosphere, an intense spiritual aesthetic, freedom from realism and the tyranny of popular taste, simplicity of plot and production, and a way to return to the poetic drama. Yeats would bring all of these features into play when he began his efforts to adapt the Nō form for his Irish theater.[37]

The Grey Lady

On January 19, 1908, Noguchi heralded the new year with a column on "Shato no Matsu," "meaning the pine tree which stands in front of the temple ground," the subject of the new year's poetry submissions, numbering some thirty thousand, it was said.[38] "Within a few days the time-honored impressive feast of the Reading of Poems will be held in the August presence of the Emperor and Empress." The pine symbolized endurance, so "it is proper at the outset of the year to sing of the pine tree and promise to be as the pine." He did not say that his column, after enduring sixty weeks, was ending. The paper's young managing editor, Tarō Yamada, had died in December, and although Noguchi's Keio colleague, Kazutomo Takahashi, was taking charge, Noguchi did not stay on.

In Yanaka-Negishi the birth of Matsuko's daughter had been recorded, according to custom, on New Year's Day. The girl was named Hifumi, spelled with characters for "1-2-3." Soon afterwards, Noguchi moved Léonie and Isamu to a two-story house at 40 Nishigoken-chō, Ushigome, an area southwest of Koishikawa. The house was much more convenient to transportation, which enabled Yone to commute more easily between his multiple lives and wives, and also made for a more active social life. Friends like Inazō and Mary Nitobe could more easily visit, and houseboy Hironobu remembered a steady stream of visitors from among the Japanese intelligentsia.

Léonie, however, did not find the new location improved her access to the world. "Here we are shut up in Tokyo," she complained to Frank Putnam on February 2, 1908, "and likely to remain so for the rest of our natural lives, unless we happen to die off young, all because—well, for no reason on earth, I should say." She made no attempt to conceal her growing sense of depression:

36. Masaru Sekine, "Noh and Yeats: A Theoretical Analysis," *ARIEL* 26:4 (Oct. 1995), 135-46.
37. For more on Noguchi's explanation, see Marx, "No Dancing," 58-62.
38. "Shato no Matsu," *JT*, 19 Jan. 1908, 6.

Have you ever heard of the 'Japanese Head?' Chiefly affects missionaries, I believe, but also other foreigners, as all we-uns are called over here. The poor things, being quite cut off from all their old associations, forget everything they ever knew, even the names of their best friends, and being debarred by their ignorance of the language, or the ossification of age, from acquiring new ones in the land of their adoption, their heads come, in the course of time, to be absolutely empty, like a blown eggshell. This may sound mythical to you. but I assure it is a dread reality. I myself have felt a touch of it.

But she had not forgotten Frank Putnam, she assured him. If she had not written in ages, it was because Yone kept insisting he would write to Frank himself. Yone, she noted, had "begun a book—prose sketches of Japanese life—childhood reminisces, etc., which he thinks will be done in a couple of months. If his typewriter doesn't get lazy. But that's a big 'if.'" Léonie was, of course, the "typewriter," and her laziness offered a small point of leverage in her relationship with Yone. Her sufferings were physical as well as cultural. "I've been quite generally miserable in my innards this winter—too cold," she complained to Frank. Isamu, too, had a perpetual cold and needed constant care. She was homesick for "fields and blossoms and breezes unscented by city odors," and she missed her garden. She refrained, however, from blaming Frank for encouraging her to come, or Yone, for conspiring to keep her a virtual prisoner in Tokyo. The Ushigome house, she told Putnam, had "quite a pretty garden . . . with a picturesque little stagnant pool and some dwarf trees. But no place left to dig, alas." By April, they had moved again, to "a tiny little house on a hilltop close by a grove of tall trees" at 90 Myōgadani (just north-west of Koishikawa). This situation, too, proved short-lived. By October they had moved to "a little house at 71 Kobinatadai-machi Sanchome."[39]

Léonie later published a cheerful account of one of these houses—probably the Myōgadani house—under the title "Home, Sweet Home, in Japan." And her letters to Catherine Bunnell were always blithely cheerful. From the grove of trees outside the Myōgadani house in April came the daily song of a nightingale that Isamu claimed was his brother and suggested she might visit. "He lives in the treetop, he explains, and I can take a train there any day." "The child is developing a tendency toward imaginativeness," she added; "Yone calls it 'lying.' That for a poet!" Yone spent half the week in Kamakura, she explained, leaving her alone with "one pretty little maidservant, and nobody to bother." She was busy with housework and typing Yone's new book, but she had spent the previous

39. LG to FP, 2 Feb. 1908, in *LG* 199-200; LG to CB, 4 Apr. 1908, in *LG* 200-2; LG to Kazuo Koizumi, Oct. 1908, quoted in Duus, *The Life of Isamu Noguchi*, 55. Hironobu Noguchi recalled moving first "to the heights in Myōgadani from Hisakata-machi and then to Ushigome Nishigoken-chō where there was easier access to transportation" (311-12).

night out with some friends, the Fujiharas, seeing kabuki.[40]

One of the items for typing that spring was the "Japanese Defense of Lafcadio Hearn" penned by Noguchi after reading the newly-published highly-critical biography of Hearn by George Gould.[41] *Concerning Lafcadio Hearn* was an odd mixture of literary admiration and personal loathing, its accusations running from Hearn's "ghoulish pleasure in the gruesome and sensualistic" to his "astonishing indifference to Occidental history and its conclusions as to sexual and social laws," supported by weak attempts at psychology: Hearn had "no constructive mind" and therefore "must needs hate Occidentalism, and exalt with a somewhat ludicrous praise the vapid and even pitiful childishness of semi-barbaric Orientalism." Noguchi's "Defense" also criticized Elisabeth Bisland's edition of Hearn's letters he had earlier reviewed favorably in the *Japan Times*, but which he now thought violated Hearn's privacy. Private letters, he argued, "are only charming when they are kept privately; but they become quite often a nuisance when they are brought out to the public gaze." He saw Hearn's letters as "a sort of confession of his worse self"; in Japan, where "true confession, however bad it be, is divine," he argued, "the best respect to pay it is to forget." He hoped that the art of biography-writing "may never invade our Japanese literature."[42]

Noguchi's somewhat ostentatious "Defense of Hearn" confirmed his role as a friend of the family. Léonie had begun tutoring Kazuo Koizumi, the eldest son, in English, and Noguchi arranged for Léonie and Isamu to spend part of the summer with Kazuo at the summer house Hearn used to rent in the fishing village of Yaidzu.[43]

In June of 1908, a letter arrived from a certain Dr. Stopes, who had read one of Yone's Hearn articles. Noguchi delegated the task of replying to Léonie, who apologized for her husband's negligence and offered some of her own impressions of Hearn and of his wife, whom, she said, she had met once. "She has a very sympathetic face," she explained, "but we could not speak each other's language." No doubt a meeting could be arranged with Dr. Stopes if he were interested, and she hoped, in any case that they would have the pleasure of meeting him some day.[44]

In fact, Dr. Stopes was none other than Marie Charlotte Stopes, an energetic and unconventional young scientist from London who was later renowned for her birth-control activism. She had come to London the previous year, ostensibly to conduct botanical research, but mainly to pursue her romance with Kenjirō Fujii, a Tokyo University scientist she

40. "Home, Sweet Home, in Japan." *Japan* 11 (June 1922): 15-19, 44-45.
41. "Lafcadio Hearn: A Sympathetic Japanese Defence of Him and Criticism of His Biographer," *New York Sun*, 2 July 1908, 6, rpt. "A Japanese Defence of Lafcadio Hearn," *LHJ*, 19-30.
42. George Gould, *Concerning Lafcadio Hearn* (London, T. F. Unwin, 1908): 104, 190, 192. YN, "Lafcadio Hearn's Despair in Tokyo," *JT*, 2 Mar. 1907, 6.
43. YN to FP, 21 July 1908, FPL 55.
44. LG to Marie Stopes, 27 June [1908], British Library.

had met while working on her doctorate in Munich. It was an ill-fated romance: Professor Fujii, unable to leave his wife as he had effusively promised, had begun avoiding the amorous botanist with feeble excuses about his health. Stopes, vindictively or perhaps merely scientifically, would respond by pseudonymously publishing their correspondence as *The Love Letters of a Japanese*, after her return.[45]

35. Marie Stopes in 1904.

None of this was, of course, known to Léonie, with whom Stopes began a polite correspondence. In late November, after missing Léonie's call, she attempted to track down the Noguchi house. There was a great deal of confusion about the address, but when she eventually found it, a polite boy who turned out to be Kazuo Koizumi came out to the gate to greet her. She found Léonie dressed in grey, and subsequently dubbed her "the grey lady." "Perhaps it was the shadow of the lamplight," she wrote in her journal, "but I received the impression that her life was in grey shadows." Léonie spoke "with such a sad lifeless voice—slowly, as though it were rather troublesome to have to speak at all, but not in unfriendly fashion." "The Brownie" (as Stopes dubbed Isamu) had somehow managed to escape being infected by the greyness: "a bright contrast—round eyes, rosy cheeks, with a woollen cap with a long point and a dangling tassel—he was like a pixy." Though barely four, he was already acting as an interpreter between his mother and the maid, Stopes observed.[46]

When Stopes invited Léonie and Isamu to lunch a few weeks later, the young botanist was delighted to be granted the rare privilege of a visit to the famed Hearn home. During lunch "the Brownie looked and acted splendidly, and was a pleasure," and when Stopes spilled breadcrumbs into her own lap after admonishing Isamu to be good and not

45. G.N. Mortlake [pseud.], *Love Letters of a Japanese* (London: Stanley Paul, 1911). Ruth Hall, *Marie Stopes: A Biography* (London: André Deutsch, 1977).
46. Marie Stopes, *A Journal from Japan: A Daily Record of Life as seen by a Scientist* (London: Blackie, 1910): 241-42.

spill anything, "his eyes twinkled a keen appreciation rare in men of four years old." At the Koizumi house, built "in the purest Japanese style, well built, with pretty woodwork," they talked at length with Setsu, whom Stopes found "less shy and quiet than most Japanese women," yet "distinctly Japanese in her shyness and quietness," and gazed upon the little family shrine, a miniature temple of unpainted wood containing Hearn's photo and a tiny lamp surrounded by miniature vases of small flowers. They stayed for dinner, served in Japanese style, as Setsu no longer prepared the Western-style food her late husband had preferred.[47]

Stopes paid a last visit to the Noguchi home in January 1909, as she neared the end of her Royal Society sponsored visit. "The grey lady is revealing herself a little—I am sorry I must go and so will not see her again," she wrote in her journal; "people who really interest one are not too many on this earth." Léonie had not told her much about her marital troubles, and Stopes had only a vague understanding that that Léonie "lies behind the poetry of that Japanese poet who wrote in English, and was so praised by Rossetti, the N[oguchi] of American fame." Nor was Stopes able to broach the topic of her frustrated affair with Kenjirō Fujii. Had the two women been able to compare notes, they would have found they had more in common than they supposed.[48]

Ninefold Clouds

Even before he stopped writing for the *Japan Times*, Noguchi was writing with increasing regularity for the English section of the *Taiyō*, a large-circulation monthly dubbed, in English, *The Sun Trade Journal*. Each month, from the fall of 1907 through the spring of 1908, he wrote about a different Japanese flower or plant: "The Lotos," "The Chrysanthemum," "The Maple Leaves," "The Bamboo," "The Pine Tree," "The Plum Blossom," "The Cherry Blossom," "The Peach Blossom," "The Iris," "The Wistaria," and "The Peony." To make the job easier he borrowed from Baptist missionary Ernest W. Clement's *Japanese Floral Calendar*, particularly the poetry selections, which Clement had borrowed from other writers. Clement, unperturbed, borrowed back: among the additions to his second edition was an "interesting story" about a maple-viewing emperor culled "from an article by Yone Noguchi in the *Taiyo*."[49] Florence Du Cane also acknowledged borrowing from "Mr. Y. Noguchi, who provided me with the flower legends and fairy tales" used in *The Flowers and Gardens of Japan* illustrated by her sister.[50]

47. Stopes, *A Journal from Japan*, 246-67.
48. Stopes, *A Journal from Japan*, 261.
49. Clement's essays first appeared in Paul Carus's *Open Court* magazine, 1904-05, and as *The Japanese Floral Calendar* (Chicago: Open Court, 1905). Noguchi is mentioned in 2 ed. (Chicago: Open Court, 1911), 49-50.
50. Ella Du Cane and Florence Du Cane, *The Flowers and Gardens of Japan* (London: Black, 1908), vi.

36. Noguchi in a 1909 Keio graduation album.

Aside from his *Taiyō* contributions, Noguchi mostly stuck to his moratorium on article writing, with one notable exception: an article on "The Mikado's Daily Life," which he sold, for a substantial sum no doubt, to McClure's Associated Literary Press syndicate.[51] Readers in such places as Buffalo, Dallas, Detroit, Duluth, Washington, and even Oamaru, New Zealand, had their curiosity gratified by Noguchi's respectfully-amused explanations of the emperor's daily routines: his six o'clock rising, activities in the "honorable mouth rinsing palace," dressing and massage, breakfast and lunch preferences, source for chopsticks, bathing and shaving methods, the special requirements during the Empress's "monthly defilement," and the emperor's fondness for horseback riding, occasional artistic efforts, and more successful practice of uta poetry writing. The details were surprisingly intimate.

> The Mikado keeps many shampooers in the palace Doctors-on-duty department, who treat him by turn or by appointment every night. He will lay himself on the lacquered bed with the design of gold chrysanthemums, which is some two feet high; and when the lady in waiting announces the shampooer he will hide his own head under the drapery, and say just one word "Un" which is the signal word "Begin." And he uses to go to sleep when the shampooer finishes his work; but if he desires once more to be rubbed, he will say nothing, but tap his own knees. Then the shampooer will start again. The Mikado is a man of few words and he rarely speaks with anybody as a rule. A certain Okamoto who has treated his body for more than thirty years was not

---

51. Yone Noguchi, "A Day with the Mikado," *Buffalo Express*, 5 July 1908, 2, 12; Yoni [sic] Noguchi, "Daily Life of the Mikado," *Dallas Morning News*, 5 July 1908, 3; Yoni Noguchi, "The Mikado at Home," *Detroit Free Press*, 5 July 1908, C4; Yoni Noguchi, "Daily Life of the Mikado Unveiled," *Washington Herald*, 5 July 1908, 5; Yoni Noguchi, "The Mikado at Home," *Oamaru Mail*, 5 Sept. 1908, 3; Yone Noguchi, "The Mikado's Daily Life," *Taiyō* 14:14 (Nov. 1908): 16-20, 142-46.

addressed by him even once in his life yet. The Emperor is silent, and the shampooer of course; and only the silk kimono's rustle is heard."[52]

"But among all those things which he enjoys," Noguchi concluded, "the making of uta poems is his first and last delight"; it was "already known even in foreign countries that he is one of the great uta poets of present Japan." He was also prolific, writing "it is said, fifty or sixty utas a day . . . no small thing at all even for a professional uta poet." The poems, Noguchi believed, had been a comfort and encouragement for the Japanese people during the late war. "His uta is not a manufactured sort, but it is his own heart." He offered one translation: "Whenever I open the ancient books, the one thing I ponder is, how goes it with the people I rule."

Noguchi knew something of the emperor's composition techniques from having visited (according to a *Japan Times* article the previous year) his poetry tutor, Baron Masakaze Takasaki, head of the *o-utadokoro* or "honorable poetry office," at his villa in Hayama, near Kamakura.[53] The old Satsuma-born warrior charged with correcting the emperor's voluminous uta production had talked on in a rambling fashion, being too deaf to take much note of Noguchi's replies, but his views were much to Noguchi's taste. "Poetry is nothing but the true heart," he told Noguchi.[54]

In 1907 and 1908, Noguchi was making further efforts to grapple with the uta, the traditional, and still-predominant, thirty-one syllable Japanese verse form also known as *tanka* (short poems) or *waka* (Japanese poems). For the *Japan Times* he had written an article on "Uta and the Imperial Court," and another on Naobumi Ochiai, a recent modernizer of the uta form.[55] He also became the first Japanese to attempt an English translation of the most popular uta anthology, the *Hyakunin Isshu* (A poem each by a hundred poets).[56] This was a noteworthy venture, but it did reveal rather clearly the limitations imposed by Noguchi's impatience for the "artificial execution" of the uta poems. On the other hand, his study of the uta poems of Naobumi Ochiai expressed a deep sympathy for the late poet's "artless songs."

> Suppose the morning stars
> Fall and Break?
> Do they sound
> Like my own song?

52. "The Mikado's Daily Life," *Taiyō* 14 (Nov. 1908): 19-20.
53. "Baron Takasaki, Chief of the Court Poets," *JT*, 21 Apr. 1907, 3, 6.
54. Skeptical readers seeking evidence that the meeting was imaginary might note the contradiction between Noguchi's comment, "it is one of the Baron's life's regrets that he cannot understand English," and Lady Lawson's assertion that "he speaks French and English well," in *Highways and Homes of Japan* (London: T. Fisher Unwin, 1910), 55.
55. "Through a Japanese Screen," *JT*, 17 Nov. 1906, 6 (on Ochiai); "Through a Japanese Screen," *JT*, 2 Feb. 1907, 6, rpt. as "Uta and the Imperial Court," *Eigo Sekai* 2:1 (1 Jan. 1908): 11-13; *SJP* 12.
56. "Hyaku Nin Isshu in English," *Waseda Bungaku* 17 (1 May 1907): 76-80; 19 (1 Jun. 1907): 53-57; 21 (1 Aug. 1907): 71-75; 22 (1 Sept. 1907): 142-46.

Noguchi was so fond of this poem that he used his own slightly altered version as the first poem of his 1920 book, *Japanese Hokkus*:

> Suppose the stars
> Fall and break?—Do they ever sound
> Like my own love song?

A few of the *Hyakunin Isshu* translations would also reappear in *Japanese Hokkus*, to the annoyance of haiku purists. Noguchi's feelings of affinity for the *uta* were transient, however, and he was finally obliged, in 1913, to come clean about his aversion to this most Japanese of poetical forms, which he blamed on the uta's tendency toward too-clever scholasticism which he labeled "poetical nonsense" in an essay on "Poetical Vulgarity." "Really I cannot see the Westerners' point of view when they take the 'pillow-and-pivot' words of Japanese *uta*-poetry kindly," he declared. He also disparaged the uta's frequent reliance on fixed poetic epithets called pillow words (*makura-kotoba*), and puns based on simultaneous uses of words with two senses called pivot words (*kake-kotoba*). Uta relying on such clever wordplay devices could easily become artificial and tiresome, and often seemed even sillier in translation. Consider, for example, Yukihira's poem in Noguchi's translation:

> Now we part. The pine-tree grows.
> There on the Inaba mountain top.
> If thou shouldst say 'pine'
> I to you will soon return.

The effect of the poem depends mainly on a conventional pivot word *matsu*, which can mean "pine" or "wait." The poem is slightly more interesting when it is noted that the name of the mountain, "Inaba," is also a pivot word, since it can mean "(even) if I leave."[57] Noguchi reiterated his opposition to uta poetics somewhat more tactfully in his introduction to *The Spirit of Japanese Poetry* in 1914: "my poetical taste," he wrote, "desires far more intensity than the *Uta* poems, whose artificial execution often proves, in my opinion, to be their weakness rather than strength." The elaborate, allusive, highly ritualized courtly form was best suited to scholarly types sympathetic to courtly culture. Noguchi was drawn rather to the irreverent, studied casualness of the itinerant haiku culture and to the boundary-crossing thrills of the foreign-influenced *shintaishi* or "new-style poetry." Even the movement to modernize the uta through contemporary language and themes—notable in the work of such poets as Shiki Masaoka, Akiko Yosano, and the young Noguchi admirer, Takuboku Ishikawa—held little interest for him.

Noguchi later told a friend that he had slighted Takuboku when he

---

57. Joshua Mostow, *Pictures of the Heart: The Hyakunin Isshu in Word and Image* (Honolulu: U of Hawai'i P, 1996), 190.

met him soon after his return to Japan. "He had written to me when I was still in the States, but I didn't remember his name at all. He thought of himself as the number one poet in Japan. So he was somewhat displeased with my ignorance. He must have thought I would at least remember his name. I was young then so I was sort of looking down on him I suppose. Maybe I could have been more polite, you know, but he seemed so conceited. He talked on and on, bragging about everything . . . it was out of the question."[58]

37. Noguchi family, neighbors and servant (left), Tsushima, circa 1909. Okuwa and Dembei seated center, with daughter Tane Hoshino behind; Hidenosuke and Yūshin standing left; Tōtarō and Yonejirō standing right.

The Pilgrimage

In anticipation of the publication of his new book of poems, *The Pilgrimage*, Noguchi began to revive his languishing foreign correspondence. On March 25, 1909, he worked up the courage to address Zona Gale, whose last, long accusing letter had remained stashed away in his drawer for the past two years. "Whenever I pull it out," he explained to her, "it is true I cannot bear to see it as it cast such a terrible accusation over me." Now he hoped she would drop a line saying 'I forgive you." His American life, he added, had become like a dream, and "my American friends are turning to be a mythology as they are." Tonight, however, his dream had returned and he wanted to assure her he was still the same Yone Noguchi she had known in New York; it was snowing, and he was sad and lonesome. He

58. Seinosuke Nishitani, "Yone Noguchi-shi no katachi" (The Figure of Mr. Yone Noguchi), *Kenkyū* 3:156-57.

told her about his home in Kamakura where, he said, he was "even living here as I did at Miller's Heights—some eighteen years ago."⁵⁹

As to the "terrible accusation" cast by Zona's last letter, "I must answer," he now wrote, "as best I can." "Mrs. Noguchi (originally Miss Léonie Gilmour of New York) and baby by name 'Isamu' are in Japan now," he explained. "We live 'separate,' but I have to come up and see them whenever I am in Tokyo." It was, he assured her, "a long story to go minutely how I married her, and at once we got separated with perfect understanding"; he had "called them to Japan as she wished to live in Japan," he explained, omitting his efforts of persuasion. This was as far as his confession was going to go, for he abruptly cut it off with: "The story is not interesting to you, so let us drop the matter for ever!" Of course the story would have been intensely interesting to Gale, who must have been hurt by Noguchi's secretiveness, especially since she and Ridgely Torrence had taken him into their confidence regarding their secret love.

> But the baby is such an interesting and bright fellow. As I send you some of his photographs you will see. He speaks already Japanese as well as English; I am very proud of him. And I live here in the temple with my poetry and meditation. Mrs Noguchi, however, appears in public as my wife; I have no objection about that at all. Isamu lives with Mother and is exceeding happy; and he comes here in Kamakura quite often and sleeps with his father.

Gale was evidently willing to accept Noguchi's plea for forgiveness even if it was made for the self-serving motive of restoring a valuable literary connection and potential supporter of his new book of poetry; having recently sent her the announcement, he was now enclosing more advertisements to distribute among her "friends who are poem-lovers and might be 'buyers.'" "This Valley Press is started with my friends; I invested some money in it; so I must sell some copies of my book," he explained. "That is sad!" he added, but as *The Pilgrimage* was his best book, he told her, he hoped it would receive some favorable criticism.⁶⁰

Noguchi's comment to Gale that his American friends were "turning to be a mythology as they are" was probably a reference to E.C. Stedman who had died the previous January, and perhaps also to Charles Warren Stoddard, who was again rumored to be dying. Stoddard had hardly written to Noguchi since the aftermath of the earthquake, and Noguchi's last two pleading letters, in May of 1907 and July of 1908, had gone unanswered.⁶¹

---

59. YN to Gale, 25 Mar. 1909, ZGP.
60. Ibid.
61. Noguchi wrote to both Stoddard and Putnam on 19 May 1907 (CEL 384; FPL 52). Fourteen months later, he complained to Stoddard, "Why don't you write me, Dad? I wrote you some time ago; I believe I wrote you at the same time when I wrote to Frank Putnam who answered me already." (YN to CWS, 26 Jul. [1908], CEL 386).

38. Charles Warren Stoddard at Monterey.

Crippled by rheumatism, Stoddard was bedridden at the sanitarium in Monterey, and could only manage brief, disheartened notes in a trembling hand. On April 23, he succumbed to a heart attack at the age of sixty-six.

The Pilgrimage was published in two volumes in May 1909, by The Valley Press, with the additional imprint of Kelly & Walsh in Yokohama. However, the colophon identifies printer and publisher as D. S. Spencer of Ginza: identifiable as Methodist missionary David Spencer, presiding elder of the Tokio Methodist Episcopal Church, and financial agent of the Methodist Publishing House in Ginza, also known as Kyo Bun Kwan. The Valley Press proved short-lived, and the second edition of 1912 listed Mitchell Kennerley in New York and Elkin Mathews in London as publishers, with The Kyobunkwan Press, Ginza, Tokyo, as printer. The book included poems written by Noguchi since his return to Japan, along with a number of previously uncollected items from his American period.

As he prepared the book for printing in March, he felt obliged to apologize to William Michael Rossetti.[62] "You were so good to give me your little preface to my book which I expected to bring out a long time ago," he wrote. "But Mr Rossetti, I could not satisfy with my poems; so I could not help myself to put my Ms. aside, and in fact, for these three years I attempted to improve myself. . . . Since you saw my Mss, I wrote some seventy poems, and from them I selected some forty pieces. And here I have a new book of poems which is more satisfactory." He was very grateful for Rossetti's preface but had not used it thus far as it had been

62. YN to W.M. Rossetti, Mar. 25, 1909, Angeli-Dennis collection, UBC.

"meant to be for my former Mss."

Though somewhat uneven in quality, *The Pilgrimage* included Noguchi's most polished poetry to date, written in a wide range of poetic styles. It opened with a "Proem" in the voice of the "Holy Pilgrims" after whom the poem was originally titled: "we, the children of prayer . . . the shadowy roamers on the holy highway"—spiritual pilgrims, "Beckoned by an appointed hand, unseen yet sure, in holy air," who "wander as a wind, silver and free."[63] The pilgrimage is an aesthetic as well as a spiritual one. The aesthetic dimension comes to the fore in the opening poem, "The New Art," which embraces a Symbolist poetics tinged with a Paterian "intensity of a moment," with art personified as "she" in a manner that anticipates Wallace Stevens' similar explorations:

> She is an art (let me call her so)
> Hung, as a web, in the air of perfume,
> Soft yet vivid, she sways in music:
> (But what sadness in her saturation of life!)
> Her music lives in intensity of a moment and then dies;
> To her, suggestion is her life.[64]

Even more remarkable as a modernist precursor is the surrealistic expressionism of "Fantasia," where Noguchi declares:

> I'll sing a song that makes the seas the hills.
> (Morality begins, I am afraid, where I stop my song.)
> So with my heart of nocturnal fear;
> I have chosen the sky red in memory and art.
> Let the stars fall in the garden rose:
> The leaves and my souls in a thousand guises
> Hurry to the ground to build a grave.[65]

Noguchi's experiments with various sorts of Japanese materials, often in the direction of the "Celtic" *Japonisme* explored in Noguchi's earlier Yeats essay, are also evident. "Out of a Kingdom's Fire" takes as its subject the ancient Japanese creation myth in which, "in the beginning of the world the god Izanagi and the goddess Izanami stood on Amano Ukihashi or Heaven's Floating Bridge" according to Noguchi's note.

> The queen of the dews and of flaming hope,
> Izanami the mother ever thinks of the day
> When, from the bridge of love and mist,
> Her first song of glory sailed to the wind . . .

Despite the evocative beginning, Noguchi's brief tale bears little resemblance to the traditional story. (No doubt this explains his reluctance to

---

63. "The Holy Pilgrims," *Chūō Kōron* 23:11 (1 Nov. 1908): 148, rpt. "Proem," *Pilg.* 1.
64. "The New Art (To Homei)," *Yomiuri*, 20 Sept. 1908, 2, rpt. *Pilg.* 2.
65. *Pilg.* 32-33.

anthologize his Japanese translation). Noguchi's poem proposes a return to the age of the Shintō gods as a rebirth out of a disastrous human history:

> Come, children, out of a kingdom's fire,
> Out of humanity's ruin and wound,
> Come where your laugh shrilled the hills,
> And set the waves dancing to the music of a star.[66]

Nature, finally, takes precedence over human hope.

The vast majority of these new poems take as their subjects aspects of Japanese life chosen specifically as signifiers of cultural difference, usually manifestations of the "Old Japan" of the Hearn school: a Japan of *koto* players, women in wooden clogs with fans, and meditating priests. It was a successful strategy; "the West fades away as he comes back to the sights and sounds of Japan, to the snows of Fuji, and to the patient smile of the Great Buddha at Kamakura," Laurence Binyon wrote approvingly in an unsigned review in the *Times Literary Supplement*. "We find in his verse, with all its modern tone, the same attitude that we find in the old singers of his country, the same feeling of the impermanence of things, the same cherishing of elusive and transitory beauty."[67] Granted, all of these aspects of Japan were part of Noguchi's world, but there was clearly a selectivity in his poetic approach which excluded the modernity of Ginza streets, rickshaws, beef restaurants, and trains. Presumably these modern features of Japan, about which he wrote occasionally in his essays, were prohibited as "manners and customs" while the more traditional features were permitted.

The Pilgrimage is not an impersonal volume. Dedicated "To Léonie," yet unembarrassedly acknowledging "the oldest yet youngest love of the Japanese girl," in whose kiss the poet tastes "the youngest soul out of the ages old," the collection is full of confessional fragments, ostensibly embodying the aesthetic of "The Poet" in which poet and poem consume each other as the roses that "live by eating of their own beauty and then die." Still, Noguchi is not as comfortable in the confessional-erotic mode as either the Symons of the Decadent *London Nights* or the Maud Gonne-besotted Yeats of *The Rose*, and chooses instead to construct an oblique poetic identity, as suggested in the poem "Ghost of Abyss":

> Who am I?" said I. "Ghost of abyss," a Voice replied,
> "Piling an empty stone of song on darkness of night,
> Dancing wild as a fire, only to vanish away."[68]

This remarkable passage was less a statement of autobiographical elusiveness than an exploration of the Zen-self, or non-self, a thematic thread of

66. *Pilg.* 107.
67. [Laurence Binyon], "Japanese Poetry," *TLS*, 10 Feb. 1910, 41-42.
68. "Ghost of Abyss," *Waseda Bungaku*, 2nd ser., no. 37 (1 Dec. 1908): 49, rpt. *Pilg.* 20.

The Pilgrimage derived, in part, from his Zen practice at Engakuji, which he had described in his recent essay, "The Japanese Temple of Silence."⁶⁹

A Japanese Hearn

Noguchi continued to be drawn to the figure of the late Lafcadio Hearn. "I think that I could do something in the same line Hearn did," Noguchi announced in a letter to Ridgely Torrence in March 1908; "—that is to say, I will start from the very point Hearn left. There are so many things Hearn was not able to do himself; these things I wish I could finish up." He thought of himself even as "a sort of exile living in Tokyo . . . trying to forget modern Tokyo as best as I can,—thus Hearn tried before me, and I wish I could live the pure Japanese atmosphere which many thousand years created." ⁷⁰

His new book (an early draft of his essay collection, *Through the Torii*) would be ready, he told Torrence, in two or three weeks, "for trial of course." He wished that Ridgely would help him place it. "As I have nobody who will manage my stuff in America, I stopped for some time to do anything at all," he explained. He was going to send the manuscript to Little, Brown and Company, but if they rejected it he hoped Ridgely could submit it to other publishers on his behalf.

39. Ridgely Torrence, circa 1904.

When he wrote Torrence next at the end of July, it was to tell him that he had decided to send *Through the Torii* to Laurence Housman, "as I thought, London would be kinder for such a book." He now wanted Torrence to take charge of his translation of Mrs. Hearn's reminiscences, which he had sent to Richard Watson Gilder at *The Century Magazine*, and the *Lafcadio Hearn in Japan* book manuscript he would send to Macmillan in a few days. If Macmillan rejected the book, he wanted Ridgely

---

69. "The Japanese Temple of Silence," *Taiyō* 14:11 (Aug. 1908): 18-24.
70. YN to Torrence, 9 Mar. 1908, Princeton.

to try Little, Brown & Company, and any publisher he liked after that. "The book has two lectures Hearn delivered in his college, beside Mrs Hearn's reminiscences which I sent to the Century, and Hearn's pictures (some twenty thumb-nail sketches in all), and also my five or six articles on Hearn."[71]

Noguchi's submissions were turned down by both the *Century* and MacMillan, and after half a year Torrence, who was suffering from ill health, had not succeeded in placing either of them. "Ridgely, I wish you will return my Hearn things," Noguchi wrote him in March 1909. "I decided to let one of Japanese publishers [publish] it,—send back the book manuscript and also Mrs Hearn's Reminiscences which you received from the Century. I am sorry that I troubled your hand with such unsuccessful [things]."[72] The plaintive request seems to have spurred some last-ditch efforts from Torrence: a few months later, "Mrs. Lafcadio Hearn's Reminiscences" and "Lafcadio Hearn at Yaidzu," appeared in the *Pacific Monthly*. Torrence had evidently called on his old Princeton classmate, John Fleming Wilson, now managing editor of the magazine, based in Portland, Oregon.[73] Another clever move was sending "A Japanese Appreciation of Lafcadio Hearn" (another chapter from the book) to the prestigious *Atlantic Monthly*, where Hearn had once been a contributor; the magazine had recently been acquired by Noguchi's former editor Ellery Sedgwick. *Lafcadio Hearn in Japan* was delayed until the fall of 1910, but the extra publicity helped make it one of Noguchi's most successful books.

Noguchi only used a fraction of the Hearn material he had assembled after Hearn's funeral. Of Hearn's former students' memoirs, "Mr. Otani as Hearn's Literary Assistant" had a chapter, but the remainder received only passing mention in "Lafcadio Hearn in His Lecture Room." Though Noguchi had translated memoirs of two prestigious former students, Bin Ueda and Hakuson Kuriyagawa, as well as Tokyo University literature department chair Tetsujirō Inoue, these were entirely omitted, as was the memoir from Hearn's junior Waseda colleague Sakusaburō Uchigasaki, which Noguchi had published in the *National*.

As Noguchi had anticipated, London did prove kinder for distributing his books, thanks to an arrangement he made with publisher-bookseller Elkin Mathews. Mathews, who had a shop in Vigo Street, near Piccadilly Circus, had established himself among London's leading literary publishers in the 1890s, and his list included such poetic classics as *The Book of the Rhymers Club* and Yeats's *The Wind among the Reeds* among others by many of the leading poets of the age, including Decadent

---

71. Noguchi to Torrence, 29 July 1908, 7 Aug. 1908, Princeton.
72. YN to Torrence, 7 Aug. 1908, March [1909], Princeton.
73. "Mrs. Lafcadio Hearn's Reminiscences," *Pacific Monthly* (Feb. 1910): 117-26, (Mar. 1910): 250-60; "Lafcadio Hearn at Yaidzu," *Pacific Monthly* 23 (Apr. 1910): 363-70.

poets like Arthur Symons, Richard Le Gallienne, Francis Thompson, and Laurence Binyon, as well as the more virile "counter-Decadents" like William Watson and Henry Newbolt. Mathews also had a keen eye for new talent, and was now taking in hand the new generation of Georgian poets and the first wayward productions of the writers who would soon be acclaimed under the Imagist and Modernist banners: young, unproven poets like John Masefield, James Elroy Flecker, James Joyce, F.S. Flint, and most recently, the young American, Ezra Pound. Mathews proved to be Noguchi's most reliable English publisher: in all, eleven Noguchi titles would be sold under his imprint. All were produced in Japan under Noguchi's supervision, thus bypassing the publication delays that had so annoyed him in the past. The arrangement proved so satisfactory that he ended up using it for virtually all of his subsequent overseas book publications. It gave him nearly complete control of the production and design, enabling him to give the books an exotic Japanese appearance without the pseudo-Oriental devices to which American and British publishers often resorted. Folded pages (printed on one side only) were bound with silk thread. Specially-commissioned color woodblock prints were used for the frontispieces. The books were wrapped in folding *chitsu* cases closed with a pair of bone or ivory fasteners. They could then be sold under the imprint of a recognized publisher or bookseller.

It was presumably the success of this arrangement that allowed Noguchi to secure Mitchell Kennerley as his American publisher on similar terms. Kennerley had gone to New York as Mathews' eighteen-year-old agent in 1896, and soon went into business there for himself, publishing books under his own imprint and (until 1905) a magazine, *The Reader*, which he also edited, to which Noguchi had contributed half a dozen poems and articles during his New York days. Kennerley's first Noguchi reprint, *From the Eastern Sea* (1910), making its long-delayed first American appearance, was followed by *Lafcadio Hearn in Japan* (1911) and *The Pilgrimage* (1912). In addition, Noguchi also added a Yokohama bookseller, Kelly and Walsh, to his stable of publishers. The firm's imprint appears on three titles, the first edition of *The Pilgrimage* (1909), Noguchi's 1910 collection, *Kamakura*, and on the second edition of *Lafcadio Hearn in Japan* (1911).[74]

Only one letter from Noguchi to Mathews seems to have survived, dated September 10, 1911. "Dear Mr. Mathews," Noguchi begins, "I was taken ill lately and confined to bed, therefore I was unable to acknowledge your letter of July 13th with money order of £16.17.9." This was not an insubstantial sum, £1 in 1911 being worth something over £100 today. This was probably due mainly to sales of *The Pilgrimage;* Hearn did not have as much name recognition in Britain and Noguchi had to urge Mathews to be patient with it: "Lafcadio Hearn in Japan is selling very well in

---

74. See James G. Nelson, *Elkin Mathews: Publisher to Yeats, Joyce, Pound* (U of Wisconsin P, 1989).

America; in fact, the book sells better there than England. I think you can sell it more; at least, the stock you have in your hand must go." He was prepared to make further contributions to advertising costs. "If you think I must go into some more advertising at Christmas, I don't mind to spend a few pounds for that purpose."[75]

Temple of Silence

Noguchi chose the Zen temple of Engakuji in Kamakura as his retreat out of desire for a peaceful, natural writing environment—a haven from the noise and domestic distractions of Tokyo: his motivation was not primarily religious. Noguchi had been raised in a family of practicing Buddhists—his brother and uncle were priests—but they were members of the Jōdō (Pure Land) sect, which shares many doctrinal points with Zen but has little use for Zen's philosophical provocations and rigorous meditative practices. Noguchi did have a longstanding interest in Zen: the poetic attitude of his beloved haiku poet, Bashō, was strongly influenced by Zen. In California Noguchi had carried with him a book of Zen master Hongzhi. His stay at the temple was also made easier by Keio's connection with the former head priest, Sōen Shaku, who had studied at the college two decades earlier.[76]

And the temple could no doubt use the rent. Zen temples were still trying to recover from the loss of patronage they had enjoyed under the old regime, when Zen's rigorous mental training underpinned the samurai warrior's "stoic composure in sight of danger or calamity."[77] Engakuji, founded in 1282, had adapted more than most temples. Through the efforts of Sōen Shaku and his followers, it had placed itself at the vanguard of a modernized and internationalized Zen. By welcoming lay followers, interested in serious Zen practice, but not aspiring to monastic life, Engakuji was reforming Zen to appeal to a wider audience. With these aims, Sōen Shaku had pursued two years of secular university life, lived among Theravada Buddhist monks in Ceylon, and served as Zen's representative at the World's Parliament of Religions in Chicago in 1893. In 1902 he had retired as head priest, in part to undertake further travels. In 1905 he traveled around the world, joined by his devoted lay disciple Daisetsu Suzuki, who had gone ahead to the United States in 1897 to learn English and assist Buddhist sympathizer Paul Carus, publisher of *The Open Court* magazine. By 1905 Suzuki was prepared to not only act as Sōen's interpreter, but also to translate and publish his *Sermons of a Buddhist Abbot*.[78] When Sōen returned to Japan in 1906, he sent a group of

---

75. YN to Elkin Mathews, 10 Sept. 1911, Papers of Charles Elkin Mathews, U of Reading.
76. Michel Mohr, "The Use of Traps and Snares: Shaku Soen Revisited," in *Zen Masters*, ed. Steven Heine and Dale S. Wright (Oxford: Oxford UP, 2010), 183-214.
77. Inazo Nitobe, *Bushido: The Soul of Japan* (Philadelphia: Leeds & Biddle, 1900), 7.
78. Soyen Shaku, *Sermons of a Buddhist Abbot*, tr. Daisetz Teitaro Suzuki (Chicago: Open Court,

seven younger disciples to the United States, led by Sokatsu Shaku, head priest of Engakuji's lay Buddhist outreach group, the Ryōmō Kyōkai. Initially they had little success, but in the late 1920s, two returned, better prepared, to the United States: Shigetsu Sasaki, better known as Sōkei-an, to New York, where he founded the First Zen Institute, and Nyōgen Senzaki, who ran a "floating Zendo" in California. Despite severe hardships, the two managed to establish the foundations for the British and American Zen movements that came to fruition in the 1950s.

Zōroku-an, the so-called Tortoise Temple, had not been Noguchi's first choice among the temple accommodations. "He first tried to rent the rooms which had been occupied by the American woman Miss Shearer. But these had been set aside for another woman expected to arrive soon."[79] Catharine Shearer, a lay Buddhist nun, had, in 1904, come "to study in the Temples of the Zen Sect, and for nearly two years she was a devout follower of the High Priest" Sōen Shaku.[80] Shearer's Buddhist odyssey had begun when she traveled to Ceylon "in the year 1898 to assist Madame [Miranda de Souza] Canavarro in the educational work started by the Maha-Bodhi Society," and stayed for several years. After leaving Japan, she continued her Buddhist studies in Burma until a fatal case of dysentery ended her pioneering work there in 1909.

Writers had stayed at Engakuji before, notably Tōson Shimazaki in 1893 and Sōseki Natsume in 1894, but usually for brief periods and with a religious purpose. Tōson, hoping to resolve his hopeless love for a student, had "shaved his head and donned priestly robes."[81] Sōseki spent two weeks meditating and receiving instruction from Sōen Shaku. Presented with the kōan, "What is your original face before even your parents were born?" he made little headway. "It seems that even after being reborn five hundred times, I am a simpleton ignorant of The Law who was unable to perceive the original state of things."[82] He would at least make good literary use out of the experience in his 1910 novel, *The Gate*. Temple accommodations were ostensibly intended for serious seekers of enlightenment, a description that did not necessarily fit Noguchi.[83] "It is said that the English poet Mr. Yoneijirō Noguchi has gone to Kamakura's Engakuji for Zen training; he is said to be studying Zen in order to aid his writing," the *Rokudai Shimpō* noted in April 1908. "However, study is

---

1906). See also Shoji Yamada, *Tokyo Boogie-woogie and D.T. Suzuki*, tr. Earl Hartman (U of Michigan P, 2022), 16-18.

79. "Ei shijin no sanzen" (The English Poet's Zen Practice), *Zenshū* 15:5 (10 Dec. 1908): 87-88.
80. "The Late Miss Catherine Shearer," *The Maha-Bodhi and the United Buddhist World* 17:6 (June 1909): 131-32; Tessa Bartholomeusz, *Women Under the Bo Tree: Buddhist Nuns in Sri Lanka* (Cambridge: Cambridge UP, 1994).
81. William E. Naff, *The Kiso Road: The Life and Times of Shimazaki Tōson* (Honolulu: U of Hawai'i P, 2011), 106-07.
82. John Nathan, *Sōseki: Modern Japan's Greatest Novelist* (New York : Columbia UP, 2018), 35
83. "Kenkyū ka jisshū ka" (Study or practice?), *Rokudai Shimpō* 245 (27 Apr. 1908), 3.

not the true function of Zen. If one attempts only to study without any intention of genuine practice, then—even if he succeeds in introducing some aspects of Zen thought to the English literary world—in the end, it contributes nothing to the cultivation of his own character. Unless Mr. Noguchi sincerely devotes himself to reverent practice, there will be no real effect."

A chance to demonstrate the authenticity of his Zen interest soon presented itself. "As this was the 14th of May I was to have an opportunity to be present at the Opening Ceremony of the 'Great Meeting with Spirit' which I had wished to attend for some long time," he explained in "The Japanese Temple of Silence," published in the August *Taiyō*.[84] A sesshin, or "meeting with spirit," in Noguchi's translation, is an intensive meditation retreat, usually lasting for some days; Engakuji continues to offer week-long Dai Sesshin several times a year. British future Japanologist Carmen Blacker gives a vivid account of sitting through one in the early 1950s, when she was herself a student at Keio.[85]

Noguchi gives a fair description of the opening event, which was presided over by "the chief priest by the name of Sokai Miyaji": "a man of sixty, heavily built, and sleepy in face, doubtless from his saturation in silence: he wore a robe of yellowish brown color, and a large scarf of old brocade across his shoulder."[86] Noguchi's account includes translations of several texts recited or used by Miyaji: "Shogaku Kokushi's words of warning" about the "three classes of students," an old Chinese dream parable, and (mercifully skipping over the Dharani of Great Mercy), the four bodhissatva vows. After tea with "some parched rice slightly sugared" is distributed and consumed he is conducted to the guest room next to the Assembly Chamber and given a paper with the following day's schedule: rising at two a.m., prayer at three, breakfast at four. Noguchi confusingly lists four sessions of "Prayer," which must, in actuality, have been sessions of zazen (seated meditation) interspersed with kinhin (walking meditation).[87]

In the guest room a kakemono in the tokonoma greets him with the words, "Hear the voice of thy hand." "It must be one of these questions of which I have heard, put by the chief priest to be answered by the student priests through their own understanding," he comments, explaining, "Here we must find our own salvation by the power of our contemplation." He is ready with a response: "Where is the voice of your hand except in yourself? And again where is the truth except in your own soul? To understand your own self is to understand the truth; the voice of

---

84. "The Japanese Temple of Silence," *Taiyō* 14:11 (Aug. 1908), rpt. "The Temple of Silence," *Kamakura*, 4.
85. Carmen Blacker, "Impressions of a Japanese University," in *Collected Writings of Carmen Blacker* (London: Routledge, 2004), 290-94.
86. *Kamakura*, 7.
87. *Kamakura*, 8-14.

truth is the voice of your own hand." Of course, contemplating a kōan on a kakemono was hardly the same as grappling with one assigned by the priest, on which one's progress, or, more likely, failure to progress, would be examined daily in what Blacker described as an atmosphere "charged with an extraordinary tension."[88]

Noguchi's prospects for enlightenment seemed hardly promising the following morning when, as he wrote,

> I could not rise at two o'clock, next morning, as I wished to; and I felt ashamed to be called up by a priest to leave my bed and sit up for breakfast. When I made my presence in the Assembly Chamber which was a dining room in turn, all the priests were already seated silently and even solemnly as on the previous evening. They muttered a short prayer before they brought out their own bowls and chopsticks from under their black robes (they are their only belongings, beside one or two sacred books); I with them had the severest breakfast ever I ate, which consisted only of some gruel chiefly of barley with rice as little as an apology, with a few slices of greens dipped in salt water. However, I enjoyed it as they did. I thought that their diet was far beyond simplicity, while I admit their pride of high thinking. And I wondered if it was asceticism to leave every human lust, and to give the way for spiritual exaltation, to fly in the air as a bird, not to walk like any other animal.[89]

Noguchi appears in tune with the general spirit of the ceremony, yet there is no indication in the essay that he stuck it out for the remainder of the week, despite his apparent enthusiasm for "*Zazen* or sitting in abstraction," which, he says, "is the way to concentrate and intensify your mind which will never be alarmed even facing thunder and mountains falling right before your eyes." Offering a description of the correct sitting posture, he advises, "Above all, you must find the place of imaginary existence of your soul right in your left palm. Then your mind will grow into silence as the Buddha upon the lotus flower—what a pure silence of the flower—swimming on the peace of the Universe, not encroached by the sense of life and death, you and nature being perfectly united." This was not always the experience of the acolytes as they sat immobile, kept in form by a stick-wielding monk who patrolled the ranks, delivering "eight terrific whacks on the back" to anyone looking drowsy or sitting badly. The trailing off of Noguchi's account suggests that he did not get this far in his observation. He had, after all, classes to teach, and wives and children to visit. "If one could stay here till the blessed day of Miroku—the expected Messiah whom Buddha promised us to give after the lapse of five thousand years!" his essay ends.[90]

---

88. Carmen Blacker, "Impressions of a Japanese University," 293.
89. *Kamakura*, 15.
90. *Kamakura*, 23-24.

If he could have stayed even until the third day, when he might have met with the priest and received his Kōan, or even until the end of the second, it would be easier to accept Yoshinobu Hakutani's assertion that "the most important tradition by which Noguchi's poetry is influenced is that of Zen."[91] As it stands, the argument for the centrality of Zen in Noguchi's work must place considerable weight on "the meaning of silence," for Noguchi rarely only sporadically returned to the topic elsewhere in his writings.

The incompleteness of Noguchi's account of the "Great Meeting with Spirit" was unlikely to have bothered readers of "The Japanese Temple of Silence," which provided a sufficient introduction to its unfamiliar subject. Noguchi's presence at Engakuji could henceforth be viewed with equanimity by the editors of *Zenshū*.[92] "Mr. Yonejirō Noguchi, known as an English poet, has recently developed a sudden aspiration to practice Zen. For this reason, he is now quietly residing in one of the dormitories of Engakuji in Kamakura, while also engaging in literary work. According to his own account, since he holds a teaching position in English literature at Keio University, he cannot remain in Kamakura all of the time, and so he stays in Tokyo about three days a week." Noguchi told the magazine that he could not say anything definite about how his Zen and English studies were interrelated, nor had he found many elements of Zen taste within English literature, but he was confident that his Zen investigations would "not only offer spiritual comfort but surely also bring much inspiration to his poetry."

The *Zenshū* article ended by noting that, "though Master Sōen is also a Keio alumnus, Noguchi says he has not yet had a single meeting with him." Sōen was no longer officially at Engakuji, having, after his return to Japan in 1905, moved across the road to Tōkeiji, an affiliated but separate temple.[93] Sōen's absence probably made little difference to Noguchi, but it did disappoint his fellow temple visitor Raichō Hiratsuka, who had trained with Sōen's disciple, Sōkatsu Shaku, and did not take to Sōkai Miyaji. "Though this may sound impertinent," Raichō wrote, "I could not warm up to him; perhaps we were not fated to be master and student. So instead of training with him, I meditated on my own and burned one incense stick after another. I stayed inside most of the time and only went out for walks."[94]

That Noguchi did not warm to Miyaji either did not apparently trouble him. He wrote of "The Buddha Priest in Meditation":

91. Yoshinobu Hakutani, "Yone Noguchi's Poetry: From Whitman to Zen," *Comparative Literature Studies* 22:1 (Spring 1985): 74.
92. "Ei shijin no sanzen," 87-88.
93. Efforts were made to reappoint Sōen after Miyaji's retirement in 1910, but Sōen, citing the need for major temple reforms, ultimately declined.
94. Hiratsuka, *In the Beginning*, 121.

> He is a style of monotony,
> His religion is aloofness,
> Is there any simplicity more beautiful?⁹⁵

Zen was certainly helping Noguchi understand and embrace monotony. Elsewhere he would write of "the beauty of the monotony of the No drama."⁹⁶ In one of the aphorisms he entitled "Netsukes" he acknowledged that "Indeed the Japanese monotony is unbearable. But wisdom will soon teach us it would be only the just proper way to escape from monotony that we bind or assimilate ourselves with it."⁹⁷

Among the poems from *The Pilgrimage* written at Engakuji were two poems overtly about the temple. One was the atmospheric "By the Engakuji Temple: Moon Night": "Down creeps the moon / To fill my cup of song / With memory's wine."⁹⁸ Hakutani argues that Noguchi wrote it "to demonstrate the state of Zen," pointing to Noguchi "giving up the ego" in the lines, "My soul, as wind / Whose heart's too full to sing, / Only roams astray . . . ."⁹⁹ The subjugation of Noguchi's ego was beautifully and simply expressed in another poem, "At the Yuigahama Shore by Kamakura," where he writes: "I am glad to be no-man to-day / With the laughter and dance of the sea-soul."¹⁰⁰ But poems like "By the Engakuji Temple: Moon Night," seem not so much a relinquishing of ego as an absorption of the world into it: a state that might qualify, at best, as a preliminary stage on the road to Zen enlightenment.

Zen acolytes almost invariably describe that road as agonizingly difficult and demanding. It was only after months of fruitless searching for her "original face" under Sokatsu Shaku's tutelage that Raichō Hiratsuka "came to the conclusion that *kenshō* or *satori*—whatever you called the heightened state of awareness—was attainable for all seekers, but the path leading to attainment, the distance, the degree of difficulty, differed with each person. I did not think that someone like myself would ever experience *tongo*, a sudden awakening; I would have to work at my own pace, with perseverance and patience."¹⁰¹ After six months, she had a breakthrough during a week-long sesshin, as the group finished reciting Hakuin Zenji's *Chant in Praise of Zazen*: "tears as large as hailstones came pouring down my face. . . . I had broken free of my finite self and reached a state of pure awareness." Noguchi's approach was more along the lines of his fond proverb, "the children who live by the temple learn how to

---

95. *Pilg.* 45. Noguchi later said, in "Sōin seikatsu no tsuioku" (Memories of monastic life), *Bishō no jinsei tokuhon* (Tokyo: Kinseidō 1933), 59-60, the poem "was not written with anyone in particular in mind, but at that time I thought of Zen masters in such a way."
96. *SJP* 56.
97. *Kamakura* 20; *TT* 188.
98. *Pilg.* 5.
99. Hakutani, "Yone Noguchi's Poetry: From Whitman to Zen," 75.
100. *Pilg.* 34.
101. Hiratsuka, *In the Beginning*, 87.

read a sutra."¹⁰² His poems seem to suggest that enlightenment might simply be absorbed through the temple atmosphere. "I that sit in your haven am a sea-tossed boat;" he acknowledges in "To a Temple Garden." "Ah, let me join to your prayer and soul!"¹⁰³ In another uncollected poem, "On the Daruma Picture," he mused on an image of Zen founder Bodhidharma, known for his extreme asceticism. "Awful thrill against thee I feel, / Then the grand rest touched by sadness:/ What countless cycles of our own lives!"¹⁰⁴

40. Engakuji Imperial Envoy's Gate).

Noguchi maintained his Zōrokuan retreat for at least four years.¹⁰⁵ In November 1910, he collected several essays and poems he had written about the area into a small book entitled *Kamakura*. Having little talent for the sort of collection of reliable facts traditionally associated with guidebooks, he surreptitiously borrowed from an old one, adding quotations from writers like John La Farge and Basil Hall Chamberlain and a

---

102. SYN 14, 37. Noguchi's mistranslation of the proverb is telling: "Monzen no kozō narawanu kyō wo yomu," means "the student monks outside the gate read the sutra untaught."
103. *Pilg.* 85.
104. "On the Daruma Picture," *Tōa no hikari* 5:4 (15 Apr. 1910): 82-83.
105. Noguchi wrote Frank Putnam from Kamakura, 26 Apr. 1911, FPL.

whole chapter by Lafcadio Hearn, along with seventeen photographs.[106] The review in the *Japan Mail* was quite favorable, but the book had few readers outside of Japan.[107] To promote some awareness overseas of his life at the temple, two articles publicizing it appeared early in 1911, one in the New York *Nation*, attributed to "S. Tsushima," the other by Noguchi's unidentified "fellow-countryman" in the *Westminster Gazette*. Both were, in all likelihood, written partly or entirely by Noguchi himself. "I am not ready to say that he has turned a Buddhist, though we often found him sitting in the Meditation Hall of the Enkakuji Temple, where he hears the Voice of the Unknowable."[108]

A more knowing knower of the unknowable was clairvoyant prodigy Chizu (or Chizuko) Mifune, whose story Noguchi gave the *Boston Evening Transcript* as "A Japanese Palladino."[109] The details of the story had circulated some months earlier in Japanese papers and the *Japan Chronicle*.[110] Noguchi took a particular interest in the efforts to link Chizu's clairvoyant powers with Zen meditation. Efforts to link Buddhism with the new Western sciences of psychology and psychical research had been underway at least since 1881, when Tokyo University appointed "defrocked eccentric" Soto Zen priest, Tanzan Hara, to teach a scientifically-informed Buddhism course.[111] Chizu's powers had been awakened by her brother-in-law, Takeo Kiyohara, a Kumamoto middle-school teacher, who, observing her hypnotic susceptibility during an experiment, and subsequent abilities to see through objects, "told Miss Chizu that if she breathed deeply in a certain way she would attain to a state of consciousness in which the distinction between ego and the non-ego would be eliminated." Tomokichi Fukurai, the Tokyo University psychologist who led the investigation into her case, approached it using the latest theories of mesmerism, while others, including Noguchi, were interested in explanations derived from Zen:

> To breathe deeply so that one can attain a certain state of mind where his ego will depart, and he will so to say, return to the very origin of soul, which soars out of the ordinary five senses—the true condition where he can perfectly be self-possessed, is rather a modern method; but such a method was called the Blessed State by Buddhists, and to

---

106. YN, *Kamakura* (Kamakura: Valley P, 1910), published Nov. 10. "A Legend of the Buddha's Tooth" and "The Wonder of Bronze" were derived mainly from a Kunitarō Sagara (1858-1899) guidebook, probably *A Chat about Kamakura and Its Environs* (Yokohama: Japan Gazette, 1893).
107. "The Bookshelf," *Japan Daily Mail* 54 (3 Dec. 1910): 704.
108. S. Tsushima, "Yone Noguchi at Enkakuji," *Nation* 92 (16 Feb. 1911): 163-64; "The Japanese Poet at the Temple," *Westminster Gazette*, 11 Mar. 1911, 15.
109. YN, "A Japanese Palladino," *Boston Evening Transcript*, 21 Jan. 1911, 3:3. The Italian medium was Eusapia Palladino.
110. See "Case For the Psychical Research Society," *Japan Chronicle*, weekly ed., 25 Aug. 1910, 341.
111. Stephan Kigensan Licha, "Hara Tanzan, Yoshitani Kakuju, and the Academization of Buddhist Studies," in *Learning from the West, Learning from the East*, ed. Licha and Hans Martin Krämer (Leiden: Brill, 2023), 133.

a great extent has been practised, particularly by the Zen Buddhists. One of the purposes for their entering into the Zendo (the meditation hall) is to soar out of the senses; and the able Buddhist can create a state for himself at any time, which is the same with a hypnotic trance when he forgets himself, being 'pure, selfless': then he can reveal a power strange and wonderful which was denied in the normal consciousness.

"Fencing masters of old," such as Musashi Miyamoto, Noguchi explained, had "always learned the Zen Buddhism for entering into the ego-less state, and to gain the superhuman power." But Chizu Mifune's superhuman powers had already ended: two days before Noguchi's story appeared, she committed suicide by poison.

The Toy Collector

One of Noguchi's neighbors in Koishikawa was the "pretty good but not very great" illustrator from his New York days, Genjirō Yeto. Yeto had returned to Japan around the same time as Noguchi, and was now known as Genjirō Kataoka. Like Noguchi, Kataoka was plying his skills as an illustrator both at home and in the U.S., with pretty good but not very great success. Noguchi was able to employ him as an illustrator for his *Lafcadio Hearn in Japan*.

While in New York, Kataoka had done some consulting work for a curator at the Brooklyn Museum, Stewart Culin, an ethnographer from Philadelphia who was among the world's leading authorities of toys and games. When not playing seriously with his toys, Culin was developing the museum's collection of Far Eastern art. He had written a number of pioneering studies of Asian communities in Philadelphia, but did not have an opportunity to travel in Asia until 1909, when he gained approval to undertake a collecting trip in Japan and China. In Japan, Culin had got in touch with his old friend Kataoka, and on July 14, 1909, he paid a visit to Kataoka's Koishikawa home. Kataoka rented a house overlooking the grounds of an old temple, a few blocks from Noguchi's house in Hisakata-machi. Kataoka was now married, and while the maid served lunch with the help of Kataoka's toy-like three-and-a-half-year-old daughter, they talked of Lafcadio Hearn. When Kataoka told Culin that he had visited Hearn's house with his friend Yone Noguchi, Culin became interested, and later jotted down in his assiduously-kept diary what Yeto told him. "Mr. Noguchi was the Japanese poet friend of Joaquin Miller. His wife was an American woman. At present he was living with priests in an old temple near Kamakura."[112]

When Culin invited Noguchi to call at one in the afternoon on the first of October, Noguchi appeared "a little after that time" and stayed until nearly six. Culin described his impression in his diary:

112. Stewart Culin, *Collecting Trip in China & Japan*, 1909, unpublished, 31-2, Brooklyn Museum.

A slender man, almost of European type, he speaks English well, and understands it so that one can address him precisely as if he was an American or European. He was greatly interested in the books and things I showed him, but has no special antiquarian knowledge. He lives at Kamakura where he hires three rooms in a small temple . . . . I made an appointment to visit him at Kamakura. His conversation, although interesting was not particularly informing. He told me nothing that I am disposed to record. He supports himself by teaching in the Keio University, where he has a small appointment, and by writing, but his heart is entirely in his poetry, he told me.

Two weeks later, on October 12, Noguchi called again, this time bringing along one of his Keio colleagues, Kochō Baba, a brilliant linguist fluent in English, French, and Russian.

41. Kochō Baba.

The scholarly Baba—no doubt busy with one of his voluminous translations, perhaps the 3,262-page rendering of Tolstoy's *War and Peace* he published in 1914—made time for the visiting toy collector in part because Culin had known his legendary elder brother, Tatsui Baba, during the latter's last years in political exile in Philadelphia. Tatsui Baba, an early Keio product, had been a brilliant political strategist of the People's Rights Movement in the 1870s and 1880s. Imprisoned for criticism of the government in 1885, he had gone into exile in America upon his release the following year, settling in Philadelphia where he wrote, before his tragically-early death in 1888, a notorious 22-page English treatise attacking the Meiji oligarchy, *The Political Condition of Japan, Showing the Despotism and Incompetency of the Cabinet and the Aims of the Popular Parties*.[113] Culin found the younger Kochō "a simple and very agreeable man." Over dinner, the three men continued their conversation, with the Nō drama emerging as the main topic of conversation. Culin was not a particularly ardent literary scholar, but drama was a form of entertainment that fell

---

113. For more on Tatsui Baba, see Eugene Soviak, "The Case of Baba Tatsui," *Monumenta Nipponica* 18:1/4 (1963): 191-235.

within the range of his interests, and he listened attentively as Noguchi explained to him about Tokyo's four Nō stages and their schedules, and the hereditary aspect of the acting profession and costumes. "The boxes are subscribed for by the year," Noguchi informed him, "and tickets are difficult to obtain, and only procurable through one of the subscribers."

On October 24, Culin returned to his lodgings to find a note from Noguchi telling him there would be a performance the following day, and that he would call at nine in the morning to take him. They arrived late at the Hōshō theatre in Kanda, missing the first play and a kyōgen. The theatre had arranged a special chair for the Westerner, but Culin preferred to sit on the tatami mats with the rest of the audience. The second play was *Sanemori*, the story of "the famous warrior Sanemori, whose ghost, unable to find rest, disturbs the country," as Culin recorded in his journal.

42. *Sanemori* in Kōgyō
Tsukioka's *Nōgaku Hyakuban*
(One hundred Nō dramas).

"In the interval between this play and the next, when another farce, kyo gen, was performed, to which no one paid any particular attention, we ate luncheon, a box of fried eels and rice, which Mr. Noguchi had ordered in the earlier interval." The next Nō was *Hajitomi*, one of several plays based on the supernatural complaints of the jilted lovers of the handsome playboy Genji in Murasaki Shikibu's famous *Tale of Genji*. As was typical, "the play concludes with her spiritual release through the invocation of the priest," Culin noted. After another kyōgen, Culin needed physical if not spiritual release: "At about three-thirty after a lapse of some five hours, sitting in a constrained position, I became tired, and decided not to remain for the fifth and concluding play."[114]

Collision

Culin met Noguchi on several occasions that year, but was never introduced to the American wife, or four-and-a-half-year-old Isamu, who certainly could have told him something about toys. One night in June 1909, while Isamu was out enjoying a street fair, Léonie took the time to write to her friend Catherine Bunnell. Isamu, she explained, was "probably bargaining for a toy at this moment. He took three large copper sen in his purse. He can buy a 'kisha' (train) or a 'densha' (trolley car) for that amount. Is he interested in locomotives? Well, I guess. And tunnels! All the sofa cushions, tables and other articles of furniture get turned into tunnels. And he likes a collision, when all the people get all smashed up." Probably Isamu was working his way though what Freud would soon name the Oedipus Complex, and Léonie, in her usual way, encouraged his free self-discovery through creative play. As she continued to write, Isamu returned from the street fair. He had selected not a *kisha* or *densha* but rather, with his remarkably intuitive feeling for the right object, "a memorandum book, bound in green, cover decorated with the Japanese and American flags in gold and a looking glass let into the cover." Perhaps he hoped the looking glass might reveal some clue to the mystery of his Japanese-American identity. He was also developing a craving for books. "He is teazing me every day to teach him to read and write," Léonie explained. But she had no intention of acceding to his demands. "I shall put that off as long as possible. He has the best eyes of any boy in his school, and I don't want him to spoil them." As a result, Isamu's eyes held up quite well, but he never did learn to spell properly.[115]

If Isamu couldn't read words, he could read his father. Yone had been playing his own version of trains and tunnels, and Matsuko was again pregnant. That autumn, Léonie and Isamu moved yet again. They were already living "separate" from Yone (as he had told Zona Gale in March) but Yone "had to come up and see them" whenever he was in Tokyo. The big smash-up coincided with the birth of Matsuko's second child, a son, Haruo, on February 1, 1910.[116] While the birth of Hifumi a few years earlier had apparently produced no great crisis, a son's birth was a more complicated matter involving questions of inheritance and the future of the Noguchi name. According to Usaburō Toyama's chronology, February 1 was also the date when Matsuko's house in Yanaka Negishi became Noguchi's official address.[117]

114. Culin, *Collecting Trip in China & Japan, 1909*, 290-92, Brooklyn Museum.
115. LG to Bunnell, 13 June 1909, in *LG* 227-8.
116. Toyama Usaburō, "Yone Noguchi no nenpu," *Kenkyū* 1:326.
117. Ibid.

Yone had dedicated *The Pilgrimage* "to Léonie," but there were few signs of affection between them. Even in her cheerful letters to Catherine she conceded she was "not anxious to invade Yone's temple," and was "glad to have him and his cigarette out of the way." "Isamu and I can run this ranch," she explained.[118]

At the time of Haruo's birth, Léonie wrote to her erstwhile intimate friend Matsuo Miyake, telling him in somewhat veiled terms of her sadness.[119] She had maintained an intimate epistolary relationship with the young Matsuo ever since arriving in Japan, although they had seen each other only once in five years—quite recently, when Miyake had been able to travel to Tokyo and Léonie cooked him a hearty dinner. The 23-year-old Miyake had himself been through much, having been left a single father when his wife died shortly after giving birth. Now, on February 5, he alluded to Léonie's own expression of despair: "You say *you have a big sorrow in your heart*. Don't think your brother does not know of his sister's sorrow," he wrote, assuring her, "I am always thinking of you and of your circumstance. I sympathize you with all my heart." Léonie took no precipitous action, but did begin to think of leaving Yone and living with Isamu on her own.

The four-year marriage had cast the desired aura of legitimacy on Isamu. Admittedly, it had been more a performance than a reality. Its last act was the charming essay, "Isamu's Arrival in Japan," an official literary declaration of marriage and paternity in California's *Sunset* magazine in November 1910, among other publications, which featured unambiguous lines like "In fact, he was born to my wife in California some time after I left America."

Isamu was well past his fifth birthday, but Léonie continued to school him at home. In April 1910, she took a job teaching English part time at the Kanagawa Prefecture Girls' Higher School in Yokohama: a first step toward independence. She began to think about moving closer to Yokohama, perhaps to Ōmori, a quiet suburb just south of Tokyo along the Tōkaidō.

On September 23, Matsuo Miyake commented on Léonie's plan to move to Omori, casually mentioning that he had remarried. "During this vacation's leisure hours," he wrote, "I have succeeded in my love affair." His new bride Fumiko was also twenty-three and was a well-known musician in Osaka. The letter must have come as a shock to Léonie, who could not have easily forgotten the idyllic dream of Kyoto domestic life painted by the ardent young journalist. Now that dream, too, was lost. Shortly after receiving this letter, Léonie poured out her sorrows to Miyake in an urgent letter, the contents of which can be inferred from his October 6 response. She had evidently announced she was planning

118. LG to Catherine Bunnell, 13 June 1909, in *LG* 229.
119. Matsuo Miyake to LG, 5 Feb. 1910, INF.

to separate from Yone, and Miyake wondered whether she was planning to separate forever, whether the separation was the "effect of economical standpoint or affection," and whether she planned to go to America or remain in Japan. He also wondered whether she would receive any money from Noguchi, who would take care of Isamu, and what she planned to do about her mother. He was still prepared to help. "If you are going to stay Japan will you come to Osaka (If I can get some good position for you) so that, if in need, you may keep household with me for saving the expenses?"[120]

How Léonie answered can be inferred from what in fact occurred: she and Isamu did move to Ōmori in December 1910. Yone's obligatory visits were now conveniently inconvenient, and the move served as public acknowledgment of their separation. For Isamu, the separation might have seemed a victory over his father, in an Oedipal sense. Now more than ever, he had to substitute for his father in his mother's affections. As Léonie recounted to Catherine Bunnell, "He told his papa the other day that he hoped to become a great man some day, but that he could not become *so* great as mama. Tonight he is busy making a book."[121] But making books was not all there was to it, and Isamu was left tormented with anxiety during his childhood, living in fear of losing his mother. His position was not secure; Léonie was indeed looking for alternate sources of emotional sustenance. No longer feeling obligated to remain faithful to her estranged husband, she had a spring fling that resulted in the birth, in January 1912, of a daughter, Ailes, named after a character in an Irish poem. She took the secret of the father's identity to her grave.

---

120. Matsuo Miyake to LG, 6 Oct. [1910], in *LG* 235-36.
121. LG to Catharine Bunnell, 23 Dec. 1910, in *LG* 240-41.

IMPERIAL JAPAN

1910-1913

Yone Noguchi now resided officially with Matsuko and their two children at 64 Naka-Negishi, Shitaya, and continued to maintain his Kamakura writing retreat at Engakuji. Negishi and Shitaya had long been "the site of quite a colony of artists and writers seeking the fresh breezes of the field and the gentle murmurings of water in the paddies," or, perhaps, the licensed entertainment quarter of Yoshiwara just across.[1] A century earlier the leading Rimpa-school artist, Hōitsu Sakai, had settled in Negishi; Noguchi could meet his descendant, Dōitsu, and even visit Hōitsu's old house, which had become a shop selling soy sauce.[2] More recently, Negishi had been the neighborhood where Kakuzō Okakura carried on the extramarital affair with Hatsu Shūzō, his employer's estranged wife, that ended his tenure as head of the Tokyo School of Fine Arts in 1898.[3] That was just before Shiki Masaoka moved into the neighborhood, where, despite failing health, he had organized the long-enduring Negishi Tanka Society.[4] Stewart Culin, visiting Noguchi's house, noted, "the quarter in which he lives is one much favored by artists, poets and literary men, who dwell here for traditional reasons. It is not healthy and there are many mosquitoes."[5] Culin also noted that "the house is near a famous old pine tree, Ogyo no Matsu, beside which there is a small temple. This tree stands on a kind of island surrounded by small canals. The place is a playground for the children of

1. Paul Waley, *Tokyo: Now and Then* (New York: Weatherhill, 1984), 131.
2. NY, *Nihon no bijutsu*, 197-98.
3. See *Kuki Shūzō: A Philosopher's Poetry and Poetics*, tr. Michael F. Marra (Honolulu: U of Hawaii P, 2004), 228-40.
4. Janine Beichman, *Masaoka Shiki: His Life and Works* (Boston: Twayne, 1982), 79-80.
5. Stewart Culin, entry for 10 June 1912, *Collecting Trip in Japan, 1912* (unpublished), Brooklyn Museum.

the neighborhood. The tree is girdled with a band of straw rope."[6] Noguchi would later reminisce about having "the good fortune to spend several years as a neighbor to the Ogyō no Matsu in Negishi."[7] "As I strolled along the little stream that flows past the roots of the Ogyō no Matsu, I imagined the peaceful age of two hundred years ago. When evening came, and I looked up at the pine in quiet reflection before returning home, I found myself touched by the mystery exhaled by this ancient tree—and I became a romanticist."

43. Ogyō no Matsu, Negishi, circa 1910.

As Japan tightened its colonial grip in Korea and Taiwan, and looked for ways to expand its presence in China with the fall of the Manchu dynasty in the revolution of 1911, Noguchi eyed the situation as a maturing political commentator. Having the opportunity to develop his views among university professors, politicians, poets, and foreign visitors, Noguchi was prepared to do his part in explaining to the English-speaking world his understanding of the politics surrounding Japan's colonial activities, as well as the ongoing crises of Japanese-American relations.

Unruly Korea

Japanese imperialistic tendencies had manifested themselves soon after the Meiji Restoration (notably in an aborted Korean effort in the early 1870s) but did not become highly visible until Japan formally entered into

6. Stewart Culin, entry for 27 June 1912, *Collecting Trip in Japan, 1912*, Brooklyn Museum.
7. "Matsu no ki no Nihon" (Pine trees of Japan), *Chūō Kōron* 40:9 (1 Oct. 1925), rpt. *Sōshiden*, 37-38.

the business of empire through the terms of settlement of the Sino-Japanese War of 1894-95, under which China had ceded its client states of Korea and Formosa (Taiwan) to Japan. In the settlement of the Russo-Japanese War in 1905, Japan had been forced to give up her new war gains in the Liaotung Peninsula and Manchuria, but her claims in Korea had been formally recognized, and the Korean emperor had been compelled to sign a treaty making Korea a Japanese protectorate.

Japanese colonialism did not greatly differ from the Western colonialism on which it was modeled, but it caused Western nations to view the rising Japanese power with a greater sense of alarm, and Japanese-American relations, already deteriorating on the West Coast due to labor and immigration issues, became increasingly tense as alarmists began to talk of the new Yellow Peril in the wake of Japan's victory over Russia. Writers like Noguchi with connections abroad were faced with the task of clarifying Japan's good intentions to the outside world. There was plenty of political rhetoric and ideology readily available for such publicity efforts, the Japanese having borrowed from their Western teachers the idea of colonialism as a great force of enlightenment and civilization created for the benefit of uncivilized peoples everywhere.

Japan had begun a series of institutional reforms in Korea as far back as 1895, but Koreans resisted Japanese rule and its often heavy-handed methods, which included appropriation of land and trade, blatant political machinations, and the Japanizing of education under the slogan of modernization. Korean resistance frustrated the Japanese, who responded with more aggressive policies, leading to greater Korean dissatisfaction: an endless, vicious circle.

Hopes had been high for Hirobumi Itō, now "Prince" Itō, appointed Governor-General of Korea after the annexation, but "Prince Ito's administration in Korea was a failure. That is our Japanese opinion," Noguchi reported on July 1.[8] The reasons, as they appeared to the Japanese, were numerous. Itō's approach had been too idealistic, too civilized, too concerned about foreign opinion; he had sought to prop up the Korean imperial house rather than demanding the emperor's abdication; Koreans had found him "rather an easy person to handle"; the Japanese and Korean officials could not work together; there had been "a hundred examples of incompetency of Japanese officials in the country towns, from their ignorance of the Korean language or other reasons, which almost appears to be a comedy." Korea was, of course, "a hard case." "And at the same time, our home statesmen and people must share its responsibility." But "whatever blunder we made or are making, we declare we are meeting Korea with honesty and truth and we must." On June 14, the aging *genrō* statesman had been forced to resign, to be replaced by the Vice Resident-General, Arasuke Sone, who, despite his four decades of

8. "Ito's Mistakes in Korea," *Boston Evening Transcript*, 7 Aug. 1909, 21.

diplomatic and political service, remained little known even to Japanese, as Noguchi explained in a November 1909 *Taiyō* article, "Viscount Sone."[9] "Above all, we must study Korea and her people thoroughly. I dare say we know, in fact, very little of them. That is the real cause whence arises every blunder."

44. **Hirobumi Itō.**

The situation in Korea went from bad to worse even before Noguchi's "Viscount Sone" article hit newsstands in November, for at the end of October, Prince Itō, traveling in northern China, was assassinated by a Korean nationalist. Itō's last words on being told the identity of his assassin were "*baka na yatsu ja!*" ("What an idiot!"), and he was at least correct insofar as the assassination helped tilt the balance of public opinion in Japan in favor of the hard-line imperialists.

In an April 1910 article on "Unruly Korea," Noguchi explained that leading figures like Count Hayashi saw "no obstacle" to annexation, citing prior agreements with Western powers and arguing it would "root out the element of dissension."[10] Advocates promised to preserve the Korean monarchy and likened annexation to a "voluntary affiliation." Yet growing unrest, including assassination attempts and rival petitions, led Viscount Sone to admit, "Unless the heart is won, the enemy in your embrace will always be your enemy." Viscount Sone, despite his reputation for "splendid health," was forced to resign as Resident-General in May 1910, due to declining health and died four months later of stomach cancer. He was replaced by Japan's Army Minister, General Masatake Terauchi.

Following Japan's formal annexation of Korea on August 22, 1910, the Itō years were reconceived as a prelude to the "real" imperialism, as Noguchi endeavored to explain in his essay on "Japan's Failure in Korea."[11]

9. "Viscount Sone," *Taiyō* 15:14 (1 Nov. 1909): 18.
10. "Unruly Korea," *Boston Evening Transcript*, 16 Apr. 1910, 3:3.
11. "Japan's Failure in Korea," *Taiyō* 16:14 (Nov. 1910): 11-14.

The real performance, with Korea as an officially annexed colony, would hopefully be better. The metaphor of imperialism as a performance was helpful in masking the contradictions between the new imperial ideology and the old. In contrast to the dirty and uncivilized Korea of the past, the new colonial Korea was Japan's long-lost relation: "Japanese and Koreans are, I think, the same race originally; the facts philological as well as anthropological tell us that we are related as a race at least in the manner of brothers." Japanese historians were making much of the historical connections between Japan and Korea, noting that "Korea has had not one day strictly independent since the day of the Chinese invasion in the Han dynasty, and the Koreans are accustomed to the idea of changes in dynasty." "I think they do not see anything different in the annexation," Noguchi commented; many in Japan were even calling it "a reunion of two parts of the same race and a return to an earlier day." Sadly, Noguchi conceded, "we did not understand Korea and the Koreans till very recently, although our relationship is thus old and historical." Itō had failed because he didn't see that Koreans were apolitical and self-serving, Noguchi thought; now, the Japanese were prepared to admit some responsibility for the failure, and hoped to do a better job. "I have ample reasons to call the Korean problem extremely sad," he concluded, "but we must feel happy, I think, that we are lucky enough to have the right to settle that sad affair. How we fought to get that right!" But his own literary efforts toward understanding Korea—much improved over the past half-decade—came to an end with "Japan's Failure in Korea."

Although the new colonies in Korea and Formosa were proving to be less satisfactory than anticipated, Japan still eyed Manchuria—with its enormous stretches of land, natural resources, and newly-built transportation infrastructure—as a great colonial prize. The ill-fated Boxer rebellion of 1900, in which the Chinese government had halfheartedly supported the violently anti-foreign Boxers, had left foreign powers, including Japan, with a much-strengthened foothold in the country, and the Chinese government saddled with a huge indemnity and increasing political instability.

In January of 1906, Noguchi had visited China. Although his English article based on the experience was rejected by Frank Putnam, he did publish a Japanese article, "*Shanhai*," in the influential *Chūō Kōron*.[12] And a few years later, when the Chinese Revolution was in the news, he recollected his trip in an article for the New York *Evening Post*.[13] Entitled "Confucian Temples Grass Grown," the article dwelled on socio-cultural failings and evidences of decay Noguchi had encountered on his trip: coolies, lack of respect for religion, lack of nationalism, lack of appreciation for poetry. The coolies were the most obvious indication of China's

---

12. "Shanhai" (Shanghai), *Keiō Gijuku Gakuhō* 100 (15 Feb. 1906): 48-52.
13. "Confucian Temples Grass Grown," New York *Evening Post*, 23 Mar. 1912, 1.

degraded condition. "I had been told much about another human class, not like you and me, called coolies, creatures fit to be compared with the summer flies that try your nerves. You should have another way, often beyond the human way, to deal with them. I was at once exposed, when the ship anchored at a certain place in Shanghai, to an almost gruesome scene enacted by these Chinese coolies (why must the reality of the "survival of the fittest" be pushed to such an extreme?), who attempted, even at the risk of life, to climb up the ship, like monkeys, with the aid of a long hooked pole. Many of them were kicked down into the water by the sailors; when they found it impossible to treat them one by one, they threw buckets of water over them. I felt sad on seeing that there were human beings in China to whom the word 'cruelty' carried no particular meaning, as they did not feel its pain: and felt still sadder to think that one would only degrade himself to show them such a high-handed contempt." "Yet, has not such been," he reflected, "the attitude of the world towards China in international diplomacy or politics at least, in the past?" "I soon became further acquainted, like all others who go to China with the coolies or rikishamen pulling dirty cars in the streets, and I even doubted whether all Chinamen were not runners, as the streets were perfectly packed with them; it was through them that I learned some fundamental Chinese characteristics."

In his *Chūō Kōron* article, Noguchi evinced some disgust for the imperial endeavor, likening it to "rats fighting for the rotten meat which is China," but did go so far as to oppose it. The Japanese advantage conveyed in the expression "same race, same script," was resented by Western powers competing for China concessions. The Japanese, he candidly suggested, "must find a way to clear up that suspicion and also get the concessions." As in his earlier English essay on "The Character of the Coreans," he showed no qualms about promoting the Japanese cause by disparaging the Chinese, harping on what he called "the sad feeling and unpleasant sense" he found everywhere, from the inhumanly-treated porters kicked from the side of the arriving boat as they fought for the privilege of carrying the baggage of the ship's passengers, to the nighttime scene in the entertainment quarter where the atmosphere of prostitution and gambling seemed to him a "revelation of the animality of human beings at its extreme." Such rhetoric, like the "civilizing mission" rhetoric of Western imperialism on which it was partly based, allowed the Japanese to persuade themselves, and sometimes others, that their exploitative colonial ventures were really for the benefit of the Chinese.

In contrast to his disdainful characterization of contemporary China, Noguchi's views of classical Chinese literature were mostly appreciative. That appreciation came partly from the long history of Japanese writers' dependence on Chinese literary models, and partly from Noguchi's unacknowledged dependence on Herbert Giles' mostly appreciative *History of*

Chinese Literature, from which he borrowed a good half of his surveys of Chinese drama and novels, more or less verbatim.[14]

Moreover, it was, as Noguchi wrote, "an open secret that the Government has been trying for some time to revive, but with no success, the old Chinese classics and the ancient ethics of filial piety."[15] He could "admit that such an attempt may not be bad," but felt "the new age should have the new literature," and dismissed such heavy-handed tactics as futile. Noguchi attributed the push to two imperial rescripts, "the Imperial Edict of 1890, known as the educational edict, and the edict of 1908,"[16] the latter being the so-called Boshin Rescript, aimed at reasserting values of loyalty, filial piety, diligence, frugality, and social harmony. Perhaps encouraged by Tetsujirō Inoue, appointed to lead the government's promotional efforts, Noguchi had grappled, in some fashion, with the Chinese classics, but concluded that "their archaic simplicity was altogether too invigorating for our modern minds." The edicts, he thought, "would be more valuable as a protest; it is still to be seen what relation they will form with our intellectual life." "What little impression this attempted Chinese revival produced on our life in general may be seen more directly from the fact that many publishers of Chinese classics failed; the unsold books are piled on the shelves of the bookstores. The Confucius vogue was only momentary." Still, he did not escape it entirely. Asked to contribute a short preface to a trilingual pocket edition of selected Confucian *Analects* (cobbled together from a recent Japanese translation and James Legge's 1893 *Chinese Classics* translation), he came up with a story of how "once some years ago when I passed the narrow streets in the outskirts of Shanghai, my restless mind and ears were suddenly calmed by the voices of Chinese children reading the *Lun Yü*. It was the first time that its musical beauty made the proper impression upon me. As mere writing, it is one of the best pieces of Chinese literature."[17] The story, if true, would have been worth mentioning when writing of China's decaying Confucius temples. But the government's Confucius promotion had little to do with Chinese views of the sage, being mainly concerned with Japanese Confucian ideals imported centuries ago.

In the fall of 1911, the centuries-old Manchu dynasty was finally toppled by a series of local rebellions assisted by the international leadership and promotion efforts of reformer Sun Yat-Sen, among others. Although sudden, the developments were not unexpected. Chinese reform efforts had stagnated since the accession of infant emperor Puyi, leaving open

---

14. "China Expects a Drama Revolution at Almost Any Time," *New York Sun*, 5 May 1912, 32; "Li Yu, Last of China's Dramatists," *Boston Evening Transcript*, 10 July 1912, 16, 24; "Chinese Novels," *Japan Mail*, weekly ed., 16 Aug. 1913, 11.
15. "The Japanese Government and the New Literature," *Academy*, 1 July 1911, 11.
16. "The Truth about Intellectual Japan," *Taiyō* 17:8 (June 1911): 8-11.
17. YN, "[Preface]," *"RONGO" (Confucian Analects) in English, Japanese, and Chinese*, tr. James Legge, ed. Yamano Masatarō (Matsumoto Gakki Gōshi Gaisha, 1912).

rebellion as the primary recourse of reformists—a recourse encouraged, and financially supported, by interested parties abroad, in the West as well as Japan.

Some in the West viewed Japan's increased Chinese involvement with alarm. Among them was Jack London, who had seen Japanese in action in China during the Russo-Japanese War and had concluded that "it is a weakness of the white race to believe that the Japanese think as we think, are moved to action as we are moved and have points of view similar to our own." The Chinese and Japanese outnumbered "the various branches of the white race"; what if, he wondered (in December 1909), they should "embark on some vast race-adventure," as English-speaking peoples were, "dreaming as all race-adventurers have dreamed." A clash of dreams—first, an economic one, and then a clash at arms, "that will-o'-wisp, the Yellow peril"—was his prophecy.[18]

Noguchi penned a quick rebuttal: "No Yellow Peril in China."[19] "A glance over the series of opinions the world has expressed on China during the last twenty years makes me wonder at the fickleness of the Western world," he began. China had been a sleeping lion, a dead lion, an Open Door for trade, a Yellow Peril, and now, the concern of the world—and Jack London—was what might happen if Japan wakened China. The fickleness stemmed from the Western world's lack of knowledge. Japan had served China for her awakening, providing an "example of how a country could rejuvenate herself," and China was now making progress toward reforming education and planning a parliament. As for becoming a Yellow Peril if awakened, there was, he pointed out, "no country except China which has no history or record of invasion into another country since the first establishment of the kingdom. . . . The Chinese ideal, if there is any, is nothing but peace."

In December 1911, with the revolution still in its early stages, Noguchi wrote to the London *Graphic* to call attention to "Japan's Share in the Chinese Revolution."[20] Japan had provided a refuge and training ground for Chinese revolutionaries in the years leading up to it. While Japan had expelled Sun Yat-sen, it educated and sheltered countless others who became key leaders, organizers, and martyrs in the uprising. Many had been students in Japan's universities, including one in Keio's literature department. It was "a blood-curdling story to follow in detail how those Chinese revolutionists paid for their existence, or when possible, for their success, and how coldly the Peking Government sent them to death."

With regional fragmentation under competing armies and shifting alliances, Japan saw great opportunities, as did Western powers. The Japanese, according to Noguchi's January 1912 letter to *The Nation* entitled

18. Jack London, "If Japan Wakens China," *Sunset* 23 (Dec. 1909): 597-601.
19. "No Yellow Peril in China," *Sunset* 25 (July 1910): 14-16.
20. "Japan's Share in the Chinese Revolution," *Graphic* 84 (23 Dec. 1911): 1004.

"A Japanese View of China," were rather skeptical of the present revolution, accustomed as they were to viewing Chinese history in terms of "changes of Emperors and a sort of series of revolutions" and saw "not one instance in China's longest history of her becoming one consolidated empire, as if she were a dragon with eight heads and tails."[21] Noguchi was dismissive of the revolution's prospects. "I should like to question what sort of a republic (though beautiful the name) those young ambitious revolutionists can make out from their own people, the majority of them ignorant, and worse than that, self-centred." Lacking patriotism, he saw little hope for a Chinese nation. "They might be taught in time the lesson of freedom, equality, and fraternity, even in the Western sense; but you must have, at the very start, a better sort of patriotism." Instead, it would be better if China were divided, he suggested. The world's policy of "Preservation of China," he argued, was merely "for the convenience of the Western nations and Japan, who have acted and will more act in China as if they had all rights they wish there."

> If I were to plan for China's own benefit, I have often thought, she should confer the places far away from her central Government, powerless to control and useless for her own purpose, upon the proper nations when such an act should not immediately break the balance of power either in the West or East; and to make her strength more easy to concentrate and more effective, she should confine herself within the provinces where the real influence of the Government could be felt. And better still, those provinces, I dare wish, should be divided into three or four countries; that, I am sure, would be the proper answer for the question of the Chinese reformation.

He was also rather pessimistic that the Chinese "love of 'empty discussion'" would lead to successful politics. "It is most sad not to have a great personality for the success of the revolution, who will at once silence the petty quarrels among the leaders and unite all the provinces by one principle, and make them act as one state." There was a glimmer of hope in the person of Sun Yat-Sen, expected in China soon from his Japanese exile; "can he," Noguchi wondered, "ever become that man?"

Many, indeed, had great hopes for Sun Yat-Sen, who had spent considerable time abroad in Hawaii, Hong Kong, and Japan. Noguchi wrote an article on Sun for the February 1912 *Taiyō*.[22] It was primarily a translation of an article by a Japanese associate of Sun, but probably also expressed Noguchi's own modest hopes for the Chinese leader: "it was good," he wrote, "that his failure took him abroad now to America, then to Europe where he learned the new knowledge and studied the Western republicanism which is to be adopted into China if the movement succeeds." Events continued at a rapid pace. Sun, elected provisional president

21. "A Japanese View of China," *Nation* (New York) 94 (18 Jan. 1912): 57-58.
22. "Sun Yatsen," *Taiyō* 18:2 (Feb.1912): 12-15.

upon his return, agreed to a peaceful transition of power under which the infant emperor would abdicate, and power would be handed over to Imperial minister Yuan Shikai. The newly emergent Chinese Republic soon became embattled in power struggles between the reorganized Kuomintang (Nationalist Party) made up largely of former revolutionists who now dominated the parliament, and Yuan, who pressed for greater concentration of power in the presidency, even advocating a revival of the emperorship. The situation was further complicated by the emergence of regional warlord-controlled factions and increased foreign pressures. Amid the distraction of the Great War, Japan presented Yuan in January of 1915, with the infamous Twenty-One Demands, which would, if accepted in full, have made China essentially a Japanese dependency; and did, in the end, succeed in gaining Japan extensive concessions in Manchuria and rights to the formerly German-held territories in Shantung. This was all construed by the Japanese as a magnanimous gesture of assistance and protection. Toward the end of 1915 Noguchi would be writing in the American press of the "Failure of the Chinese Republic," blaming, as usual, the "self-seeking of the Chinese and their general lack of public spirit" as well as "the Chinese conservatism."[23] It would be better, he thought, to "create a centre of inspiration which might consolidate the national mind": "Yuan Shi-Kai as Emperor, but not as President," he suggested, "might make the country more straightforward in conduct, and more compact in her life."

Future of Japanese Art

Since his return to Japan, when he had observed in the exhibition of the *Hakuba-kai* painters an effort to adapt European methods to Japanese subjects, Noguchi had been following with interest developments in the Japanese art world. Within a few years, he had formed friendships with many of the country's leading younger artists. His occasional English writings on the latest exhibitions and developments in the art world offer intriguing glimpses into the embattled Meiji art world, where nationalist and internationalist factions were fighting it out in battles which closely paralleled those of the literary world. The battle lines were evenly drawn between practitioners of *Nihonga* (Japanese-style painting) and *Yōga* or *Seiyōga* (Western-style painting), with a number of artists attempting occasionally-successful fusions between the two.

Within these two broad divisions there were a number of influential schools, movements, and societies. Japan's first official art academy, the Tokyo School of Fine Arts (*Tōkyō Bijutsu Gakkō*), founded in 1889 by a group that included Ernest Fenollosa and Kakuzō Okakura, attempted to bridge East and West, employing many of the leading artists of the day in both styles. Not surprisingly, it became a hotbed of controversy with

23. "The Failure of the Chinese Republic," *Nation* (New York) 101 (16 Dec. 1915): 709.

various schools competing for primacy. Okakura's affair with a superior's wife did not help matters; in 1897 he resigned as director, and with the support of some of the school's other disaffected artists (including Gahō Hashimoto, Taikan Yokoyama, and Kanzan Shimomura) formed the Japan Fine Arts Academy (*Nihon Bijutsuin*).

Gahō Hashimoto, the last of the famed Kanō school painters, became the chief professor of the new Academy. In the 1880s, Fenollosa and Okakura had discovered Gahō and Hōgai Kanō living in poverty. The two painters had struggled on despite the loss of their daimyō patronage, and Fenollosa and Okakura had been impressed at the way they had absorbed Western influences while retaining an essentially Japanese style. They became the models for a new generation, Hōgai, who died in 1888, through his example and Gahō through his direct teaching. Gahō's younger colleagues at the Academy, Taikan Yokoyama and Kanzan Shimomura, had been his star pupils at the School of Fine Arts.

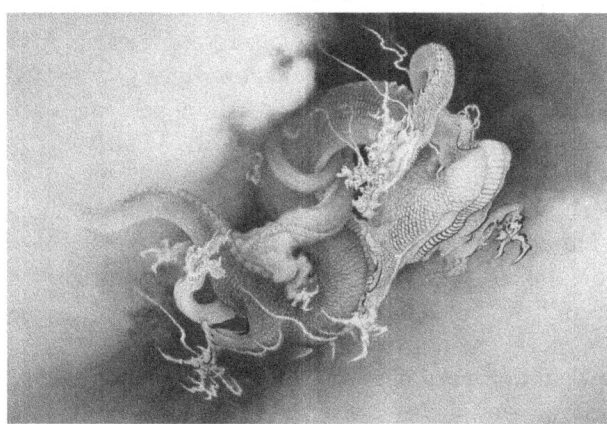

45. Hōgai Kanō, *Two Dragons*, 1885.

Meanwhile, Japanese Western-style painting had been gradually transforming from exotic novelty to serious art form. Like so many other cultural products of the West, Western-style painting had come into vogue in the early decades after the Meiji Restoration. The more prominent of the early Western-style artists emerging in the 1870s and 1880s—Chū Asai, Hōsui Yamamoto, and print artist Kiyochika Kobayashi—had studied under either Charles Wirgman (a correspondent for the *Illustrated London News* in Japan from 1861) or Antonio Fontanesi (an Italian artist appointed by the Japanese government to teach at a Kobe art school from 1876 to 1878). A number of artists studied abroad. But with the rise of cultural nationalism in the 1880s came a backlash against imported art forms. "The popularity which the Western art seemed to have attained had a great setback when the pictures were excluded from the National Exhibition in 1890," Noguchi noted; "but in the reaction the artists of the Western school gained more vigour and determination."[24] Japan's first

24. SJA 107.

internationally-recognized painter in the Western style was Kiyoteru (Seiki) Kuroda. He and another artist, Keiichiro Kume, had studied in Paris from 1886 to 1893 and formed a studio on their return; and in 1896 they had formed the Hakubakai (White Horse Society). The same year, the Tokyo School of Fine Arts decided to form a separate Western-style painting department: Takeji Fujishima (who had studied Western painting under Hosui and other first-generation practitioners) and Eisaku Wada (a student of Kuroda) were appointed to teach the subject. In 1898, with the Okakura exodus, more *Yōga* specialists were brought in: Hakubakai founders Kuroda and Kume, as well as Chū Asai. Eisaku Wada left to study in France.

Noguchi had written approvingly of the Hakubakai exhibition of 1904. Items on display had included Fujishima's delightful Pre-Raphaelite-influenced *Chō* (Butterflies), and Wada's Genroku-period piece *Aru ka? Naki ka?* (Is There Any Thorn? Is There Not?) for which two famous Shinbashi geisha had served as models. Said to be "the best painting that has appeared in Japan for some five years," Noguchi agreed it was "a great achievement." But by 1907, when the first annual government-sponsored exhibition was mounted as part of an industrial exposition held in Tokyo, he had lost much of his enthusiasm for the Westernists. "The *Nihon ga* or Japanese art, however poor it be, will tell you something of history or of the nature you see about you; but European art in Japan is no more than a grafted tree, rather sad to see," he had written in the *Japan Times*. Compared to the "dreaminess or reflection" of the Nihonga artists, the Seiyōga artists were full of "the seriousness of artistic purpose." Seriousness of artistic purpose was not, in Noguchi's view, a good thing: "unhappily with spasmodic effort of mistaken zeal they excessively finish and elaborate their work; the sickness of over-study which marks it is perfectly unbearable."[25]

But neither was Noguchi much impressed with the *Nihonga* displayed at the 1907 exhibition. Part of the problem was the exhibition space itself. The fragile *kakemono* (hanging scrolls) and *byōbu* (painted screens) were poorly suited for the Western-influenced exhibition styles of the day, where multitudes of closely-packed, framed paintings jostled for wall space. Noguchi "felt extreme sorrow on seeing those 325 pictures making such an uncomfortable appearance in the art hall," observing that Japanese art was better suited to, and had developed in perfect harmony with "the soft and mellow grey atmosphere of the Japanese house." And he feared the "moral effect on the artist's mind" of the exhibition itself, which encouraged artists to "attempt to devise something to attract the eye in colour, form, subject, and even in title," and thus depart from traditional

25. "Japanese Artists Ignore the War: Reflections Suggested by a View of the Autumn Exhibition in Tokio," *National Magazine* 21 (Mar. 05): 671-74; "Upon the Exhibition Oil Paintings," *JT*, 16 June 1907, 6; "The Exhibition Pictures Again," *JT*, 23 June 1907, 6.

artistic ideals of simplicity, nobility and beauty. But exhibitions had come to stay, and that October, the first of the annual Mombushō Bijutsu Tenrankai (Ministry of Education Fine Arts Exhibitions), or Bunten for short, opened in Ueno Park.

By that time, Noguchi had become critical of both the Yōga and Nihonga schools. His evaluation of the situation was summed up in a September 1907 column on "Japanese Art." "There are many people who declare that they are tired of the *Nippon ga*," he explained; "we will say that we feel in them only the faded scent of an older art and refinement, which are not quite true to Nature, and are too far away; they have somehow degenerated to a mechanic art: we want more the artistic reality; we demand some unmistakable end to all art." Japanese Western-style paintings "might be poor or a poor imitation at the best," he conceded, and he was sure that "Western people can not help feeling as if they were looking over some valueless debris of civilization in their own home." But then, he had observed that "many poor Japanese pictures receive extraordinary praise in Western countries," and therefore "we cannot believe what Westerners say on our art without reservation." Western artists and art critics were beginning to criticize Western methods and look to Japanese methods as a solution to Western art's mechanical realism and artistic egotism, but then Japanese art, Noguchi thought, suffered from a "poverty of artistic subjects," and it "would not be unwise to advise our Japanese artists to study Nature or the realism of life; and there is no question of their incompetency in their drawing of figures."[26]

Art in Japan was, in other words, being pulled in a number of opposed directions, and when Noguchi assessed the 1911 government exhibition, he diagnosed what he called "the nervous debility of Japanese art."

> The best possible course art can follow in the time of its nervous debility might be that of imitation; I know, of course, there is a moment even for imitation, when it almost becomes creation. The question is how you imitate. And what does the Japanese art imitate? What it imitates is the Western art as the life here copies the civilization beyond the seas. When it tells something, I thank God, it is from its sad failure; indeed, the present Japanese art is a lost art, since it explains nothing, alas, unlike the old art of idealistic exaltation, but the general condition of life. It is cast down from its high pedestal.

Western-style art was now in the ascendant. "This morning," Noguchi notes in the same article (dated February 9, 1912), "I was informed by the press that the four Government Exhibition jurors of the old Japanese school had suddenly resigned, saying that their opinions and desire to preserve the time-honored art intact had been always insulted, jeered, and laughed at by the other jurors of the Western initiation, who always outnumbered them. The resigning jurors published their proclamation to

---

26. "Japanese Art," *JT*, 1 Sept. 1907, 6.

the effect that the real Japanese art was dying."[27]

The modern Nihonga school lost Ernest Fenollosa in 1908, Gahō Hashimoto in 1910, and Kakuzō Okakura in 1913, nearly ending the Japan Fine Arts Academy. A Hōgai Kanō memorial exhibition in October of 1910 which Mary Fenollosa helped to arrange, did provide a reminder of its influence and potential, inspiring one of Noguchi's few enthusiastic art reviews of these years.[28] "His art is the art of freedom of his own mind," Noguchi wrote, "in another word, the art of the 'thing itself.'"[29]

As for the Western school, Noguchi had, at least for the moment, tired of it. "I have ceased for some time to expect anything great or astonishing from Wada or Okada or even Kuroda," he wrote in a 1913 article inspired by that year's exhibition.[30] Nevertheless, he had not given up on it entirely. "We most eagerly look forward to the sudden appearance of some genius at once to frighten and hypnotise and charm us and make the Western art more intimate with our minds." Moreover, he remained conscious of the positive impact of Western art, not least in the broadened sense of color and perspective. "There are many other lessons we received from it; it seems to me that the best and greatest value is its own existence as a protest against the Japanese art. If the Japanese art of the old school has made any advance; as it has done, it should be thankful to the Western school; and at the same time the artists of foreign method must pay due respect to the former for its creation of the 'Western Art Japonised.' It may be far away yet," he concluded, "but such an art, if a combination of the East and West, is bound to come."

46. Eisaku Wada, Ōna (Old woman), 1908.

27. "The Nervous Debility of Japanese Art," Nation 94 (28 Mar. 1912): 313, revised in SJA 113-4. The Japan Mail, in "Mr. Yone Noguchi," weekly ed., 25 May 1912, 605, doubted Japanese art had ever been free of foreign influence: "The truth is that Japan borrowed her art, whether pictorial art or applied art, from China, and that the more closely she approached her foreign model, the greater her achievement was considered to be."
28. "The Hogai Kano Exhibition," Taiyō 17:1 (Jan. 1911): 11-13.
29. What Noguchi meant by "this Japanese expression," he explained, was "that he and the subjects he painted were perfectly one, the subjects with all his temperament he wished to reveal."
30. "Western Art in Japan," Academy 85 (27 Dec. 1913), rpt. in SJA 104-05.

Blue Wave

Pondering the complexities of Japanese art, Noguchi hardly suspected the future of Japanese art was currently enrolled in an Omori kindergarten. In the experimental school, run by wealthy Yokohama merchant Ichizaemon Morimura, children were taught to do things with their hands. "My first sculpture was made there in the form of a sea wave, in clay and with a blue glaze," Isamu Noguchi later recalled.[31] To his great pride, it was "shown around." "Somehow or other I knew about waves. It was a kind of prophecy . . . On a boat, coming here, I saw waves." From the beginning, Isamu's artistic fame emerged from his conflicted identity, the space of separation between his American and Japanese selves. From the beginning, it borrowed something from his father, the poet from the Eastern Sea whose books had waves on their covers.

The success of Isamu's first sculpture, at the age of five, was no accident: Léonie had in effect been preparing for this first public exhibition for years. When Isamu was barely fourteen months old, she had written Yone of her recurring thought to bring Isamu to Japan: "I would like to put him to an Art school somewhere, where he will have eye and hand trained to express his idea—No matter if he become artist or not." The idea became gradually fixed in her mind, and her determination was at times extraordinary. Nearly twenty years later, when the well-meaning Dr. Rumely tried to put Isamu through medical school, Léonie would raise an "awful row," accusing him of "turning a boy of artistic temperament toward a career for which he was entirely unsuited." [32]

It is often supposed that Léonie was channeling her own frustrated creativity into her children. In fact, she was subjecting them to the educational philosophies with which she herself had been raised. The strongest influence came from the innovative educator who founded the kindergarten and elementary school that had rescued her from a life of poverty: a German-Jewish immigrant named Felix Adler. In 1878 Adler founded his Free Kindergarten in New York. In two years, it was expanded into the Workingman's School. (Later it was known as the Ethical Culture School). Léonie had been a graduate of the first class. "The educational objects aimed at are to cultivate the eye and the hand, to develop skill, to call out the active side of the pupil's nature," Adler had written in one of his early manifestos. He wanted his school to bridge the gap between manual training and intellectual idealism: indeed, to turn manual training into a kind of idealism.[33] He determined to "exclude as far as possible the use of text-books, to deprive teacher and pupils alike of those props of indolence, to make them construct their text-books as they go along." He thought school should be "a gymnasium of the faculties," "'the midwife'

31. ASW 11; Duus, 59-60.
32. LG to YN, 24 Feb. 1906, quoted above; LG to Catharine Bunnell, 27 Mar. 1927, in LG 329.
33. Felix Adler, "The Democratic Ideal in Education," Century 38:6 (Oct. 1889): 929.

of the soul in its process of self-manifestation." He thought schools should be more respectful of the "specific differences by which human beings are distinguished from one another" instead of trying "to fashion all alike upon a preconceived and arbitrary pattern." [34] Léonie followed Adler's ideas almost to the letter. But Isamu's "process of self-manifestation" would be a complicated business, for wherever he went, he was different from everyone else, and after kindergarten, the available schools did not suit Léonie's educational philosophy. As Léonie saw it, only an art school could take Isamu where he needed to go.

Ōmori, where Isamu's kindergarten was located, was then a coastal town just beyond Tokyo's southern edge. Since April 1910, Léonie had been teaching at a prefectural girls' school in Yokohama. "This place is halfway between my former home and my school, and I spend alternate days riding on the train or trolley to school and to Tokyo, where I still have some pupils."[35] During the slightly less than a year they lived there, Léonie became pregnant, perhaps in in Tokyo, Omori, or Yokohama.

When the Berkeley, California-based writer, Charles Keeler (Catherine Bunnell's cousin by marriage) arrived in Japan in September of 1910 for a stay of some weeks at the outset of a lengthy international lecture tour, Léonie's advanced pregnancy made it difficult for her to spend much time with him. "Yone took him on a trip to Nikko, said he was glad to have seen him and glad it was over," she reported to Catharine in January, after Keeler had "come and gone like a comet." Yone, she explained, was "not equal to the strenuosity of the average American, and C.K. may have an extra amount of the blizzard ingredient." But she believed Keeler had "made a brilliant sensation."[36]

47. Yone Noguchi and Charles Keeler, 1910.

34. Adler, "Democratic Ideal," 930.
35. LG to Catherine Bunnell, 23 Dec. 1910, in *LG* 240-41.
36. LG to Catherine Bunnell, 15 Dec. 1912, in *LG* 246.

Near Heaven and Town

In the early months of 1905, when the poet had, with his fading O Yuki San, "walked away from the city and noise, into the valley of Love and silence," he had set his mind to imagining his ideal study, "a tranquil place, not far from town yet near to heaven, only five or six blocks from the human world," where he might sit by the coolness of a pine tree, surrounding himself with favorite works of literature. On one of his Kyoto trips soon after his return, he visited the home of the writer Gekkō Takayasu, on the west bank of the Kamo River. "I remember sitting with you, Gekkō-kun, in your upstairs room, and—borrowing your own expression—conversing with Higashiyama spread out before us on the desk."[37] Takayasu then guided him up into the eastern hills, around Ichijōji village where Buson had tried to reconstruct one of Bashō's dwellings near Kinpukuji. Buson's description, as Noguchi put it, "dwelt reminiscently upon the place with its solitary old mosses and dozing birds among the trees, though sufficiently humanized by a grog-shop and a bean-curd seller."[38] And Jōzan Ishikawa, a retired 17th century official, "jealously guarding the solitude of forty years' self-confinement, built here Shisendo, the 'Hall of the Poets,' where he read the classics and studied calligraphy." By 1912 the romantic mists and dreams had faded, but the Higashiyama-influenced ideal home, "not far from Heaven and yet not far from town," seemed more attractive than ever.[39]

With Tokyo's population increasing at a rate of fifty percent per decade, one had to go far beyond "Far-beyond Street" to find a quiet, peaceful neighborhood with any proximity to Heaven. Access considerations kept most of the city's population living somewhere near the center, but this was starting to change, thanks to new transportation options. Following the Railway Nationalization Act of 1906, the new Chūō line, which went far west of Tokyo, was brought further into the city center: first, in 1912, to the new station opened at Manseibashi (near Kanda, where streetcars were plentiful), and then to the new Tokyo Station that opened in 1914. Noguchi had a good source of information on such developments in his railway-engineer brother, Hidenosuke.

In 1912 the town of Nakano seemed far enough down the line to escape the bustle of Tokyo, being two stations past Shinjuku, itself "still a backwater post town, with brothels lined up on both sides of the street," a station where a woman on a train might announce to her child, "We've arrived in the countryside now."[40] Nakano, he rhapsodized, had "a scenic

---

37. "Takayasu Gekkō kun," *Yomiuri*, 2 Dec. 1917, 7, rpt. *Geijutsu no tōyōshugi* (Tokyo: Daiichi Shobō, 1927), 72-81.
38. "My Ideal Home," *Spectator* 154 (15 Feb. 1935), rpt. *LE* 25, originally published as "Risō no ie" (My ideal home), *Yonejirō dokugo* (Yonejirō monologues), 1926.
39. "Shi no kondo wa yaburete," *Tsuyoi chikara yowai chikara* (Tokyo: Daiichi Shobō, 1939), 143.
40. "Shi no kondo wa yaburete," 151.

beauty with a carpet of wheat and barley responding in golden rhythm up to the bluest sky in summer, and in autumn, with such a hill of red pulpy persimmons that would surely please a screen-artist like Korin or Hoitsu."[41] Sadly, he underestimated the speed of Tokyo's accelerating urban sprawl. "Like a crab scuttling sideways, Tokyo just spreads out broadly and flatly. It's like a wildfire racing across a field."[42] It would be a decade before the most dramatic growth period began, under the pressure of post-earthquake resettlement. But changes were already underway: in 1917 Noguchi's Kashiwagi station, with its shelterless, rotting, wooden bench, was renamed Higashi Nakano (East Nakano).[43] His neighborhood of open fields, grassland, and scattered farmhouses, known simply as Hara ("The Fields") became Sakurayama (Cherry Blossom Mountain)—despite the scarcity of cherry trees. An overseas friend's envious praise of the new name left Noguchi panicked: "what if they came to Tokyo and visited me?" he wondered.

Kites circled in the sky above the train station, and in evenings sparrows twittered in the roadside zelkova trees. Owls were heard in summer and crickets in autumn. The air smelled of manure. In winter, the high ground would be shrouded in mist, with crimson moonrises reminiscent of London. The road to the site where he built his house had until recently been a narrow footpath between rice fields. "How pleased I was then to take a little walk about and look at the cottages of my neighbouring farmers over a hedge or through a bamboo thicket!" "I was so glad that the farmers, honest lovers of the seeds among the ridges, were hardworking and true, and revealed a silent history of simple lives between their clumsy fingers; I looked at their tough skin in reverence, that for many long years touched with manure."[44]

As he would later say, "The house was built during my penniless younger days with older-brother-borrowed money. It was badly designed—just rooms lined up, you might say, watching over the garden."[45] "The house and its garden," explained a visitor, "formed, roughly speaking, a square, the house occupying two sides of the square. A platform ran along the garden side of the house. The rooms opened by sliding *shoji* off the platform." Noguchi's study, the farthest from the door, was divided into two parts: six mats in the front, four-and-a-half mats in the rear. "The front portion of it, which opened on to the garden and stepping-stones, was used for reception purposes. The back portion, which could be isolated by sliding screens, was the poet's sanctum. Ordinarily it was part and

---

41. "Japanese Poet Deplores Ravages of Westernism," *Nichibei Shimbun*, 1 Feb. 1929, 8.
42. "Shi no kondo o yaburete," 145.
43. Mayumi Itoh, *The Origins of Contemporary Sino-Japanese Relations: Zhou Enlai and Japan* (New York: Palgrave Macmillan, 2016), 46.
44. "Japanese Poet Deplores Ravages of Westernism," 8.
45. "Shi no kondo o yaburete," 145.

parcel of the outer room, but differed from it by having a writing-table and chairs, and a lounge."[46] A south-facing window looked out over vast wheat fields and the Musashino forest. Through a west-facing window it was possible—for a few years—to glimpse Mount Fuji. With shojis opened, the oval writing desk looked out on the garden pines, and a small planted hill.[47]

The site started as "a cluttered wasteland overgrown with miscellaneous trees and tea bushes."[48] When Noguchi first saw it, with "the afternoon sun filtered softly through the leaves, casting golden rays like fluttering butterflies over the modest tea flowers," he was delighted by its quiet rustic charm. Surrounded by open fields and flat farmland, "it didn't seem like a place where one could easily build a settled home"— but that, he thought, was part of the appeal. One could make a garden simply by removing the unwanted trees. His choice puzzled the local farmers: "There are better spots available," they said. "What a strange fellow to choose this one." In autumn, Noguchi brought his carpenter to inspect the site and discovered "a different natural beauty: among the trees stood about eight persimmon trees, each laden with golden fruit." "Ah, how splendid!" they agreed. "Our first priority is a wide, perfectly square garden," Noguchi informed the carpenter, "The house is not so important—just build it along the garden in an L-shape. Cypress is too expensive, so use hemlock, and make sure to use Mikawa roof tiles; the rest is up to you." But fitting a 60-tsubo (200 square meter) single-story house into the 250-tsubo (.2 acre or 830 square meter) plot meant "half the persimmon trees had to be moved, two-thirds of the miscellaneous trees cut down, and even the beloved tea bushes had to be burned away." In any case, the landscaper informed him, "persimmon trees don't make good garden trees"; he might keep two if he must. For the heart of the garden, pine was of course necessary. "Bring whatever trees you think best," Noguchi told him. The landscaper then planted two Japanese black pines, a fully-grown maple brought by ten men from some distant place, a two-century-old boxwood, and, for the entrance, a towering umbrella pine.[49] "We've put in some truly magnificent trees!," the gardener declared when it was finished. "No one would have thought this neglected thicket could become such a magnificent garden!" But the budget overrun was painful.

A substantial garden was necessary for Yone, who needed a convenient place to contemplate nature, and also for his children. As Noguchi wrote in an early Japanese poem, his fairy-like daughter Fumi-chan was

---

46. James Cousins, *The New Japan*, 34; Noguchi Hironobu, "*Noguchi Yonejirō sensei no omoide*," 310-11.
47. Hironobu Noguchi, "Noguchi Yonejirō sensei no omoide," 310-11.
48. "Shi no kondo o yaburete," 157.
49. In "Rain," *Matsu no ki no Nihon* (1925), 44, Noguchi wrote, "Ten years ago, when I bought two black pines at the Araiyakushi plant market, a free wisteria came as a bonus."

a great admirer of the outdoors, holding up her hands as her sign she wanted to go outside, even before she could properly walk. "Lively little Fumi / starts to walk out and falls down flat: / a human butterfly that can't yet fly," he wrote, amused.[50]

The house was finished in the spring of 1912. On April 5, Noguchi wrote to Léonie enclosing "some twenty five or six yen." "So sorry to hear Isamu is ill. Hope he is well by this time. Yesterday your postcard came—yesterday morning, when we were so busy—moving to our new house." The house, he told her, had not been cheap. "I am somehow under a heavy debt," he told her. "I built a house which was too expensive altogether."[51] A few months later, he mentioned his move to Charles Keeler, describing the house as "quite large with a quite large garden attached to it."[52]

On the walls of the study he hung favored artworks, including a Yoshio Markino London watercolor and a woodcut print by his friend Goyō Hashiguchi, the leading print artist of the day. Naturally there were many books, filling many bookcases and eventually lining the tatami mats along the walls. Hironobu, who had the job of cleaning the books, was surprised to discover that they all seemed to have been read.[53]

In later years Noguchi would dub the house and its garden "Shi no Kondo," meaning "Golden Hall of Song," borrowing the idea, perhaps, from Sarojini Naidu's "Golden Threshold."[54] Noguchi first mentioned the name in a poem, "Shi no Kondo," published in 1927,[55] which holds the distinction of being the subject of Noguchi's only known surviving voice recording.[56]

The description of the house and garden in the poem is celebratory, religious even, in its veneration of this little refuge of poetic suburbia, with its "small-as-a-pussy's-brow garden" full of interesting plants, and an atmosphere of esoteric Buddhist contemplation: "Dainichi Nyōrai's holy place." "Here, a mere 7 or 8 minutes by train from the city center . . . I build the Golden Hall of Song memorializing eternity, healing poetry-less living things, drawing them into the mandala world." Although never mentioned, there was more than a hint of Miller's "sanctum or Holy Grotto" in Noguchi's conception of the ideal home. But a year or two later, he was decrying the "Destruction of the Suburban Beauty"

50. "Fumi-chan," *Ringo hitotsu otsu* (Tokyo: Genbunsha, 1922), 172.
51. YN to LG, 5 Apr. [1912], in LG 251-52 (misdated as 1913). According to LG 255, Yone's 25 yen contribution was around a third of Léonie's 70 yen monthly salary.
52. YN to Charles Keeler, Keeler Collection, Box 4, Huntington Library.
53. Noguchi Hironobu, "Noguchi Yonejirō sensei no omoide," 310-11.
54. Naidu's house in Hyderabad. She had earlier used the phrase to describe her youthful attainment of an authentic Indian poetic voice under the tutelage of Edmund Gosse.
55. "Shi no kondo" (Golden hall of poetry), *Shinchō* 24:10 (1 Oct. 1927): 84.
56. *Shi rōdoku: Shi no kondō* (Poetry recording: Golden Hall of Song) (Nippon Columbia, 1940), NDL Digital Collections <https://dl.ndl.go.jp/pid/3571576>, also in *Yomigaeru jisaku rōdoku no sekai II* (Rediscover the world of poets reciting their works II) (Columbia, 2008).

in essays written in both Japanese and English.[57] The extended catalog of nostalgia and complaints in the longest of these, "Shi no Kondo wa yaburete" (The Golden Hall of Song Ruined), ran to eighteen pages.[58]

Looking back, Noguchi was inclined even to praise the inconveniences of his semi-rural life, finding few reasons for gratitude in the town's modernization and eventual incorporation. Even the arrival of running water and a sewage system "were no reason for thanks," as the kitchen well had to be closed up, and the garden well reduced to a "decorative ruin." The widened road—praised by car-traveling visitors, but of little benefit to him—meant an extra twenty yen a year for twenty years, in property taxes. To widen and pave the road in front of his house, he had to pay half the cost and give up a meter of land. Land taxes rose from "practically nothing" to eighty yen a year, plus a hundred-yen-a-year tax on the house, "leaky roof, rattling shutters and all," and then income tax. The five electric street lamps installed around the house, paid for by the neighborhood association's monthly dues, made the street "so bright that, to exaggerate a bit, you could see an ant crawling by," and rendered unnecessary the charming custom Noguchi had devised of equipping visitors with small paper lanterns to navigate the pitch-black road. Gone were the days when one might glimpse in the darkness the eyes of wild raccoons and badgers.

It was all he could do to hold the line against the incursion of the telephone. On the morning of May 3, 1913, when Matsuko went into labor at 3 a.m., Noguchi ran through the dark streets to Nakano searching for a public telephone in order to call a midwife in the city. Returning to find Matsuko groaning terribly, he went out again and woke a neighboring farmer, who located a shabby-looking midwife, who delivered their second son, Masao. The next morning, the Tokyo midwife belatedly arrived. After this episode, Matsuko "became a passionate believer in the telephone," providing regular updates on the steadily-increasing prices of telephone lines, while Yone dug in his heels. "If I'm sitting at my desk trying to gather my thoughts," he would respond, "and that bell starts ringing nonstop, what then? The telephone is a tyrant—it barges in uninvited and demands a response."

Noguchi found some charm, as well, in the single shop that sold fruits and vegetables, and the arrangements with local farmers who reserved for their family a small plot of daikon radishes, and helped them plant eggplant and cucumber in a corner of their own garden. He was charmed by the daikon farmers, who in late November "tied up the pulled roots in

57. There are three versions of the English essay: "Japanese Poet Deplores Ravages of Westernism," *Nichibei Shimbun*, 1 Feb. 1929, 8 comprises the first half of "Destruction of the Suburban Beauty," *India and the World* 3:5 (May 1934): 130-31, a manuscript copy of which may be found in the Marianne Moore papers at the Rosenbach Library, Philadelphia.
58. "Shi no kondo wa yaburete," *Tsuyoi chikara yowai chikara* (Tokyo: Daiichi Shobō, 1939), 143-61.

rope and stacked them like hedges to dry in the sun"—a sight that was "beautiful in the moonlight." On dark nights, they kept sleepless watch by lantern light, and their "loudly sung folk songs" sometimes reached Noguchi's house. As New Year approached, the farmhouses erupted in the noisy pounding of mochi, mixed with shamelessly-shouted obscene songs surprising to hear so close to the modern metropolis. "These farm girls shamelessly shouting out such bawdy songs, their heads tied round with twisted hachimaki" would soon be sporting permanent waves, Western dresses, and high heels.

To preserve the sanctity of his poetic refuge, Noguchi surrounded the garden with a hedge of hinoki cypress.[59] Bought for a mere twenty sen apiece, the trees grew into "upright, disciplined soldiers," giving the home a quiet dignity. Though the house "was designed with so many flaws that it's almost unlivable," Noguchi wrote, a decade or so later, "I take pride in the hedge I planted around the garden, which I consider a success." "For someone like me, who moved here longing for the quiet atmosphere of suburban life, it has ended up just another rude, trash-strewn extension of Tokyo. I feel as though I am under siege by the encircling attack of destruction, holding out behind my defenses, guarded by those hinoki hedge soldiers."

Carpenter's Apprentice

The difficulties of Isamu's "process of self-manifestation" became more apparent in the months after the birth of his sister on January 27, 1912. After the birth, they moved again, from Omori to Chigasaki, a seaside town beyond Yokohama: "a place so small as to be unnoticed on the railway timetable, but rather famous for its clear air fragrant of the sea and pine woods which make it a resort for consumptives," as Léonie told Catherine.

48. Isamu and Ailes, 1912.

---

59. "Ikegaki" (hedges), *Ai no sen* (Oct. 1924), rpt. *Matsu no ki no Nihon*, 87.

Isamu was at the age when childhood freedom customarily gives way to powerful social constraints in Japan, but Léonie could not have known how to socialize Isamu to conform to Japanese norms even if she had wanted to—and she most certainly did not want to. Her insistence on individualism insured that Isamu's relations with his new peer group started off badly and deteriorated quickly, as he found himself the subject of the merciless bullying customarily dished out to Japanese non-conformists. Perhaps Yone felt some sympathy for his son's plight, for in a rare moment of paternalism, he paid a visit when Isamu caught the measles in the spring.[60]

In the summer of his eighth year, Léonie approached Isamu with the question, "Which would you like better, a trip to the mountains this summer, or to have a teacher of 'making things' to give you a few lessons at home?" Isamu, whose "undirected efforts at 'making things'" included, at this stage, "warships clumsily and painfully hewn out of rough pieces of wood, bristling with nails and sticky with pitch, . . . automobiles loosely patched together of old cardboard boxes, with spool wheels, . . . primitive airships, cameras and other inefficient apparatus," replied, "of course you know, Mamma, what I like best." In five lessons a "young man who knew how to make things" who taught at the Kamakura Normal School gave the boy "a few ideas to help him on his lone road." In two lessons on clay modelling they made vases, cups, elephants and warships, then "a very good and strong automobile" made out of cardboard with an exterior made from red paper. (Isamu, already inclined to outdo his teachers, "decided to make one all his own, with improvements" such as "a real glass panel in front and an instrument to measure the distance," which, though it did not match the teacher's model in neatness and strength, could comfortably accommodate his beloved Teddy Bear in the back seat. They used Dan Beard's *The Jack of All Trades* for the final two days' projects: a bright yellow paraffin-waterproofed pasteboard houseboat, and a "home-made circus" consisting of "a wooden water-wheel that turned a bar on which danced a monkey, a boy, and a horse." In their usual spirit of can-do optimism, Léonie typed up the story as "Manual Training in the Summer Vacation: A Boy's Play-Work" while Isamu spent the next day in his usual fashion, trying to make "another water-wheel far bigger and more splendid, which will not only dance monkeys, but lift heavy weights such as a toy bucket of sand or the like." Léonie was "watching to see if he will carry it to completion." She does not seem to have found a publisher for the article.[61]

Isamu's troubles, as he headed into adolescence, did not catch Léonie

60. LG to Catherine Bunnell, 14 July 1910, 23 Dec. 1910, 3 Nov. 1911, INF.
61. "Manual Training in the Summer Vacation: A Boy's Play-Work," typescript, dated "Kowada, Chigasaki, Kanagawaken, Japan. Aug.31.1913," INF. D.C. Beard, *The Jack of All Trades: New Ideas for American Boys* (New York: Scribner, 1900).

entirely unprepared. Since 1910 she had been teaching at a school in Yokohama, and in September 1913, she enrolled Isamu in a French Jesuit school there called St. Joseph's. The move offered Isamu the chance to escape his tormenting Japanese peers and develop his American side (he enrolled as "Isamu Gilmour"), but it was a move out of the frying pan and into the fire. It was unlikely Isamu would fit very well in a Catholic school, even such a multicultural one as St. Joseph's. His mother had raised him on a good Adlerian diet of Greek and Irish mythology, William Blake, and Uncle Remus (fairy tales, Adler said, "reflect the unbroken communion of human life with the life universal," stimulating the imagination and quickening the moral sentiments").[62] So it was hardly surprising that Isamu "became terribly confused" when he "learned later of God and Santa Claus." Léonie must have seen this coming, and wisely continued to offer him alternative educational opportunities on the side. As Isamu later put it, "there came a reprieve. Mother decided to build a house, and insisted that we must do it together." She had found an oddly-shaped seaside plot wedged between the palatial estates of the wealthier residents on the edge of a pine grove. There, with Isamu assisting the carpenters and reporting to his mother on their daily progress, they built "a semi-Japanese house with a round window on the second floor, which on a clear day would frame Mount Fuji off to the west."[63] Later, when Isamu refused to return to St. Joseph's, she even had him apprenticed to a Japanese carpenter.

The idea to build a house was partly an attempt to keep up with Yone and his new house in Nakano. It gave them something in common, namely, debt: Léonie had borrowed $400 from her friend Catharine Bunnell to build her house, and Yone, too, was "under the debt," and had to postpone his trip to England another year. "But I expect that I will be soon all well even in that money matter," Noguchi told her.[64]

Black-Visaged Sneak

As Yone and Léonie retreated to their separate houses, and Isamu bitterly contemplated his conflicted identity, the relationship between Japan and America was deteriorating dramatically. In May 1911, when Noguchi wrote up an amusing conversation of a group of cosmopolitan Japanese intellectuals entitled "Japanese on America and Americans," the main topics revolved around the usual amusing misunderstandings encountered by Japanese traveling in the United States. Granted, talk of war between the United States and Japan was occasionally bandied about amid talk of the "Yellow Peril" and the "Japanese Invasion," but it was hardly worth taking seriously. "We, America and Japan," an admiral

62. Felix Adler, *The Moral Instruction of Children* (New York: Appleton, 1912), 79.
63. ASW 11-12
64. YN to LG, 5 Apr. [1912], in LG 251-52 (misdated as 1913).

involved in the conversation comments, "are sane enough, earnest enough and strong enough to rise above any misunderstanding that we may have in the future; and how can we forget our historical relation?" Another participant (a philosopher), suggests that war would be a great benefit to Japan "on this condition that we shall be badly beaten," for Japan, as he saw it, was "suffering from being the 'glorious victors over Russia.'" He added that America, too, might benefit from war on the same assumption. "No cost, I dare say," he explained, "is too dear for her to get the experience of centralization of the nation's mind; is she not too scattered physically and morally?" "How, I should like to know," wonders a third, "will this Japan-American war end if both parties are to be beaten?" Such topics were clearly being discussed, even if no one seemed to be taking them seriously.[65]

When the Japanese government agreed, at President Theodore Roosevelt's request, to stop the emigration of Japanese laborers to the United States in 1908 in what became known as the Gentlemen's Agreement, it was thought that the problem was solved. But the Japanese already in California were becoming a powerful presence, particularly agriculturalists who, becoming successful, were buying their own farmlands. Moreover, a new immigration practice emerged through a loophole in the Gentlemen's Agreement that permitted the immigration of family members of already established residents, thus encouraging the immigration of "picture brides," a practice which led to increases in the numbers of Japanese born in America, who were automatically entitled to citizenship. Xenophobic Californians, hearing reports of Japanese imperial expansion, regarded these developments with alarm.

"Apparently the Californians are satisfied that the restrictions on immigration are duly observed, since we do not hear complaints on this score," the *Japan Chronicle* observed in April 1913, "but the feeling against the Japanese invasion is evidenced by the large bundle of anti-Japanese Bills now awaiting the attention of the State Legislature."[66] While the bills were being discussed, Noguchi wrote an angry letter to the *Boston Evening Transcript*, sending it also to the London *Times*, which printed an excerpt.[67] Noguchi had always approached American racism with philosophical humor, but now, for the first time, he wrote of the feelings of the Japanese facing the "almost daily fight in the streets with the urchins who called them 'Japs' at unexpected moments," the particular fear of harassment on Sunday afternoon or the Fourth of July, and the painful irony of being blamed for not participating in American activities from which they were forcibly excluded:

65. "Japanese on America and Americans," *Taiyō* 17:6 (May 1911): 10-16.
66. "The Japanese in California," *Japan Chronicle*, weekly ed., 17 Apr. 1913, 695.
67. "A Japanese on the California Case," *Boston Evening Transcript*, 3 May 1913, 3:5; "Terms of the Californian Land Bill," London *Times*, 2 May 1913, 5.

> When we were not permitted to associate freely with the white people in California, we were naturally obliged to cling to each other, in happiness as well as sadness; as we were never given any chance to develop our attachment to American history, on their national holidays we found little joy, and on our own, like the emperor's birthday, we even made the Japanese flag fly in the American air and shouted banzais to their displeasure. We had to open our own barber shop, as we were not welcomed at the American's, and for the same reason we dined at the Japanese restaurants. But as a consequence the Americans cast the most displeased look on us, and declared that, like the Chinese, we would never make good Americans and should be sent back to our own country. How could we become 'good Americans,' when we were not allowed to?

Noguchi also added accounts of many of the well-known racist incidents that had occurred in California. Although most of these happened after his departure, he had been present for some of them, such as the long fight against discrimination by Japanese laundry shop proprietor Matsunosuke "George" Tsukamoto "which started in 1899 [and] does not see yet its official settlement." Tsukamoto had "sustained many injuries at the hands of the laundry union, which was backed even by the city officers," he and his employees having been repeatedly arrested on their attempts to open the business. "In such stupidity is no meaning, except that the laundry union, with unmistakable official backing, attempted quite successfully to exterminate Mr. Tsukamoto's business."[68] Noguchi also described more recent incidents that had occurred after his departure, including discriminatory health inspections of Japanese female passengers aboard the *America Maru* in 1900, harassment of scientists like seismologist Fusakichi Ōmori and geologist Tadatsugu Kochibe, and spurious plague claims in Chinatown in 1911. There was little help in law ("we find quite often that the so-called American justice of California fails in the most selfish fashion"), nor was the Japanese government protecting the interests of the Japanese abroad ("it seems that the Japanese Foreign Offices have firmly decided to sacrifice the actual interest of the Japanese there, and also the spiritual dignity of the race, for the sake of keeping the good will between Japan and America"). The pretense of respect between the two nations was a sham: "what use it is that courtesy and respect are continually exchanged between the Governments of Tokio and Washington, when our brothers, more than fifty thousand, are not given equal right as a people from a first-class nation of the world, and in fact are treated with such humiliation, so to say, like dogs in the yard," he wondered.

68. Tsukamoto had taken his case all the way to the U.S. Supreme Court in 1902 but gave it up when it was remanded to the California Supreme Court, choosing instead to operate his laundry illegally despite continual arrests and harassment from white laundry unions. See David E. Bernstein, "Two Asian Laundry Cases," *Journal of Supreme Court History* 24:1 (1999): 95-111.

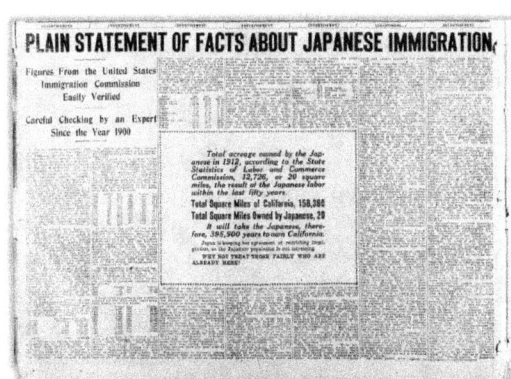

49. Pro-immigration advertisement in the San Francisco *Call*, May 1, 1913.

But over such objections, the exclusionists prevailed, and on May 19, 1913, the California legislature passed and signed into law the first Alien Land Law, which was soon imitated by the state of Washington and several others. Previous attempts at passing such laws had been struck down as unconstitutional, but this time the authors had taken advantage of a racial clause built into the first American immigration law of 1790, which provided that any "free white person" could be naturalized (people of "African descent" were added in 1870) and could thus be interpreted as excluding non-white Asians from becoming naturalized citizens. Taking advantage of this racially-biased 18th-century immigration law already on the books, the exclusionists could achieve their long-cherished goal by simply preventing "aliens ineligible to citizenship" from owning land in the state. The brilliance of the new formulation was the way it avoided any reference to the Japanese, whose interests were vigorously defended in Washington. Though the Japanese Embassy lodged a formal complaint, charging that the law made use of a political distinction to deprive the Japanese of property rights, placing them in a disadvantageous position compared with other aliens, they were unable to overturn it.

After the law's passage, Noguchi took a calmer view of the situation, sending, on May 25, another letter, this time to the *Nation* on the subject of "The Naturalization of Japanese."[69] Although continuing to argue the Japanese claim for "equal treatment with other Western people," he did not mention the new land law specifically, but took up the underlying question of citizenship. "As for the question of American naturalization being extended to Japanese," he wrote, "I doubt, as a Japanese, whether it would not be a damaging affair equally for America and Japan." The justification for this surprising position was twofold, both points deriving from his own experience. Taking up the controversial question of whether a naturalized Japanese-American would be "able to assimilate himself with America," he suggested that "true assimilation can come

---

69. "The Naturalization of Japanese," *Nation* 96 (19 Jun. 1913): 616-17.

only from intermarriage." "Now to ask more directly," he continued, "can Japanese love the American women admirably and honestly?—the women psychically as well as physically larger than their home women, besides being born and bred so differently from themselves?"

> What will be the result if a Japanese marries an American woman? The answer is short: collision, that is all. Even where there is no terrible clash, certainly there will not be a true harmony of understanding between them. How can they thoroughly understand each other since they were born from different roots?

This concern seems somewhat exaggerated—assimilation, though certainly aided by intermarriage, was possible without it, and Japanese men who intermarried did not always encounter terrible clashes and disharmony. Noguchi's second argument also derived from his own experience—that of draft-dodging: "If it is understood that any Japanese can become naturalized in America, I believe that many young Japanese, mainly to escape from military duty, would try to enter the country across the ocean." Here again, the argument seems overblown. Although Noguchi himself had managed to avoid military service during the Sino-Japanese War by remaining overseas, there is little evidence that draft-dodging emigration had been perceived as a problem in any of Japan's wars. It is surprising to note the willingness of Noguchi—who had more than once contemplated becoming an American citizen himself—to deny the Japanese capacity for assimilation. But opposition to emigration had been an official Japanese government position since the "Gentlemen's Agreement" of 1908, and Noguchi was evidently in favor of the policy. Still, he was prepared to allow for the possibility in the future:

> The time will be changed in the next fifty years under the Western education and invading civilization; our Japanese minds will certainly make the foreign assimilation easy; so I think that that question of naturalization should be left to the wise hand of time and wait for some fifty years. Even without our asking it, I am sure that America will give it to us; perhaps then we shall be able to answer more truthfully and properly to her invitation.

By shifting perspective, Noguchi was suggesting that American exclusionist policy was not as opposed to Japanese interests as it appeared when viewed from the immigrants' perspective, as he had done in his earlier article. Moreover, his prediction proved correct, as Japanese exclusion did end within fifty years without Japanese intervention, through the 1952 and 1965 immigration acts, although Asian immigration remained subject to restrictive quotas.

Time's Change

Japanese intellectuals faced a more immediate problem of restrictive laws at home in the form of government censorship. Censorship had a long history in Japan: in the Edo period, criticism of the Shōgunate, Emperor, and Confucian values had been prohibited; after 1613, there had been a ban on Christian books, a category eventually expanded to include all Western books; sexually explicit materials had long been banned (albeit ineffectually); and the Meiji government, though reintroducing Western books, had expanded and systematized censorship laws, particularly in the new laws governing newspapers that had forced the Japanese-American newspapers Noguchi worked on in California to repeatedly change their names. But the problem had recently become more serious, as Noguchi wrote in 1911: "we have no precedent in our literary annals that the writers and the Government presented such an opposite front."[70] "Since the war," he explained, "particularly in the last three years, the Japanese Government has had two objects—namely, to stamp out Socialism and 'naturalism,' which, both of them, insist on perfect individualism." The government had been using "every possible power of the police and Press law toward her end," and "many writers were supposed, in fact, to be as dangerous morally and socially as anarchists."

To some extent the writers, accustomed to being marginalized, had been pleased by the attention, at least initially. Hakuchō Masamune, the literary brother of Noguchi's artist friend Tokusaburō, wrote a story entitled "Kiken Jinbutsu" (The Dangerous Man), recounting "how the author was followed secretly or openly by detectives on his way home." More than sixty stories, magazines, and books had been suppressed the previous year in the government's effort to stamp out the bad literature, which Noguchi supposed would actually gain strength from the publicity: "when it is known that a certain story or book has been suppressed," he observed, "that story or book always grows more known in a mysterious way." The bad literature was certainly not worse than much that was being published in the West. "If Bernard Shaw were in Japan, he would have endless trouble with the Japanese Government; I see quite a number of European writers who would hardly escape from her punishment."[71]

The government had also been cracking down on the literary clubs devoted to the new literature, and one group, the Rindo-kai, had been "obliged to stop its regular meeting, as the members could not talk freely, and felt uncomfortable with the police in the next room on every occasion." An incident at a meeting of the influential *Pan no kai* (alternatively the Bread Club or the Pan Club) was characteristic:

> There is a little literary society, mainly of young writers and artists, called the Bread Club. It had a dinner party the other evening, when one young artist who was about starting to Europe for his art-study made a speech saying that he was going to a big, big world like the sea; while another young man who was called to be a soldier said, on the contrary, that he

70. "Some Phases of the Modern Japanese Literature," *Independent* (Boston) 71 (27 Jul. 1911): 186-88.
71. "The Japanese Government and the New Literature," *Academy*, 1 July 1911, 11.

was going to a narrow, narrow place like a hole. As they were playful, jolly young people, one of the artists painted the edge of the *menu* black on the spot, meaning, as I fancy, to make it appear as a death-report of that young writer who was going to "a narrow, narrow place like a hole." Now such a harmless fun-making was reported by the police to the effect that the Socialist writers cursed the soldiers, and sent their colleague to the Army with a funeral song. As a consequence, many of them were duly examined by the authorities.

Meanwhile, the government was continuing continuing to press its revival of Confucian classics as the solution to the problem of social decay. "It seems to me almost incredible that the Japanese Government, who recognises and encourages the material Westernisation, is so despotic against the new thoughts. The time is changing, but I am not ready to prophesy what the result will be for the Government who does not realise the Time's change, and even flatly denies its existence."

"For some time past the Japanese Government has been attempting to oppress the dangerous elements of thought and literature under her administration of militarism," Noguchi explained in an essay for the London *Graphic*. This was the government of Tarō Katsura, the unpopular conservative army stalwart who had spent most of the past decade as Prime Minister, after Hirobumi Itō proved unable to form a cabinet in 1901. "Is there, or was there, any Government like this of Katsura's, which endeavours to consolidate the present Japanese mind with the old Oriental Ethics? While we all laughed at its attempt of stupidity, we could not help recognising its official power under which we all were obliged to modify our attitude." The chilling effect was particularly felt among playwrights experimenting with imported European plays, like the recently staged Shaw play translated by Ōgai Mori. Noguchi had heard that "many phrases in the latter part were erased, as they doubtless would displease the Government, which might at any time stop the play,"[72] as happened the following year when the censors objected to the anti-patriarchal ending of Sudermann's *Magda* and "the Japanese translator was forced by the Government to make Magda meekly reconcile and surrender before the final curtain dropped."[73]

Government repression of radical intellectuals reached new extremes in January 1911 when twenty-four accused of plotting to assassinate the emperor were rounded up by police, given a summary secret trial resulting in quick execution for half, and imprisonment for the remainder, in what was known as the High Treason Incident. The bomb plot was real enough, but involved only three of the accused, with scant evidence tying it to the alleged mastermind, Shūsui Kōtoku, a well-known promoter

---

72. "The Artistic Interchange of East and West," *Graphic* 83 (18 Feb. 1911): 248.
73. "Sun's Japanese Critic on Drama of the New Sort and Its Troubles in Japan," *New York Sun*, 13 May 1913, 6. See also "Stage Censorship in Japan," *Japan Chronicle*, weekly ed., 20 June 1912, 1102.

of socialism, pacifism, and, lately, anarchism, who had been waging an uphill battle against the Katsura government and police since the suppression of his 1901 tract against imperialism. Noguchi was not alone in regarding Kōtoku as a "misguided, though learned" idealist. "When he stood firm for his anti-war principles at the time of the Russia-Japan War, his splendid style with the pen was universally recognized. We regret that we have rarely read his writing since he turned it is said, anarchist, as the Government fettered him with the Press Law."[74]

The incident had galvanized opposition to Katsura's government. "I passed along Ginza, the main thoroughfare of Tokyo, on the day of Kigensetsu, the [February 11] anniversary of the birth of the Imperial Throne, where people were reading the extra of the royal Rescript with its gift of 1,500,000 yen as a relief fund for helpless invalids. All of them exclaimed: 'Kotoku did not die in vain, did he?'" Acknowledging the "change in the economic condition of the nation" (presumably a reference to the ruinous postwar taxes under which the country, the lower classes, especially, still struggled), the Rescript observed, "In such a state of affairs the thoughts of people are apt to take a misguided course and to deviate from the proper way." But poverty could not be the main factor motivating the socialist and anarchist extremists, who, more often than not, they came from the middle class, Noguchi argued. When the Government went to such extremes to punish them, it only called attention, and thereby promoted, their views. By such short-sighted policies, the government was "attempting to carry out the policy of spiritual seclusion; it is not necessary to be a far-sighted prophet to foresee her failure. If she does not adopt a new method modified to the new age she has only to expect a rebellion."

There was ample evidence of these trends on display at the Maruzen bookshop near Nihonbashi, where Noguchi kept tabs on sales of foreign books. He recounted one such visit in his November 1911 essay, "The Truth About Intellectual Japan":

> I saw only a little difference between the books of today and those of one week ago; in place of a large stock of Pinero's plays the books of Phillips and even John Galsworthy (whose name was first mentioned in the press only a few days ago) were found; as before, Walter Pater and Nietzsche and George Brandes and Tolstoy are placed side by side.
>
> "Sale of Shaw is slightly falling lately, sir," the clerk said. "Chesterton is the coming man in Japan."
>
> "How about Wilde?" I ventured.
>
> "We carry quite a stock of 'Dorian Gray' and 'Salome,' as you see. However, I think the Japanese literary taste is at the turning point now; the wonder is about Maupassant, who never fails to interest Japanese students.

---

74. "Kotoku's Last Word," *Boston Evening Transcript*, 3 May 1911, 21; "The Japanese Government's Policy of Spiritual Seclusion," *Spectator*, 29 July 1911, 176.

By the way, did you read Maeterlinck's latest, 'Mary Magdalene'?"

I thanked him for his suggestion, but I had grown somewhat tired of this author, and the "Blue Bird" is still left on my table unopened. I kept my slow walk amid the books by Ibsen, Kropatkin, Strindberg, Carl Marx, Dostojowski, Wedekind and a hundred others; I observed that the work of D'Annunzio was holding a little table at the other side.[75]

In another corner were piles of unsold, government-supported Chinese classics. Buddhism, too, was going through hard times. "There is no greater decadence, I mean in relation to the intellectual Japanese life, than that of Buddhism." Buddhist priests, Noguchi noted, "neither pray, nor do they preach," Zen had come to be regarded as "an old curio," and the Buddhist temples were in a state of disrepair. "The temples that are vassals to Enkakuji, more than ten," of which Noguchi's Zōrokuan was one, "barely support themselves by letting their rooms; their impoverished condition is often appalling." And the old ethics of Bushido were "too expensive for our present life." Westernism, in contrast, remained populer. "There is nothing so easy, nothing so cheap to buy as the Western wisdom."

Our Modern Life

Noguchi sat pondering this same problem at the annual Keio faculty dinner on December 14, 1911, "the customary year-end banquet before we hasten to slip into our little nest for a wintery rest," at one of Tokyo's foreign restaurants.[76] He was suffering from acute boredom while his colleagues chattered on about the latest European cultural trends. "I read the menu from top to bottom, and again from bottom to top; when I could not find anything special, I set my eyes on the date printed at the top, 'December 14th, 1911,' as if on the name of some strange new dish." December 14, as every Japanese schoolboy once knew, was the night in which those famed paragons of Bushidō, the loyal forty-seven rōnin, carried out their long-awaited revenge plot in the year 1702.

> I raised my face to the looking-glass on the opposite side, where a large part of the scene of the banquet (What a monkey show, indeed!) was reflected, all the guests in Western dress, quite skilful in handling knives and forks, looking even natural as if they were born with butter and bread; I presently asked myself as in a dream if this was real Japan where our fathers, only fifty years ago, wore two swords in the place of the gold watch of to-day, and ate rice gruel in place of beef and lobster. Oh, what a change! And then I questioned again how true Japan could be related with the Western luxuries; I am sure that real Japan would do very well without Chamberlain's single eyeglass and

75. "The Truth about Intellectual Japan," *Taiyō* 17:8 (June 1911): 8-11.
76. "The Fourteenth of December," *Westminster Gazette*, 14 Dec. 1912, 1-2. The essay appears in slightly revised form in *TT* 66-73.

Turkish cigarette. My mind, which suddenly hated and loathed our modern life, tacitly declined to take the asparagus when they were passed round, simply from the reason of their being of foreign origin, and tried to live (bless my soul) on the very thought of the fourteenth of December.

Noguchi's mind drifted back to the days of childhood "when we little boys used to gather in the prayer room of Kojoji temple, and read, all through the night, the whole history of the loyal spirits of those forty-seven ronins under the candle lights" and were fed with rice gruel in remembrance of the ronins' dawn meal the next morning at the palace of Prince Sendai on their way to pay respects at the grave of their lord at Sengakuji Temple, "only a quarter of a mile from here where we are dining in Western fashion." "Nobody, I am sure, would believe if he were told that the *ronins* accepted with many thanks Prince Sendai's treat, suppose, of oyster patties or soft-shell crabs." As he struggled through the rather tough roast beef, he thought of the hokku poems written on the occasion by Gengo Otaka:

> It's light—
> The snow upon my hat,
> When it's mine.

The reverie was finally interrupted by Noguchi's neighbor inquiring about his silence, a signal for him to pay his obligatory respects to the assembly, after which he headed out into the cold wind and darkness, thinking how prosaic modern Japanese life had become.

Clearly the departure, earlier that year, of Basil Hall Chamberlain, professor emeritus of Japanese at Tokyo Imperial University, had not saddened Noguchi. He had some justification for his resentment of the venerable Japanologist. In 1898 the *Japan Mail*, noticing a Japanese magazine profile of Noguchi, had quoted his early poem "The Midnight Winds" published in *The Chap Book*. Chamberlain had picked it up as an amusing example of "English as she is Japped" to include among the many examples of such in the revised, third edition of his highly popular, sardonic cultural compendium, *Things Japanese*.[77] While he did not name Noguchi as the author, the poem remained in the fourth edition of 1902 and even in Chamberlain's fifth and final revision of 1905, where it was supplemented by a note in the "Books on Japan" section newly acknowledging that "several Japanese educated abroad have written books in European languages," among which he included, "though they have little relation to Japan—the so-called poems of Y. Noguchi, which have made a sensation (in California)."[78] Noguchi responded in kind, slighting Chamberlain's "single eyeglass and Turkish cigarette," and asserting that

---

77. "Monthly Summary of Current Japanese Literature," *Japan Weekly Mail*, 10 Apr. 1897, 366.
78. Basil Hall Chamberlain, *Things Japanese*, Fifth ed. (London: Murray, 1905), 73, 143.

Chamberlain had "failed when he tried to translate waka."[79]

The Meiji era came to an end in October of 1912 with the death of the emperor Mutsuhito, whose reign (beginning in 1868) had encompassed the whole trajectory of Japanese responses to the West: from desperate resistance and rebellion to enthusiastic embrace and imitation. The mood Noguchi was now chronicling seemed a kind of weariness with the whole business. The hero of the day was General Nogi, "the Hero of Port Arthur, who committed suicide, or *junshi*, to use our Japanese word meaning a royal death, in following his master (the late Mikado) to the other world, on the very same evening when the Imperial hearse left the Palace." There was a medieval simplicity in this unexpected gesture of Nogi—and of his wife, who followed him (though this did not receive much comment)—that caught the attention of Japan and the world, and seemed to prove Nitobe's claim that the spirit of Bushidō was not entirely lost in the modern world. Even Noguchi was moved to new heights of nationalist eloquence: [80]

> General Nogi died as a protest against the modern tendency of imbecility and effeminacy, and as the encourager of the old Bushido precepts. He was right when his old Samurai heart grew restless and wounded from seeing the real fact that, not to China this time, but to Western nations, we were making kowtows and indiscriminately importing their literature and philosophy, even the dangerous individualism which would upset the Empire's spiritual foundation; and he saw enough, I fancy, to know that even the soldier class, who have promised life's whole devotion to the Mikado and his country, were growing to be lovers of money and Western luxuries, and I believe that he wished to warn us of the danger, and to point out to us, before it was too late, the true, only road we should follow, as Japanese.[81]

The fourteen-year reign of the new emperor, Yoshihito, known as the Taishō era (1912-1926), would be an even more tumultuous period for Japan and the world.

---

79. "Gyosei no Eiyaku hiyō," 42.
80. "On the Suicide of Gen. Nogi," *Nation* (New York) 95 (17 Oct. 1912): 352.
81. "Why Count Nogi Died: The Soul of a Samurai," *Graphic* 86 (26 Oct. 1912): 614. See also "Home of Gen Nogi in Tokio Now a Place of Pilgrimage," *New York Times*, 19 Oct. 1913, C4.

5

Distinguished Lecturer

1913-1914

Noguchi had been strengthening his connections with the British press since 1909, when he began sending illustrated articles to a popular large-format weekly, *The Graphic*. In 1910, after *The Academy* had favorably reviewed his Hearn book, calling it "the most valuable contribution that has at present appeared on this fascinating subject," he had sent off a letter to the magazine on the subject of Bushidō. His friendship with Inazō Nitobe having cooled, Noguchi was now prepared to divulge that Bushidō, the basis for all manner of recent theories about the Japanese, was commonly regarded in Japan as "a sort of fiction." He refrained from opining whether it had ever existed, but was sure "it does not exist in the present heart of Japan. . . . Our present Japanese life has . . . nothing to do with Bushido."[1]

The provocative letter was well-timed. A colossal Japanese-British Exhibition had opened in London in May 1910, in anticipation of the expected renewal of the Anglo-Japanese Alliance. And *The Academy* had recently "passed into the hands of a new proprietor" (having been sold off by Lord Alfred Douglass to pay off legal debts) and was to be "conducted on original lines" in hopes of increasing circulation.[2] Noguchi was soon a favored contributor, placing more than twenty essays over the next two and a half years, most of which he used in his collection, *Through the*

1. "Correspondence," *Academy* 79 (24 Dec. 1910): 630. An American journalist who later publicized Noguchi's "leaving his gifted 'American' wife to rear in brave fight against terrible poverty his gifted children," added: "never, however, would [Léonie] permit a word to be spoken against [Yone]—which estranged her from the indignant Mrs. Nitobe, who bristled at mention of the name of Yone Noguchi." Upton Close, *Challenge: Behind the Face of Japan* (New York: Farrar & Rinehart, 1934), 173.
2. *Academy*, 2 July 1910, 3; *The Autobiography of Lord Alfred Douglas* (London: Secker, 1929), 219-25; Harford Montgomery Hyde, *Lord Alfred Douglas: A Biography* (London: Methuen, 1984), 171.

Torii. Around the same time, in late 1910, he began contributing also to the London weekly, *The Nation*, beginning with "My Boyhood Sorrow," a translation of a story by Doppō Kunikida, whose authorship he omitted to mention.³ Three pieces went to *The Open Window*, a short-lived little magazine that began in 1911 and lasted a year. *Rhythm*, an avant-garde magazine founded in 1911 by John Middleton Murry, who edited it with his sometime partner, Katherine Mansfield, lasted nearly two years before their publisher ran off with the magazine's funds, leaving them unable to pay Noguchi, who had been asked to "send . . . a letter from Japan and write regularly."⁴ Even so, he sent a final contribution, "Daibutsu," for the magazine's successor, *The Blue Review*, before it, too, ceased publication in 1913.

Lest any still doubt his Anglophilia, Noguchi wrote two obsequious poems in honor of the coronation of King George V in 1911: a coronation poem that appeared the *Japan Mail* and *The Graphic*,⁵ and a poem entitled "To England," in the *Taiyō*, which ended:

> England, thou who only knowest Eternity's Promised Land,
> Hold our sad and true hearts in thy safest hands!⁶

"I received many good letters from England; but I might postpone one more year, I mean my going to England," Noguchi wrote Léonie in April 1913.⁷

By that point, the new poet laureate, Robert Bridges, was busy arranging an invitation for Noguchi to lecture on Japanese poetry at Oxford. Back in 1903, Noguchi had included Bridges among his pamphlet recipients and "jolly companions." In the spring of 1913, Bridges wrote to Laurence Binyon, now head of the Department of Oriental Prints and Drawings at the British Museum, asking if Noguchi was a suitable choice for the invitation. Binyon consulted his Japanese connections and informed Bridges that "there is general agreement that while Noguchi is not considered to be a man of very great erudition, he is thought highly of as an interpreter of the spirit & genius of Japanese poetry." Binyon had read enough of Noguchi's articles to feel confidence in the Japanese poet's knowledge, and thought him capable of giving excellent lectures.⁸

Some glimpses of preparations for Noguchi's departure may be found in Hōmei Iwano's diaries.⁹ On October 15, an early Noguchi farewell party, with Ariake Kanbara, Tokusaburō Masamune, and Gekkō

3. "My Boyhood Sorrow," Nation 8:9 (26 Nov. 1910): 365-67. An earlier version in Taiyō 14:12 (Sept. 1908): 20-24, acknowledged "This is from Kunikida's Doppo Shu," Doppo having died of tuberculosis in June of that year.
4. John Middleton Murry and Katherine Mansfield to YN, 11 Dec. 1912, CEL 398.
5. "Japan's Salute: A Coronation Ode," Graphic 83 (27 June 1911): 52; "Coronation Song from Japan," Japan Weekly Mail 55 (24 June 1911), 775.
6. "To England," Taiyō 17:10 (July 1911): 19.
7. CEL 400; "Correspondence," Academy 79 (24 Dec. 1910): 630.
8. Laurence Binyon to Robert Bridges, 16 June 1913, Berg Collection, NYPL.
9. Iwano Hōmei, *Hōmei zenshū* 12 (Tokyo: Kokumin Tosho, 1921), 199.

Takayasu, was held at Sanchasō (Mountain Teahouse). Over the next week and a half, Noguchi continued to correspond with Iwano, who was rushing his translation of *The Symbolist Movement in Literature* through the press so Noguchi could personally deliver a copy to Arthur Symons. On the 23rd, Iwano went to Shinchōsha, picked up two copies, and then visited Noguchi. The two then went to visit Ariake Kanbara, who joined them for a farewell party in Ginza, followed by a second party at a cafe called the New York Kitchen, where someone named Kurimoto joined them. At 9 p.m. Noguchi was sent off on his journey.

The following day, Iwano sent to the ship his latest revision of the English translation of his article comparing Confucian scholar Wang Yangming with the American writer Ralph Waldo Emerson. Iwano had been consulting Noguchi about the piece since spring, and had alreadyhad it rejected by *The Open Court* in Chicago and *East and West* in Bombay. It was still unpublished when Iwano died six years later. "This English writing was the so-called Iwano-style English, clear but not excellent as English. No English magazine wanted to publish it, so I still have the manuscript," Noguchi recalled.[10]

Noguchi had plenty of reading time during the month-and-a-half voyage. After a delay occasioned by a slight collision in Yokohama Bay, the *Kamo Maru*, one of the larger (8,500 ton) steamers on the Tōyō Kisen Kaisha's European line, headed off to Kobe. The ship reached Shanghai on October 29, followed by Hongkong, Singapore, Penang, Colombo, Suez, Port Said, before reaching its destination of Marseilles on December 9.[11] "Mr. Yone Noguchi, the Japanese poet, has left Tokyo for a lecturing tour in England, where he expects to arrive about the middle of December," the London *Times* reported in late November.

A Perch for Fowls

In the several years since *The Pilgrimage*, Noguchi had continued to use Elkin Mathews as his London bookseller. Mathews had taken on *Lafcadio Hearn in Japan* in 1910 and a new edition of *The American Diary of a Japanese Girl* in 1912. Now in preparation for his trip he assembled a selection of essays written over the last half-decade, to be called *Through the Torii*, to be printed in Japan for release on his arrival in England.

The *torii*, the distinctively shaped gate, usually painted bright vermilion, marking the entrance to a Shintō shrine or sacred space, is another of the symbols of passage and crossing used by Noguchi as a general title for his literary efforts. The origin of these distinctive structures, found throughout Japan, remains the subject of debate. In his essay on Kamakura's famous Hachiman shrine written around this time, Noguchi gives the following explanation of the torii:

10. "Iwano Hōmei kun o itamu (I mourn for Hōmei Iwano)," *Waseda Bungaku* 175 (1 Jun. 1920): 175.
11. London *Times*, 26 Nov. 1913, 11.

It is merely an assemblage of four lines of stone (often of wood); but it is one of the creations of art, like the obelisk or the pyramid, quite an impressive and original symbolic gate. Whether it came from the sacred heart of Northern India or elsewhere, there is something of the beginning of man, when he lived and talked with the birds. As the name Torii indicates, it may be nothing but a perch for fowls; is it not right to fancy then, that it is the very place where they hail the daybreak? There is no other sight like the daybreak that takes one's mind at once back to the age of mythology and nature-worship when our ancestors (nay gods) lived primitively like the fowls on that Torii, under the thatched roof of *kaya* grass; if there is a proper entrance to a Shinto shrine, the shrine of our ancestors or heroes, that is the Torii; primitiveness only inspires reverence pure and simple, that you never feel before a Buddha temple. You will become awestruck by the silence that flows from the complexity of Buddhism; but we have a human strength in the simplicity of Shintoism.[12]

Through the Torii is, of the books Noguchi published in his lifetime, the one that gives the widest sense of his range as a prose writer. The thirty-six essays—not, in all cases, his best—fall into five categories: Japanese places, criticism of contemporary Japan, Japanese attitudes toward nature, Noguchi's thoughts on Western literature and art, and Noguchi's philosophical thoughts on themes like "art," "life," and "truth." They may also be divided according to the very different publications in which they were originally printed: the bilingual *Taiyō*, the solidly English *Academy*, Horace Traubel's radically Whitmanistic *Conservator*, and the London avant-gardism of John Middleton Murry and Katherine Mansfield's *Rhythm*. But none of the essays from Noguchi's American period were included, nor any of the pieces from the *Japan Times*.

On his arrival in Marseilles, Noguchi sent letters to friends announcing his impending arrival. One was to his old friend Yoshio Markino to whom he had promised a quick return to London ten years earlier. "You must be very much changed," he wrote. "At least I am." He wondered whether Markino—now a successful illustrator, publishing his memoirs, and living in fashionable South Kensington, would be as good a friend to him as before. "Markino, ten years ago at Brixton!" Noguchi exclaimed. "Have you ever thought of our Brixton days? I have very often."[13] Another letter was to an American photographer in London, Alvin Langdon Coburn, with whom he had been corresponding since the previous year.[14] And a third was to Edmund Gosse, to whom he had dedicated *Through the Torii*, an advance copy of which he sent under separate cover. "The day after tomorrow," he told Gosse, "I will be in Paris, and I hope to see London on the 15th." "Dear Professor," he entreated Gosse, "can't I

---

12. *Kamakura* 74-75.
13. "Yoshio Markino," *JT*, 4 Mar. 1917.
14. Alvin Langdon Coburn, "Yone Noguchi," *Bookman* (London) 46 (Apr. 1914): 36.

call on you on the 15th? If it is not inconvenient to you, please give me your hour (when you can see me)." "You are the first person I must make my homage in London," he explained. Noguchi's promotion of Gosse to the first rank among his literary associates had several likely causes: first was Gosse's admiration of *The Pilgrimage:* "your delicate fancy and your tender sympathy with rare and elusive forms of beauty have become more intense, and command a wider and surer vocabulary," he had written, appreciating how Noguchi aimed to "preserve the attitude and the expression of Japanese while employing with increasing mastery the language of England."[15] Noguchi would also have read the introduction to Sarojini Naidu's latest collection in which Gosse recounted how he had shown Sarojini "the way to the golden threshold" of poetry by entreating her to become "a genuine Indian poet of the Deccan, not a clever machine-made imitator of the English classics."[16] Gosse recognized Noguchi too as a poet who did "not attempt to imitate Western thoughts and feelings," aiming to deliver to Western readers "the impress of the purely Japanese imagination."[17]

50. Edmund Gosse.

When the overnight train from Marseilles deposited him at the Gare de Lyon, Noguchi found a Paris that "looked still sleepy, although it was quite late in the morning."[18] The season, early winter "when nature turns her eyes down to the ground," felt like the wrong time to visit the city. He was struck by "how different is the French atmosphere from that of England," there was "exquisite charm" he admitted, but also "much of what is false and what is called blasé"; he supposed "the artificial world called

15. Gosse to YN, 6 Mar. 1910, *CEL* 392; Gosse, "Introduction" to Sarojini Naidu, *The Bird of Time* (London: Heinemann, 1912), 5.
16. Edmund Gosse, "Introduction," in Naidu, *The Bird of Time*, 1-8.
17. YN to Edmund Gosse, 9 Dec. 1913, author's collection.
18. "Time by 'Rapide,' about 12 hours" according to *Bradshaw's Through Routes* (London: Blacklock, 1913), 117; YN, "A Japanese Impression of Paris," *Japan Weekly Mail*, 14 Feb. 1914, 200.

Paris is merely a creation of sensuousness and insincerity." And he "could not help feeling sad and uncomfortable with the people here who never looked real enough but impressed my mind as a thing even morbid."

On his first night in Paris, Noguchi had trouble sleeping. "I felt so stupid next morning that I could not get up early; as I had only a day or two to stay here, I could not assume a role of a Parisian who wishes to spend all the morning in musing on the absurdity of the last night; besides I had to fulfil my friend's desire in seeing Carrière's portrait of Paul Verlaine at Luxembourg."[19]

He was happy that England seemed already to begin at the *Gare du Nord*, where he could buy his "beloved old Punch" with English money before boarding the train to the channel.[20] "People in Paris must have thought me an idiot or something quite superhuman," he confessed, "as, when I took a 'bus or bought a picture postcard or a necktie, I had to spread out the French money in a row upon my palm and let them take whatever they liked." The porter who carried his Japanese bamboo portmanteau to his train compartment happily received what was left over. The familiarity of the American travelers who surrounded him in the dining car was less welcome; listening to the "terribly nasal voices" chattering about the prices of chickens and pigs, Noguchi wondered whether he had not somehow boarded a train bound for Chicago or Pittsburg. Escaping to his cabin, he tried his best to dream of "dear old smoky London" (now said to be somewhat less smoky) after an absence of ten years.

His seasickness crossing the Channel was not improved by the continual reappearance of "the old smiling boy" announcing the time remaining, an unmistakable reminder of Noguchi's return to the troublesome world of tipping. Characteristically, Noguchi found himself without the requisite coin, and felt obliged to part with a golden half sovereign. On the night train from Dover, when Noguchi's "sense of time and direction had all been lost under the heavy mantle of dark clouds or rocks," London seemed no dream city but rather the hallucinatory nightmare of Thompson's "City of Dreadful Night." "The bare trees of the roadside against the dark sky looked as if a sentinel was guarding the pass to hell." With a terrible burst of noise the train pulled into London, and moments later Noguchi found himself out on the Strand, where ten years ago, his soul, "A ghost from the unknown air, a fay from the mist into the mist," had strayed down "the torrent of life." Now again he was going to cast the chance of his "Eastern gondola of soul" against the high tide of the West.

19. "A Japanese Impression of Paris," 200. The Verlaine painting, acquired by the Musée du Luxembourg in 1910, was moved to the Louvre in 1933 and to the Musée d'Orsay in 1977.
20. "Again in London," SYN 139. Six daily express trains left Paris-Nord for London, via Calais or Boulogne, a 6½ hour trip with one hour at sea, according to *Kelly's Manufacturers and Merchants Directory* (London: Kelly's, 1914), 508.

Old and New Friends

At his hotel, the first letter he found was from Markino. "Yes, ten years ago!," Markino wrote. "I cannot help thinking that we two are taking a part in a play. Our Brixton days were our first act. Now the curtain of the second act is rising. Indeed, these ten years seem only ten minutes interval between the two acts." "My 'phone rung on Saturday morning" (actually, it was Sunday), "and a voice said: 'I am Yone. I arrived last night.' I told him to come to my studio at once, and I waited his coming very impatiently."[21]

As Noguchi recalled it: "It was late Saturday night that I arrived here; and on the Sunday morning I already found myself in Markino's Studio at No. 39 Redcliffe Road, South Kensington." He had donned his kimono and traveled by taxi. Markino, who was on the balcony waiting for him, waved as he stepped out, shouting, "O-i, Noguchi I am here; can't you see?" There were tearful embraces, comparisons of hair loss and graying, and sad discussions about the death of their mutual friend, the artist Bushō Hara, and more recently, of Noguchi's father.[22]

51. Yoshio Markino.

The conversation was interrupted by the arrival of a reporter—probably the *Daily News* reporter whose story ran with Markino's account the next day.[23] "It was luncheon time when the interviewer was gone," Markino

21. Yoshio Markino, "Yone Noguchi," London *Daily News*, 15 Dec. 1913, 6.
22. YN, "Yoshio Markino," *JT*, 4 Mar. 1917.
23. "Poet's Servant Who Became Professor," London *Daily News*, 15 Dec. 1913, 2.

wrote. "I suggested that we should eat something in my room instead of going out; for we were too excited and quite unfit for a restaurant. Yone agreed with me, so we two ate my usual daily humble food—beefsteak and potatoes—and smoked the commonest Virginia cigarettes, which Yone said 'reminded him of our Brixton days very much.'"

Over the ensuing months, Markino's new studio, fifteen feet square with a little bedroom attached, and full of beautiful furniture—£263 worth, he told Noguchi—became the visiting poet's refuge "whither I at once escaped when I was bored by people."

Markino had made his breakthrough in 1907 with the publication of a book of his London paintings, *The Colour of London*, with text by antiquarian William John Loftie, accompanied by a simultaneous exhibition of the original paintings. The success of the book had led to a steady run of pleasant assignments for illustrated books on Paris, Rome, Oxford, and Italy, as well as a quirky tribute to English womanhood entitled *My Idealed John Bullesses* (with his own text), and three volumes of autobiographical writing beginning with the highly successful *A Japanese Artist in London*.[24]

52. Alvin Langdon Coburn, self-portrait.

Noguchi did not remain long after lunch, for he had worn his Japanese kimono at the request of photographer Alvin Langdon Coburn. "And so on a bright December morning he came," Coburn wrote, "looking more like a poet in his Japanese garments than I believed it possible for any human being to look in these modern times. We talked of books and art through the morning and afternoon, and I made the much desired and long anticipated photographs."[25]

24. Yoshio Markino, *A Japanese Artist in London* (London: Chatto & Windus, 1910).
25. Alvin Langdon Coburn, "Yone Noguchi," *Bookman* (London) 46 (Apr. 1914): 33-36. Coburn's portrait of Noguchi looking over his shoulder was used in several *Daily News* articles as well as Coburn's Noguchi essay in the *Bookman*. A frontal portrait with left arm extended illustrated "Mr. Kimono on Cockaigne," *Graphic* 89 (10 Jan. 1914): 70. A portrait of Noguchi reading a copy of *Seen & Unseen* was included in Coburn's 1922 portraiture volume, *More Men of Mark*. Other images from the Coburn session are in the George Eastman House archives.

53. Noguchi photographed by Alvin Langdon Coburn, December 14, 1913.

Edmund Gosse had also received Noguchi's letter and responded by inviting Noguchi to a night reception at his home at Hanover Terrace. When Noguchi arrived, it was already after ten o'clock and the room was full of guests. "With my own name, which was loudly announced at the door, I confess, I was somehow frightened; this was my first experience after fully ten years, with the so-called reception."[26] Noguchi found himself drawn out by Gosse and his wife and daughters, "skilful in introducing one guest to another, quietly chucking in a little bright saying to make the party interested." Noguchi soon found himself talking with Holbrook Jackson, the editor and art critic whose famous book on the 1890s would shortly be published.[27] Jackson pointed out the well-known humorist Max Beerbohm. As Noguchi expected, Beerbohm "looked quite a dandy in appearance, with all the correctness in dress and even with a touch of poseur most natural for the most matured person." Noguchi, upon being introduced, humbly declared what an honour it was to know him personally, at which Beerbohm "strangely smiled," and in his smile Noguchi "read at once his reproof of the rawish and green language of mine which was forbidden in the cultured English society." Beerbohm was "an incarnation of quietude," as was his old friend Laurence Binyon who "was standing with his wife by the door, quite aloof from the tumult of the room."[28]

26. YN, "Literary England Before the War," *Japan Times*, 7 Aug. 1917.
27. That Coburn also attended Gosse's party with Noguchi is suggested by Noguchi's comment, in "Kōban" (Coburn), *Kiri no Rondon* (Tokyo: Genbunsha, 1923), that Coburn introduced him to Holbrook Jackson. He also credited Coburn with introducing him to the poet [W.H.] Davies, arranging his lunch with George Bernard Shaw, and taking him to the home of John Masefield, and, on many occasions, the theatre.
28. Noguchi introduced Beerbohm to Japanese readers in "Ei bundan no datesha" (A dandy of the literary world), *Yomiuri*, 6, 7, 8 Oct. 1915, 6, rpt. *Ōshū* 88-99.

54. Georg Brandes, 1913.

The Danish scholar George Brandes was more forceful, assaulting Noguchi like a Northern Viking with outstretched hand saying, "I know you, I know you, since I have read your book of poems, the 'Pilgrimage'"; Noguchi soon discovered that not only had Brandes received the copy of the book but that he had even reviewed it in a Danish magazine, and wondered whether the review hadn't been translated yet into Japanese. "Oh, how I wished that his English were more easy to take hold of," Noguchi lamented. "He was throwing over me an avalanche of speech whose meaning I had only to imagine, when Gosse pulled his arm and led him away, saying: 'Brandes mustn't monopolize Noguchi, nor Noguchi Brandes.'" Later, when saying farewell after refreshments had been served, Brandes told Noguchi that he "was an object of particular interest, because he had seen a Japanese before only once in the person of a certain captain, perhaps of a pirate ship."

In Noguchi's account of "My First Night in London," written for the *Daily News* a few days later, and reprinted as the first part of "Again in London" in his autobiography, Noguchi omitted all of the interesting events of the day, dwelling instead on the uncomfortable channel passage, the ever-present "smiling boy" waiting for tips, his own habit of overpaying, and the pain in his legs from the hard pavements.[29] His complaints did not go unnoticed by his old nemesis at the *Japan Chronicle*, Robert Young, who wrote, in mock commiseration:

> Instead of having clean and soft, nicely-made roads, such as Mr. Noguchi is used to in Japan, the pavements in London are so hard that the poor poet got terrible pains in his legs after a five minutes' walk. How he must have longed for the sweet, soft mud of Dai Nippon's roads! One can imagine him sitting wearily on the steps of one of the Clubs in Pall Mall, taking off his boots, and nursing his poor feet in one hand while writing poetry with the other:—

---

29. YN, "My First Night in London," London *Daily News*, 19 Dec. 1913, 6, rpt. "Again in London: I," *SYN* 139-44.

> The air of London,
> It is the colour of rubies; but—
> O! my poor feet.³⁰

At least Noguchi had provoked Young into writing a half-decent haiku.

Noguchi's successful debut appearance naturally led to an invitation to the January meeting of the Poets' Club, the group Gosse and Henry Newbolt had founded in 1908, which met at Mayfair's United Arts Club for monthly dinners accompanied by readings and speeches. The Poets' Club was an important meeting place for both established and aspiring poets. But it had all of the deficiencies that might be expected of such an institution, and was virulently disliked by younger writers like Ezra Pound, who dismissed it as an "arthritic milieu" inhabited by "Gosse's generation" whom he called "contemptible" and "mingy" (though usually not to their faces). Pound had been delighted when F.S. Flint attacked the club in the *New Age*, contrasting its "suave tea-parties" to Verlaine and his contemporaries "conning feverishly and excitedly the mysteries of their craft"; soon afterward, he and Flint had joined together with T.E. Hulme—then the club's secretary—to form an alternative group which met Thursday nights in the more Verlainesque surroundings of the Tour Eiffel restaurant, where they lamented the state of English verse and experimented with alternative forms—free verse, tanka and haikai—transforming themselves into *les Imagistes*.³¹ In 1911 after Hulme began a relationship with Ethel "Dolly" Kibblewhite, the meetings became a Tuesday night salon in her father's elegant residence at 67 Frith Street.

As it happened the day after Gosse's party was a Tuesday, and no time was lost in presenting Noguchi with an invitation. Harold Monro, owner of the Poetry Bookshop and editor of the *Poetry Review* (to which Noguchi had contributed a brief statement the previous year), apologizing for not writing earlier, offered a last-minute invitation to a performance of Ibsen's *The Wild Duck* at the St. James Theatre, "& afterwards to my friend Hulme in Soho, where you will meet several painters & literary folk."³² "The house in Soho Square where I was taken," Noguchi wrote,³³ "had the most wonderful twisted staircase, which alone was a sufficient proof that the house had once belonged to a Venetian minister as well as to Hazlitt. The general atmosphere with a Latinised touch made an interesting background for the young insurgents of London, literary or artistic, who talk desultorily on the movements of the day, or read their own prayers. Here I found Joseph Epstein, the sculptor, whose Wilde Monument at Pere Lachaise cemetery made him a subject of discussion; Wyndham Lewis, the

---

30. F.A.G. [Robert Young], "Stray Notes," *Japan Chronicle*, weekly ed., 22 Jan. 1914, 134.
31. Humphrey Carpenter, *A Serious Character: The Life of Ezra Pound* (Boston: Houghton Mifflin, 1988): 113, 115, 118.
32. Harold Monro to YN, 16 Dec. 1913, *CEL* 401.
33. "A Japanese Poet in Literary England," New York *Evening Post*, 14 Apr. 1917, 3:1, 14.

cubist, of whom I once impolitely wrote that he was at least as bad as Alma Tadema, and also T. E. Hume [sic], who had, to use Ezra Pound's prefatory words, set an enviable example to many of his contemporaries in publishing complete [poetical] works of five pages.[34] Through the smoke Japanese ladies, or geishas of Utamaro or Kiyonaga on the wall, peeped with their little coquettish eyes, while our talk exhausted our vocabularies of laughter and sneering over the English stupidity." Noguchi seems to have had mixed feelings about these "young insurgents," and they about him. He mentions "my young philosopher friend, Hulme" again in his Japanese essay on Beerbohm, but that is all. For their part, the Imagists as a group were less enthusiastic than might have been expected in their embrace of the visiting Japanese poet. Yoshinobu Hakutani has described the "accord between the imagists and Noguchi" in terms of shared principles and patterns of likely influence of ideas.[35] But it seems to have been an uneasy alliance. Pound never mentioned Noguchi in print, nor did Hulme, Flint, or Aldington. Noguchi returned the favor, neglecting to mention Imagism in accounts of his trip, although Pound's anthology, *Des Imagistes*, came out in February while he was in the U.K. When Noguchi did come to write about Imagism, in a 1918 essay for a special magazine issue on the topic, he denied knowing much about it, and only mentioned D. H. Lawrence and Amy Lowell by name.[36]

Noguchi did describe the salon in two Japanese essays. One was about his experiences with women in the literary world. "Near Soho Square in this area, the poets and painters of the new school host soirées every Tuesday night. I, too, have been a few times, accompanied by my poet friend Monro, and on the walls of the room, there are woodblock prints by Japan's Utamaro and Hokusai, as well as old Dutch-made plates on display. On the central table, there's a whisky bottle, soda water, a tall pile of fruit, and men and women gathered in the room (at such soirées, there are often more women than men, with a ratio sometimes as high as 7 to 3) freely drinking and eating as they please. Of course, smoking is allowed, and the conversations are far from ordinary. Some women even debate politics, there's talk about art, and evaluations of plays. I saw the prominent cubist painter Lewis, who is famous in modern-day England, being mercilessly criticized by the women."[37] The other essay, about Henri Gaudier-Brzeska, was published after Noguchi received news about the artist's death in 1915. "I found it quite enjoyable to sit across from Brzeska, who, though rough in manners, was pure at heart and proud of his inner

---

34. "The Complete Poetical Works of T.E. Hulme" was a five-page appendix to Ezra Pound's *Ripostes* (London: Swift, 1912).
35. Yoshinobu Hakutani, "Ezra Pound, Yone Noguchi, and Imagism," *Modern Philology* 90 (Aug 1992), 68.
36. "Shashōshugi shaken" (My view of Imagism), *Gendai Shika* (Modern poetry) 3:2 (Mar. 1918), rpt. NY, *Shosai no shōsoku* (News from the study) (Tokyo: Daiichi Shobō, 1927): 104-11.
37. "Bungeikai no Ōfujin" (Women of the literary world), *Ōshū* 67-68.

cleanliness, even if his clothes were dirty. As the time neared midnight, everyone started drinking punch and whiskey recklessly, but as I had no connection to alcohol, I focused on my cigarettes, sitting back in a chair before the wall where four or five paintings of courtesans by Utamaro hung, and I discussed art with him. The room, thick with smoke and growing dim, seemed to deepen the atmosphere of mental tension, almost enhancing the intimate interest of the drawing room. During my time in London, I had entered many drawing rooms, but I had never witnessed such a tragically heavy and solemn gathering that stimulated one's eternal anguish. We were always about fourteen or fifteen people here, each carrying our own solitude. As the night deepened and we talked in the dimly lit room, filled with the smell of liquor and cigarette smoke, I began to think that the assembled group were not simply individuals shaped by personal ideas, but rather embodied spirits of young artists starving for the desire for vibrant art."[38]

Noguchi had many opportunities to attend the theater during his visit, and he had no objection even to such Christmas fare as *Babes in the Woods* and *Sleeping Beauty Reawakened*, finding in them an "innocent English enjoyment" in contrast to the modern plays with their troubling obsessions with life's difficult questions.[39] He did not avoid those, taking in two Shaw plays—*The Doctor's Dilemma* and *Pygmalion*—as well as the obligatory "Oriental play" (*Mister Wu*, at the Strand, which gave him an opportunity to complain about the actresses "who may have never seen a Chinese girl except on a paper label on a box of tea") and also plays by the ever-popular Granville-Barker and Arnold Bennett. He also satisfied his curiosity about the latest of cultural imports, the tango, newly arrived from Latin America and rearing its naked thighs in the saucy *Hullo, Tango* on view at the Hippodrome. If only to determine whether the fuss was exaggerated, he attended, and found the dancers with little skirts "as if they were dancing half naked or only in their loin cloth which we Japanese call imoji; the sight was highly improper indeed. Only a skilful man would be able to make the dance interesting when he has only to touch his lady's fingers, take a short walk away from her, then return and again walk round her with a strange gaze."

On December 23, Robert Bridges wrote to explain about the Oxford lecture. He had discussed it with Dr. T. Herbert Warren, the president of Magdalen College and professor of poetry, and thought one of the last four days of January would be best. He thought Dr. Warren would invite Noguchi to stay at his house, and Bridges would be glad if Noguchi would also stay a night at his home, although it was somewhat inconveniently located five miles out of town. As for the topic of the lecture,

38. NY, "Seinen chōkokuka no senshi" (A young sculptor's death in battle), *Yomiuri*, 3, 4, 5 Nov. 1915, 7, rpt. *Ōshū* 231.
39. YN, "A Japanese on the English Stage," *Japan Times*, 29 Apr. 1917.

which was to last one hour, he thought the audience would want to hear what Japanese poetry sounded like, and recommended that Noguchi prepare a handout with transliterations of some suitable poem.

"About a week after I arrived in London, I was invited by Yeats to have dinner at a hotel near Euston Station."[40] Noguchi brought up the dinner only to explain how it happened that Yeats had told him some interesting news: "Right now, the Indian poet Sarojini Naidu is in London."[41] Naidu's absence from Gosse's party was perhaps due to the medical treatment for which she had come to London. "She isn't seriously ill," Yeats explained, "but for the past few days, she has been resting at a sanatorium on Park Lane, on Hyde Park, to recuperate from her fatigue." "I saw her at a tea party a few days ago and we had a good talk. She was very pleased to hear you had come to London and is hoping to meet you soon." Some four or five days later, Noguchi received a letter from Naidu, asking him to visit.

Noguchi had first heard of Naidu from Edith Thomas in New York. Thomas, having met the young Indian poet during a London visit, gave Noguchi her address in Hyderabad, telling him "you two Easterners must come together." But he had forgotten about it until seeing her first book of poems, *The Golden Threshold* (1905), with its glowing introduction from Arthur Symons. Noguchi praised the volume warmly in a *Japan Times* review, and may have initiated a correspondence with her at that time.[42]

When Noguchi visited her in London, it was, he wrote, a foggy December afternoon. "She took hold of my hand and said, 'I have longed to meet you for so long a time: ten, maybe fifteen years.'" They were, he thought, like birds or butterflies that had lost their way and found each other in a distant land.

55. John Masefield.

40. "Tō joshijin Naijiu" (The fighting poetess Naidu), *Sōshiden* (1943), 294-95. One should, of course, approach such stories skeptically, but as corroboration, there is a copy of *Through the Torii* in Yeats's library carrying the dedication "To W.B. Yeats/Yone Noguchi/ Christmas Night 1913." See Edward O'Shea, *A Descriptive Catalog of W. B. Yeats's Library* (New York: Garland, 1985), 191.
41. Edward O'Shea, *A Descriptive Catalog of W. B. Yeats's Library* (New York: Garland, 1985), 191.
42. "Sarojini Naidu's Golden Threshold," *JT*, 22 Dec. 1907, 6.

Before New Year's, Noguchi went with an unidentified friend up to Hampstead to visit the poet John Masefield, intending also to pay homage to one of his English poetical heroes, John Keats, who had lived there. He found Masefield looking younger than expected (at 35, Masefield was Noguchi's junior by three years), "with a beautiful clear glow in face denoting great sensitiveness or morbid refinement, [he] came out to receive me in the entrance hall; his soft voice, with the manner matching to it, gave me an impression that he was a dreamer of beauty and that when he sang the ugliness of street gutters he wrote as an outsider, a prince incognito stretching out his nose, from his whim perhaps, into the brutal smell." Masefield had made a name for himself with poems like *The Everlasting Mercy* (1911), depicting the lower classes in colloquial language which seemed to refined readers shocking in its vulgarity. The combination of Masefield's personality and subject matter had struck others, besides Noguchi, as strangely incongruous. Max Beerbohm had famously drawn Masefield, in his *Fifty Caricatures*, "lengthening his slender body, tall like a dream, over the roof to peep down to the fighting gutter-bloods below," as Noguchi described the picture, with the caption:

> A swear word in a rustic slum
> A simple swear-word is to some,
> To Masefield something more.[43]

56. John Masefield, caricatured by Max Beerbohm, 1913.

43. Max Beerbohm, *Fifty Caricatures* (London: William Heinemann, 1913), 12.

Noguchi had heard from playwright Granville-Barker that Masefield was writing a verse play adaptation of the Japanese *Chūshingura* story, the revenge tale of the forty-seven rōnin, entitled *The Faithful*. He told Noguchi he was using F.V. Dickins' 1876 translation, and Noguchi was surprised to learn that "although the forty-seven samurais are connected with the play, he was going to bring out only a few people on the stage, because he was going to make his Japanese play mainly develop around the great struggle in the heart of Oboshi" (aka Oishi Kuranosuke—the chief retainer who leads the plot to avenge lord Asano, who had been forced to commit suicide). Noguchi "thought it would be most interesting to watch as a Japanese how this Ronin story will gain a spiritual exaltation through a western baptism," but after the play appeared in 1915, he wondered whether Masefield had not gone too far in adapting his play to a Western point of view.[44]

Japan Society and Oriental Club

On January 14, 1914, Noguchi gave a lecture on "Japanese Poetry" at the Japan Society in Hanover Square.[45] As Colonel Sir Wyndham Murray, the Chairman of Council, explained, Noguchi, "well known for his poetical works and essays written in English, had come to England to deliver some lectures at Oxford," and had kindly agreed to present his paper to the Society as well. The lecture, later printed in the Society's journal, was essentially identical to the version published in *The Spirit of Japanese Poetry*, except for some interesting autobiographical comments from a recent essay entitled "My Own Poetry," in which Noguchi had discussed his own poetry in relation to "the question whether one can attain a success with one's language of adoption." Here, Noguchi spoke in defense of his own poetics and use of the English language, in contrast to his usual apologetic dismissiveness. "There are beauties and characteristics of any language," he argued, "which cannot be plainly seen by those who are born with them; it is a foreigner's privilege (or is it the virtue of capital-lettered Ignorance?) to see them and use them, without a moment's hesitation, to his best advantages as he conceives it." To be sure, he still stopped somewhat short of defending his own poetry, choosing rather to form his argument as a proposal for how Japanese poetry might come to have an influence on English poetry, just as Japanese art had had an impact on Western art through such artists as Whistler. "Even Japan," he argued, "can do something towards the reformation or advancement

---

44. "A Japanese on Some English Poets," *Living Age* 290 (12 Aug. 1916): 420-25. Noguchi's detailed critique of *The Faithful* appeared as "Mesufuwīrudo no Chūshingura" in *Mita Bungaku* 7:3 (Mar. 1916): 93-100, and as "'Chushingura' in England" in Motosada Zumoto's paper, *The Herald of Asia* 1:4 (15 Apr. 1916): 111-12.

45. "Japanese Poetry," *Transactions of the Japan Society of London* 12 (1914): 88. Similar to the chapter in *SJP* this version includes additional material from "My Own Poetry," *Academy* 84 (15 Feb. 1913): 198-99.

of the Western poetry, not only spiritually but also physically," the point developed in the lecture being that English poets waste too much energy in "words, words, words," and might do well to emulate the simplicity of Japanese forms.

For *Japan Chronicle* editor Robert Young, Noguchi's success, and self-promoting self-defense provided further evidence of the British public's "inexhaustible appetite for pidgin English."[46] "We had hardly expected a Professor of English Literature to condescend to the disguising of the poverty of his thoughts in a garb of pidgin," wrote Young, apropos of a recent Noguchi essay in *The Academy*. Noguchi, Young supposed, was perfectly capable of writing English, but it was "too much to expect a man who finds apparently sane and sensible people ready to admire and pay for his antics not to succumb to the temptation. We only wish for Japan's sake that Mr. Noguchi could see the indignity of posturing for people who think that it is Japan's chief charm to be a little bit grotesque, a little bit ignorant, a little bit clever, and a little bit deformed." He could, however, wholeheartedly endorse Noguchi's claim that "the very best poems are left unwritten or are sung in silence." "Judging from the awful samples I have seen, not only by my Japanese friends, written in English, but by English-speaking people who should know better—I consider it absolutely certain that the only poems worth writing are left unwritten, or at any rate unpublished."[47]

Noguchi reported to Léonie that the lecture had "turned out in quite a good shape." The Japanese Ambassador, Kaoru Inouye, and his wife had been in attendance. Prof. Joseph Henry Longford, a sixty-five-year-old "old Japan hand" who had studied Japan's penal codes back in the 1880s and was the author of three recent books on "Old Japan," "New Japan," and, for good measure, "Japan of the Japanese," opened the discussion. Having read Noguchi's paper in advance, he had been "struck by two or three points in it which are not in harmony with our ideas of what is worthy of admiration in poetry," and took up the defense of English poetic tradition against Noguchi's attack on the poetic inefficiency of "words, words, words" by proceeding to lecture Noguchi on the indispensability of Milton's *Paradise Lost*, reiterating, in passing, the tiresome observation that Noguchi's own poetic thoughts "would have carried greater force and made more impression if they had been conveyed in one of the rhythmic forms to which we have been accustomed." The professor then proceeded to expound his own views on Japanese poetry, in which he found "a great deal of real beauty," but also an "extreme conservatism" along with a regrettable tendency to exclude what he referred to as "the dourness of life" which combined to produce a poetry which took as its subject "all the softer aspects of nature and all the more tender elements

46. [Robert Young], "Western Art in Japan," *Japan Chronicle*, weekly ed., 29 Jan. 1914, 154-85.
47. F.A.G. [Robert Young] "Stray Notes," *Japan Chronicle*, weekly ed., 12 Feb. 1914, 266.

of human passion" rather than "the hard features of life" that intrepid English poets made it their business to confront in what Longford clearly felt was a more manly fashion.[48]

Ignoring the implicit condescension in Longford's polarization of hard England and soft Japan, T.G. Komai, who had recently published an article on Japanese poetry in the *Poetry Review*, took this opportunity to assert his presence in the society by helpfully offering some florid translations of several Japanese poems, including one that Noguchi had already translated in his lecture.[49] This was followed by a long commentary by Osman Edwards, author of the pioneering theatre book, *Japanese Plays and Playfellows* (1901). Edwards lamented the somewhat limited range of Japanese poetry available in the translations of Dickins, Porter, and Chamberlain, and expressed his frustration—directed partly at the translations and partly at the poetry itself—that Japanese poetry was "so epigrammatic that it requires explanatory notes," and also that, being "confined to lyrics and epigrams," it seemed to have "no chance of being epical or dramatic." Noguchi might complain about the English poet's "words, words, words," but as for Japanese poetry, Edwards suggested, "it is as if English poetry had stood still at the sonnet." He wondered what was happening with "the younger writers who had been influenced by foreign poetry," asking particularly about Bansui Tsuchii, translator of Milton and Carlyle, whom Edwards had met in England a few years earlier, and about Hōmei Iwano, whom Edwards understood to have written "a sort of Japanese 'Lady of the Lake' in no less than three thousand lines." There is no record of Noguchi's responding to any of the comments, leading one critic to conclude that "Noguchi apparently stood on the podium without saying a word in response."[50]

Around the same time as the Japan Society lecture, as Noguchi noted, "Wilson Crewdson of St. Leonards-on-sea invited me to a dinner at the Oriental Club Hanover Square, where I was promised to meet Robert Bridges, the Poet Laureate, Lowes Dickinson of Cambridge and Edward F. Strange of the South Kensington Museum."[51] A number of other Orientalist types turned up for what promised to be a lively

---

48. YN to LG, 17 Jan. 1914, in *LG* 259-60; "Japanese Poetry," *Transactions of the Japan Society*, 101; "Japanese Poetry," London *Times*, 15 Jan. 1914, 5.
49. T.G. Komai was Gonnosuke Komai (1877-1956), a recent arrival to London who occasionally wrote on Japanese topics for the London *Times*. As Gonnoské Komai, he published a book of overwrought translations from Chinese and Japanese poetry, *Dreams from China and Japan*, in 1918, and a book of essays, *Fuji from Hampstead Heath*, in 1925). His 1921 marriage to dancer Nora Howard drew considerable gossip.
50. Norimasa Morita, "Yone Noguchi (1875-1947)," *Britain and Japan: Biographical Portraits*, v. 8, ed. Hugh Cortazzi (Folkstone, Kent: Global Oriental, 2013), 414.
51. "A Few English Clubs," *JT*, 19 Aug. 1917. Crewdson was the author of *The Dawn of Western Influence in Japan* (London: Japan Society, 1903), Strange, a Japanese art specialist at the South Kensington Museum, and Lowes Dickinson a Cambridge political science lecturer recently returned from a year of Asian travel.

gathering, including Laurence Binyon, and Japanese-art critic/novelist Arthur Morrison (famous for his "slum novels" including *Tales of Mean Streets*).

It was Noguchi's first meeting with Bridges, the two having previously only corresponded. The tall, slender sixty-nine-year-old poet ("You mustn't call me the Poet Laureate," he insisted) seemed to Noguchi like "an old plum tree blossoming above the snow or a fearless pinetree amid the frosts"; he felt (recalling a phrase from a sonnet by Edmund Gosse), "braced by hope's high alpine atmosphere." Noguchi considered Bridges to be as striking in his way as Joaquin Miller, an "exceedingly interesting British type of poet" as he wrote Léonie a few days later.[52]

57. Robert Bridges.

When the conversation turned to the question of Japanese poetry, the subject of Noguchi's upcoming lecture, Arthur Morrison "tried to impress the mind of the Poet Laureate with the reticence and noble pathos of Japanese poetry," taking as illustration the sad farewell of Michizane, expressing the sadness of departure in taking leave of his beloved plum tree:

> Where the spring breeze comes and passes,
> Load her with perfume, O my plum-tree,
> Though thy master be far away.
> Forget Not thou to Bloom.

Bridges, though something of a nature enthusiast, was not much moved by this melancholy scene of arboreal parting. He advised Noguchi to focus on the *form* of Japanese poetry—the Oxford audience would be delighted to hear how it sounded "from real Japanese lips"—and defer "the spiritual question." "We know absolutely nothing of Japanese poetry," he told Noguchi. "And Oxford is so ignorant; she has to be educated."[53]

52. The sonnet is "R.B.," in *The Autumn Garden* (London: Heinemann, 1909): 50.
53. "A Few English Clubs." On the Michizane poem, see "Japanese Poetry," *Living Age* 264 (19 Mar. 1910): 745.

With this chastening pronouncement, the conversation turned to other things Japanese. "Lewes Dickinson as the one most recently returned from Japan was naturally full of talk on Japan and the Japanese," Noguchi recalled. "Why," Dickinson asked, "is Japan trying so hard to uglify herself after the Western fashion?" Noguchi could hardly have agreed more. "Really that was the very question I wished to ask somebody and be answered." As East was becoming West, so West was becoming East: when the topic of Zen Buddhism came up, Laurence Binyon made the case that George Meredith's "Reading of Earth" could be understood as expressing a Zen doctrine of contemplation. "For the Zen sages, as for Meredith," Binyon declared, "the contemplation of nature was no sentimental indulgence, but an invigorating discipline." (Whether Binyon actually said this in conversation is doubtful, since it was taken verbatim from his book, *The Flight of the Dragon*).[54] Noguchi suspected that Binyon's own affinity to certain aspects of Japanese thought stemmed from his Quaker background. (Joaquin Miller, too, had come from a Quaker family).[55]

Lunch at Shaw's, Dinner with Yeats

On January 16, Noguchi was invited to lunch at the home of Bernard Shaw at Adelphi Terrace along with Alvin Langdon Coburn. The playwright's sumptuous home afforded an interesting view of Cleopatra's Needle and was luxuriously furnished with superb carpets and bookcases filled with *éditions de luxe* apparently meant more for decoration than for reading. Shaw was that rare thing, a successful but serious writer, but the bourgeois trimmings seemed out of place in the home of "the curser of conventionality and sophistry." "Even with his bust by Rodin upon the large table," Noguchi wrote, "the room failed to convince me it was Shaw's."[56]

The bust was all of Shaw to be seen at the time of their arrival, but Noguchi was glad to find Mrs. Shaw "the most pleasing person, with jolly wrinkles round her typical Irish eyes." Finally, Bernard Shaw entered the room as Noguchi "hoped he would, as if a guest who had made a delay of half an hour only to make his entrance more impressive." Noguchi had expected Shaw to exude a sort of dark and slightly cynical austerity matching his writerly tone; instead he was pleasantly surprised to find that the playwright's light-colored hair and reddish complexion gave him "a certain optimistic gaiety," and that "his Irish eyes like those of his delightful wife already danced before he began to talk."

It was Shaw's famous and often-imitated manner that interested Noguchi most, and he observed with careful attention as Shaw began pronouncing his opinions on the Granville Barker production of *A*

---

54. Laurence Binyon, *The Flight of the Dragon* (London: Murray, 1911): 38.
55. "A Few English Clubs," *JT*, 19 Aug. 1917.
56. "Bernard Shaw," *Bookman* (London) 47 (Dec. 1914): 75-77.

Midsummer Night's Dream at the Savoy: it was "perfectly absurd" though it was "Granville Barker's art always to get something quite good out of those absurdities," he declared, stopping to gauge the impact on Noguchi and Coburn and then walking back to the table "where his own statuette poised like a stuffed eagle." He seemed rather restless, and Noguchi considered that "it would not be any wonder if we could find ten thousand Bernard Shaws in London alone, since his peculiarity or eccentricity in manner as well as thought is the easiest kind to imitate." Shaw's manner had become so commodified that even Noguchi had taken to exclaiming, "what a miserable Shaw!" when confronted with examples of it; now, confronted with the genuine article, he was on the verge of exclaiming it again when he was rescued by a crisply-aproned maid announcing luncheon.

58. George Bernard Shaw, September 1914.

Over soup, Shaw turned to Noguchi and exclaimed, "Why, I should like to know, do you Japanese, who live in such a lovely country of art and natural beauty, ever go to America, the country of all sorts of barbarities? What do you gain there?" Shaw was disgusted with what he had heard about Japanese modernization. "My beautiful dream of Japan is spoilt. I have no desire to go there."

Noguchi found it more interesting to feed the fire than to stop it. "I dare say," he interrupted, "you would have a still greater reason for your fear in going to Japan; I mean that you would surely encounter your books badly translated, and your plays most horribly acted."

"My plays here are horrible enough," Shaw replied, expressing little interest in the topic.

"Is it possible now to see the real old Japanese plays?" inquired Mrs. Shaw, intervening to change the subject.

Noguchi could not wholeheartedly affirm it, and explained to her, or rather to Shaw, as well as possible the changed artistic conditions in Japan since the 1880s, during which "the East and Japan always retreat before the Western invasion," an invasion in which Shaw himself had had no small part, he added.

"How sad!" Mrs. Shaw sighed. Shaw apparently lacked any concern about the fate of his own plays in Japan.

The vegetarian Shaw, looking like the chief guest at Mrs. Shaw's luncheon, remained silent, being busy with the vegetables on his plate. But after a time he inquired of Noguchi whether literature paid in Japan, which led into a long reminiscence of his unsuccessful efforts as a novelist in the early years of his career.

Shaw had a committee meeting to attend, but before leaving said to Noguchi, "I wonder what you ever learn from England, stupid, silly, with her eternally unchanged mind. I often doubt if England has any mind at all."

"You have to go to Ireland," Mrs. Shaw added, "if you wish to see a real human mind."

"You are a perfectly wonderful man if you can live in Japan," said Shaw. "I am Irish," he added, "but I cannot live in Ireland." Looking at his watch, he bid them farewell, and like a blast, banged the door and ran off. Mrs. Shaw valiantly attempted to keep the party going by consulting Noguchi and Coburn on the subject of the upcoming fancy dress ball, which she planned to attend in the costume of Holbein's *Duchess of Milan*, a reproduction of which she showed them. But bereft of its main energy source, the party grew "quiet and indifferent" and soon broke up.

"Yesterday I was invited by Bernerd [*sic*] Shaw and tonight am going to take a dinner together with Yeats," Noguchi wrote happily to Léonie on January 17. "And so on—you see, I am splendid in condition, but not financially." He had moved to an address at 29 Montague Street on Russell Square in Bloomsbury. He was not without a paternal thought for Isamu, to whom he had promised to send picture-cards. "Please tell him: 'His papa is tremendously busy, but tomorrow, no, the day after tomorrow, he will go to some shops and buy something for him.'"

William Butler Yeats had been spending most of the winter in a borrowed cottage in rural Sussex with Ezra Pound serving as his secretary, in hopes of preserving the Irish poet's failing eyesight and providing a rejuvenating poetic influence. Periodic returns to his studio at Woburn Buildings in Bloomsbury, a few blocks from Noguchi's hotel, allowed him to remain connected to the literary and social worlds. This particular weekend Pound was organizing a memorable dinner in honor of the quirky anti-imperialist poet Wilfred Scawen Blunt at Blunt's Sussex estate; they would rent a motorcar from Harrod's to drive there, bringing fellow poets T. Sturge Moore, Victor Plarr, Richard Aldington, and F.S. Flint. "The population of the car represented Pound's and Yeats's collective determination of those in the world of letters eligible to pay tribute to Blunt," explains Lucy McDiarmid. Pound had planned the event back in November; D.H. Lawrence, Padraic Colum, James Joyce, and Rupert Brooke were also invited, but were all out of the country at the time. "Pound suggests our bringing Nagochi [sic] the Japanese poet, as 'he will make it known among men of letters in Japan,'" Yeats explained to Lady Gregory five days before the dinner. But Noguchi did not attend the historic event. McDiarmid supposes that "Yeats was reluctant to invite someone like Noguchi, who might never have heard of Blunt and therefore 'might show ignorance and so spoil the compliment.'"[57]

59. W. B. Yeats, 1911.

Perhaps as a consolation, the night before the Blunt excursion Yeats invited Noguchi to dinner: Pound and his French sculptor friend Henri Gaudier-Brzeska also came. Noguchi's account of the evening, published the following year by Holbrook Jackson in *T.P.'s Weekly*, to which Yeats was also a contributor, is probably fairly reliable.[58] He begins with his arrival at Yeats's studio, where "my bell was soon answered by a slow old-fashioned footstep descending the stairs; when the entrance door was opened, the dimly lighted narrow hall revealed a rather heavy figure, somehow stooped like a dream; our shaking of hands seemed to confirm a friendship of thirty years' standing. He was Yeats in whose song of the "phantom beauty in a mist of tears," I was glad to believe, I found at last my own Japanese song." They headed off to dinner at a nearby grill-room, where Noguchi, uncertain whether he was with a real person or "an ageless Celtic ghost," contemplated the "melancholy but pleasing" face of the forty-eight-year-old poet, spectacled, with grey hair combed sideways, his "proud, innocent eyes, shaking perfectly clear of the nets of right and wrong."

57. Lucy McDiarmid, "A Box for Wilfrid Blunt," *PMLA* 120:1 (2005): 170; Yeats to Lady Gregory, Berg NYPL 916 series, box 12, quoted in McDiarmid, "A Box," 167; Lucy McDiarmid, *Poets and the Peacock Dinner* (Oxford: Oxford UP, 2014), 52-3, 56-7.

58. "Shijin Eitsu to aimameru no ki" (Chronicle of meeting with poet Yeats), *Jiji Shimpō*, 10, 11, 14, 15 Aug. 1914; "W.B. Yeats" *T.P.'s Weekly* 25 (9 Jan.1915): 35; "A Japanese Poet on W. B. Yeats," *Bookman* (New York) 43 (June 1916): 431-33.

The conversation turned immediately to the subject of the Nō drama. It was now more than five years since Noguchi had proposed Yeats undertake a serious study of Nō in the fall of 1907. Nothing had immediately come of the suggestion, but Mary Fenollosa's visit to Japan in the summer of 1910 had set the wheels in motion. Anticipating her arrival, the *daijin sensei*'s former students prepared to help his widow revise her husband's monumental *Epochs of Chinese and Japanese Art*, planned a Hōgai Kanō memorial exhibition to help finance her trip, and debated what to do with the professor's notebooks of Nō translations and Chinese poetry studies. Noguchi may also have been in contact with Mary Fenollosa, who had been a member of his short-lived Iris Club; in any case, his close friends among the former Fenollosans would have kept him informed. Perhaps anticipating some involvement he published his first attempt at a Nō translation the month before Mary Fenollosa's arrival, and then republished his series of articles on Yeats and the Nō two months later.[59] The choice of Pound to edit Fenollosa's notebooks was hardly an obvious one. Pound's interest in Asia had been, until recently, little more than a flirtation, developed through visits he and his fiancée, Dorothy Shakespear, had made to the British Museum's Oriental Print Room during the past two years.[60] But Pound had been a serious student of philology and had experience translating poems out of old English, medieval French, and ancient Greek. This, combined with his emerging position as a leader of the poetic vanguard made him an interesting choice, potentially better able than an Oriental literature specialist to turn Fenollosa's studies into something of general interest. Moreover, Pound's closeness to Yeats meant that Yeats would finally have access to the translations he needed for the Nō-influenced theatrical regeneration Noguchi had prescribed a few years earlier.

Yeats had been working with Pound on Fenollosa's Nō notebooks since early December. By the middle of the month, Pound had reported to Dorothy Shakespear that he had "cribbed part of a Noh (dramatic eclogue) out of Fenollosa's notes," and that Yeats called it "charming."[61] The play was *Kinuta*, in which a merchant's wife, separated from her husband for three years, dies of sorrow just before his return, reappearing as a ghost to bewail her fate only to receive a lecture from the Buddhist chorus on the need to restrain false desire. Now as Yeats was beginning to incorporate the Nō into his own view of drama, he explained to Noguchi (according to Noguchi's account of their pre-dinner conversation) that he was delighted at the way the Nō incorporated what he called "the

---

59. "The Morning Glory," *Mita Bungaku* 1:1 (1 May 1910): 9-11; "The Japanese Mask Play," *Taiyō* 16:10 (Jul. 1910): 4-9.
60. Edward Marx, *The Idea of a Colony* (Toronto: U of Toronto P, 2004): 98-103.
61. *Ezra Pound and Dorothy Shakespear, Their Letters, 1909-1914*, ed. Omar Pound and A. Walton Litz (New York: New Directions, 1984): 287.

folk element," which was, in his opinion, "alone worthy of any poetry; by that," he explained, "I mean that the true literature should be a folk literature invigorated, not weakened, by the cultured elements." Yeats was himself attempting a difficult fusion of aristocratic theatre based on Irish folklore. "These two opposite elements," he told Noguchi, "often clash with one another in a poor literary hand; but one who holds the secret or key of the real literature will at once harmonise them, and make them grow more beautiful by their marriage." And yet, it was critical for Yeats to achieve this marriage of folk elements and cultured elements while remaining true to the idea of a national tradition as well. "The literature of any country should remain as itself," he told Noguchi, "whatever culture, whatever universality it likes to embrace." And now, turning the tables on Noguchi, he asked, half-innocently, "Tell me about your literature and Japanese literary life; above all, whatever do you learn from our Western literature?"

It was, of course, an often-made accusation—made even by Noguchi himself—that Japan was guilty of borrowing indiscriminately from the West, as attested by his vigorous assent a few weeks earlier to Lowes Dickinson's observation at the Oriental Club that Japan seemed to be trying hard "to uglify herself after the Western fashion." Now Yeats, with his polite but pointed question, wanted to know why Noguchi should not be held guilty of the same charge.

Noguchi's response was to tell Yeats that Japan's age of transition was "approaching well nigh to its end" and that the Japanese were "at present . . . rearranging or rather destroying what we once learned from the West," a sort of Japanese version of Irish anti-colonialism. Recently, there had been a stronger reaction against Western literature. He explained, "We should keep some Western literature, not because it is new and strange for us, but because we can find our own Japanese passion and imagination more beautifully, more precisely, expressed in it." The problem with "the so-called modern education" in Japan, he told Yeats, was that "it does not teach people to become real and sensible. From the teaching of a useless mass of stupidity they grow at once spiritually lost."

The conversation drifted for a while to Irish politics until the two poets were joined by Ezra Pound and his sculptor friend Henri Gaudier-Brzeska, "who looked delightfully barbarous as if they had left but a moment before their hidden shelter covered by ivy vines." Noguchi confessed to feeling almost ashamed of his "stupid formality in a stiff extent of shirt front, which was perfectly out of place in the company of poets whose songs echo down the road of wind."

Noguchi had been acquainted with Pound for several years. He had initiated a correspondence with the young American in 1911, when Pound was traveling through Europe in search of authentic poetry and the spirit of romance, having been fired from his teaching job at a small

Midwestern college in 1908 after being found with an actress in his room. Then twenty-two, he determined to embark on a literary career, traveling to London and then Venice, where he self-published his first collection of poems, *A Lume Spento*; two more small collections, *A Quinzaine for this Yule* and *Personae*, appeared in London the following spring. His reception was in many ways like Noguchi's; the reviewer on the *Evening Standard & St James's Gazette* thought *Personae* "queer" and often "incoherent," but was "attracted occasionally by the lines which are almost, if not quite, nonsense." "Our conclusion is that Mr Pound is a poet, though a fantastic one."[62] Pound gradually gained entrée into London literary circles, meeting Yeats in 1909, and gave a series of lectures on Provençal poetry at the London Polytechnic, which he published as *The Spirit of Romance* in 1910.

60. Ezra Pound, 1913.

In July 1911, Pound published his third book of poems, *Canzoni*. That month, Noguchi sent him a letter:

> Dear Mr. Pound:
> As I think you may not know my work at all, I send you, under a separate cover, my new book of poems called *The Pilgrimage*. As I do not yet acquainted with your work, I wish you will send your book or books which you like to have me to read. This little note may sound quite businesslike, but I can promise you that I can do better in my next letter to you.
> Yours truly,
> Yone Noguchi
> P.S. I am anxious to read not only your poetical work but also your criticism.[63]

62. Humphrey Carpenter, *A Serious Character: The Life of Ezra Pound* (Boston: Houghton Mifflin, 1988), 108.
63. Kodama Sanehide, ed., *Ezra Pound & Japan: Letters & Essays* (Redding Ridge, CT: Black Swan, 1987), 4.

Pound received the two volumes a few weeks later and, intrigued, described Noguchi's letter, with minute attention to grammatical quirks, to Dorothy Shakespear. "His poems seem to be rather beautiful," he commented. "His matter is poetic & his stuff not like everything else, he is doubtless sent to save my artistic future."[64]

Pound sent a warm reply to Noguchi on September 2. The books had delighted him, he said, but he confessed he did not yet know what to say of them. He had seen Noguchi's books in Elkin Mathews' shop—Mathews was also Pound's publisher—but knew little of Noguchi other than the fact that he was somewhat older (ten years) and had been in New York. He sent along his two most recent poetry collections, commenting on the similarity between his work and Noguchi's: "You are giving us the spirit of Japan, is it not? very much as I am trying to deliver from obscurity certain forgotten odours of Provence & Tuscany." He did not send his one volume of criticism, *The Spirit of Romance*, because, he said, it "has many flaws of workmanship." "It might be more to the point if we who are artists should discuss the matters of technique & motive between ourselves. Also if you should write about these matters I would discuss your letters with Mr. Yeats & likewise my answers." He conceded that he knew "almost nothing" of Japan, but "surely if the east & the west are ever to understand each other that understanding must come slowly & come first [through] the arts."[65]

Pound's volumes of early poems gave few clues that the author would soon be hailed as a groundbreaking modernist. On the contrary, the poems appeared ultra-traditional, absorbed in multilingual wordsmanship, and demonstrations of intricate poetic forms: as T.S. Eliot later put it, "rather old-fashioned romantic stuff, cloak-and-dagger kind of stuff," adding, "I wasn't very impressed by it."[66] Nor, it would seem, was Noguchi, who sent a polite curt reply on October 22: "Many thanks for your kind letter [together] with *Exultations* and *Canzoni*. I was glad to be acquainted with *Exultations*, and what a difference of your work from mine! I like to follow closely after your poetry." The promise to "do better" in his next letter had been forgotten; nor did he take up Pound's friendly invitation to discuss artistic technique and motive. Pound must have felt somewhat slighted. Noguchi's failure to cultivate Pound's friendship would cost his reputation dearly over the following decade, when Pound emerged as the most powerful figure in the world of modernist poetry, and its most vocal proponent of Japanese poetics.[67]

Now, the three men left the electricity and ice cream of the modern

---

64. Pound to Dorothy Shakespear, [24 or 31 Aug. 1911], in *Ezra Pound and Dorothy Shakespear*, 44.
65. Pound to Noguchi, [2] Sept. 1911, CEL 395.
66. Carpenter, *A Serious Character*, 140.
67. Noguchi to Pound, 22 Oct. 1911, in Kodama, *Ezra Pound & Japan*, 5.

hotel restaurant for Yeats's fire-lit studio. There, as Noguchi described it, Pound, "a present day faun in appearance with his uncombed hair where pigeons might like to be nesting, sat on a couch"; Noguchi was "glad that he knew well the place where he fitted perfectly." Gaudier-Brzeska, "who had run away, he said, from army service in France and taken upon his hand the reformation of the dull English mind, artistically, sat in a little chair, casting his youthful shadow on the dark wall where pictures and sketches in oil or water colour or what not congregated in pleasing confusion."

For Noguchi, "the poetical atmosphere gradually thickened" when Yeats, sitting in his customary wooden chair, began to talk on "spirit and deathlessness." Yeats informed Noguchi that he was an ancestor-worshipper "almost as if a Japanese," and began comparing the practices of Western mediums to those of traditional Japanese ritual. "The medium, or the American medium," Yeats told Noguchi, "practises your Japanese ancestor-worship. He or she has no Christian God or Holy Ghost in mind; when we have no particular ancestor to whom we are bound to go, we will go quite freely to any dead spirit of our own choice. Is it not the same ancestor-worship you practise in Japan?"

Noguchi considered this, and found it plausible. "Our ancestor-worship," he told Yeats, "is not so free as yours. But yours is more true and real."

Pound had limited patience for Yeats's psychical research and the spiritualists he referred to as "the charlatans of Bond Street," but saw supernatural psychology as a key to understanding the Nō plays. "Some will be annoyed at a form of psychology which is, in the West, relegated to spiritistic séances," he apologized in his comment on the play *Suma Genji*.[68] "There is, however, no doubt that such psychology exists.... If the Japanese authors had not combined the psychology of such matters with what is to me a very fine sort of poetry, I would not bother about it."

The conversation turned to other matters, such as Noguchi's first impressions on arriving again in the West. As the candles were burning down Noguchi thought of the comment Mrs. Shaw had made the previous day and said to Yeats, "I was told at Adelphi Terrace that I should go to Ireland if I wished to find a real mind. What is the real Irish mind?"

"The real Irish mind that Shaw perhaps means," Yeats replied after a moment, "is the mind which all true Irish are trying to get away from."

Madman Symons, Indian Nightingale

Since arriving in London, Noguchi had thought often of the poet Arthur Symons who had so helpfully delivered a poem dedicated to him during the short life of *The Iris*. Noguchi had been among the first to hear of Symons's nervous breakdown a year or two after that. (In early 1909,

68. Pound and Fenollosa, *"Noh" or Accomplishment*, 44.

Symons's friend Yeats had reported that Symons was writing continually but in handwriting that nobody could read; a few months later he believed himself to be in heaven, where he was busy preparing the reception of the late Swinburne).[69] Noguchi had thus lost touch with Symons, who had since been in and out of mental institutions. His Japanese admirers, Bin Ueda and Hōmei Iwano undoubtedly among them, were keen to know the real nature of Symons's illness. Noguchi was relieved when he received an invitation from Sarojini Naidu to join Symons in visiting her at the Park Lane nursery home near Piccadilly.

The visit took place on January 18.[70] Sarojini was surrounded in her small room by plants and flowers which seemed to Noguchi an effort to recreate a warm Indian atmosphere in the winter grayness of London. Symons, stretching out his legs, with his "high but tender brow and such sensitive fingers like those of a painter or pianist," seemed to evoke an artificially sweet atmosphere. "He had not fully recovered yet, so his words sounded strangely muffled and unclear. Sarojini repeated them to me one by one." Sarojini, a tiny figure with "such remarkable eyes in which her whole life concentrated," dressed in clinging clothes of Indian silk, her long black hair hanging straight down her back, sat cross-legged on the small bed in a manner that reminded Noguchi of Kannon, the Buddhist Goddess of Mercy.

61. Sarojini Naidu.

69. James Longenbach, *Stone Cottage* (Oxford: Oxford UP, 1988), 14-15.
70. The account of this meeting is reconstructed from four slightly different versions: "Kyōjin Asā Shimonzu" (The madman Arthur Symons), *Yomiuri*, 7 Feb. 1915, 4 rpt. as "Shimonzu" (Symons)," *Kaigai no kōyū* (Overseas friends) (1926); "A Japanese on Some English Poets," *Living Age* 290 (12 Aug. 1916): 420-25; "Arthur Symons," *JT*, 1 July 1917, and "Sarojini Naizū," *Senkusha no kotoba* (1924), 217-39. The date, given incorrectly as November in the Japanese article on Naidu, is given in the Japanese article on Symons.

Symons presented Noguchi with a copy of his book *Knave of Hearts*, in which he had included the poem "Japan" dedicated to Noguchi. Noguchi too had brought a gift for Symons, a copy of his friend Hōmei Iwano's Japanese translation of Symons's *Symbolist Movement in Literature*, just published in November. Symons was pleased, remarking afterwards to John Quinn that it was "jolly to be in Jap language."[71]

62. Arthur Symons.

The conversation (in Noguchi's account) began with Noguchi informing Symons of the considerable influence of modern French poetry in Japan, which seemed to please Symons; when Noguchi asked him if there was any such influence in England, however, "he declared that there had been almost nothing of it." The Rhymers' Club of the 1890s had been an attempt to "bring a Latin Quarter into London," Symons explained, adding, "I dare say that it was the first attempt to create a literary atmosphere, even a movement if possible, in this impossible city; and I think it was the last England ever had in her literary annals." But the English air, "half proud, and half self-deceiving," had not been congenial to "the true literary atmosphere where life's restrictions should be unbuttoned." Noguchi had become somewhat better informed about French poetry and pressed Symons for his opinions. "There is no question about Verlaine's being the greatest poet modern France has produced; if I chose the other poets," Symons declared, "there are Villon and Charles Baudelaire." Noguchi found that "there was no other subject which so excited Symons's sympathy and interest," and it seemed that Symons's face, "with such eyes of Welsh dreaminess, was strangely assuming a Verlainesque irregularity accentuated by somnolent fire." But Noguchi accurately sensed the Victorian limits of Symons's decadence: in place of Verlaine's impulsive, anti-intellectual abandonment, Symons could not wholly forget a sense

---

71. Symons to John Quinn, 30 Jan. 1914, in Carl Beckson, ed., *Selected Letters of Arthur Symons* (Iowa City : U of Iowa P, 1989): 284.

of morality which "only looms up to frighten him." He seemed pleased, however, to learn from Noguchi that his English Verlaine translations were regarded as the best by Japanese.

Returning to the topic of English poetry, Symons was asked to name his selections among the modern poets. At once the name of Swinburne came to his lips, and he began to reminisce about the poet, who had died in 1909. "How nervous Swinburne was," he declared. "Every fibre of his was rhythm, wave-like swing fire and passion." As for the present poets, there was "no poet worthy of consideration except Yeats; but Yeats is a sort of shadow, not a reality," he observed. Here, Sarojini broke in saying that "glamour" was the word for Yeats. "Even when Yeats sings love and woman," Symons explained, "he means a shadowy love and shadowy woman; his dreams are so heavy." But there was no other poet at present but Yeats, Symons repeated. The name of W. H. Davies was proposed, perhaps by Naidu, but although Symons was happy to take credit for discovering Davies, he had trouble remembering what he had ever written about him. Noguchi politely replied that to be discovered by Symons was something. Beyond poetry, there was Joseph Conrad. "Although he is not English," Symons declared, "his prose carries a mighty swing of colourful vision." Conrad was a great visionary, but also a realist, whose vocabulary was alive with a strong impulse, and who had alone brought into English literature "a mighty song of soliloquy." He was a prose writer any age might be proud to possess.

The conversation turned to the stage, with Symons asked to pronounce on the subject of great actresses. Symons talked of the Italian actress Eleanora Duse, then a dominant figure of the European stage. But he was not forgetful of the Japanese actress [Kawakami] Sada Yacco, whose performance he had once reviewed, and whose impression he told Noguchi, was still fresh in his mind. Noguchi thought of Yeats, and asked Symons what he thought of Yeats's opinion that a poetical drama would be realised within the next ten years. Symons, whose attempts at poetical drama had not found much popular interest, was skeptical.

As the afternoon grew late, Noguchi felt it time to go, and said his farewells. As he pressed the button for the elevator he considered Symons's condition. If Symons was indeed mad, he concluded, it was a benign insanity like that of Blake.

Sarojini also joined Noguchi to attend several Poets' Club dinners. ("I will be a guest of honour at Poets Club's dinner, and am hoping to read some poems of mine, or will lecture on Japanese poetry," he told Léonie on January 17). Women made up a large proportion of the poet-diners, and Noguchi had been informed that many would be beautiful, although he was struck more by their eccentric and often inelegant dress (particularly one with blue-dyed hair), and the boisterous atmosphere. Listening to club members reciting their poems could be trying. "I silently derided the mediocre works of the female poets lined up before me. Sarojini must have felt the same way, for when she thought no one was looking, she gently nudged my elbow." "For foreign visitors, he explained, "such invitations must be accepted as a kind of tax we must pay."[72]

Readings and Lectures

On the night of January 21, as the London *Times* reported, "Mr. Yone Noguchi, the Anglo-Japanese poet and critic, was the guest of the Poets' Club at dinner at the Café Monico." As Noguchi described it, this was "the grand hall of a pretentiously decorated restaurant near Piccadilly in London, with brightly shining electric lights, and red velvet upholstered chairs." Welsh poet Ernest Rhys, founder of the Everyman's Library, presided as Noguchi read a version of the Hokku lecture he was to give in Oxford, after which "Miss Enid Rose recited a selection of Mr. Noguchi's English lyrics."[73]

63. The Poetry Bookshop.

A more appealing venue for poetry enthusiasts, especially those of the disgruntled younger generation, was the new Poetry Bookshop on Devonshire Street, off Theobald's Road in Bloomsbury, opened in January 1913 by Harold Monro, publisher of the popular *Georgian Poetry* anthology and the magazine *Poetry and Drama* (formerly *Poetry Review*). Regular, unadvertised readings on Tuesdays and Thursdays in an old out-house in back typically drew an audience of twenty-five or thirty. Although conveniently located in Bloomsbury, Devonshire Street was "certainly very obscure" (Monro's biographer notes); Noguchi found it "forgotten, even ruined, with neglected children on the doorsteps." Nevertheless it was, Noguchi wrote, "a congenial background with its honest simplicity born

72. "Sarojini Naizū," *Indo no shijin*, 367; "The Japanese Lyric," London *Times*, 22 Jan. 1914, 8.
73. "Sarojini Naizū," *Indo no shijin*, 367; "The Japanese Lyric," London *Times*, 22 Jan. 1914, 8.

out of tragic reality; here would be the place where one will gladly deal with modern poetry whose song of rejuvenation and revolt gains, as once I wrote, its real exaltation from its flat falling to the ground."[74]

Noguchi found his reading there to be a curious experience. Monro, impatient at the door (the room was already filled) immediately conducted him through a dark passway into the room at the back, with its "cold severity of the wooden benches and bare floor, as if a Quaker meeting room or a meditation hall of Zen priests." Here, Noguchi states, "I had to disclose a few of my literary essays as if they were contraband." His mind was "undecided and wavering at first, but calmed down presently on seeing the audience, most of them young women plainly dressed who looked intensified under the mysterious darkness of the room, now hushed as in a chapel before the service; I proceeded to read my work by a little light from the shaded lamp set by the reading table." The room was quiet and the audience sympathetic:

> I felt as if reading alone in some secret recess with absolutely nothing to confuse and harass my imagination, widely separated from the world and noise; some occasion I had, in truth during the course of my reading, when I was almost frightened at the loudness of my own voice and felt extremely strange. I hardly thought myself that I was reading my own work, but something written by an unfortunate writer perfectly forgotten in dust. And then I thought that unfortunate sad writer who lived a thousand years ago was myself; now as the ghost, I thought, I was appealing to the audience for their sympathy. When I finished my reading I was as if awaking from a dream; the audience thanked me, making a soft commotion and whisper.

Noguchi's visit to the Poetry Bookshop had, in short, become a kind of Nō play.[75]

Noguchi's Oxford lecture was fast approaching. The London *Times* formally announced on January 22 that Noguchi was at present in England and had accepted an invitation from Mr. Robert Bridges, the Poet Laureate, and the President of Magdalen College to deliver a lecture on Japanese Poetry, to be given in the Hall of Magdalen College on Thursday, January 29, at 3 o'clock. On the day before the lecture Noguchi traveled by express to Oxford where he was met by Bridges, who took him by landau to his college, Corpus Christi.[76] As there was some time before dinner, Bridges wished to take him for a walk around the town. They set off through the lanes into High Street; Noguchi soon found Bridges to be "quite the quickest walker I ever found myself in company with" as the Poet Laureate commented on the points of note that they were passing, or rather, had just passed—"we had now already left

---

74. Joy Grant, *Harold Monro and the Poetry Bookshop* (Berkeley: U of California P, 1967), 61; "A Few English Clubs," *JT*, 19 Aug. 1917.
75. "A Few English Clubs," *JT*, 19 Aug. 1917; "Hobby," *Adelphi*, Ser. 2, 11:2 (Nov. 1935): 110-11.
76. "My Impressions of Oxford and Stratford-on-Avon," *Blackwoods* 199 (June 1916): 535-39.

behind University College, which was silly enough, Bridges said, to erect a monument to Shelley whom she had driven out." There were "the so-called Oxford dons, half monks, half magistrates of mediaeval court, specimens of whom I had already seen," who "most gracefully matched with the town, particularly the town of wintry desolation," and of course, the undergraduates, one of whom, a decade later appointed to teach in Tokyo still remembered the sight: "Noguchi, a short-legged tortoise, runs for life after Bridges, a long-legged stork."[77] The streets were wet and slippery, and in bad condition. "We have the town committees, but they never happen to see how bad the streets really are," Bridges informed him; it was the fault of democracy and modernity. "There's nothing more awful than turning democratic," he lamented.

In the Common Room at Corpus Christi a tremendous large old-fashioned fireplace, "decorated perhaps with many pictures of Bishops" reminded him that the college was founded in honour of "the most precious Body of our Lord Jesus Christ, of His most spotless Mother, and of all the Saints." "When I thought to myself that I was a mere bundle of heathenish mind from the forgotten East, the feeling that I was doubtless out of place here almost shivered my soul." Bridges eased his mind somewhat by telling him "there was among the *alumni* A. B. Walkley, who declared that 'nothing on the English stage is sacred except the dancing of Adeline Genée.'" Thus comforted, Noguchi accompanied Bridges and the college dons "who to my greatest comfort did not address me in Greek" into the Dining Hall where only the old ceilings, Bridges informed him, were worthy of attention. Noguchi sat between Bridges and a great Hegelian of Exeter College, feeling "as if I were leaning against a pair of Roman pillars," but found the dinner "unusually bright, contrary to my expectation . . . falling into a sort of horse-play even of an American brand."

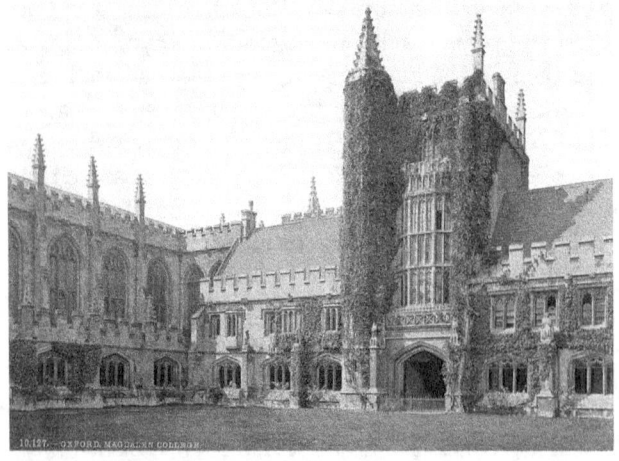

64. Magdalen College.

77. "Hobby," *The Adelphi* (Ser. 2) 11:2 (Nov. 1935): 110-11.

The next morning began, naturally, with more walking: three miles from Bridges' house to Magdalen, where he was welcomed by Dr. Warren, who told him to prepare for a large audience in the afternoon. Although slightly tired, he accepted Bridges' suggestion to see some of the other sights of the town. Bridges continued to point out the deleterious effects of democracy on architecture for Noguchi's edification, at one point exclaiming, "See that building! It's ugly. Nobody would like it; I don't in the least. It was built by my father-in-law." The Bodleian Library, where they stopped for a brief rest, possibly escaped censure. Back on High Street, they proceeded to a certain drug store "where, according to Bridges, we could get any poison we wished" and refreshed themselves "perhaps with poison" before returning to the College where Noguchi was happily permitted, after luncheon, to rest for two hours before the lecture in the room he had been given for the night.

65. Dr. Herbert Warren, circa 1912.

"I was conducted by Dr Warren and Robert Bridges, both of them wearing caps and gowns, through the cloisters full of shadows and silence (I felt myself turning half a monk who knew nothing but prayer) up to the Hall where all the eyes of a tremendously large audience were directed on me at once," Noguchi wrote. (The London *Times*, reporting on the lecture the following day, also noted the "crowded audience.") Noguchi was pleased with their "intellectual sobriety," and thought afterwards that he had been "somewhat able to impress their minds with my points." Indeed, the gist of it was apparent even to the *Times* reporter, who diligently reconstructed the major points from notes, in spite of the novelty of the topic and Noguchi's characteristically diffuse treatment:

> Mr. Noguchi, who stated that his subject was specially the Japanese 17-syllable "Hokku" poetry, began by quoting Mr. Walter Pater, saying that art struggled after the law of music, and that lyrical poetry approached nearest to that condition. The 'Hokku' poems were not lyrical poetry in

the Western sense, but often realized this definition of Mr. Pater's. The 'Hokku' poems were sometimes hardly connected with the thing or matter actually stated, but aimed to cast a light on the poetical position in which the writer stood; they depended so much on the intelligent sympathy of their readers. In Japanese poetry the readers assumed an equally responsible place, and they could become, if they liked, creators of poems which in fact were not their own work. Although there was a prodigious number of productions in Japan, the very best 'Hokku' poems could not be, in his opinion, more than half a thousand, perhaps not more than 250 in number, from all the work written in the last 300 years.[78]

The reporter erred in one point: Noguchi had said that that "each reader can become a creator of the poem by his own understanding as if he had written it himself." That was not the same as saying they could become "creators of poems which in fact were not their own work." Was this a simple misunderstanding, or a tongue-in-cheek allusion to Noguchi's own creative habits?

The point had actually come up in a discussion of the multiplicity of interpretations accorded to Bashō's most famous haiku—

> The old pond!
> A frog leapt into—
> List, the water sound!

—a poem "regarded in some quarters as a thing almost sacred," Noguchi had noted, "although its dignity is a little fallen of late," and read variously as (among other things) "a picture of an autumnal desolation reigning on an ancient temple pond whose world-old silence is now broken by a leaping frog," or, alternatively, as a Zen poem in which "Basho is supposed to awaken into enlightenment now when he heard the voice bursting out of voicelessness, and the conception that life and death were mere change of condition was deepened into faith." The latter interpretation may seem a stretch, but Noguchi was by no means exaggerating the philosophical weight the old frog had been made to carry over the years. "It is true to say that nobody but the author himself will ever know the real meaning of the poem; which is the reason I say that each reader can become a creator of the poem by his own understanding as if he had written it himself."

Throughout the lecture, Noguchi crossed back and forth between haiku and English poetry, drawing out comparisons and contrasts, and sketching out philosophical backgrounds to haiku with particular emphases on Zen and Taoism, ending with a nod to Arthur Ransome's theory that poetic language operated on two levels, which Ransome called kinetic and potential speech. Kinetic speech encompassed the prosaic, factual and narrative effects of poetic language, potential speech its

---

78. "Hokku Poetry: Lecture by Yone Noguchi," London *Times*, 30 Jan. 1914, 5.

suggestive associations—a division not unlike that of later philosophers of language who distinguished between denotation and connotation, or reference and sense. Clearly Ransome's conception of the potential element owed much to his Noguchi-influenced understanding of hokku. No doubt some of the audience would have preferred less philosophy and more exposition of the actual practice of haiku poetry, an important topic Noguchi avoided, as usual, in the lecture. At the reception following the lecture, Noguchi seems not to have been assaulted with pressing questions; rather, he drank tea with Tennyson's niece and listened to an old professor talk of how he had once met Wordsworth. This was followed by dinner in the Magdalen dining hall and smoking in the Common Room. He was pleased that the name of Joaquin Miller was known to many of the dons, but his announcement that he planned to visit Stratford-on-Avon the next day to see Shakespeare's birthplace produced strange looks. "I thought perhaps they considered Stratford to be outside of the English domain and Shakespeare a foreigner," he noted.[79]

66. Stratford-on-Avon.

In fact, Stratford did look much like "a dusty suburb of Shanghai or Chicago," and the Shakespeare pilgrims seemed to be mainly Americans; there was even an American flag on one house. Finding no guidebooks, he asked directions from "a little bare-footed street urchin" and finally reached "the literary Mecca in Henley Street" (Shakespeare's birthplace) where he found, as he expected, two American women exclaiming "in the most informal manner at each step: 'Oh, wonderful! How wonderful!'" He was troubled also by "a huge iron pipe, which ran through this shrine of the Elizabethan age for heating purposes... perhaps for the American

79. "'Hokku Poetry': Lecture by Mr. Yone Noguchi," London *Times*, 30 Jan. 1914, 5; "The Japanese Hokku Poetry," *SJP* 33-53.

visitors." What Noguchi would have made of today's busloads of Chinese and Japanese tourists is an interesting question for speculation, but at the time, the American tourist reigned supreme, and even Noguchi was taken for an American by the barmaid when he attempted to visit the Red Lion pub memorialized by Washington Irving, whose account of the town was much on his mind. Asked to sign his "American address," he rose to the occasion with: "Yone Noguchi from Chattahoochee," a name he had borrowed from a Whitman poem.

Artists and Playwrights

As Noguchi returned to London toward the end of January, reviews of *Through the Torii* were piling up, nearly all of them enthusiastic. The Japanese binding thrilled. "It would be difficult to imagine a more pleasurable book to handle. The soft paper takes the ink in a peculiar way, and the Eastern method of printing on folded pages gives a new and fascinating sensation to the (to me) always delicious experience of running the leaves of a book through thumb and finger. These Eastern books are made to be caressed in this way, and when they happen to contain matter printed in English one is in luck's way." Then, there was "the quaintness of his English." This quaintness, however, did not reach "the decidedly humorous proportions of Yoshio Markino's adventures in English," nor was it "quite so tiring after the first flush of amusement or interest. The reason is not far to seek—Yone Noguchi has more to say, and his mastery of our language is a triumph."[80] In the inevitable comparisons Noguchi's English easily bested Markino's. "Mr. Markino writes a quaint broken English," wrote Dixon Scott; "Mr. Noguchi's prose is merely bent. It is bent as a stick seems to be when you thrust it into clear water; there is an almost uncanny refraction." Where "Markino learnt his English in the actual London streets . . . Mr. Noguchi learned our language from our literature, reading and lecturing in the Universities of Japan."[81] Francis Bickley in *The Bookman* raved, "Mr. Noguchi has perfectly realised [the essay's] possibilities, and has used it in a manner which makes our most delicate masters seem rather heavy-handed."[82] The *Times Literary Supplement* in another blurb-worthy rave, declared it "a book that you like before you have read it and love when you have finished it."[83] "Mr. Noguchi's English is a little less secure and perfect than Mr. Tagore's," the reviewer conceded, "but, like Mr. Tagore's, it has the freshness and the new force of an unfamiliar medium. . . . On ears dulled with the noisy monotony of our 'vulgar' tongue it falls with the cool music of an Elizabethan lyric, or of the rain which croons and whispers so often through the

---

80. Bernard Lintot, "At Number I, Grub Street," *T.P.'s Weekly*, 23 Jan. 1914, 105.
81. Dixon Scott, "Yone Noguchi Essays," *Liverpool Courier*, rpt. JT, 5 Apr. 1922, 2.
82. Francis Bickley, "Yone Noguchi's Essays," *Bookman* 45 (Feb. 1914): 275.
83. "Mr. Noguchi's English Studies," *London Times*, 5 Feb. 1914, 65.

gentle greyness of Mr. Noguchi's book." Only the *Athenaeum*'s reviewer demurred, saying the book would "do little to enhance Yone Noguchi's reputation as a writer of English" and suggested that if he really wished to be regarded as an artist in the medium of words "it behoves him to look to his English grammar a little more carefully."[84]

Comparisons between Noguchi and the Indian poet Rabindranath Tagore were also inevitable. Tagore had arrived in London a year ahead of Noguchi and taken the literary capital by storm. Though regarded as the preeminent poet of his native Bengal, he was virtually unknown in the English-speaking world until W.B. Yeats took up his case after being shown Tagore's notebook of translations undertaken on the sea voyage; in a little over a year, Tagore had several English books to his credit and had received the Nobel Prize in literature for 1913. When Noguchi arrived in London in mid-December, the Tagore craze had reached its peak following the November announcement of the prize, and had begun forming a kind of backlash; now adulatory articles shared space with articles with titles like "Do Prizes and Petting Spoil Poets?" expressing the anonymous author's hope that Tagore would "drop a certain tendency to affectation," adding that Yoshio Markino "whose idiosyncracies and way of writing English get rather on one's nerves" might do the same, while another piece in the *St. James Gazette* found humorous poetic matter in the question "How Do We Pronounce Rabindranath Tagore?"[85] Beneath such dry efforts at humor lay anxieties about "natives" and "orientals" forgetting their place. Regardless of whether Japan ought to become a British colony as Shaw had half-jokingly suggested, Noguchi could hardly hope to become the next Tagore—he lacked the prophetic demeanor, the melodious speaking voice, and the sheer literary talent of the Bengali writer—but Tagore's success represented a great breakthrough for Anglophone Asian writers and indicated a new receptivity toward their work. With Tagore's prize, Noguchi's Oxford lecture, Markino's books and paintings selling, and Sarojini Naidu in town for good measure, England in 1913 seemed a promising place for Asian writers of English. Noguchi's "Eastern gondola of soul" seemed to be making progress against the Western tide. Although England still held to an "unshakeable belief that she is the first country of the world," the reviews of *Through the Torii*, like the early reviews of Tagore, showed England in a new spirit of self-criticism and eagerness to look to the East.[86]

On February 2, "Some Stories of My Western Life," an account of his California days first published in the *Taiyō* three years earlier, appeared

84. "Through the Torii," Athenaeum (7 Feb. 1914): 199.
85. "A search for a genius: Do Prizes and Petting Spoil Poets?," *Daily Citizen*, 3 Jan. 1914, 4; "How do we pronounce Rabindranath Tagore?" *Evening Standard* and *St. James's Gazette*, 4 Jan. 1914, rpt. Kalyan Kundu, Sakti Bhattacharya, Kalyan Sircar, eds. *Imagining Tagore: Rabindranath and the British Press (1912-1941)* (London: Tagore Centre, 2000): 134, 136.
86. SYN 142, 164.

in the *Fortnightly Review*, the second of his autobiographical essays to appear there.⁸⁷ Arrangements for the publication of a volume of Noguchi's autobiographical essays, originally entitled *My Own Story*, were taken in hand by the capable Douglas Sladen, a cosmopolitan travel writer, editor of *Who's Who* (in which Noguchi was included the following year), and a longtime friend of Yoshio Markino. Sladen arranged for the book to be brought out by Chatto and Windus, publisher of several of his and Markino's books; it would appear, illustrated by Markino, in time for the Christmas season as *The Story of Yone Noguchi*.⁸⁸

67. Charles Ricketts and Charles Shannon, 1903.

With the Oxford lecture finished, Noguchi's attention turned towards his interests in art and theatre. He visited the shared studio of Charles Ricketts and Charles Shannon, whose work still held ties to the 1890s world of Aubrey Beardsley and Oscar Wilde. They were long-time associates of Yeats: Ricketts was currently designing Japanese-influenced costumes for a new production of *The King's Threshold*. Noguchi had met them at a 1903 dinner with Laurence Binyon, a few days after Binyon had showed him his collection of poetry books with covers Ricketts had designed.⁸⁹ Ricketts was eloquent while Shannon was quiet. "Neither of them is a complete person alone, but together they present a rare phenomenon," he explained.⁹⁰ "Ricketts is an enjoyable conversationalist, and how stark the contrast with the sympathetic silence of Shannon, with whom he shares a brotherly bond and lives together."⁹¹ As a gay couple,

87. *Fortnightly Review* 101 (2 Feb. 1914): 263-76. "My London Experience" had appeared in *Fortnightly Review* 95 (Apr. 1911): 608-16.
88. "Some Stories of My Western Life," *Fortnightly Review* 101 (n.s. 95) (2 Feb. 1914): 263-76. Douglas Sladen had first become aware of Japan while living in Australia three decades earlier; a subsequent one-year stay in Japan provided sufficient material for three books: *The Japs at Home* (1892), *A Japanese Marriage* (1895), and *Queer Things About Japan* (1903). He had befriended Markino during the artist's penurious days and the two had become intimate friends, twice traveling together through Italy on Markino's two illustration assignments there.
89. "Rikettsu" (Ricketts), *Yomiuri*, 9 June 1918, 7, rpt. *Nihon no bijutsu* (Tōkyō: Daitōkaku, 1920), 359.
90. "Shanon," *Yomiuri*, 21 July 1918, 7, rpt. *Nihon no bijutsu* (1920), 369-81.
91. "Gaka Rikettsu sensei" (The artist Ricketts), *Ōshū* 193-99.

Ricketts and Shannon escaped censure through their shared vocation and discreet lifestyle. Both had impressive art collections and were great admirers of Japanese prints. "Shannon is also famous as a collector of Hokusai. When you enter his room, you see many magnificent Hokusai prints on the walls. In the first few visits, he was too reserved to show me, but as we became more acquainted, he began showing me his collection of what he called 'naughty pictures,' which are erotic prints. Some of these prints were once owned by Goncourt."[92] He saw the pair several times during his stay, and towards the end of his stay, they invited him to a special dinner, served on dishes of old silver, the table adorned with freshly blossomed spring flowers, and the walls of the small dining room hung with Rembrandt etchings."[93]

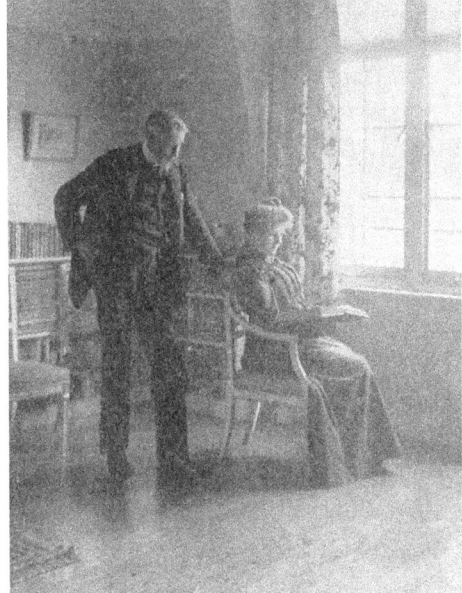

68. Joseph Pennell's studio.

There was also an atmospheric visit to the Adelphi Terrace studio of American artist Joseph Pennell: "The time," Noguchi wrote in an article in the *Graphic*, "should be in January or February, the hour between 5:30 and 6 o'clock." He had gone to take afternoon tea and was surprised when Mrs. Pennell called his attention to the lights along the Thames. "Oh, what a Japanese colour-print effect!" Noguchi exclaimed, reminded of Hiroshige's Ryōgoku Bridge, as well as Whistler's Japanese-influenced paintings. "Indeed it was Whistler that found a Japanese colour-print effect in London," Pennell said. "But he never imitates Hiroshige."[94]

On another occasion he took up an invitation from poet and dramatist Gordon Bottomley to visit him at the home of Robert Trevelyan

92. "Shanon," 379-80.
93. "Shanon," 381.
94. "The Beauty of London," *Graphic* 89 (13 June 1914): 1082.

near Dorking. Bottomley, who suffered from a chronic lung malady, had been a Japan enthusiast for many years. He had been fascinated with *From the Eastern Sea*, and wrote Noguchi a dreamy poem in 1906 about having "seen bending ladies in a mist / Gathering dewy butterflies with fans"; and like his friend W.B. Yeats, would also experiment with Nō-influenced methods in his plays. Noguchi made the short train journey one Monday to Oakley, where he was met by Mrs. Trevelyan, who took him, wrapped in a thick rug, by carriage through the rainy Surrey landscape to the house, commanding "a grand view through the break of a forest leafless but looking almost blossoming in purple in the blue of the mists." There the rain-soaked poet soon found himself sitting before the highly entertaining fire, with Bottomley and Trevelyan and their respective wives. "There were many things I wished to ask Bottomley; but still more subjects Bottomley had to ask me about," Noguchi notes. Trevelyan, a Cambridge-educated classical translator and minor poet, spoke of his recent trip (with his friend Lowes Dickinson) to Asia, and showed Noguchi two or three color-prints hanging on his walls that, he said had once belonged to Edmond de Goncourt.[95]

69. Savage Club smoking room.

Some English Clubs

In contrast to his earlier trip, London's doors were now wide open to Noguchi, even the elite private clubs. Recalling Joseph Addison's description of the "modern celebrated clubs . . . founded upon eating and drinking . . . in which the learned and illiterate, the dull and the airy, the philosopher and the buffoon, can all of them bear a part," Noguchi envisioned "a long procession of handsome young dandies gayly clad in satin with exquisite

95. "A Japanese on Some English Poets," 425.

ruffles, ever ready to rise up with the sword on any possible provocation." He found the modern clubs changed but nevertheless fascinating. "While losing the adventurous romanticism, the present clubs certainly have gained a sure claim as institutions through their own worth; hardly an Englishman, I believe, can live without their convenience," he wrote. One evening, Arthur Morrison, whom Noguchi had met at the Oriental Club, invited him to dinner at the Savage Club, which offered "more democratic freedom in art and life than any other club in the so-called West End." The house dinner was "a boisterous affair quite free from restraint," interrupted only by the Chairman of the evening announcing, "You shall smoke." "Then you have to obey and sing or play on instrument when you are bidden by him; and if you are artist, you can have a large thick piece of paper ready for your activity of fingers."[96]

Noguchi was introduced by Arthur Diósy to an even more curious club called "Ye Sette of Odd Volumes," which held its 337th meeting at Oddenino's restaurant on January 27.[97] There, Noguchi recalled,

> I was greeted by the Rev. Rosedale as the master of ceremonies, carrying a long staff in hand; "Brother Ralph Straus, Scribbler," as President, with a big silver medallion on his breast (what an innocent ornament), was seen making a social bow to every member and guest of the evening. When the dinner was announced, a certain huge key was brought in before Straus the President, with which he opened, I presume, the regular proceedings of this evening; and also a large wooden hammer in shape of 'Odd Volumes' with which the President will make the people silent or call order when it is necessary.

At dinner, Noguchi was introduced to a collector of Japanese *netsuke*, who as Diósy predicted, revealed his hobby to Noguchi by producing a small ivory curiosity from his coat pocket "as if a magician who brings out unexpected things at an odd moment," while the man across from him implored him at some length of the necessity of seeing the blue bells of Kent in the spring, telling Noguchi: "you will be surprised to see the whole hill covered, leaving hardly any spot to step in." "Although I was not quite sure where was that Kent," Noguchi notes, "I promised him that I should use my first opportunity for the blue bells in Kent when the real spring set in here." Taking a break from the conversation, Noguchi turned his attention to deciphering the curious note on the menu:

> After ye disappearance of much goodlie Victuals, and of many flagons sparklynge Wine, there shall be a short time for restynge. Then ye

---

96. [Joseph Addison], *Spectator* 1:9 (10 Mar. 1711), 43; YN, "A Few English Clubs."
97. Ellen Crowell, "'We Are Odd! Ye Archive of Ye Sette of Odd Volumes," *The Center & Clark Newletter* 54 (Fall 2011), 9, explains, "formed in London in 1878 by prominent bookseller and bibliophile Bernard Quaritch, and in continuous operation from 1878 through the 1940s, the group's name derives from bibliophilic parlance: bound volumes not paired with others in their 'set' were 'odd,' and thus less valuable than when united."

Brethren re-assemblyage, and all being readie, His Oddshyppe shall exhorte and commande
   Brother George C. Williamson
      (Horologer)
to entertaine and instruct ye companie concerning Ludowick Muggleton, the Story of his Life, and the Sect he founded, and to illustrate ye same with fine and rare pictures.

Before the lecture began, however, each of the guests were introduced; Noguchi was pleased that "when Diosy introduced me with his usual eloquence, there was a little commotion and handclapping as a sign of good feeling toward myself." The interesting lecture on religious dissenter Muggleton[98] produced a lively discussion, and Noguchi was pleased to see again his friend Holbrook Jackson, who pessimistically commented that the existence of many such sects revealed "the hereditary character of Englishmen who live to deny others."

70. **Edmond Xavier Kapp,** *Seer of Visions: Yone Noguchi,* 1914.

Modernists

And there were more private invitations, one from the Fabian reformers Beatrice and Sidney Webb, in mid-February.[99] Another from Marie Stopes, who wrote inviting him and Léonie to visit, elicited an awkward reply. "Don't you know that we never lived together?—I lived at Kamakura, she at Koishikawa where you called on her." Stopes would have to write Léonie in Chigasaki, but he would be happy to take up her invitation sometime in March, if it were convenient for her.[100]

98. Muggleton was a religious dissenter who had moved from a Cromwell-era apocalypticism to a less blasphemous form of anti-Quakerism. His doctrines questioning the utility of prayer in a world forsaken by God retained a dwindling grass-roots following in the early twentieth century.
99. Sidney Webb to YN, 5 Feb. 1914, *CEL* 406.
100. YN to Marie Stopes, 16 Feb. 1914, British Library.

There was another meeting with Ezra Pound: "Yone Noguchi dined with me on Tuesday; interesting litterateur of the second order," Pound wrote his mother in an undated letter. "Dont like him so well as Sung, or Coomaraswami," he continued, alluding to two Asians known to his parents, a Chinese Finance Ministry official who had recently offered to find Pound and his father jobs in China, and British-Ceylonese geologist-historian Ananda Coomaraswamy. "Still you neednt repeat this, as the acquaintance may grow and there's no telling when one will want to go to Japan."[101]

71. Jacob Epstein, January 1914.

Among the artists Noguchi met, he was perhaps most interested in the young sculptor Jacob Epstein. Although Noguchi was still prone to anti-Semitism ("I was [mightily] pleased that he never looked, in his face, an Isaac or even a Jacob," he wrote), he was glad to find "quite an Oriental archaism, even the Japanese simplicity of Old Japan, in his work," and Noguchi was to find in him, among the modern artists, "perhaps the only one person whom I could trust, whose language well echoed to my senses." Epstein, a Polish Jew born in New York, had settled in London in 1905, taking British citizenship two years later. During 1912-13, he had met Picasso, Brancusi, and Modigliani in Paris, and had there designed the Tomb of Oscar Wilde, perhaps his most famous work, in the Cemetery of Père Lachaise. Back in London—he was living temporarily in the attic above Harold Monro's Poetry Bookshop—he had held his first solo exhibition at the Twenty-One Gallery, which he had invited Noguchi to see. It was perhaps his interest in non-Western art forms, then in vogue in Paris, to which Noguchi responded. In Epstein's art, "the West magically becomes the East," and "the Voice has heightened into the real silence."[102] Returning to London from Paris, Epstein had

---

101. Ezra Pound to Isabel Pound, undated (1914), quoted in Kodama, *Ezra Pound & Japan*, 216. On Far-san T. Sung (Song Faxiang), see Zhaoming Qian, *Ezra Pound's Chinese Friends* (Oxford: Oxford UP, 2008), 1-8. Pound wrote his father on January 19 that he had "seen Sung, pleasant chap." *Ezra Pound to his Parents: Letters 1895-1929* (Oxford: Oxford UP, 2010), 318.

102. "A Japanese on the Western Newest Art," *JT*, 22 Apr. 1917.

founded the London Group, "a considerable body of artists in often unintelligible but merry mood," whom Noguchi had the opportunity to meet during the latter part of his visit at the Goupil Gallery. There, Epstein spoke of his aim "to make his work 'something solid and durable, like the art of the old masters,'" as Cézanne had once proposed. Noguchi was interested in "Epstein's scraw [sic], in red sprawling lines resembling a totem pole of some American tribe or Whitman's barbarous ideograph," which somehow "seemed concerned with eternity or the eternal verities of things."[103] Noguchi lamented that such artistic attitudes were not yet widely understood and appreciated. Yet the general misunderstanding of Epstein was not, Noguchi felt, in the sculptor's Gauguinesque declaration that "barbarism was his restoration to health," but rather in the fact that "modern Western people are not simple enough to see his simple statement of things observed."

72. Roger Fry, February 1913.

Noguchi visited another enthusiast of non-Western and primitive art, Bloomsbury Group member Roger Fry, with his "wonderful hair and intense eyes," at his Omega Workshops. There he found a large screen "you might say in Japanese style, where the cubistic shapes of figures and tent invited you to imagine anything you pleased." The tent, Fry told Noguchi, was "no actual tent, but enough tent to suggest something else, perhaps a green field or a blue sky." Fry told Noguchi that the so-called new art was "even classical" and that the difference from other art was its "greater freedom and desire for real expression." Fry showed him numerous cubist-influenced designs on such tables, curtains, bedspreads and cushion covers, which "in the most cases reminded me of our Japanese work," and Noguchi concluded that "Cubism when it is treated as an applied art shows its artistic revolution (or is it evolution?) very well justified. When it fails, I believe, as an art in its titanic understanding, it will certainly gain as a design which explains the modern sensibility of the artistic mind, and even a science in its most advanced sense if you like."

103. He was probably referring to Epstein's *Totem*, circa 1913, acquired by the Tate Gallery in 1986. <http://www.tate.org.uk/art/artworks/epstein-totem-t03358>.

At one of Hulme's Tuesday night salons, probably on March 3, Harold Monro introduced him to a man with a pale face and delicate, slender fingers—no typical beef-eating Englishman—saying, "This man is a famous English Cubist painter." According to Noguchi's later recollection, they briefly conversed, the painter, none other than Wyndham Lewis, inquiring whether there was any Cubist art in Japan, to which Noguchi replied, "We don't have Cubists like you have here, but for the past two centuries, there's been a something called the *Nanga* style, which looks something like Cubist landscape painting. People sometimes call the paintings 'mashed potato landscapes.' I wonder what they call you in this country." At the time, as Noguchi noted, the works of Lewis and his fellow cubists "aroused not praise or approval, but a kind of strange artistic curiosity."[104]

Noguchi gained respect for Lewis the following week when he read in the *Evening News* Lewis's piece arguing that "Englishmen were the first Futurists, not in paint but in Life; for machinery is chiefly our invention or fashion." It was a clever way of dispensing with arguments that British modernist art was both backward and derivative. Lewis saw the present art movements as "a reaction against the naturalistic chaos of the Impressionists and analytic painters of the last fifty years." "The gush of reverence for Mother Nature is over," he declared. It was not that the modernists had forgotten nature: "we have her in us as a son his mother's blood." But "just as every mother inevitably becomes old-fashioned, so too has nature become old-fashioned. . . . While we respect our mothers' unfashionable clothes, we certainly want our wives to dress stylishly."[105] Such eloquent arguments had impressed Noguchi before he had a chance to see Lewis's paintings, which (at a London Group exhibition) came as a shock.[106]

> It is perfectly amazing to hear such sensible language from the mouth of an artist who calls a coloured tessellated pavement in picture "Christopher Columbus." Certainly that is too much. I think I have a right to say that Wyndham Lewis (putting aside the question of his artistic eligibility) is at least as bad as Alma Tadema. The artist who only argues as the first and last thing is a lost artist; I am sorry that Lewis cannot prove, at least to my mind, his artistic conviction with his own picture.[107]

Comparing Lewis's designs to those of the late Sir Lawrence Alma-Tadema (known for his idealized and often erotic paintings of classical scenes) bordered on cruelty. But Lewis's large canvases had few admirers

---

104. "Shin-geijutsu Tyronism." The term "tsuku-imo sansui" (potato landscape) had been popular since the 1880s.
105. Wyndham Lewis, "Englishmen the First Futurists," London *Evening News*, 10 Mar. 1914, 4. Noguchi may have been the only critic to discuss the article.
106. "A Japanese on the Western Newest Art," *JT*, 22 Apr. 1917; "Shin-geijutsu Tyronism" (A new art, Tyronism), *Kaiga Seidan* 9:12 (Dec. 1921): 1-5.
107. "A Japanese on the Western Newest Art."

even among his modernist confrères: Hulme dismissed them as "mere arbitrary arrangements of bright colours and abstract forms" which failed to "produce as a whole, the kind of coherent effect which, according to the theory, they ought to produce."[108] And Noguchi did not mean his suggestion that Lewis's designs "would look well in a linoleum or carpet or shawls," such as those he had seen at Fry's workshop, as an insult. Lewis's most successful recent project was the Futurist Dining Room he had designed for wealthy British socialite Lady Drogheda. If architects and painters could collaborate, Lewis thought, "the present movement should produce a finer crop of wall paintings than any since the early Italians."[109]

73. Henri Matisse, Joaquina (1911).

Noguchi saw more examples of "so-called Futurists and Cubists" at the Doré Galleries (on New Bond Street), and also the work of Henri Matisse, to which he had a mixed reaction. He thought some of Matisse's oil paintings, like the portrait *Joaquina* (1911) failed, because oil had a "heavy exactness" like the English language or Western clothes. He was better pleased with Matisse's work in watercolor, a medium "much like a Japanese robe," and particularly liked Matisse's crayon drawings, purchasing a lithograph of one. He was also delighted to find a lithograph of "Boys Bathing," by his "beloved" Cézanne, a picture he had unsuccessfully tried to purchase from a German artist during his earlier stay in Paris.

One afternoon as spring approached Noguchi took up Henri Gaudier-Brzeska's repeated invitation to visit his studio by the banks of the Putney Bridge.

> After getting off the train, I wandered around five or six streets and finally discovered his studio, which was one of the warehouses beneath the railway tracks. Peeking through the torn door at the entrance, I saw the sculptor with torn shoes showing beneath his work clothes, which had turned completely

---

108. T. E. Hulme, "The London Group," *New Age*, 26 Mar. 1914, 661.
109. See "Lady Drogheda's Futurist Dining-Room: Decorations," *The Sketch*, 4 Mar. 1914, 265.

black. His shoes were completely white with plaster dust. Inside, there wasn't a single chair to sit on, so as I walked back and forth, Brzeska pulled out two or three dirty newspapers, spread them over a box, and said, 'Take a seat.' There wasn't even a single broom, so it was clear the warehouse had never been swept; the floorboards were covered with dust and plaster. He stopped his work on a bust of his friend Pound and, saying it was already noon, suggested we have a meal together. He took a piece of beef from a paper wrapping, wiped a dirty pot with the paper, put the meat in, and, since he had no firewood, broke apart the lid of a box to make a fire and cook. Even after the meal was prepared, there was only one plate, and no more than two bowls, so after I had eaten, Brzeska ate his meal, and I drank strange coffee from the bowl he had used. When poverty reaches this level, it becomes almost charming. While saying he wanted to give me something as a souvenir before I returned to Japan, he pulled out a piece of art from among the scrap papers in a box—a painting of something swimming, though it was unclear whether it was a person or something else. At the time, I thought little of the picture, but today, it has become a memento of him."[110]

On the afternoon of March 10, "an interesting lecture on the 'No' drama, the Japanese Plays of Silence, was delivered," the London *Times* reported, "in the rooms of the Royal Asiatic Society by Mr. Yone Noguchi."[111] The lecture (later published in *The Spirit of Japanese Poetry*) was mainly taken from his 1912 *Taiyō* essay on the subject, in which Noguchi had given a general introduction to the characteristics of the Nō theatre and its appreciation, proposing it as an antidote for "minds tired from the burden of the spectacular show in the West." "Indeed," he predicted, "the time may be already at hand, or at any rate quite near, when the Western stage will heed the lesson of Japanese simplicity, particularly of this *No* drama, whose archaism might give a divine hint how to sift the confusion and to rhyme beauty and life with emphasis." The London *Times* reporter was intrigued but not convinced:

> In simplicity of stage effect and stage trappings some approach has been made of late years in this country to this particular aspect of the 'No' drama, and the virtues of contemplation have long been recognized in some of the monasteries of the Western world. But not even Mr. Granville Barker has as yet attempted to carry contemplation into the theatre to the extent of filling the auditorium with rows of silent 'appreciators.' On the other hand, London has for a long time been moved by the Russian ballet, and Mr. Bernard Shaw is so far a prophet of the drama of silence that he objects to applause during the performance of his plays. One thing, however, is certain. As a character-forming influence the theatre of contemplation can only succeed on spiritual lines; the optimist who would venture to run it in latter-day London as a commercial speculation is probably not yet born.

In this case the *Times* reporter was mistaken: such an optimist did exist in

110. "Seinen chōkokuka no senshi," *Ōshū* 241.
111. "Drama of Silence," London *Times*, 11 Mar. 1914, 10.

the person of W.B. Yeats (then on tour in America), whose Nō-inspired theatre of contemplation would be successfully staged in London in only two years' time.

Noguchi's objections to the ordinary English theater were not as severe as his lecture suggested, especially when armed with director Harley Granville-Barker's free pass. He took in Barker's production of Shaw's *Doctor's Dilemma*, and saw his *Midsummer Night's Dream* three times.[112] He also saw performances by the leading ballet stars of the season, Nijinsky and Adeline Genée.[113]

By March, Noguchi was making arrangements with Douglas Sladen to have Chatto & Windus publish a book tentatively entitled *My Own Story*. "Many thanks for your last letter," Noguchi wrote Sladen on March 12.[114] "How much Chatto & Windus could give for my book? Fifty pounds, I wonder. I have an idea they are not bad as publishers for such a book of mine." He was eager to move quickly. "I may leave here on the 25th of April; so I like to have my book or books perfectly arranged before my departure."

One of the pleasures of the trip for Noguchi was the fact that he was able to stay long enough to see the English spring. Although he did not make it to Kent to see the bluebells as he had promised at Oddenino's, he did get to Kew Gardens to see "the real beginning of spring" on March 27th. "The gateman directed me to the place where the Japanese cherry trees were blooming. 'Cherry blossoms already in March!' I exclaimed." With the sun going down casting long shadows on the grass by the Chinese pagoda, "I could not properly control my own mind and sang a Japanese popular ditty." He determined to make weekly return visits to see how the beauty of English spring was advancing: "each week I found there a greater beauty of growing leaves and blooming flowers." He was particularly impressed by the blooming almond trees that looked as if covered by snow and reminded him of California.[115]

On April 1, he gave a second lecture at the Japan Society, this time on an artist: "Yoshitoshi, the Last Master of the Ukiyoye School." Ukiyoe specialist Edward F. Strange of the Victoria and Albert Museum, who chaired the talk, said he was looking forward to getting "the real Japanese point of view" from Noguchi. In fact, there was rather little in the way of a Japanese point of view on ukiyoe at this time, as the print genre was only gradually being recognized as a serious art form under the persistent pressure of Western interest; Japanese scholarship on the subject rarely went beyond informal anecdotal reminiscences about artists. Noguchi's

---

112. "Bākā no Saogeki" (Barker's Shakespeare play), *Tōa no Hikari* 10:3 (Mar. 1915), rpt. *Ōshū* 210-18.
113. *Ōshū* contains essays on both performers: Genée's *Robert the Devil*, and Nijinsky's *Les Sylphides* and *Le Spectre de la Rose* both opened in March.
114. YN to Douglas Sladen, 12 Mar. 1914, Collection of Sammy Tsunematsu.
115. "The Beauty of London," *Graphic* 89 (13 June 1914): 1082.

choice of subject was an excellent one for two reasons: first, Yoshitoshi Tsukioka (1839-1892) was not yet widely appreciated in the West, and secondly, the artist's cult popularity in an age of newspapers meant there was more information concerning his life in circulation than was the case with most earlier print artists, so that Noguchi was able to give a fairly comprehensive account of his life and work. Noguchi said he had himself had been a Yoshitoshi fan in his youth:

> I can distinctly remember even to-day my great disappointment, now almost twenty-five years ago, as a most ardent admirer of Yoshitoshi, when, calling at his publisher's house as early as seven o'clock in the morning after I had read the announcement of his new picture of a dancer, I was told that the entire set of copies was exhausted; his popularity was something great in my boyhood's days.

Noguchi was appreciative of Yoshitoshi's haunting works like the famous *One Hundred Views of the Moon* series, one of which he pasted on a screen when still a schoolboy, and less enthusiastic about the gory pictures that were a hallmark of the artist's style in the violent 1870s, images that anticipate the violent *manga* of late twentieth-century Japan. "He helps, more than any other artist, the historian of Japanese art to study the age psychologically," Noguchi suggested.[116]

74. Yoshitoshi Tsukioka, *Genji Yūgao no maki* (The Yūgao chapter of Genji) from *One Hundred Views of the Moon*, 1886.

---

116. "The Last Master of the Ukiyoye Art," *Transactions of the Japan Society of London* 12 (1914): 146-55, rpt. (without illustrations) in SJA.

In early April Noguchi received a note from Sarojini Naidu inviting him to tea at the Lyceum Club on the 9th. "I hear you are soon leaving England and I should so much like to have one more opportunity of seeing a poet for whose beautiful talent I have such great admiration," she wrote. The Lyceum Club was a sort of literary women's club with membership limited to "those who have published original work in literature, journalism, science, art, and music, who have University qualifications, or who are wives or daughters of men distinguished in these branches," the first of its kind in the world. The club was open to women of all nationalities.[117]

There was some truth to the rumor of Noguchi's departure from England. On the following day, April 10, he boarded a train for Edinburgh. He wrote an account of the trip in both English and Japanese.[118] He does not explain his reasons for visiting the city, and his activities were those of an ordinary tourist: visiting the castle, Holyrood Palace, John Knox's house, the Walter Scott monument. He went to a double feature of American films he had already seen in London. He found the street urchins "delightful" and marveled at the wind and rain.

There is no suggestion in his essay that he stayed long in Edinburgh. How he spent the last three weeks of April remains unclear, but he seems to have spent at least part of it in Paris, for he wrote Léonie from London on May 4 that he had "returned here from Paris for a few days to attend to some business—Then to Berlin & Moscow." He was, he told Léonie, "awfully tired of Europe—nothing in it. Japan is the better country to live."[119] With war only three months away, his prediction proved correct. But his European trip was not finished: he was planning to go back to Paris before Berlin and Moscow, although he did not mention this to Léonie.

He may also have needed to put in some work on the three books he had in preparation—*The Story of Yone Noguchi*, which Sladen and Markino would see through the press later that year, and the two books for Cranmer-Byng's pocket-sized "Wisdom of the East" series: *The Spirit of Japanese Poetry* and *The Spirit of Japanese Art*. The autobiographical volume was a haphazard collection of previously published essays. But the "Wisdom of the East" books were expected to make some effort at covering their ostensible subjects. The lectures that formed the core of *The Spirit of Japanese Poetry*—on Japanese Poetry, Hokku Poetry, and the Nō—left gaps which were only partially filled by "Some Uta Specimens from the Hyakunin Isshu" (recycled from his own 1907 translation), and an updated version of his "Poets of Present Japan" essay. So he added a chapter on "The Earliest Japanese Poetry" which discussed the *Kojiki*

---

117. Sarojini Naidu to YN, 5 Apr. 1914, CEL 405.
118. "A Japanese Impression of Edinburgh," *JT*, 17 June 1917; "Ejinbara" (Edinburgh), *Kiri no Rondon* (Tokyo: Genbunsha, 1923), 41-48. No dates are mentioned, but the films Noguchi saw (*Beauty Unadorned* and *The Gusher*) played from April 7 to 10.
119. YN to LG, 4 May [1914], CEL 407.

using lengthy, unacknowledged helpings from Basil Hall Chamberlain's translation. The book was to come out at the end of May.

Noguchi was also writing new essays about his experiences in Britain. He had written to Holbrook Jackson on May 1, explaining he hoped to arrange a final meeting on the 4th as he was planning to leave on the 8th.[120] As editor at *T.P.'s Weekly*, Jackson had published Noguchi's essay on "Bernard Shaw in Japan" and welcomed "The Return of Yone Noguchi" with an enthusiastic article by F. Hadland Davis. As an authority on *The Eighteen Nineties*, his book of the previous year, Jackson likely encouraged Noguchi to write about his own interactions with writer and artist friends of note. Noguchi delivered at least three of these—on Yeats, on Symons, and on the artists Ricketts and Shannon—but only the Yeats essay made it into the magazine.[121] As for his Japanese accounts of the trip for various periodicals, these would take many months to complete after his return, but he did make a start with an essay on Oxford for the April number of *Mita Bungaku*, presumably to show his university colleagues his long sabbatical had not been a waste of time.[122]

For his final travel essay for the *London Daily News*, Noguchi put aside complaints about the present state of Europe and went all out in appreciation of "Things that are Most English." Oxford came to mind first, with its capped and gowned dons, afternoon teas, and common-room talk. The patience and self-control he admired at the college boat race, he found also at city restaurants, where, on one occasion, he was "perfectly surprised to notice that one young woman, evidently a wage-earner at some store, was reading Bergson's philosophy." And then there was a story that had touched many Londoners, "the death of a little boy at Holloway on Bank Holiday, from stopping a runaway horse... England will never fall, I am sure," he concluded, "as long as she has such a wonderful boy in her land."[123] This was too much for the *New Age*, one of the more influential modernist magazines, which dismissed the article as "infantilism," "trash," and "childish prattle." Noguchi was "another treacly Jap," an unfriendly comparison to his artist friend: "have we not suffered under Yoshio Markino?"[124] In case Noguchi missed the article during his travels, Robert Young kindly reprinted it in the *Japan Chronicle* after his return.[125]

Noguchi had explained to Laurence Binyon his "desire to stay some days longer in London" to see the Royal Academy of Arts exhibition

---

120. YN to Holbrook Jackson, 1 May 1914, Poetry and Special Collections, SUNY Buffalo.
121. F. Hadland Davis, "The Return of Yone Noguchi," *T.P.'s Weekly* 23 (2 Jan. 1914): 7. YN, "Bernard Shaw in Japan," *T.P.'s Weekly* 23 (16 Jan. 1914): 67; YN, "W.B. Yeats" *T.P.'s Weekly* 25 (9 Jan.1915): 35.
122. "Okkusufōdo shisō no shōrai" (Future thought of Oxford), *Mita Bungaku* 7:4 (Apr. 1914): 119-23.
123. "Things That Are Most English," London *Daily News*, 13 May 1914, 6. Thousands attended the funeral of twelve-year-old Albert Hatswell who died on Easter Sunday, April 12.
124. "B.," "Another Treacly Jap," *New Age* 15:5 (4 June 1914): 119.
125. "Mr. Yone Noguchi's Return," *Japan Chronicle*, 30 July 1914, 217.

opening on May 1. Binyon, after staring at him for a moment, said he "did not see at all the exact point why." Yoshio Markino was also skeptical, explaining that the reason he attended the special opening day each year was not to see the pictures, but rather, the English ladies' dress, which was "ten times more advanced than the English art." Noguchi, after being "obliged to hear a great deal of sad opinion on the exhibition in general before it opened," was well-prepared "not to be frightened by any bad picture in the exhibition." Thus fortified, he managed to enjoy several paintings, particularly George Clausen's *Primavera*, and John Singer Sargent's *San Geremia*.[126]

Farewell to Europe

The *Japan Times* reported that Noguchi "left London May 10 for home . . . returning via Siberia and will probably arrive in Tokyo in June."[127] Despite his weariness of Europe, he would stop again in Paris before taking the long land route home through China by the Trans-Siberian Railway.

75. Shimazaki Tōson.

In early May, Tōson Shimazaki, who had been in France for the past year, was looking forward to Noguchi's visit. "I have received word from Yonejirō Noguchi, who is staying in London, that he will be coming to Paris around the beginning of this month, but he has not yet arrived," he wrote in his diary.[128] This time around, Noguchi found the season to be as he hoped: "The Paris I saw was peaceful," he wrote, "and being in mid-May, was at its best."[129]

Tōson Shimazaki, three years Noguchi's senior, had left his well-to-do farming family in Magome, a Nakasendō post village, to study at Meiji Gakuin, a Protestant college in Tokyo, from which he graduated in 1891.

---

126. YN, "A Japanese Impression of the Royal Academy," *Westminster Gazette*, 2 June 1914, 1-2.
127. "People and Things," *JT*, 27 May 1914, 8.
128. *Shimazaki Tōson zenshū* 13 (Tokyo: Chikuma Shobō, 1956), 103.
129. "Sensō mae no Pari" (Paris before the war), *Mita Hyōron* 2:2 (Feb. 1915): 38-41.

For five years he remained in Tokyo, becoming part of an influential literary coterie associated with a famous but short-lived journal, *Bungakukai* (1893-98), where he established himself as one of the first true devotees of the new-style poetry. Tōson's first collection of verse, *Wakana-shū* (Collection of young herbs, 1897), had, Noguchi wrote, "enthroned him at once as the master of Shintai-shi." He was "a poet of sentiment, almost inclined to be sentimental . . . always delicate, and often sad."[130] In 1896 he left Tokyo to teach, first in Sendai and then in Komoro, and soon gave up poetry for novel-writing. He established himself as a leader of the realist and naturalist schools with his second novel, *Hakai* (The broken commandment, 1906), the story of a *burakumin* (out-caste) schoolteacher's concealment and eventual confession of his origins, and his 1910 novel, *Ie* (The family), which explored the decline of two provincial families. He had come to France to escape after impregnating his niece, Komako, a secret his family would assist him in keeping uncomfortably concealed until he acknowledged it in his 1917 novel, *Shinsei* (New life).

By the time Noguchi arrived, a minor novelist named Kizan Ikuta had come from Berlin to stay with Tōson at his Montparnasse boarding house. In contrast to Tōson, who spent his days writing and had yet to even visit the Louvre, Kizan had already explored every corner of the city.

The three set off towards the Luxembourg Gardens, Tōson instructing them on the proper way—along the outer path like true Parisians, not through the park as country people did—tapping their canes as they strolled. Their destination (although it would have been more Parisian not to have one) was the statue of Verlaine in the Luxembourg Gardens. (Noguchi concluded that, while he preferred Carrière's painting, the statue was probably a better likeness). Tōson, who had been studying French history, tried to evoke the scene of the palace and gardens in the days of the Revolution. When rain suddenly began falling, Tōson informed them that Parisians regarded running as unbecoming, so they walked on leisurely as the rain drenched their only fine clothes. At a bookshop near the Odéon Theatre, which offered a respite, Noguchi contemplated an expensive illustrated book on the Russian dancer Karsavina, but left it for Tōson. They drank terrible coffee at a nearby café supposedly frequented by Odeon actresses, admiring the female passersby. Then they walked along the Seine to Notre-Dame, and watched the chess players.

On another day, "aimlessly wandering through the city under Ikuta's guidance," they "crawled like snails from Napoleon's tomb towards the Seine." Seeing some splendidly adorned soldiers, they "learned that it was the day the King of Denmark arrived in Paris after his visit to England." That would have been May 16. In Tōson's travel memoir, *Étrangers*, Noguchi and Ikuta are two among a multitude of visiting Japanese, most of them artists. "Noguchi and Ikuta, whom I had known for some time,

---

130. "The Younger Poets of Present Japan," *JT*, 20 May 1905, 6, revised in *SJP* 94.

never expected that we would meet in Paris. Noguchi, weary from his journey in England, stayed at my lodging for about nine days," Tōson recalled, adding that they "had stayed up until dawn at a Japanese restaurant with [painter Kanae] Yamamoto and others."[131]

Noguchi was able to make a brief stop in Berlin on his way to St. Petersburg to begin his Trans-Siberian journey. "When the train crossed the German frontier, the view of nature, with the trees intense in color, with such large open fields of corn or wheat, reminded me at once of the Western country of America, not from the point of magnanimous wealth, but from its extravagance," he later wrote. Berlin seemed to him a European Chicago: "common and businesslike, in sack-coat, with the inartistic regularity of her buildings and the equally inartistic statues of soldierly rigidity at nook or corner." His impression of Germany and the Germans was not, apparently, a favorable one, but by the time he wrote about it for an American magazine, Germany was at war with England, and Noguchi no doubt felt encouraged to give his criticisms full reign, writing of the Germans' "incommunicable crudeness and uncouth self-expression," their civilization "a civilization without gentlemanly culture, whose eye is set on life's strife and contest."[132]

His impression of Russia was somewhat better.[133] The journey by train from Berlin to Moscow was both beautiful and entertaining, as Noguchi shared a compartment with three multilingual Russians. The capital that would soon be transformed by revolution was, to Noguchi, a city "of innocently striking colour, somewhat tropical, therefore incongruous with its loudly painted walls and roofs, its audacious cupolas of gold, its irregularities and fantasies, with temples, dirty small cottages neighbouring with pretentious pillars, its narrow, winding streets, where the passers-by were seen tracing a sacred cross on their breasts." He filled out his brief glimpse of the city with material drawn from Arthur Symons's Moscow chapter in *Cities* (1905). Moscow, Noguchi agreed, was a "town of uncivilized people who give the impression of civilization," but "how like is Moscow to our Kyoto, where the savage extravagances are softened to harmonise with the civilized aspect!" It also had a feeling of being "quite an Oriental town" due to its "multitudinous colours, distinguished by dissimilarity rather than by contrariety" and "the warm, even elemental sense" which "pervades here like a glowing atmosphere, and makes us feel crushed under it, as if a heavy cloud were fallen from above." He found the Kremlin "an extremely characteristic sight of Russian devotion

---

131. *Etoranzee: Furansu ryokō-sha no gun* (*Étrangers*: A France travel group) (Tokyo: Shunyōdō, 1922), ch. 57.

132. "A Japanese Scholar on Western Civilization," *Nation* (New York) 101 (29 July 1915): 145-46.

133. "Russian Psychology," *JT*, 10 Dec. 1916. A Japanese version appeared as "Nichi-Ro ryōkokumin no kokoro" (Japanese and Russian mentality), *Yomiuri*, 23 July 1916, 7, and "Shimonsu no Roshia kokumin-ron" (Symons's theories about the Russians), *Yomiuri*, 26 Nov. 1916, 7, reworked as "Rokokujin" (Russians) in *Suwaru ningen no hyōron* (Tokyo: Kaizōsha, 1925), 42-48.

in religion, grotesque rather than simple with immense crowds of country pilgrims, sandal-footed, carrying a cotton quilt on their backs, the occasion being to commemorate somebody's accession to a saintship." At the Chudov monastery he was awestruck to find an almost endless line of people waiting to be admitted within, with not a word of complaint, "but only realising their own religious courage or strength" with "motionless patience, or perfect disregard of time." Again, he found a parallel with Kyoto, where "patience and aloofness above time" were also characteristic. Perhaps, he thought, Russia could be said to share the qualities of Celticism he had previously been interested to discover in Japan, although he thought that in contrast to the Irish, the Russians had "a barbarous turn that makes them unable to resist their too wild impulses."

On June 12, Noguchi was back at Tokyo's Shinbashi Station.[134] On the 16th he was visted by Hōmei Iwano, to whom he presented a copy of Romain Rolland's *Tolstoy* as souvenir.[135] On the 17th he gave a press conference. He had, according to the *Japan Times*, "many interesting things to tell of his observations" on "a wide range of subjects, all the way from the popularity of old Japanese paintings in England, the novel features of the British stage, the introduction of 'No' performances in Europe, and so on, to his appreciation of the Irish poet William Butler Yeats."[136] But it was "his reference to the practice of literary piracy in this country" that drew most of the comment. When Noguchi had told George Brandes that some of his works had become very popular in Japanese translation, "the Danish scholar expressed himself as quite surprised to learn of the fact, as he had never been communicated with about the matter, although he said he was glad that his productions are being read in so distant a land." George Bernard Shaw had also heard there had been Japanese translations of some of his works, and his question to Noguchi as to whether they were "well done" hinted, Noguchi thought, "at the impropriety of giving a Japanese version of his work without asking his permission." Shaw also "emphatically objected to staging his dramas" saying he "hoped this would never be done in Japan," a comment that must have surprised Noguchi, who had enthusiastically reviewed a Japanese Shaw production for *The Graphic* a few years earlier. "Mr. Noguchi says that to translate a foreign work without first writing to its author is something that should not be done by a civilized people." The *Japan Times* writer thought it a timely rebuke. Noguchi's own extensive career as a literary pirate was not mentioned, nor the irony of his appearing as a spokesman for the anti-piracy cause.

134. "Zappō Noguchi Yonejirō shi no kikyō" (Miscellaneous Reports: The Return of Mr. Yonejirō Noguchi), *Gakutō* 18:6 (20 Jun. 1914): 21-22.
135. Iwano Hōmei, *Hōmei zenshū* 12 (Tokyo: Kokumin Tosho, 1921), 250.
136. YN, "Literary Piracy," *JT*, 17 June 1914, 4; YN, "The Artistic Interchange of East and West," *Graphic* 83 (18 Feb. 1911): 248.

6

OUR MODERN MINDS

1914-1918

"What does the present European war mean to us Orientals?" Noguchi wondered on September 7, 1914, addressing readers of the New York magazine, *The Nation*, to which he was a regular contributor.[1] "It means," he answered, "the saddest downfall of the so-called Western civilization; our belief that it was built on a higher and sounder footing than ours was at once knocked down and killed; we are sorry that we somehow overestimated its happy possibility, and were deceived and cheated by its superficial glory." News of the war had come at a time when Japanese cultural nationalism had firmly taken root, reawakening opposition to internationalism; Noguchi's weariness with Europe during his recent trip was one manifestation of it. The news that Europe was embroiled in war thus provoked a further devaluation of the ideas of Western civilization, which were now interpreted by a generation of well-informed and often foreign-educated intellectuals. "We now see," Noguchi wrote, that the so-called Western civilization "was merely a mirage or optical illusion of a thing which, in its truest sense, never existed; or if it ever existed, it was simply a changed form or crafty masquerading of an avaricious instinct of primitive barbarism." Battles over colonial possessions revealed the hypocrisy of the idealistic rhetoric about colonies supposedly established to spread civilization and enlightenment. The war confirmed the suspicion that "the Western people, with all sorts of colleges and institutions in their most advanced order, are, after all, like their naked friends in far-away Asia or Africa, as it proves now, only a hungry piece of flesh, who, to use a Japanese saying, has just three more hairs than a monkey."

Japan had been criticized as a "warlike nation," declared a threat by Americans, and labeled another "Yellow Peril" by the German Kaiser,

---

1. "The Downfall of Western Civilization," *Nation* (New York) 99 (8 Oct. 1914): 432.

but "what that German Emperor is doing now," Noguchi pointed out, "is certainly a mighty peril against all the humanities of the whole world." And it was not only Germany: "Who can deny when I say that the Western people, when they are so strong and savage, are the pure believers in Machiavellism?"

The present war, Noguchi believed, would set a new standard for international relations, a standard that he feared would be emulated by Asian nations. He foresaw an ominous escalation of imperial violence. "It is not too much to say," he wrote apocalyptically, "that the present European war is the beginning of the dark age of the whole world."

He himself had been "losing for some long while his respect towards the West and Western civilization." "I have seen enough proof that the Western life was not to lead one to soul's content and peacefulness but always to disturbance and pain," he wrote. His recent trip had reinforced his views. "Having much dissatisfaction with the Western life, I returned to a country whose immediate, most important determination should be a refusal to the Western invasion; I believe I know too much to be surprised by the present European war."

Rising Tides

Noguchi probably intended his essay as a wake-up call to American idealists, but it also served as a provocation to the Machiavellians. For Lothrop Stoddard (no relation to Charles Warren), Noguchi's essay affirmed the threat of awakened Asia. Japan represented the vanguard of *The Rising Tide of Color Against White World-Supremacy*, as Stoddard titled his influential manifesto. Like Noguchi, Stoddard saw "the heart of the white world ... divided against itself" as the beginning of "an ominous cycle ... whose end no man can foresee." After the war's end, an "unconstructive peace" would leave the white world "debilitated and uncured," at the mercy of the colored world's "rash dreams and violent action."[2]

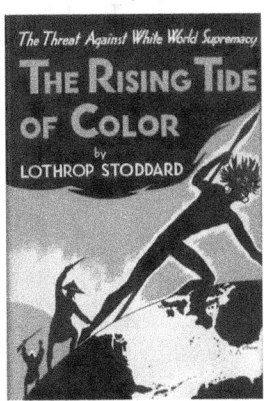

76. Lothrop Stoddard, *The Rising Tide of Color Against White World-Supremacy* (1920).

2. Lothrop Stoddard, *The Rising Tide of Color Against White World-Supremacy* (New York: Scribner, 1920), 14-16.

Noguchi's attack on Western superiority was, for Stoddard, one among a number of wake-up calls to recognize the Japanese desire for world domination: one of the most militarily potent threats of the "colored world." The Japanese were "fired by a fervent patriotism; resolved to make their country a leader among the nations"; they "writhe at the constriction of their present race-bounds." "Japan must find lands where Japanese can breed by the tens of millions if she is not to be automatically overshadowed in course of time, even assuming that she does not suffocate or blow up from congestion before that time arrives. This is the secret of her aggressive foreign policy, her chronic imperialism, her extravagant dreams of conquest and 'world-dominion.'" China seemed the natural outlet for such dreams—Stoddard was inclined to relinquish white dominion in Asia to maintain the purity of the "White race" in America—but "a Japanese imperialist pronouncement written in the autumn of 1916," stating that "North America alone will support a billion people" and "that billion shall be Japanese with their slaves," was another matter. There was, he thought, a "very imminent danger that the white stocks may be swamped by Asiatic blood." Stoddard's views were by no means dismissed as the views of a raving extremist; on the contrary, during the 1920s, along with Madison Grant (who wrote the introduction to *The Rising Tide of Color*), Lothrop Stoddard enjoyed a respected position among the leading American representatives of the widely-accepted "science" of Eugenics.[3]

Grand political topics, such as "The Downfall of Western Civilization" became something of a specialty for Noguchi during the First World War. For the New York journal, *The Nation*, he compared Germany and England in "A Japanese Scholar on Western Civilization," explained "The Impracticability of Sending a Japanese Army to Europe," "The Failure of the Chinese Republic," "The Future of the Anglo-Japanese Treaty," and "The Future of Japanese Shintoism." For readers of the London *Graphic* he wrote "What Japan Thinks of the War," "The Effect of the War on Japan," "The Effect of Britain on Japan," and the "Spiritual Effect of the War on Japan." No longer merely a purveyor of spurious translations and imaginary battle scenes, his faults were now of a milder variety: a tendency to overconfidently overgeneralize about topics out of his range of expertise. Provocative phrases, sometimes exaggerated for effect, like "the downfall of Western civilization," helped Noguchi punch above his weight in the mainstream American and British magazines for which he wrote political journalism during the First World War.

Racism and xenophobia were nothing new in the United States, of course, but they were enjoying a new popularity, bolstered by the growth of wartime nationalism and new scientific efforts at rationalization, particularly within the emerging Eugenics movement. The Japanese, in

---

3. Lothrop Stoddard, *Rising Tide of Color*, 48, 301.

addition to their ongoing efforts at racial self-definition, were also coping with the inevitable conflicts between rationalism and the Shintō-based nationalism promulgated since the early years of the Meiji era. A decade earlier, Noguchi had attended a ceremony at Yasukuni Shrine where "the ten thousand spirits of our Japanese soldiers who were killed by Russians in the Manchurian field" had been "called back here to the Yasukuni shrine (the sacred home for the soldiers dead for the country's welfare) by the august wishes of the Emperor, and enshrined in it," becoming "no more dead soldiers, but gods."[4] "It may sound to you Western people hopelessly heathenish or barbarous," Noguchi conceded. "But we Japanese do not mind what criticism you may fling upon us. . . . We are ancestor worshipers, and also worshipers of the brave fighters who sacrificed their lives for the country. They are the men of men, and very properly we regard them as gods." "The secret of uniting harmoniously Occidentalism and Orientalism only Japanese know . . . that secret made Japan victorious in the last war. We must remain Oriental forever, and at the same time we must be Occidental spiritually." Noguchi had found the opposing beliefs hard then to reconcile, and harder now. In "The Future of Japanese Shintoism," he pointed to the "unmistakable evidence of agitation in the general conception of Shintoism or ancestor-worship in the Japanese minds of to-day," and wondered "how the belief in Shintoism, simple and archaic, can harmonize with modern education."[5] Evidence of this disharmony had recently cropped up in a curious way in a troubling public debate over the correctness of an Imperial decision to appoint a successor to the Nogi family which had been left, by the General's express wish, without an heir following his famous suicide. Nogi had taken an unusually strict view of Shintō ancestor worship, going so far as to call the common Japanese practice of adoption "unnatural and even unreasonable": since his sons had died in battle, he argued, his family line should become extinct. Had the Imperial decision to override his wishes been the correct one? Moreover, the choice of the heir had an odd provocativeness about it: it was a younger brother of Arinori Mori, Japan's first envoy to America, who had been assassinated by a Shintō fanatic after violating the sanctity of the Imperial shrine at Ise, attempting to demonstrate the pointlessness of Shintō superstitions. What did it mean? Noguchi regarded it as an indication of a weakening shift in the conception of ancestor-worship, produced by sociological shifts of descendants away from ancestral homes (as had happened in his own family, where the eldest son lived in Tokyo), by "the modern tendency of individualism and the evolutionary theory, which incline to encourage the idea of regarding the descendants as superior to and greater than the ancestors themselves," and finally, by what he called "the inner destitution" of

4. "The Making of Gods," *Los Angeles Times*, 24 Jun. 1906, VI:18.
5. "The Future of Japanese Shintoism," *Nation* (New York) 102 (11 May 1916): 512-13.

the ancestral spirits, by which he seems to have meant their decreasing relevance in their children's lives in a rapidly changing society. "When the ancestral spirits cannot reveal their worldly action as in their lives, bestowing on us physical prosperity and peace, our modern minds, more or less touched by science and philosophy, would only recognize them through our emotion." This was not a complete disaster for ancestors and *kamisama*. Even if ancestor worship were reduced to merely an emotional feeling toward the ancestors, "such a sense will be real and true," he argued—employing a phrase he had used to describe Yeats's ancestor worship—"as far as the imaginative reality goes." He did, however, think that "the ancestor-worship as a religion," even though "highly encouraged by the Imperial House," was "becoming a thing of the past." If this were to happen, it would be necessary to rethink "Japanese Patriotism or devotion to the Imperial House"; "our world-famous loyalty to the Throne, if we still keep it then, should be understood differently." But there were many ifs, and Noguchi himself seemed ambivalent about the outcome. Should such a shift in thought take place, "even the Imperial House would be powerless against our changing conception of ancestor-worship." But he thought it "both right and wise for the Imperial House to remind us that it is the very descendant of the ancient god or goddess; certainly this is the strongest self-protection it could find," and moreover, "the spiritual insularity which once has been broken cannot be so easily mended." As it happened, in an increasingly isolated Japan, pragmatism would continue to hold the edge over rationalism, keeping State Shintō out of immediate danger. Noguchi had probably overstated the threat presented by "science and philosophy"; after all, Shintō had managed to coexist fairly peacefully with the contradictory system of Buddhism for centuries.

Overseas Friends

Now that Noguchi had declared his vehement dissatisfaction with Western life and affirmed his support for Japan's "refusal to the Western invasion," he devoted himself, paradoxically, to writing about his recent European trip, both in English and in Japanese. English articles on Shaw, Yeats, "the madman Symons," Oxford, and the London art scene and theatre world appeared in the London *Bookman*, Holbrook Jackson's magazines (*T.P.'s Weekly* and *To-day*), New York's *Nation* and *Living Age*, and the *Japan Times*, to which Noguchi contributed a weekly column between 1916 and 1918. "I've been a little busy typewriting Y.N.'s new book on 'Blessed England,'" Léonie noted in a November 5, 1914 letter.[6] But the travel experiences of a Japanese poet, for all their novelty, were not what wartime Britain was clamoring to read. It did not help that Noguchi was still prone to occasional inventions, such as an impossible

---

6. LG to Catherine Bunnell, 5 Nov. 1914, in *LG* 272.

meeting with poet James Elroy Flecker, who had left England in 1912.[7] The book never saw print in English.

In Japan there was considerable interest in what Noguchi had learned about the latest developments in British literature and art, his encounters with writers and artists, his pioneering Oxford lecture, and even his ordinary travel experiences. The essays in Japanese were easy to publish. They went to the two Keio magazines, *Mita Bungaku* and *Mita Hyōron*, *Gakutō*, and a variety of newspapers: most often the *Yomiuri*, but also the *Asahi*, *Jiji*, *Kokumin*, and *Osaka Mainichi*. Twenty of the essays were anthologized as *Ōshū bundan inshō ki* (Impressions of European literary circles) in 1916, a slightly different selection as *Kiri no Rondon* (London mists) in 1923, after which they continued to reappear in various collections.[8] The trip had stimulated his interest in British and Irish literature. Among living writers, he was mainly interested in those he (or his friends) knew or had known. He also began to look more closely at British writers of the previous century: Shelley and Byron, Browning, Carlyle, Dante Gabriel Rossetti, and George Meredith. He continued to be interested in the works of nineteenth-century American writers: Poe and Whitman, as in his younger days, but now also Hawthorne, Emerson, and Thoreau. The writers he took up were mostly canonical—presumably topics he taught at Keio—but some were whimsical, like the essay on Claude Duval, highwayman hero of dime novels he had devoured in his youth.

77. Eunice Tietjens.

7. "A Japanese on Some English Poets," *Living Age* 290 (12 Aug 1916): 420-25. "One more poet whom I cannot forget is Flecker, who died somewhere in the near East since I left London in the summer of 1914," Noguchi added at the end of his article, "A Japanese on Some English Poets." "It was by accident that I met him in the street near Bloomsbury, whither I had moved from a hotel in Pall Mall." Noguchi said had been looking for the house where Stoddard, Miller, and Mark Twain had stayed many decades earlier when "a man covered by a heavy overcoat tapped my back and exclaimed: 'I cannot tell you where your American friends lived. But I will point out where Disraeli used to live.' Then we stole into a little restaurant near by, and sat before the coffee for a long hour." Flecker last left England on Christmas Eve, 1912, according to John Sherwood, *No Golden Journey: A Biography of James Elroy Flecker* (London: Heinemann, 1973): 166.

8. *Ōshū bundan inshō ki* (Tokyo: Hakujitsusha, 1916); *Kiri no Rondon* (London mists) (Tokyo: Genbunsha, 1923).

Noguchi had no thought of refusing the Western invasion when overseas writers like Eunice Tietjens came to visit. The thirty-one-year-old aspiring poet from Chicago had become an "office girl and general nuisance" at the newly-inaugurated *Poetry* magazine after separating from her husband a few years earlier. She and her mother, sister, and four-year-old daughter had embarked on a long journey: first to San Francisco for the Panama-Pacific Exhibition, and then to China, by way of Japan, to visit another sister working there as a missionary. She arrived in Yokohama in early November, left her family in Tokyo, and secured the last available berth to Kyoto in time to see the so-called coronation of the new emperor, Yoshihito, which she had been commissioned to write up for *Vogue* magazine. Noguchi was there too, writing up the event for the *Nation* in New York, though they probably did not meet until Tietjens returned to Tokyo, when she began (as she says in her autobiography) "taking lessons in modern poetry" from him at his home in Nakano. Noguchi was at that time "the leading interpreter—in a psychological sense—between his country and the West in matters of literature and manners," Tietjens explained, and indeed, in the November issue of *Poetry* magazine, Alice Corbin Henderson had praised *The Spirit of Japanese Poetry* as "a key to a vast store-house of treasure." But Tietjens was among the first to see Noguchi as simply a modern poet rather than a Japanese curiosity. "His floating black hair, his startlingly brilliant eyes and surprising accent in English, for all he wrote it so well, had impressed me with the fact that sometimes a person's profession seems more obvious even than his nationality. Noguchi was to me far more apparently a poet than a Japanese."[9]

India's Messenger

One of the major events in the Japanese intellectual world in 1916 was the June visit of the Bengali poet Rabindranath Tagore. Noguchi had heard much about Tagore in London two years earlier when the news that Tagore had been awarded the Nobel Prize for literature was the talk of the town. Tagore had arrived in England in 1912 carrying a notebook of translations he had made of his own poetry while passing the time on the voyage from his native Calcutta; though famous in India, he was at the time virtually unknown abroad. His poems, shown by Will Rothenstein to W.B. Yeats, had overwhelmed the Irish poet, who wrote an introduction to the volume. For several months all of literary London had clustered around the handsome, spiritual, white-bearded poet who wore flowing robes and spoke his poems in a musical voice, or sang them in the original Bengali. Noguchi's success in Britain was a polite clap in

9. Eunice Tietjens, *The World at My Shoulder*. New York: Macmillan, 1938): 22, 78, 95; Noguchi, "The Coronation of Emperor Yoshihito," *Nation* 101 (23 Dec. 1915): 740; A[lice] C[orbin] H[enderson], "Japanese Poetry," *Poetry* 7:2 (Nov. 1915): 89-95.

comparison to the deafening applause that surrounded Tagore. Even the usually critical Ezra Pound conceded that the "very great Bengali poet" made him feel "like a painted pict with a stone war club." After Tagore won the Nobel Prize in literature in November 1913, his works achieved an unprecedented popularity, as his poems, fiction, plays, and essays sold briskly not only in English translation but in dozens of other languages worldwide, including, of course, Japanese.[10]

Tagore had an earlier connection to Japan, however, via Kakuzō Okakura, "a great original mind from these shores" who had come to India in 1902, staying with Tagore's family, and traveling with his nephew. "He was our guest for a long time and he had immense inspiration for the young generation of Bengal in those days," Tagore reminisced.[11] Three leading artists from Okakura's Bijutsuin—Taikan Yokoyama, Shunsō Hishida and Shōkin Katsuta—had followed, as emissaries of an artistic exchange that proved productive in both directions. When Okakura, "almost mortally ill and intending to come back to his native soil" met Tagore again in Boston in 1913, he had promised to take him personally to see not only Japan but also "the real China which is not quite evident to the shallow curiosity of the ordinary tourist mind." Before Okakura's death from kidney disease only months later, Tagore "came to know both of these countries from the personal relationship with this great man whom I had the good fortune to meet and accept as one of my intimate friends."

Noguchi had probably heard of Tagore's planned visit when he wrote his first letter introducing himself in February 1915. "I was so often told of you while I was in London some months ago," he explained, mentioning their mutual friends, W. B. Yeats and Ezra Pound. He had often thought of Tagore and was eager to learn more about his personality. He enclosed some of his own poems in hopes that Tagore would read them.[12]

"I know your name through your English poems," Tagore replied a few months later. "I hope to have the pleasure of seeing you, and I am glad to think that I shall have the chance." His trip was to be the following year. "I only hope there will be no obstacles next autumn when I intend to visit Japan in the season of the chrysanthemums. . . . I earnestly hope to understand real Japan by the help of true poets when I visit your country."[13]

As a prelude to Tagore, Noguchi met another Bengali visiting Japan:

10. Pound to Dorothy Shakespear, 1 Oct. 1912, in *Ezra Pound and Dorothy Shakespear, Their Letters, 1909-1914*, 163. For an account of Tagore's Western popularity see Edward Marx, "The Tagore Era," in *The Idea of a Colony* (Toronto: U of Toronto P 2004): 63-83.
11. Rabindranath Tagore, "Address to the Indo-Japanese Association," *Visva-Bharati News* 1:8 (Feb. 1933): 71. On Okakura's Indian travels, see Surendranath Tagore, "Kakuzo Okakura: Some Reminiscences," *Visva Bharati Quarterly* 2 (Aug 1936): 65-72.
12. YN to Tagore, 5 Feb. 1915, qtd. in Hori, *'Nijūkokuseki' Shijin Noguchi Yonejirō*, 349-50.
13. Tagore to YN, undated, qtd. in "Great Indian Poet to Visit Japan," *JT*, 29 May 1915, 1.

28-year-old sociologist Benoy Kumar Sarkar. Sarkar had heard about Noguchi when in England and had read *The Spirit of Japanese Poetry*. Noguchi met him at his Tokyo hotel and brought him by tram and train to his Nakano house, which to Sarkar's eye resembled a picture on a kakemono: a cottage surrounded by farmhouses, rice fields, and vegetable plots, with a Buddhist temple not far off. Entering Noguchi's study from the garden, Sarkar admired Noguchi's literary mementos, including a photograph of Robert Bridges and a handwritten letter from W.B. Yeats. Noguchi's wife entered, bowing to the floor, and his children, doing the same. Sarkar was surprised that his wife spoke no English. Noguchi informed him that, having spent his younger days abroad, he now preferred a more traditional Japanese lifestyle, as did his wife. Sarkar returned to his hotel believing that Noguchi could at least partially fill the place left vacant by the death of Okakura.[14]

There was much anticipation surrounding Tagore's visit to Japan, and a great deal of public discussion. An anthology of his English writings had already been translated into Japanese, running through four editions in 1915, and two biographies in Japanese and several books on his general philosophy had appeared. Following the announcement of his impending visit in the spring of 1915, a number of magazines ran special Tagore numbers. An anthology on *How Famous People View Tagore*, which included an entry by Noguchi, had also appeared in 1915.[15]

Even before his arrival, however, many Japanese intellectuals were sharply questioning the relevance of Tagore's pacifist spiritualism to Japan. This element of doubt turned into consternation when it became clear that Tagore would be taking up a strongly anti-nationalistic position in his lectures. Tagore argued against emulating "the political civilization which has sprung up from the soil of Europe and is overrunning the whole world, like some prolific weed." This political civilization was "carnivorous and cannibalistic in its tendencies," a "wholesale feeding of nation upon nation" which "tries to thwart all symptoms of greatness outside its own boundaries, forcing down races of men who are weaker, to be eternally fixed in their weakness." He offered Japan, instead, the civilization of China and India, "whose basis is society and the spiritual ideal of man." "Though it may look feeble and small, judged by the standard of the mechanical power of modern days, yet like small seeds it still contains life and will sprout and grow." Tagore's vision was wise and remarkably prescient, but he had arrived just as Japan, having enthusiastically joined the "wholesale feeding of nation upon nation," was sitting down to dine,

---

14. Sugata Bose, *Asia After Europe* (Cambridge, MA: Harvard UP, 2024), 59-61; Benoy Kumar Sarkar, *Nabin Asiar Janmadata Japan* (The birth-giver of new Asia: Japan) (Calcutta: Grihastha, 1923), 169-71.

15. Kiyozawa Iwao, ed., *Meishi to Tagōru kan* (Famous people's Tagore views) (Tokyo: Jōnansha, 1915). See also Stephen Hay, *Asian Ideas of East and West: Tagore and His Critics in Japan, China, and India* (Cambridge, Mass.: Harvard UP, 1970): 85-89.

as it were, on China while the Western powers were occupied elsewhere. The course Tagore was suggesting was inconceivable to most Japanese intellectuals, as it went against Japan's great effort, since the arrival of Commodore Perry, to stand up to the West as an equal. Many, including Noguchi's friend Hōmei Iwano, became strong critics of Tagore. Noguchi, however, was prepared to embrace Tagore's views, and was, as Steven Hay notes, "so excited at Tagore's arrival in Japan that he somehow managed to get into his fellow poet's train compartment to talk with him on the last part of his journey from Kobe to Tokyo."

On the evening of June 5, a crowd of twenty thousand waited outside Tokyo station to greet the arrival of the Bengali poet in his distinctive white robes, escorted by Noguchi and Taikan Yokoyama, Tagore's host during his Tokyo stay.[16]

78. Tagore's arrival at Tokyo, escorted by Noguchi and Yokoyama.

Noguchi wrote up his "Talks with Tagore" for the magazine *Bunshō Sekai*,[17] and helped arrange for Tagore and his entourage to attend a Nō performance on June 12, after which he used Tagore's comments about the performance for an article on "Mr. Tagore and the Nō."[18]

Despite all the fanfare, most Japanese intellectuals, Noguchi's friends included, regarded Tagore with skepticism and suspicion. Chōkō Ikuta, a translator and social critic who would soon be coediting a magazine with Noguchi, conceded he had read nothing of Tagore's but "judging

16. Hay, *Asian Ideas of East and West*, 12.
17. "Tagōru-shi to kataru" (A Talk with Mr. Tagore), *Bunshō sekai* 11:7 (July 1916): 202-07.
18. "Tagōru-shi to nō" (Mr. Tagore and the Nō), *Yōkyokukai* 5:1 (Jul. 1916): 50-52.

by what has been written thus far about Mr. Tagore by the Japanese who wished to introduce him to Japan, I do not recognize any need to know more about him." Hōmei Iwano, the "fiercest of all Tagore's critics among Japan's literary leaders," called it absurd for Tagore "to deny material civilization with the petrified ideas of ruined India when he comes to an independent and developed country like Japan." Tetsujirō Inoue, the former chair in philosophy at Tokyo University, thought Tagore's voice was "like the song of a ruined country." While a writer like Yeats could speak of Tagore's lyrics as "the work of a supreme culture," nearly every Japanese critic spoke of India as "ruined," a sign of the deep-seated fear of colonial domination that continued to motivate vehement Japanese efforts to "escape from Asia," as Yukichi Fukuzawa had long ago recommended. Japan was at this stage fully committed to Western-style science, materialism, and imperialism. Inoue warned: "Tagore wants to reverse the current of civilization; I do not want this opinion to spread."[19] Noguchi promptly took a poem he had written for Inoue's journal some years earlier, "Symphony Born But Not Fashioned" and rewrote it as an extended paean "To Rabindranath Tagore," whose "song looms above time and place . . . a light born of dream and hope."[20] Noguchi told Calcutta's *Modern Review* Tagore's Japanese audience had been split: "While some, adherents of the so-called Western civilization in Japan . . . called Sir Rabindranath merely a propagandist of negativism or willful dreamer . . . others, delightfully awakened into the so-called Japanism or Orientalism endorsed by the exposed weakness of the present European war, thought that Sir Rabindranath agreed with their first principle in encouraging the real individualism to assert the inner development of the nation."[21] These, he acknowledged, included "the Japanese chauvinists" who were encouraged by Tagore's eviscerating critique of Western politics, particularly his attack on the California exclusionists, "inhospitably shutting out aliens through those who themselves were aliens in the land they now occupy."

On June 15, Tagore left Tokyo for the outskirts of Yokohama where he would spend a relatively quiet two months at the home of Taikan's wealthy art collector friend, Tomitarō (Sankei) Hara. Adopted into his wife's family of wealthy silk merchants, Hara had developed a tract of land into the Sankeien, a resplendent lake garden filled with old buildings, some brought from distant Kyoto. The Hara family occupied a house in the private inner gardens, while the outer gardens had been opened to the public as a park in 1906.

19. Chōkō Ikuta in *Rikugō zasshi* (July 1916): 92, qtd in Hay, *Asian Ideas of East and West*, 95; Hōmei Iwano in *Shinchō*, qtd in Hay, 96; Tetsujirō Inoue in *Rikugō zasshi* (July 1916): 27, qtd in Hay, 107.
20. "To Sir Rabindranath Tagore," *Far East* 9 (24 June 1916): 352; "Symphony Born But Not Fashioned," *Tōa no Hikari* 4:8 (Aug. 1909): 112-3. Noguchi called the Japanese version, "Sono tetsujin ni ataeru" (to a philosopher).
21. YN, "Tagore in Japan," *Modern Review* 20 (Nov. 1916): 528-29..

79. **Entrance to Sankeien.**

Eunice Tietjens recalled her summer visit with Noguchi in her autobiography. "One night as I lay on my *futon* under the mosquito netting, I was awakened by a great pounding on the door which proved to be a boy with a telegram." Opening it, she read: "Today at two o'clock we go to see Rabindranath Tagore." It was signed, "Yone Noguchi." Tietjens was quite eager to see Tagore, having joined *Poetry* magazine too late to meet the Bengali poet during his 1912 visit to Chicago. At Hara's house, "a veritable palace," they found several people waiting in the anteroom, and Tietjens had a moment of culture shock when the great poet arrived and "Noguchi, who had always seemed so westernized when with me, suddenly dropped from my side to his knees and bowed his head to the ground," and "all the others did the same, leaving me alone high in the air, lost to all civility." Among those bowing ceremonially at her feet was "a white man, a tall thin English man in kimono and *tabi*, who presently rose to his feet and rescued me by offering me his hand": no doubt W.W. Pearson, Tagore's disciple, formerly of the London Missionary Society. Tagore "sat that day on a cushion on the floor, at the head of a long table only a few inches high, on which were various exquisite pieces of oriental carving." Tietjens and Noguchi "sat on cushions farther down the table, in places of distinct oriental inferiority," she felt, though this suited her feelings perfectly, for "Tagore was impressive beyond anything I could have imagined by the very simplicity and sincerity of the man, one of those people who 'convince by their presence.'" He was wearing a Japanese *haori* over a simple Indian garment, and his long, curly hair was then quite striking, for "surprisingly it was not black, not white, but both, so that one lock was black and the next white, with no shading of grey."

He spoke in a high and gentle voice, and his face seemed to shine with an inner light of peace. Afterwards, Tietjens did not remember much that he said, "only how I felt in his presence." She remained an admirer, though she did not become like Pearson, a disciple, preferring the opinion of Sarojini Naidu who later told her "most amusingly that Tagore was 'a fine lyric poet,' but that it was absurd of the West to insist on looking at him as a 'living Buddha.'"[22]

It was during Tagore's 1916 visit that Noguchi had to contend with an unexpected and devastating family tragedy. Afterward, it became connected in his mind with the banana tree he had planted in his garden after moving to Higashi Nakano, as he explained in a poem, entitled Bashō ("Banana Tree"). The tree was his favorite, not only for its connection with his beloved poet, but also because it reminded him of the tropics, with its large leaves unfurling like flags out of a magician's box to point at the summer sun. Japanese banana trees bear no, or at most, inedible fruits, so it was surprising when two or three appeared.

> One afternoon, a stranger passed behind my house,
> gazed at the fruit of this banana plant, and commented, 'This is a good omen... but I hope it's not the opposite,'
> which made my wife, who overheard it, nervous.
> Then, not two weeks later, on a Sunday morning . . . my house suddenly donned mourning clothes.
> My eldest son, six years old, had died of a brain stroke in a space of ten minutes.
> And then, strangely . . . one or two banana plants in the garden also withered,
> not only the fruit-bearing shoot, but the whole stalk, withered within ten days.[23]

Haruo died on June 25. The summer was a sad one for the Noguchi family, now reduced to eight-year-old Hifumi and three-year-old Masao, and of course, Matsuko, who would soon be pregnant again.

Adding to the shock was the unexpected death of Noguchi's literary confrère, Bin Ueda, on July 9 from kidney disease. "I confess that during your lifetime, I always acted somewhat formal and distant toward you, and lacked a genuine sense of grief," he wrote in his post-mortem confessional memoir.[24] "But at your funeral, at least, I mourned your spirit with a sincere heart, and I take great comfort in that. In fact, I had lost my eldest son, Haruo, just three weeks prior, and from that experience I felt a fervent sympathy for your bereaved family. There at the funeral, I wept inwardly together with them." Eulogies showing Ueda's capacity

---

22. Tietjens, *The World at My Shoulder*, 96.
23. "Bashō," *Sanjō ni tatsu* (Tokyo: Shinchōsha, 1923), 86-79.
24. See NY, "Ueda Bin-kun," *Jiji Shimpō*, 22, 25, 26 July 1916, 5. Ueda's Kyoto University literature department chair was filled by his younger colleague, Hakuson Kuriyagawa.

for warmer friendships spurred Noguchi to explain the inhibitions in his own relationship with the late scholar, which he attributed to their meeting after they had both passed the age of forming deep friendships. Tekkan Yosano, who as editor of *Myōjō*, had known Ueda longer, only partially agreed with his assessment.[25] "Some have called you a pedant, or—using Mr. Noguchi Yonejirō's phrase—'a man who talks with a cloud of tobacco smoke between him and others,' suggesting that you were difficult to open up to," Yosano wrote, in his own *Mita Bungaku* tribute. "Such views are clearly the misunderstandings of those who have not known you well over time. You were raised in a household of Edo-period scholar-gentlemen, steeped in tradition, and nurtured in the intellectual tastes of the French school as a refined scholar. It is hardly to be expected the character of someone with cultivated special qualities such as yourself could be easily grasped by country folk like us, raised in a rougher climate, newly arrived in Tokyo, who occasionally encountered you."

As the furor over Tagore gradually faded over the summer, Noguchi did what he could to counter public criticism of the Bengali poet. In "A Few Words at Tagore's Departure" Noguchi conceded that Tagore's lectures had a certain sentimentalism, but held to the view that they "spoke out what the real intellectual Japanese minds wished to speak from their patriotism." Tagore's words had been "nothing new, in fact, even commonplace; but there is no time like today when we so urgently need the commonplace honest criticism which will lift or split the covering clouds to let us come to a realization of our true selves." He noted that Tagore was not singling out Japan; for "the Great Republic over the Pacific Ocean"— the United States—"has also to listen to a prophet whose transcendental arguments would show the way of emancipation." Tagore departed on September 3 for the United States, where his audiences would be far more receptive to his harsh criticisms.[26]

Are You in the Nō?

In April 1916, W.B. Yeats's Nō-inspired *At the Hawk's Well* debuted to genteel applause in the drawing rooms of Lady Cunard and Lady Islington, ushering in a new international vogue for the medieval Japanese drama. Ezra Pound, Yeats's young American poet friend, had, after two years of work on Ernest Fenollosa's Nō translations and essays, enough material to fill a book or more. In Tokyo, Yone Noguchi observed these developments from a distance, continued to take foreign friends to performances at Tokyo's Nō theaters, and made his own attempts to put Nō plays into English form.

25. Yosano Hiroshi, "Ko Ueda Bin hakase" (The late Dr. Ueda Bin), *Mita Bungaku* 7:9 (Sept. 1916): 136.
26. "A Few Words at Tagore's Departure," *Osaka Mainichi Shimbun* 1, 2, 3, 5, 6 Sept.1916, 5. Tagore departed on September 3.

The announcement that Tagore and his entourage would, on June 12, attend a Hōshō school performance of *Yamanba* and *Hagoromo* was greeted with excitement in *Nōgaku Gahō*, one of several monthly illustrated Nō magazines. "After Tagore watches the Nō performance, he will surely offer some remarkable insights into Nō theater; he may even contribute something great to Nō."[27] Noguchi had the honor of accompanying the poet-saint's entourage and reporting on his comments for another Nō magazine, *Yōkyokukai*. While it was true that some in the group had complained of boredom, Tagore, at least, had found the experience interesting. "Only those who do not pay attention to the mental art of contemplation find the superficial monotony in Nō," he told Noguchi. "I was amazed at the variety of spiritual energy and the visible and invisible colors that Nō expresses."[28]

Yōkyokukai (Nō-Chanting World) was a relatively new addition to the monthly assortment of Nō magazines. Eager to test the possibilities of Noguchi's reputation among the apparently-increasing foreign Nō enthusiasts, the magazine included in its July number, along with Noguchi's Tagore interview, Noguchi's "Nō Play" essay under the title "An Appreciation"—in both English and Japanese. For the August number, he offered "A Further Appreciation," along with an English version of *Nakamitsu*, the play actor Manzaburō Umewaka was to perform at a special performance at Yasukuni Shrine on September 9. Diverging from the decades-old translation of the play by Basil Hall Chamberlain, Noguchi recast it as a prose narrative with a new title, *Koju's Loyalty*.[29] Over the past year, Noguchi had done at least seven other Nō plays in similar fashion for *Japan* (a monthly tourist magazine issued by the Tokyo Imperial Hotel), Calcutta's *Modern Review*, and the London *Nation*.[30]

Noguchi had published a pioneering collection of *Ten Kiogen in English* in 1907. "These translations of ten ancient Japanese farces are very well-done," the *Japan Mail* had enthused. "On one side of the page is printed the original in Japanese on the other side the English translation, thus making the book invaluable to students."[31] But Nō plays were far more difficult. He had serious doubts about how well Nō plays could be

---

27. Muzen Koji (Beardless Gentleman), "Zuiji zuigen" (Random comments), *Nōgaku Gahō* (illustrated magazine of Nō) 10:2 (1 June 1916): 52.
28. "Tagoru-shi to nō" (Mr. Tagore and the Nō), *Yōkyokukai* 5:1 (Jul. 1916): 50-52.
29. "Koju's Loyalty," *Yōkyokukai* 5:2 (Aug. 1916): 1-6. In the play, the anger of an overbearing father, Nakamitsu, is diverted from his wayward son, Bijō, by the sacrifice of his loyal retainer, Kōjū.
30. *Ukai*, as "The Cormorant-Fisher," *Japan* 54 (Apr. 1915): 26-29; *Sesshōseki*, as "The Perfect Jewel Maiden," *Japan* 57 (July 1915): 24-28; "Semimaru, the Blind Musician," *Japan* 58 (Aug 1915): 26-31; *Hagoromo*, as "By Miho's Pine-Clad Shore," *Japan* 59 (Sept. 1915): 26-29; *Kantan*, as "The Magic Pillow," *Japan* 60 (Oct. 1915): 29-32; *Yokihi*, as "The Everlasting Sorrow," *Nation* 17:6 (8 May 1915): 174; and *Ebira* as "The Quiver-Adorning Plum Blossom," *Modern Review* 19 (May 1916): 480-82. *Japan* (not to be confused with *The Japan Magazine*), had been started as *The Musashino* in 1911 by Yaekichi Yabe, a pioneer of jujitsu, and, later, psychoanalysis.
31. "The Bookshelf," *Japan Weekly Mail*, 25 May 1907, 567.

understood and appreciated by Westerners and even non-specialist Japanese such as himself. "Occasionally I find myself at a loss when trying to explain Nō to foreigners. Even foreigners well-versed in Japanese literature can hardly grasp the intricate diction of many Nō plays," he wrote in 1917. "It seems proper to say that no English literature scholar could accurately translate the original texts of plays like 'Yuya' or 'Matsukaze.'"[32]

Noguchi had been exploring various ways of Englishing the plays, short of full translation. The inaugural issue of *Mita Bungaku* in 1910 carried *The Morning Glory*, based, loosely, on the play *Asagao*, "a dramatic fragment on the subject after my own fashion," as he later described it.[33] The following year, his attempt at a verse translation of *Sumidagawa* appeared in *The Open Window*.[34] Retitling the play *The Willow Tree*, he had extensively reworked it, shortening it considerably, simplifying the language, removing difficult poetic allusions, but retaining the main elements of the story (about a mother's quest for her kidnapped son) and some phrasing. (He subsequently dispensed with the verse lineation in a later version of the same play for the *Pacific Monthly* entitled *The Willow*.[35])

The efforts of Yeats and Pound forced him to reconsider his approach. "Now these difficult and untranslatable Nō plays began to appear in the English-speaking world in English versions," he wrote, in March of 1917. "I myself have attempted to translate about ten Nō plays, though I have yet to complete them,". "And recently, I have been considering publishing them in the Western literary world."[36]

Nō was, quite literally, in *Vogue*: the July 1916 issue to be precise, which carried an article entitled "Are You in the Nō?" featuring a photograph of exotically-dressed Michio Itō caressing an enormous Japanese-style mask (actually by Edmund Dulac). At the center of the reported excitement was Yeats's *At the Hawk's Well*, a play seen only by the "princesses, duchesses, and other personnages décoratifs, [who] crowded Lady Islington's drawing-room recently," though "in due time New York must see it." In the meantime, "to those coming under the charm, or wishing to come under the charm of these newly-presented old plays of the east, rich and informative material is being made accessible by Mr. Ezra Pound. . . . from the manuscripts of the late Ernest Fenollosa . . . This work of accomplished scholarship," the writer concluded, "may be relied upon to

32. "Gaikoku ni okeru nō no kenkyū" (Nō Studies Abroad), *Yomiuri*, 28, 29, 30 Mar. 1917, rpt. *Teki o aise*, 176.
33. Noguchi's "The Morning Glory," SJP 68-70, first appeared in *Mita Bungaku* 1:1 (1 May 1910): 9-11. As Michael Watson, in his useful compendium of Noh translations, <http://www.meijigakuin.ac.jp/~pmjs/biblio/noh-trans.html> notes, "comparison reveals little or no use of the plot or language of the noh play."
34. "The Willow Tree," *Open Window* 2:9 (June 1911): 129-35.
35. "The Willow," *Pacific Review* 1:3 (Dec. 1920): 310-13.
36. "Gaikoku ni okeru nō no kenkyū" (Nō Studies Abroad), 183.

complete one's surrender to the flower-like beauty and imaginative appeal of the Nō drama."[37]

With full versions of the plays being offered, sometimes in verse, by Pound, and with less fanfare, by Marie Stopes, the appeal of narrativizations was diminished. For the next issue of *Yōkyokukai*, Noguchi offered his own full free-verse translation of *Sesshōseki*, as *The Perfect Jewel Maiden*, giving the play a more inviting title than Chamberlain and Aston in their more literal *The Death-Stone*, which, Noguchi, surprisingly, seems not to have used.[38] Full free verse full translations of *Ukai*, as *The Cormorant Fisher*, and *Ikkaku Sennin*, as *The Delusion of a Human Cup*, followed in the October and November issues. For the latter, he did borrow extensively from Kenzō Wadagaki's earlier translation.[39]

Unlike Wadagaki, Noguchi had no opportunity to study *utai*, or Nō chanting. Fenollosa and his senior colleague, Edward Sylvester Morse had, of course, under a leading actor, Minoru Umewaka, and his sons. Minoru had died in 1909, and his eldest son Manzaburō, who now headed the school, had emerged as one of the greatest actors of the age, "perhaps the most gifted No actor of today," as Noguchi wrote, "endowed by Heaven's blessing with a remarkable voice, . . . large, round, deeply vibrating . . . at once spontaneous and well-calculated."[40] A week after seeing *Yamanba* with Tagore and his entourage, he attended Manzaburō's performance of the same play, and was duly impressed. "As the season was the month of June, the afternoon sky blue suddenly darkened with heavy rain-carrying clouds, and even the soft, whispering, ghost-like winds were felt blowing into the hall from the gloomy looking Sumida River beside which the Umewaka stage stood; the atmosphere sad and almost threatening furnished us the most appropriate situation to see such a play as this Yama Uba, whose imaginary flight into eternity or phantasmal symbolism is so grotesque." In his 1914 Royal Asiatic Society lecture he had talked of the play, saying "we are souls much troubled in a maze of transmigration, indeed, like the Mountain Elf, who, it is said, spends all the dark night circling round the mountain," which, he understood, was "a symbol of life itself." For a long time he had felt it "would certainly make a splendid subject for a modern interpretation."[41] He was still working on his translation—"The Mountain She-Devil," to appear in dramatic form as the first English version of the play the following year, without fanfare.[42] "What interested and highly delighted me in this play," he wrote,

37. "Are You In the No?," *Vogue*, 1 July 1916, 69.
38. YN "The Perfect Jewel Maiden," *Yōkyokukai* 5:3 (Sept. 1916): 1-9; Basil Hall Chamberlain, "The Death-Stone: A Lyric Drama from the Japanese," *Cornhill Magazine* 34:2 (Oct. 1876): 479-88.
39. Kenzō Wadagaki, "Monoceros, the Rishi," *The Far East* 3:24 (Jan 20, 1898): 46-51.
40. "Manzaburo Umewaka, Famous No Actor," *JT*, 15 Oct. 1916.
41. *SJP* 66-67.
42. "The Mountain She-Devil (A Japanese Noh Play)," *JT*, 20 May 1917; rpt. in "Three Translated Selections from the Noh Drama," *Poet Lore* 29 (Autumn 1918): 447-51. For an extraordinary

"was the part where Manzaburo as the Mountain Elf looking over the imaginary valley at midnight, sang the following lines: 'Mountains over mountains! What artist carved such shapes of green rocks! Waters and again waters! Who dyed such colors of the bluest depth!' Noguchi was still tinkering with his translation.[43] "The whole audience sat still, now charmed and then terrified by the sublimity personified through the art of Manzaburo."[44]

80. Manzaburō Umewaka as Yamanba at the June 1916 performance.

Despite these efforts, Noguchi remained unconvinced that full dramatic translations were always the best approach. For three months he reverted to prose narratives, with *Semimaru (The Blind Musician)*, *Ataka (The Sadness of the Warriors)*, *Hagoromo (By Miho's Pine-Clad Shore)*, and then returned to dramatic translations for *Yokihi (The Everlasting Sorrow)*, *Miidera (The Moon Night Bell)*, and *Koi no Omoni (Love's Heavy Burden)*. But even in his ostensibly full dramatic translations, he continued to shorten and simplify.

Ezra Pound, since his first May 1914 publication of *Nishikigi* in *Poetry* magazine, had published two translated plays in the *Quarterly Review*, another seven in *The Drama*, and most recently, *Awoi no Uye* in the first

---

"modern interpretation," see Gary Snyder's "The Mountain Spirit," in *Mountains and Rivers Without End* (Berkeley: Counterpoint, 1996), 142-49.

43. "Yama mata yama. Izure no takumi ka seigan no katachi wo kezuri naseru? Mizu mata mizu. Tare ga ie ni ka hekitan no iro wo someidaseru?" In the published version it became "Lo, mountain over mountain! What carver carved such a wonderful shape of green granites? Lo, water on water! What dyer dyed such a pleasing colour of blue brocade?" (*Poet Lore*, 449).

44. "Manzaburo Umewaka, Famous No Actor," *JT*, 15 Oct. 1916.

issue of the *Quarterly Notebook*, in June. Pound apparently sent this last translation to Noguchi, who wrote a critique of it for *Yōkyokukai* in October and the *Japan Times* in November.[45] By this point the Cuala Press, run by Yeats's sisters, had printed four plays in a small volume with W.B. Yeats's introduction, *Certain Noble Plays of Japan*. Numerous other plays were more or less complete. Pound probably sent *Awoi no Uye* hoping Noguchi's comments might shed some light on the curious supernatural story, which had baffled the Fenollosas; Pound—unaware that Kenchō Suematsu had, back in 1882, translated the "Aoi" chapter of *Genji Monogatari* on which the play was based[46]—tried to talk his way around the problem in a preface claiming that "the 'Princess Rokujo,' the concrete figure on the stage, is a phantom or image of Awoi-no-Uye's own jealousy. That is to say, Awoi is tormented by her own passion." Actually, the figure on the stage is the "living spirit" of Rokujō, Aoi's rival. Noguchi attempted to clarify this while preserving some of Pound's language: "Although the play is entitled Awoi no Uye or the 'Court Lady Awoi' (Flower-of-the-East), the heroine does not appear in the scene; but her struggle on death-bed which is, in truth, nothing but a torment of her own jealousy of the Princess Rokujo, the other and later co-wives of Genji, is represented on the stage by a red, flower-brocaded kimono." Noguchi's explanations could have enabled Pound to fix the errors, had Pound not taken up Macmillan's offer for a longer collection of plays and put the book into almost immediate production.[47]

Noguchi also offered in his Fall 1916 "Awoi no Uye" essay a harsh assessment of the plays' limited interest for modern Japanese, which he attributed to the overbearing "mystical influence of the Buddha and deities" in all matters. "The spontaneous appearance of demons and spirits for a mystical story would be even proper; but when the human passion and natural love are to be connected, as in the usual case with the literature of this Muromachi period, with the spiritual superstition, it would never be too much to say that such literature is nothing but a lost literature," he wrote. Moreover, he argued, "It is really pitty [*sic*] that this play which most interestingly started finally ended in a commonplace fashion, that is to say with the demon's surrender against the holy names. That is a stereotype of the No plays; and again that is the point which makes our modern minds dissatisfied with them."[48]

45. "Aoi no ue o hyōsu" (Evaluating *Aoi no Ue*), *Yōkyokukai* 5:4 (Oct. 1916): 85-90; "Awoi no Uye, a 'No' Play," *JT*, 19 Nov. 1916.
46. Suyematz Kenchio, *Genji Monogatari: The Most Celebrated of the Classical Japanese Romances* (London: Trubner, 1882), 164–72. Suematsu included a lengthy note on 'living spirits' (168-69).
47. Andrew Houwen, *Ezra Pound's Japan*, 170.
48. YN, "Awoi no Uye, a 'No' Play," *JT*, 19 Nov. 1916. Andrew Houwen observes that the stereotypical ending diverges even from the novel, in which "Aoi dies, while Rokujō leaves Kyoto": in the play, a Tendai Buddhist holy man "drives the jealousy out of Rokujō's spirit through prayer to the four Buddhist guardian kings and the Buddhist deity Fudō-Myō-ō, thus enabling her to achieve enlightenment" (*Ezra Pound's Japan*, 163-64).

The arrival of the Pound/Fenollosa book, *'Noh' or Accomplishment* (published by Macmillan in January of 1917) spurred a series of articles in March. For the *Japan Times*, a brief note on "Fenollosa on the Noh."[49] And in Japanese, a review on "Fenollosa and Minoru Umewaka" for Maruzen's *Gakutō*, was followed by a three-part *Yomiuri* article on "Nō Studies Abroad."[50]

The *Japan Times* review was quite favorable, praising both Pound, who had "cleverly gathered in this book the papers or notes the late Ernest Fenollosa had written on the subject," and Fenollosa: "It is true that he knew more of it than anyone who has yet written in English tongue. For us Japanese it is highly pleasing to hear that many western writers find the Noh plays very wonderful, and they become to them even intelligible if 'they read them all the time as though they were listening to music.'"[51]

The Japanese essays were not quite as enthusiastic. "Fenollosa and Minoru Umewaka" began with a slightly less harsh assessment of the plays' limited interest for modern Japanese than the one ending his "Awoi no Uye" essay; now, instead of declaring the Nō "nothing but a lost literature," he merely said that Nō's tendency to force religious interpretations on all aspects of human life made it "uninteresting." But there were "some examples among the Noh plays in which rational progress and mystical taste are blended beautifully, like a splendid garment," such as Utoo and Yamamba, which he briefly summarized with quotations, mentioning his own attempts at English translation.[52] This brought him to the Pound/Fenollosa translation of *Nishikigi*, which he summarized in detail, apologizing that he did "not have the original text at hand for comparative study." "Fenollosa's attempt to undertake such a formidable task is admirable, and it also vividly reveals the contrast between English literature and classical Japanese aesthetics, making the effort highly rewarding. I don't want to pass judgment here on the quality of the English versions by Fenollosa and Pound (though somewhere in the book the name of Mr. Hirata appears once or twice—it's likely that Fenollosa sought his assistance). I've recently begun translating this Nō piece myself and am now personally experiencing just how difficult it is." Nevertheless, he had some criticism of Pound's editorial efforts. "It says that while the initial translation was crude, it was Pound himself who polished it into elegant English. I don't know who Arthur Waley is, but he is said to have corrected the Japanese in the text. Nevertheless, regrettably, numerous errors remain in the Japanese text. It's disheartening to find so many typographical mistakes in a serious book of this sort." He was

---

49. "Fenollosa on the Noh," *JT*, 18 Mar. 1917.
50. "Fenorosa to Umewaka Minoru," (Fenollosa and Minoru Umewaka), *Gakutō* 21:6 (20 Mar. 1917): 1-8. "Gaikoku ni okeru nō no kenkyū" (Nō Studies abroad), *Yomiuri*, 28, 29, 30 Mar. 1917, rpt. *Teki o aise*, 176-83.
51. "Fenollosa on the Noh," *JT*, 18 Mar. 1917.
52. "Fenorosa to Umewaka Minoru," 1-2.

also troubled by Pound's tendency to retain Japanese words he clearly did not understand. "Perhaps the intention was to signal that this is a scholarly work (Pound does have that kind of eccentricity—an affected scholar's quirk!). But to insert random Japanese words throughout the text and have half of them be incorrect, is a lamentable dilettantism." He had few criticisms of Fenollosa's study of Nō, which "was not the kind of superficial, irresponsible work often produced by Westerners, nor was it a haphazard collection of vague opinions. He admired Minoru Umewaka and pursued his study of Nō in the same way he studied Japanese painting—by seeking its inner spirit." In fact, the excerpts from Fenollosa's diaries interested Noguchi more than the translations themselves. He though the book would be extremely helpful to Japanese scholars of English unfamiliar with the art of Nō.

In his *Yomiuri* article on "Nō Studies Abroad" Noguchi offered a more detailed critique of Pound, who he described as "a rather reckless and self-willed poet" who "passionately praises Nō as the most astonishing and commendable art."[53] "Reckless and self-willed" likely reflected his dissatisfaction with Pound's unimproved *Awoi no Uye* commentary, addressed by Noguchi in two paragraphs that revisited points raised in his earlier essay on the subject. Pound, Noguchi claims (skirting around blaming Pound and Fenollosa for simply misunderstanding the play) "says it is difficult for Westerners to perceive the demon as anything other than a spiritual entity embodying soulful power." (In a later Nō lecture, Noguchi employed the same strategy, skirting around the misreading while extensively quoting the Pound/Fenollosa *Awoi* translation and Pound's comments on psychology and translation[54]). Pound's discussion of the Nō as "a theatre of which both Mr. Yeats and Mr. Craig may approve" elicited Noguchi's approval. "There is no doubt that Nō is something Yeats would love and wish to understand. Although I haven't yet seen the book, I hear Yeats wrote the preface to a book entitled *Certain Noble Plays*, which compiles several of Fenollosa's English translations of Nō plays. . . . it would surely be enjoyable reading to see how Nō appears through Yeats's eyes."[55]

For whatever reason, no copy of *Certain Noble Plays* had arrived. But he did receive the May 1917 issue of *To-day*, in which editor Holbrook Jackson discussed and reprinted the part of Yeats's preface describing his use of the plays as a model for his own.[56] Writing glowingly of how the

53. "Gaikoku ni okeru nō no kenkyū," 177. In Noguchi's phrase, "zuibun muteppō de dokudanteki na seinen shijin," the word *"muteppō"* ("reckless"—literally, "gunless") suggests a samurai, armed perhaps with a sword, charging into a gun battle, and *"dokudanteki"* literally ("self-willed"), tending to make decisions without consulting others.
54. "History of 'No' Drama Told by Japanese Poet," *Nichibei Shimbun*, 10, 11, 12, 13 Apr. 1929, 8.
55. "Gaikoku ni okeru nō no kenkyū," 180-81. It is difficult to believe Yeats would have neglected to send Noguchi a copy of *Certain Noble Plays*, in recognition of Noguchi's advice on the subject, as well as appreciation for the copy of SJA Noguchi had sent him the previous year.
56. W. B. Yeats, "Instead of a Theatre," *To-Day*, 1:3 (May 1917), 98–102. *To-day*, edited by Holbrook Jackson, had merged with *T.P.'s Weekly*, to which Noguchi had been a contributor, in 1915.

Nō had offered a theatrical model to rescue him from the popular theatre where his muses had been "but half-welcomed," Yeats proudly called it "my discovery" without so much as a nod to Noguchi, although "our Japanese dancer Ito, whose minute intensity of movement in the dance of the hawk so well suited our small room and private art" did get a mention.[57] Noguchi seems to have puzzled over the meaning of Yeats's apparent silence for some months before arriving at an appropriate response. Ten years earlier he had published "With a Foreign Critic at a No Performance" and "Mr. Yeats and the No" in his weekly *Japan Times* column. Now he was again writing a weekly *Japan Times* column, which offered him a convenient position from which to launch a few suggestive comments about his own role in bringing together "Yeats and Japan."[58]

> I am very glad to see that this Yeats has realized my own idea since I wrote in the 'Spirit of Japanese Poetry': 'I dare say, however, it will delight minds tired from the burden of the spectacular show in the West; indeed, the time may be already at hand, or at any rate quite near, when the Western stage will heed the lesson of Japanese simplicity, particularly of this Noh drama, whose archaism might give a divine hint how to sift the confusion and to rhyme beauty and life with emphasis.'

Was Noguchi claiming he had actually influenced Yeats, or simply that there had been a confluence of ideas between them? Readers unfamiliar with his earlier essays would have assumed the latter, and that was no doubt as he intended: the ambiguity allowed him to show his awareness of what had transpired without going so far as to accuse Yeats of ingratitude.

It took another six months for Noguchi to publish his Japanese "Yeats and the Nō" essay.[59] "It seems that today the word 'Nō' has spread over the general educated class because of the fact that Yeats adopted Japanese Nō," he wrote in the essay, one of a number addressed to a friend identified as H-kun, many of which appeared in the *Yomiuri* newspaper, although this one in the *Kokumin Shimbun*.[60] "H, you will wonder how [Yeats] acquired a knowledge of Nō. He himself writes that he acquired almost all his knowledge from the Nō translations which have come to be regarded as important these days as Fenollosa's posthumous manuscript." The Nō had provoked in Yeats a surprising reconsideration of the old problem Noguchi had discussed in "The Japanese Mask Play":

---

57. Yeats, "Instead of a Theatre," 101-2.
58. "Yeats and the Noh Play of Japan," *JT*, 2 Dec. 1917.
59. "Eitsu to Nō" first appeared in the *Kokumin Shimbun* in late June or early July 1918, according to the July *Eigo Seinen* and August *Waseda Bungaku*, neither of which specifies the date. It is reprinted in Noguchi's *Teki wo aise* (Love the enemy) (1922) and *Nōgaku no kanshō* (Appreciation of the Nō) (1925).
60. The honorific suffix "-kun" is less formal than "-san." Many Japanese names begin with H, making it difficult to determine H-kun's identity. Tokuboku Hirata seems a likely prospect, but Hōmei Iwano, Hakuson Kuriyagawa, and Kōnosuke Hinatsu are all plausible.

Yeats's vacillation between popular arts and aristocratic arts. "He publicly switched over from the popular arts (having thought for a long time that Irish true self-awareness needed the revival of popular arts) to the aristocratic arts." It had been a conflict between discontent and idealism, as Noguchi saw it. The discontent had driven Yeats to become involved in political art, but his idealism made it impossible to achieve his artistic goals without compromise. Yeats had "come to accept that it had been a mistake in the first place to demand the understanding of the general public," and it was at that point, that Yeats had discovered the Nō. Although Yeats's knowledge of the Japanese drama was far from perfect, it was perhaps adequate for his purposes: "I know from letters from England that he is quite satisfied with the results."

In December of 1917, Noguchi wrote to Ezra Pound, requesting a copy of his book on Gaudier-Brzeska, telling Pound he wanted to review it for his weekly *Japan Times* column.[61] "Some months ago I recommended your Noh book to our readers," he told Pound; "also I had written a Japanese article on the book. Your Noh book is now quite well-known in Japan," he added.

Noguchi was being pointedly polite about Pound's book being "now quite well-known in Japan": he must have seen Pound's angry exchange of letters with Robert Young in the *Japan Chronicle* after the editor scathingly reviewed it. Young had devoted nearly a page to questioning Pound's qualifications as "translator," derisively laughing at his ignorance of all things Japanese: language, geography, historical figures, furniture, sports: Pound had "not even read Lafcadio Hearn" and had been unable to make sense of a reference to Sumo. All of these faults were "in spite of 'Mr. Arthur Waley, who has corrected a number of mistakes in the orthography.'" Young also ridiculed Pound's uses of colloquial language, as when "the ghost of the poetess who represents to the Japanese mind all that is fine and cultured" tells a priest, "There's a heap of good in your prayers." "So far as the reader can judge," Young concluded, "the work gains nothing by Mr. Pound's labours, arduous as these quite possibly were."[62]

The attack on Waley gave Pound an opening to respond, ostensibly so that "no stigma can attach to Mr. Arthur Waley or to his accuracy in Japanese scholarship. The entire MSS.," he explained, "was not submitted to him. Nothing but extreme kindness caused him to look through certain parts of it and correct certain errors." Fenollosa's notes, he explained, had been "left on a mass of loose sheets, and in dilapidated notebooks, in faint, often illegible, or even partially obliterated lead pencil." It seemed to Pound insignificant "that there should be some thirty small errors in the course of the book . . . which any philologist

61. YN to Pound, 8 December 1917, in Kodama, *Ezra Pound and Japan*, 13.
62. [Robert Young], "A New Book by Fenollosa," *Japan Chronicle*, 26 April 1917, 678-79.

could, or can, easily correct before the work goes into a second edition." He himself was "not interested in *Kunstwissenschaft*," having "wasted enough of [his] life in a university." His main intention had been to "indicate the poetic beauty of Noh (No, Nogaku, Yokioku. etc., etc.), a beauty which the philologists have done a good deal to conceal from the Occidental." None of these arguments carried much weight with Young, merely confirming his view that "the wretched production of [Fenollosa's] work" had been "entirely due to the ignorance of Mr. Pound," who glories in his ignorance of Japanese, yet spoke of himself in his preface as a 'translator!'" "We should have spared ourselves the trouble of wasting more words upon this egregious person," he added, "but in Maruzen's latest book-list we find advertised *Certain Noble Plays of Japan*, which are "chosen and finished" from the MSS. of Fenollosa by Mr. Ezra Pound—more of Fenollosa's pearls trampled under foot! The pity of it!"

Noguchi, a frequent fellow victim of the irascible Scotsman's ire, made no mention of it in his letter, continuing cheerfully: "Perhaps you had seen some specimens of my Noh translation; how did you like one I published in the Egoist? The Quest and the Poetry Review also published my Noh plays. I like to talk about this subject further with you."[63]

Noguchi's contribution to the October 1917 *Egoist* had been a dramatic translation of *Yokihi*, a Nō play about a Tang Dynasty emperor's tragic love for a beautiful courtesan, Yang Guifei, based on Bai Juyi's 9th century poem, "The Everlasting Sorrow," the title of which Noguchi used for his play. Noguchi had previously published a narrative version, with the same title, in the London *Nation*, with—as usual—no mention of its source, but drawing heavily on Herbert Giles's translation of the Chinese poem in his *History of Chinese Literature*. For the revised dramatic version, he did explain in a Japanese note to the *Yōkyokukai* version that he had "combined the Nō play *Yōkihi* and Bai Juyi's *Everlasting Sorrow*."[64] Although more a reconstruction than a direct translation, it was Noguchi's most complete version of a Nō play thus far, and its publication coincided with an article in *The Dial* exploring Arthur Waley's interest in Bai Juyi, the Chinese poet who "derided the formal themes and treatment of his great predecessors and complained of the lack of freshness and lack of drawing from nature in his contemporaries."[65] Pound was intimately connected with *The Egoist*, his friend T.S. Eliot having recently replaced his former love interest, H.D., as assistant editor, under Dora Marsden and Harriet Shaw Weaver. Eliot did not entirely share senior editor Marsden's enthusiasm

---

63. YN to Pound, 8 Dec. 1917, in Kodama, *Ezra Pound & Japan*, 13.
64. "Eibun Yōkihi ni kanshite" (Regarding the English *Yōkihi*), tr. in Andrew Houwen "The 'Everlasting Sorrow' of Yone Noguchi's Nō Translations, *Yone Noguchi Society Newsletter* 9 (2025), 11.
65. Edward Garnett, "A Great Chinese Poet: Po-Chu-I," *Dial* 63 (25 Oct. 1917), 381-83.

for Noguchi. "I have above me a nice but timid person who likes to stick to old standbys, or else take the remains of Arthur Symons and Yone Noguchi," Eliot apologized to a female writer friend whose work he was unable to print.⁶⁶ But he had been much impressed by Yeats's *At the Hawk's Well* and what he had learned of Nō from Pound's book. "The European stage does not stimulate the imagination; the Japanese does," he had written in a review of it.⁶⁷ No correspondence is known to have survived between Eliot and Noguchi, but Noguchi's three contributions to *The Egoist* under Eliot's assistant editorship attest to a productive working relationship.

Nor does any further correspondence from Pound to Noguchi survive, leaving the question of Pound's attitude toward Noguchi's Nō efforts unanswered. There is some evidence of Pound working against Noguchi: in particular, a 1914 letter to in which Pound had made efforts to keep Noguchi out of Harriet Monroe's influential new *Poetry* magazine by telling assistant editor Alice Corbin Henderson that the two pieces Noguchi had given him were "bad jobs," and that "if he has anything worse, it may as well come here for rejection."⁶⁸

Fortunately, although Pound was then serving as the magazine's international editor, Henderson and Monroe did not always heed Pound's advice, and formed their own more positive opinion of Noguchi. Henderson's enthusiastic review of *The Spirit of Japanese Poetry* had appeared in 1915, and two of Noguchi's poems ("The Poet" and "I Have Cast the World") were included in the magazine's important 1917 anthology, *The New Poetry*. "The study of Japanese poetry is probably at least in part responsible," the *New York Times* reviewer wrote, for the "very many short poems" in the anthology with a "tendency to produce a vivid impression with as few words as possible," a tendency the reviewer had qualms about, as "the direct attempts to create English equivalents to the hokkus of the Japanese poet" were "on the whole disappointing," due, presumably, to "the difference in languages." They were "like a ballet dancer poised on a single toe, pleasing in a way, but too exotic to be of real value, not inherent, not belonging to the genius of the language."⁶⁹ Despite such doubts, Noguchi could congratulate himself on the impact of both his hokku promotion efforts, and the recognition of his own verse.

66. A[lice] C[orbin] H[enderson], "Japanese Poetry," op. cit.; *The New Poetry: An Anthology*, ed. Alice Corbin Henderson and Harriet Monroe (New York: Macmillan, 1917); Eunice Tietjens, "Yone Noguchi," *Poetry* 15 (Nov. 1919): 96-98. Eliot to Mary Hutchinson, 17 Sept. 1917, *Letters*, v. 1, 197.
67. See also T.S. Eliot, "The Noh and the Image," *Egoist* 4 (Aug. 1917): 102-3, and Carrie J. Preston, "Sweeney Agonistes in Noh Mask," *Neohelicon* 46:1 (2019): 97-113.
68. Pound to Henderson, 27 Jan. 1914, in Ezra Pound, *The Letters of Ezra Pound to Alice Corbin Henderson*, ed. Ira B. Nadel (Austin: U of Texas P, 1993), 66.
69. "A Birdseye View of 'The New Poetry,'" *New York Times Book Review* (11 Mar. 1917), 1-2.

Egoists and Drunken Slaves

In a March 1918 essay for *Gakutō*, Noguchi introduced readers to *The Egoist* for the purpose of introducing the little magazine's most significant publication to date, James Joyce's novel, *A Portrait of the Artist as a Young Man*, serialized in the magazine for two years and then published in book form by The Egoist Press in defiance of censorship laws.[70] Though available for the past year, the novel remained unknown in Japan until the appearance of Noguchi's article.[71] He began by introducing the magazine. "Until recently, Richard Aldington, recognized as a leading figure among Imagist poets, served as its assistant editor alongside his wife, who is known by the initials 'H. D.' However, with Aldington now engaged in war duties, the position of assistant editor has been taken over by a new poet, Eliot (who may be American). The special novel currently being serialized in this small magazine of less than 16 pages is *Tarr* by Wyndham Lewis, a painter who startled people in England with his Cubist works. Even the decision to serialize this novel requires more intellectual rigor and determination than most magazines possess. Yet, the serialization of James Joyce's *A Portrait of the Artist as a Young Man* required even more daring and deep commitment. This occurred a few years ago, but now it can be purchased as a single volume." He went on to quote from two reviews of the novel, before offering his own detailed assessment of it, concluding, "I believe that anyone who reads this novel will immediately recognize it as a modern masterpiece written in English."

Noguchi was also "the first [Japanese] to become familiar with Eliot,"[72] whom he introduced to readers of *Mita Bungaku* in April 1918,[73] after encouragement from Poetry Bookshop owner, Harold Monro. "I'm sending you a copy of my recent publication and Eliot's new collection *Prufrock*. Once you've read the latter, I'd appreciate your thoughts on it. Eliot would surely be interested in your critique." Noguchi had written of the Poetry Bookshop's lecture room, comparing it in "Some English Clubs" to "a Quaker meeting room or a meditation hall of Zen priests where silence is the highest virtue."[74] Now, Monro wrote:

> It has been three years since a candle was last lit in the lecture room that you once compared to a Japanese Zen hall. This alone shows how deeply the war has impacted poetry. I had hoped to fill this room

---

70. NY, "Ichi gaka no shōzō" (A Portrait of the Artist), *Gakutō* 22:3 (20 Mar. 1918): 6-11.
71. Eishiro Ito, "'United States of Asia': James Joyce and Japan," in *A Companion to James Joyce*, ed. Richard Brown (Oxford: Blackwell, 2008), 196.
72. Shunichi Takayanagi, "'In the Juvescence of the Year': T. S. Eliot's Impact and Reverberations in Japan 1930-2005," in *International Reception of T. S. Eliot*, ed. Shyamal Bagchee (London: Continuum, 2007): 181; Akitoshi Nagahata, "The Reception of Ezra Pound and T. S. Eliot in Prewar Japan," *Oxford Research Encyclopedia of Literature* (Oxford: Oxford UP, 2018), 11.
73. NY, "Yopparatta dorei" (Drunken slaves), *Mita Bungaku* 9:4 (Apr. 1918): 131-35.
74. YN, "Some English Clubs."

> with pure silence, but I never expected it would be filled with such a painful, almost dead silence for three years. The bare floor remains unswept, and the wooden benches are covered in dust. You likely know it has been four years since the publication of my magazine, *Poetry and Drama*, ceased, and that, like other writers, I've been engaged in military service. As a result, I haven't stepped into this lecture room for over a year.[75]

Monro had kept the lecture series going until a month after enlisting for home duties in the summer of 1916. In March 1918, still mobilized but back at home while serving at the Labour Supply Department in London, he had briefly reopened the lecture room for a reading of Siegfried Sassoon's poems.[76]

"I've known the name of this new poet T.S. Eliot for about a year, as the assistant editor of *The Egoist*," Noguchi noted in his article. Eliot, he explained, "lives today in London and believes that 'being a foreigner everywhere was probably an assistance to his native wit.'"[77] Noguchi, who had "once enjoyed the pleasures of cosmopolitanism" could understood Eliot's perspective. He saw in a poem like "Rhapsody on a Windy Night," "a vivid image of urban decay, reflecting his freedom to exercise the privileges of being a foreigner. 'Living as a foreigner'—there is hardly anything more bittersweet than that."

Five poems by Eliot were featured among the many modernist poems in Ezra Pound's *Catholic Anthology* of 1915. They did not please the *Quarterly Review*'s poetry critic, Arthur Waugh, who, in October 1916, attacked "the unmetrical, incoherent banalities of these literary 'Cubists.'"[78] These New Poets might serve as a warning, Waugh suggested, like the "classic custom in the family hall, when the feast was at its height, to display a drunken slave among the sons of the household, to the end that they, being ashamed at the ignominious folly of his gesticulations, might determine never to be tempted into such a pitiable condition themselves." Eight months later, Pound made his counterattack against "the silly old Waugh" in *The Egoist*.[79] Anacreon too, he pointed out, had been called a "drunken helot." He praised "the freshness, the humanity, the deep quiet culture" of the anthology, and concluded, "Let us sup with the helots." Noguchi agreed: "I, too, feel as though I would not mind being called a 'drunken slave.'" But he feared he was not yet qualified. "For us Japanese, Eliot's collection is written in such difficult English (he himself might say it is not ordinary English, but 'Eliot's own English') that it cannot be lightly read and understood."

---

75. NY, "Yopparatta dorei," 131.
76. Dominic Hibberd, *Harold Monro: Poet of the New Age* (Palgrave, 2001), 196.
77. As Eliot had written, "In Memory of Henry James," *Egoist* 5:1 (Jan. 1918), 1-2.
78. Arthur Waugh. "The New Poetry." *Quarterly Review* 226 (Oct. 1916): 365–86.
79. Ezra Pound. "Drunken Helots and Mr. Eliot," *Egoist* 4:5 (June 1917): 72–74.

So Much to be Desired

At the fourth Nikakai exhibition in October 1917, Noguchi found that the modernist art he had seen in Europe three years earlier had begun to have a significant impact, and the result did not please him. It seemed "a sad worn-out remainder of last year; this Japanese Cubism, even when it is successful, will never be more than a childish imitation." And moreover, "the Cube of Cubism in Europe had been swept away already in 1913 as a nightmare of frivolity." Adoption of foreign styles, he knew, could occasionally produce "a happy fusion between the spirit of the original and the mind of the adopter; then the result is not exoticism but rejuvenation." But he could not fathom "what Mr. Seiji Togo and one or two others want to represent by those poorly-coloured badly-arranged piles of planes on their canvases."

81. Seiji Tōgō, *All about Her*, 1917.

This was perhaps a bit hard on the twenty-year-old prodigy who had taken home the Nika Prize at his first exhibition the previous year. Founded in 1914 in opposition to the conservative tendencies of the annual government exhibition, the Nikakai had a decidedly French flavor; prominent among its members were two of Chū Asai's former students recently returned from Paris: Sōtarō Yasui who came back after seven years under the spell of Cézanne, and Ryūzaburō Umehara, who had spent six years working at the Académie Julian and studying under Renoir. "Nearly all the exhibitors at the 'Nika' exhibition have hidden idols [to] whom they burn incense and candles, a Cézanne, a Renoir, a Matisse or whatnot," Noguchi noted in his review of the exhibition.[80] He was not a great fan of the influential Yasui—"I cannot help hating his naked women, as this grape-coloured figure suggests me something at once animal and vegetal in life like Gauguin's poor picture." But he appreciated Yasui's

---

80. YN, "The 'Nika' Exhibition," *JT*, 30 Sept. 1917.

"careful watching for nature, not troubled by journalistic fancifulness," and thought Yasui "might be able to bring us health and a sort of renaissance by bringing before us an ideal, as some critic says, akin to that of the Venetian decadence."

82. Sōtarō Yasui, *Woman Washing her Feet*, 1913.

He had similarly mixed feelings about Umehara: "Some one rightly said that Mr. Ryosaburo Umehara was caught by a chronic laziness; indeed it is a pity, since he is a rare possessor of such brilliant Renoir-like colour. But beyond his magical handling of those colours, what has he to express, I like to know." Still, he found Umehara's pictures "not so naked and foolish as those Japanese Cubists or Futurists." He was most impressed by the work of his friend Tokusaburō Masamune, the most recently returned of the Nikakai Francophiles, who had studied with Matisse during his 1914-1916 stay. "Perhaps Mr. Tokusaburo Masamune might carry the first trophy through his hardest labour," Noguchi suggested, adding, "it goes without saying that he labours under an almost blinding weight of his egotism. But who among the 'Nika' exhibitors is not egoist?"

Nor was Noguchi very enthusiastic about the official *Bunten* government exhibitions, where the Kyoto faction continued to hold sway. At the 1916 exhibition, as usual, Noguchi reported, "the women of Madam Shoyen Kamimura [sic], Mr. Ikeda and his talented wife, and many others,—indeed the same women only different in objective attitude and dress—are the centre of popular interest."[81] Noguchi's misreading of the name of Shōen Uemura—one of the few successful women artists of the day—reveals the limitations of his knowledge about the Kyoto school. Uemura and the Ikedas (Yoson and Terukata) were Kyoto-based former

---

81. YN, "The Mombusho Fine Art Exhibition," *JT*, 12 Nov. 1916.

students of Seihō Takeuchi: a late but important descendent of the famed Shijō-Maruyama school (so named after the Shijō-street studio of the school's eighteenth-century founder, Maruyama Ōkyo). Uemura, though not regarded as particularly original or profound, chose appealing subjects, mostly *bijin* (beautiful women), and executed them with an extraordinary technique. But Noguchi was not greatly impressed by these quasi-traditional Kyoto productions. "I cannot help feeling an artistic danger from the reason that their monotonous exhaustion of subject-matter and thought mars and disfigures (perhaps inevitably as a result of the not so great gift and education of the artists) the spontaneous development of Japanese art whose procreative infinity should be guarded." He was more impressed with the work of another Gahō Hashimoto student, Eikyū Matsuoka, who had been active that year creating societies to revive interest in the old Yamato-e and Tosa styles. Matsuoka's painting of courtesans in an antique style seemed to Noguchi "remote yet actual enough, decorative yet quite symbolic"; it was "not an art of compromise, because it is a picture of visionary idealism beautified by a pervading musical harmony," and he was "glad to see it at the exhibition where the real art seems perfectly drowned under the technicality." Such favorable comments were increasingly rare in Noguchi's art criticism. "I am sorry to say that there is so much to be desired for the present art of Japan," he concluded.

83. **Eikyū Matsuoka,** *Ladies in a Room,* **1916.**

Even the work of his old friend Taikan Yokoyama at the 1917 Japan Fine Arts Academy exhibition seemed to him to exhibit all manner of defects, from a "too glaring realistic effect" to "hasty exaggeration," regardless of whether the eclectic painter pursued an Eastern or Western style.[82] In one painting Yokoyama's artistic honesty seemed "quite doubtful," while, in a six-paneled screen, Taikan "failed to reduce facts to symbols" and revealed his "old weakness to play with pigments." The Academy's other leading painter, Kanzan Shimomura, "did not exhibit this year," Noguchi noted; "perhaps he was wise, because the artistic world of present Japan is perfectly wrapt by darkness, and no artist would know when the clear dawn shall be expected." Perhaps this clear dawn never arrived for Noguchi, since he seems to have largely withdrawn from writing about the contemporary art scene around this time, turning away from its sad

82. YN, "Taikwan Yokoyama and Others," *JT,* 23 Sept. 1917.

failures to the more satisfying arts of Japan's earlier ages.

These historical art interests of Noguchi's were becoming broader in range; although ukiyoe remained his major subject, his Taishō-era writings reveal a strong interest in the *Rimpa* school: named after the seventeenth-century artist Kōrin Ogata, although the term is sometimes taken to include the earlier work of Kōetsu Hon'ami and Sōtatsu Tawaraya—from whom Kōrin's style developed—as well as that of Kenzan Ogata, Kōrin's younger brother. "There is no other Japanese school so interesting, even from the one point of style in expressive decoration, as the Koyetsu-Korin school, the much-admired branch of Japanese art in the West," Noguchi wrote in the introduction to his 1914 *Spirit of Japanese Art*, in which he included chapters on Kōetsu and Kenzan but begged for more time to "make myself able to write on great Korin." (Noguchi did, in fact, produce a book on Korin in 1922). Noguchi was by no means alone in his appreciation of the school: the Kōrin-influenced Rimpa styles, much admired by Fenollosa and his art-collector friend Charles Freer, as well as Okakura and his followers, had become highly valued in Japan, and were exerting a strong contemporary influence on the Nihonga painters.[83]

Columnist and Editor

From October 1916, Noguchi was once again contributing a weekly column to the *Japan Times*. A decade earlier, he had called his column, "Through a Japanese Screen," now, with a nod to architectural modernity, it was "From a Japanese Window."

His return to the *Japan Times* was the result of another chaotic management turnover. At the center of the chaos this time was Irish journalist John Russell Kennedy, who had come to Japan as an Associated Press agent (after London and New York) in 1907, and after showing himself unusually sympathetic to Japanese concerns, was "anointed foreign architect of the Foreign Ministry's early English-language press network" (in Peter O'Connor's words), "to lay the foundations of the Foreign Ministry press network in East Asia."[84] According to the 1870 Ring Combination agreement, global telegraph lines were controlled by four companies, each with its own territories. The AP controlled the American lines, while Reuters, "believed to be a British foreign-office adjunct," held a vast territory encompassing most of Europe and Asia, giving it leverage over the other wire services. Japanese observers could see that "the major nations each possessed news agencies, under government control, for filtering the news," and that, in order to protect Japanese interests, "the Island Empire must also own and operate her own news agency."[85] So in 1913,

---
83. SJA 11.
84. Peter O'Connor, *The English-Language Press Networks of East Asia, 1918–1945* (Folkestone: Global Oriental, 2010), 36.
85. Harry Emerson Wildes, *Social Currents in Japan, With Special Reference to the Press* (Chicago: U of Chicago P, 1927), 168.

with funds "gathered by [Eiichi Shibusawa] and his main contact at the Foreign Ministry, [Nobuaki Makino]," the Kokusai Tsūshin Sha, Japan's first international news agency, had been created, and the cosmopolitan Kennedy appointed as its general manager. But Kennedy had other interests; he not only still worked for the AP, but had also taken over as Reuters' agent in 1914, and had, moreover, bought a half interest in the *Japan Mail* after the death of its longtime owner, Frank Brinkley, and in addition, acquired the *Japan Times* in 1914 on behalf of the Foreign Ministry. Motosada Zumoto had reluctantly turned over management of the paper to Kennedy for the sake of future Japanese international relations. But Kennedy had overplayed his hand. "The basic problem," O'Connor writes, was "one of credibility, arising from the fact that Kennedy wore so many hats: President of the *Japan Times*, General Manager of Kokusai and the Reuters correspondent." As a news service, Kokusai needed to at least give the appearance of impartiality and independence. So, "in 1916 the board of the *Jyapan Taimuzu Kabushiki-gaisha* decided that Kennedy should resign from the *Japan Times* presidency and from the board of directors and that Kokusai and the *Japan Times* should become separate companies."[86] Kennedy soon departed for Europe, leaving the paper with no managing editor.

To fill the gap, the paper brought in Baron Jirō Miyabara, a retired naval engineer, educated for three years at the Royal Naval College, Greenwich, a decorated member of the House of Peers of impeccable standing, but no real journalistic experience. According to an official *Japan Times* history, Miyabara "remained at the helm between September, 1916, and March, 1918,"[87] but in actuality, the Vice Admiral's editorship ended with his death on January 15, 1918. Miyabara's death threw the paper's management into chaos once again. Noguchi's column, which had run from October 1, 1916 to January 13, 1918, came to an unceremonious end. John Russell Kennedy was called back to Japan to resume his previous position, and plans were made to merge the *Japan Times* with its old foreign rival, the *Japan Mail*, which had for several years operated out of the same building. The newly rechristened *Japan Times and Mail* began publication in April. During Kennedy's four years in charge, Noguchi did not return as a contributor.

Noguchi published some sixty-five columns during his sixteen-month tenure, around the same number he had published in the *Taiyō* over a longer eight-year period. Even after discounting the many reprints of material published elsewhere, the articles still represent a substantial addition to Noguchi's English prose writings. Nine articles recount

---

86. Peter O'Connor, *The English-Language Press Networks of East Asia, 1918–1945* (Folkestone: Global Oriental, 2010), 79.
87. *Short History of the Japan Times in Commemoration of the 15,000th Issue of the Daily and Revision of Its Title* (Tokyo: Japan Times Ltd., 1941), 37.

experiences of his 1913-14 trip. About two dozen are concerned with art—exhibitions and art history in general—and another dozen with drama: recent developments in the Nō drama abroad, and Nō translations. The remainder are comprised of book reviews, reprinted nature essays, and as a finale: a three-part article on the culture of the Genroku period, an "age of revolution and renaissance . . . general insolvency and foolishness" when "all the people led lives most careless, luxurious, and absolutely thoughtless of the morrow."[88]

The cessation of the column enabled him to devote more time to a new project he had co-organized toward the end of 1917 together with two professors who had been closely connected with Ernest Fenollosa—Kenzō Wadagaki and Tokuboku Hirata—to form a new semi-academic literary magazine entitled *Eigo Bungaku*.[89] Wadagaki, fifteen years Noguchi's senior, had been one of Fenollosa's first students at Tokyo University, graduating in both literature and economics, after which he had studied abroad in London, Cambridge and Berlin; he had subsequently been appointed to the Faculty of Law, and Chair of Economics at Tokyo University, and remained active in the literary field. He had written a preface to the Fuzanbō edition of Noguchi's *From the Eastern Sea* in 1903 and had been Noguchi's neighbor in Koishikawa. He listed *utai* (Nō singing) as his hobby, and had translated at least one Nō play, as well as plays in other genres, and various styles of Japanese poetry. Tokuboku Hirata was closer to Noguchi's age (a year or two older). He had been Fenollosa's junior colleague during Fenollosa's later period in Japan, and had served as Fenollosa's Nō translator (although Noguchi expressed doubts about this[90]). He had subsequently spent three years in England and had since taught in various universities in Tokyo. The group soon added a fourth editor, 37-year-old Chōkō Ikuta, a brilliant and prolific Tokyo University educated scholar, translator, literary and social critic and occasional novelist and playwright.

As a journal intended for teachers and serious students of English literature, *Eigo Bungaku*'s independence from any a particular university or literary society had both advantages and disadvantages. There was already a journal, *Eigo Seinen*, which published short notes on topics related to English literature, culture and education. *Eigo Bungaku* also coincided with the birth, in 1917, of the English Literary Society of Japan, which began publishing its *Studies in English Literature* in 1920. There were by

---

88. "Once More Again on Genroku Period," *JT*, 13 Jan. 1918.
89. Literally "English Literature," but the magazine also carried the English title *The Lamp*.
90. "Nō Studies Abroad," 177, has the parenthetical note, "It is said he was indebted to Mr. Hirata, but where it says Mr. Hirata might be meant Suzuki." ("*Hirata-shi ni ou ga aru to kaite aru ga Hirata-shi to ieba Suzuki-kun no koto de arō*"). The assertion is mystifying since Hirata's presence was well documented by Mary Fenollosa, and there is no mention of a Suzuki. It is possible that Suzuki was a student assistant, since he is named with the informal Suzuki-kun, contrasting with "Mr." Hirata (Hirata-shi).

this point legions of junior academics trained in English literature to draw on for contributions and subscriptions. *Eigo Bungaku* published a wide variety of materials ranging from research notes, cultural diatribes, translations of English texts (with Chōkō Ikuta throwing in a few French and Russian topics for good measure), to short prose sketches and original poetry. The contributors included rising young academics like Junzaburō Nishiwaki, Makoto Sangū, Sōfū Taketomo, and Minoru Toyoda, a few of them women, including Jōdai Tano, fresh back from her Master's degree studies at Wells College, who would later become president of Japan Women's University. The magazine offered an opportunity for the exchange of ideas on significant works in progress, like Tokuboku Hirata's translation of *At the Hawk's Well*, or Takeji Wakameda's translations of tanka from his forthcoming translation of the *Kokinshū*, or Noguchi's own series of bilingual "Little Poems" and Nō translations. The journal might have gone on to greater glory had it not been for the death of Kenzō Wadagaki in July of 1919; Noguchi's departure a few months later for an American lecture tour reduced the editorial staff still further, and though Hirata and Ikuta struggled on for another year, the journal finally folded in 1921.

84. *Eigo Bungaku,* **September 1918.**

In the pages of *Eigo Bungaku*, Noguchi published a number of otherwise unpublished articles and poems, and it was here that he began to transform himself into a true bilingual poet.

Mésalliances

As 1917 rolled around and the Great War continued, Noguchi's disillusionment with "the so-called Western civilization" had deepened. He had even, he said, lost hope for the Anglo-Japanese Alliance, through which, he had once thought, "Japan would be influenced by the calm consciousness of the English mind, which never departs from the sense of justice." It remained "a mere piece of composition on paper, an agreement between two Governments of West and East"; it did "not represent the mutual understanding of one race with another"; he had "no hesitation in declaring it a failure." "Only the Western nation who will forget her Western prejudices against the East, and stretch out her arms of humble love," he declared, "shall be a true conqueror of our part of the world."[91]

Nor did his disapproval of the war mean he approved of the United States' continued isolation and deepening xenophobia. The Immigration Act of 1917 established an "Asiatic Barred Zone" from which undesirable immigrants were to be refused; Japan was implicitly included, but escaped being named by virtue of an "existing treaties" clause which turned the polite "Gentlemen's Agreement" of 1908 into a humiliating exclusion law.

Rather than addressing American political or racial questions directly, Noguchi did so indirectly through essays on Whitmanism (a proxy for American democratic ideals), and American humor (a convenient indicator of American isolation and complacency). No doubt these were topics he was also able to make use of in his Keio lectures.

Whitman, he explained, was "the American poet most beloved by the young Japanese today."[92] But Whitman's Civil War era democratic idealism had limited application, he thought, in the present international era. "The Whitmanism which strengthened the human mind of half a century ago with its simplicity of prophetic idealism, . . . was too absolute, because it was not built on practical execution; it was too dreamy." "How will this Whitmanism, if it insists to stay with us, meet with those confused civilizations and cultures freely invading from all Europe and even from Asia?" "Truly America of the present time is, I dare say, dangerous more than interesting; in truth she is stepping into a perilous age since the Civil War. The Civil War was a thing that could be settled nationally; but the question which America is now confronting has to be solved internationally. The country with such a difficult problem to settle certainly cannot be spinning, as an innocent child, the same old literature."

Noguchi did not explicitly link the problems he saw in American humor—optimism, complacency, irresponsibility—to American neutrality and isolation, but that was the obvious implication.[93] American humor was "merely a joke or horse-laugh not backed by life's tragedy or tears" "fed by the unreality of the so-called American optimism," having "naturally, no footing on life's inevitable realism." It often failed when needed most, as "the other day we were told that a certain American senator had declared that to have Japanese inhabitants in California meant to keep and feed hateful spies in the domain. What a lack of 'the sense of humour'!" Noguchi "would advise the world-famous American humour that it should be more serious if it wants to act, with other phases of

---

91. YN, "The Future of the Anglo-Japanese Treaty," *Nation* (NY) 102 (13 Apr. 1916): 402.
92. "On the Failure of Whitmanism," *JT*, 1 Oct. 1916; revised as "Whitmanism and Its Failure," *Bookman* 49 (Mar. 1919): 95-97.
93. "The Future of American Humour," *Egoist* 4 (Feb. 1917): 25-26.

American literature, in solving the destiny of the nation."

Noguchi had fallen out—or at least out of touch—with many of his American friends, and was no longer contributing to American magazines and newspapers. But the occasional visits of American poets still delighted him. In the spring of 1917 two American poets, Witter Bynner and Arthur Davison Ficke, arrived, along with Ficke's wife, Evelyn. Noguchi had met the Davenport, Iowa-born Ficke in 1904, when Ficke was a young Harvard graduate traveling around the world with his parents. Ficke had married in 1907, joining his father's Davenport law firm, though he also wrote poetry, which Noguchi described as "romantic" and "Tennysonian" (a polite way of saying "old fashioned") and had acquired some expertise on ukiyoe, which he had demonstrated in his 1915 book, *Chats on Japanese Prints*. Like his more talented Harvard classmate, Wallace Stevens, who escaped the tedium of the small-town insurance office with occasional trips from Hartford to New York, Ficke sought cultural escape from Davenport in the metropolis of Chicago.

Witter Bynner, another Harvard classmate, was a native New Yorker who, after graduation, had worked for a few years as an editor at *McClure's*, then settled in New Hampshire where he worked as a publisher's reader, wrote unsuccessful plays and poems, and traveled around the country, giving occasional lectures that often touched on war and women's rights (Bynner was a pacifist and supporter of the women's suffrage movement).

Bynner's last book of verse, *The New World*, had been "a Whitmanesque song in praise of the new America" organized around "a figure named Celia, based upon a writer friend of Bynner's, Herselia A. Mitchell-Keays."[94] Celia remained at the center of his soon-to-be published *Grenstone Poems*, a verse cycle set in "a kind of Vermont or New Hampshire complement of Spoon River," with "similarities to 'A Shropshire Lad.'"[95] Although his mostly free-verse poems fit more easily than Ficke's more formal verse within the growing modernist movement, Bynner found himself "feeling not only skeptical but resentful" about the "vagaries of various 'schools' such as the 'Imagist', 'Vorticist' etc.," the antics of which, in his view, had interrupted "the coming of a period when a very large audience would be soundly and properly interested in poetry."[96] His disapproval had erupted into parodic hostility on a February 1916 Chicago visit, when, attending a Ballet Russe performance of *Le spectre de la rose* with Ficke and two other friends, he had interrupted an intermission discussion of Imagism and other recent movements by inquiring whether his companions had heard of the Spectrists in Pittsburgh (through which he had recently passed); the

---

94. James Kraft, *Who is Witter Bynner?: A Biography* (Albuquerque: U of New Mexico P, 1995), 36-37.
95. William Marion Reedy, "What I've Been Reading," *Reedy's Mirror*, 23 Nov 1917, 736.
96. Witter Bynner, "The Story of the Spectric School of Poetry," *Palms* 5:6 (Mar. 1928): 207-210, rpt. in *The Selected Witter Bynner* (Albuquerque : U of New Mexico P, 1995), 164-66.

Spectrists, he insisted, were the ones to watch. Ficke was quickly drawn into the joke, and the two were soon holed up in a hotel room composing Spectrist verse and a manifesto, written under the pseudonyms of Emanuel Morgan and Anne Knish, which was eagerly snapped up by most of the major poetry magazines and discussed at length by leading poets of the day. *Spectra*, the first anthology of the new "movement," had been published by Mitchell Kennerley in June 1916. As Bynner and Ficke set off together on their Asian holiday in March 1917, the hoax continued, for the most part undetected, except by the poet Marjorie Seiffert, who became the third Spectrist, "Elijah Hay."

"Two American poets, Mr. Arthur Davison Ficke and Mr. Witter Bynner, arrived at Yokohama on the 27th by the S.S. Empress of Asia," the *Herald of Asia* reported. "They will stay in Yokohama for a few days and will lecture on contemporary English poetry at Keio University when they come up to the Capital. They will visit Kyoto, and from thence go to China." "Mr. Ficke," the *Chronicle* explained, "is the author of 'Chats on Japanese Prints.' He visited this country 14 years ago in company with Mr. Yone Noguchi, the poet, when the latter returned from America. He is accompanied by his wife. Mr. Bynner is an editor of McClure's Magazine, and is visiting this land for the first time."[97]

On April 7 (coincidentally the day the United States' entry into the war was announced in Japan) Noguchi held a welcome party for Bynner and the Fickes at his home in Nakano, inviting a number of his Japanese literary and artist friends, along with a photographer. Two photographs of the event survive. One, in the Bynner collection at Yale, shows the Fickes and Bynner seated on the veranda with Noguchi, his wife and daughter Hifumi.

The second shows the same group on the veranda surrounded by eleven Japanese guests: Ryūkō Kawaji and Sangū Makoto are seated at the far left, Gekkō Takayasu beside Matsuko, and Hōmei Iwano beside Witter Bynner. Rounding out the group are a novelist, an ukiyoe scholar, and several literature professors. As Noguchi informed Bynner in a note sent the following day: "The photograph which was taken yesterday is expected to appear in the May number of 'Shincho' a literary monthly."[98]

He sent the letter to Ficke with a Japanese newspaper clipping and note: "This paper is 'Yomiuri'. The editor wishes me to tell how we spent a day at Hyakkayen Garden, and how we enjoyed an evening together at Kyoto, ten years ago, and some other things. So I managed to say something about them. Sorry you cannot read Japanese language."[99]

---

97. "Notes and News," *The Herald of Asia*, 31 Mar. 1917, 3.
98. YN to Bynner and Ficke, 8 Apr. [1917], Bynner Papers, Houghton Library, Harvard. "*Saikin raichō no Beikoku shijin nishi shōtai kai (Noguchi Yonejirō taku ni oite)*" (invitation party for two recently-arrived American poets [at Yone Noguchi's house]), *Shinchō* 25:5 (May 1917).
99. "*Raichō seru Fikku kun*" (Ficke has come to Japan), *Yomiuri Shimbun* 8 Apr. 1917, 7.

85. Arthur Ficke, Matsuko Noguchi, Witter Bynner, Yone Noguchi, Hifumi Noguchi, Evelyn Ficke.

86. Seated, from left: Ryūkō Kawaji, Makoto Sangū, Yone Noguchi, Nobutsuna Sasaki, Shukotsu Togawa, Kizan Ikuta, Gekkō Takayasu, Matsuko and Hifumi Noguchi, Arthur and Evelyn Ficke, Witter Bynner, Hōmei Iwano, Katsunosuke Nagata, Asatori Katō; standing, from left: Yajirō (possibly Genjirō) Kataoka, Saian Shibata.

Bynner and the Fickes remained in Japan for another three weeks before continuing on to China on April 29, and stopped over in Japan again on their return. Bynner afterward told a friend, "I had several interesting sessions with Yone Noguchi, the poet, who took some of his American furniture out of storage and insisted on furnishing a room in his house in American style for me."[100]

Feminine America

While Noguchi was formulating his critique of the United States, Léonie, to his annoyance, was trying to find a way to send Isamu there for school. In February 1916, she told her friend Catharine Bunnell that Isamu was "begging [her] to let him go over to America next winter, spend two or three years, perhaps returning when he is old enough to enter an art school here."[101] A year later, she reiterated that Isamu "wants to go to America" adding "he wants to know if you would have him—and if there's a school in the neighborhood."[102] In Isamu's recollections, however, the plan was Léonie's. "When I was thirteen years old, my mother decided that I must go to America to continue my education."[103] Isamu's Japanese schools worried her, as did the prospect of military service. "If he is here when he is 18 years old the Japanese government may seize him for military service—a brutalizing and demoralizing service, I am told by Japanese who have been through it," Léonie explained, adding "Yone is opposed to sending Isamu to America so soon—but he is ever averse to doing anything in a hurry." Yone did have a point—Isamu would not be at risk for another five years. The war had provoked anxiety and heightened awareness of nationality among the foreign community of Yokohama, where Léonie had moved her family the previous year to ease her and Isamu's commute. "I have been seeing the American consul, as there was a notice to American residents to do so," Léonie told Bunnell. The consul thought there might be difficulty in establishing her American nationality because, under Japanese law, women took their husband's nationality. Léonie had filed papers pleading an "irregularity" in her marriage on the grounds that it had not been registered. She was still waiting for a reply from Washington, but the consul had advised her not to be optimistic, for, "as various police reports have been signed by me and Mr. Noguchi together it is equivalent to a registration." If the plea failed, she would be unable to obtain a passport to leave the country, and could only get one, with difficulty, by applying to the Japanese government.[104]

---

100. Guido Bruno, "The Orient: Seen by an American Poet," *Pearson's Magazine* 38:5 (Nov. 1917): 204-05.
101. LG to Catherine Bunnell, 24 Feb. 1916, in *LG* 278-79.
102. LG to Catherine Bunnell, 20 Feb. 1917, in *LG* 285-86.
103. *ASW*, 13.
104. Duus, *Life*, 74; LG to Catherine Bunnell, 20 Feb. 1917, in *LG* 287.

87. Léonie and Isamu in Chigasaki.

It was under these anxious conditions that Léonie became determined to send Isamu to America. "Having been born in America, if by the time he is 21, he can show that he has lived some years in America, he can claim American citizenship," she told Catharine.[105] She was starting to look into an alternative plan, an experimental school in Indiana she had read about in *Scientific American*, called Interlaken, run by a German immigrant named Edward Rumely.[106]

Meanwhile, Yone put together a mostly-critical eight-page "Analysis of the Americans" for the *Chūō Kōron*.[107] The article began with a discussion of American complacency. "Will America's participation in the war help Americans find their true selves?" he wondered. "Or will it leave them as haughty as before, childish optimists?" Thackeray had once written that the chief characteristic of ignorance is self-satisfaction, and Noguchi was sure that Americans "possess this characteristic in a perfect condition." He could offer plenty of examples from his own experience in the country and reports of recent Japanese travelers, who continued to be astonished at Americans' lack of knowledge about Japan. Then, Noguchi argued, America was provincial. American literature offered few great writers, and was, for the most part, "an amateur literature." The American education system was run by low-salaried women. And this brought Noguchi to his central point: "American civilization is throughout a feminine civilization—as American literature is a feminine literature." American men were unable to escape from "woman worship."

---

105. LG to Catherine Bunnell, 20 Feb. 1917, in *LG* 287.
106. "The Daniel Boone Idea in Education," *Scientific American* 109 (3 Nov. 1916): 361-62.
107. "Beikokujin no kaibō" (Analysis of the Americans), *Chūō Kōron* 32:10 (Sept. 1917): 108-15.

They would never be rescued from this "strange religion" until women themselves were prepared to abandon their anti-realistic idealism. American men had devoted themselves exclusively to material pursuits, leaving the women responsible for maintaining American culture, which had become a culture of sentimentalism, an escape from the world of reality into an irresponsible world of optimism, a fairy tale world of ideal love stories that had no relation to reality. When both sexes were sufficiently disillusioned, America might wake up from its lazy slumber. Noguchi's jabs at American provincialism were certainly well-founded, and many of the gender-related arguments had in fact been raised by prominent American writers. Lafcadio Hearn had made an attempt at elucidating the strange phenomenon of Western woman-worship in a university lecture entitled "The Insuperable Difficulty."[108]

If it was Noguchi's intention to vent his anger, he got more than he bargained for when the *Japan Advertiser*, a competitor to the *Japan Times*, ran an unauthorized translation of the full article on September 21. "AMERICAN MEN MERE RUSTICS—WOMEN SENTIMENTAL, SAYS POET" declared the headline, followed by the subhead: "Yone Noguchi Flays the Country Which Helped Him Get His Start as 'Undeveloped' and 'Woman-Ridden.'"[109] The translation was preceded by an introductory paragraph which explained that the article was of interest because the author "is often referred to as a poet and is well known as a writer in English. He would be world famous if the foreign public held as high an estimation of Yone Noguchi as he does of himself." The article, the introduction continued, was "all the more interesting because the author was the recipient of many kindnesses in America, where he married an American girl whom he brought to live in Japan. His moral conduct and treatment of his wife led to a separation. His former wife is living in Japan and is supporting herself and her child by teaching. Mr. Noguchi is now married to a Japanese." The facts, indeed, seemed to contradict Noguchi's assertion that "generally speaking, American men are laboring machines, and American women consider it their very duty to lead a life of irresponsible pleasure."

Léonie, however, leapt to Noguchi's defense, at least in regard to the personal side of the attack. "Your correspondent has been misinformed. I, as the former wife of Mr. Noguchi, who know the facts, assure you that this statement is utterly untrue," she wrote in a letter to the editor.

---

108. Noguchi had quoted from the lecture in *LHJ* 325: "The attitude of man toward woman in Western countries might be very well characterized as a sort of worship," Hearn had explained. "In the upper classes of society, and in the middle classes also, great reverence toward woman is exacted. Men bow down before them, make all kinds of sacrifices to please them, beg for their good will and their assistance." The full lecture is in Lafcadio Hearn, *Books and Habits* (London: Heinemann, 1922): 1-8.

109. "American Men Mere Rustics—Women Sentimental, Says Poet," *Japan Advertiser*, 21 Sept. 1917, 6, 10.

"Though I was not happy as Mr. Noguchi's wife, I did not consider myself to be ill-used. On the contrary, he used such courtesy toward me as I should expect from one of my own countrymen. Nor was the moral conduct of either of us the cause of our separation." To this perhaps overly generous assessment, Léonie added the acid observation that "a thoughtful reader of Mr. Noguchi's article in the Advertiser might find in the author's own mental attitude and inability of appreciation of Western ideals a clue to the hopelessness of a union between such a thinker and an American woman." Mr. Noguchi, she added, "contributes regularly toward our support," and as teaching had been her chosen profession for many years before meeting him, her working life was "hardly a matter for commiseration."[110] However, another letter two days later, signed "U.S.A.," commended the paper's treatment of Noguchi's "absurdly childish, too contemptible" article, lamenting that the "esteemed 'poet,'" who had been "most cordially received" in America, now "bites the hands that fed him!"[111]

Noguchi's weekly *Japan Times* column offered him a convenient perch from which to defend himself from the charges.[112] The *Japan Advertiser* was a "provincial paper," "un-American and even ungentlemanly," whose editor ("whoever he be, a Jew or Christian," Noguchi noted) had "violated not merely the libel laws but also the sense of journalistic ethics." Invoking libel laws and journalistic ethics was certainly a bold move for a man who had three months earlier passed off a translated Junichirō Tanizaki story as his own,[113] but Noguchi did have a point. He calmly recounted the charges made in the article and professed himself "pleased to trust on the intelligence of the readers for the judgement of its sanity." He had nothing to retract in his own article; "the fact that American woman-worship is carried to the widest extreme," he pointed out, "is written up almost every day in paper or magazine by an American writer."

Noguchi's ability to defend himself in print had improved significantly in the twenty years since Jay William Hudson's attack in the *Chronicle* had driven him into hiding in Sausalito. His new critical confidence was likely encouraged by Tagore's recent success criticizing Western materialism during his recent lecture tour. Noguchi's main complaint was with America's failure to live up to its democratic principles, a failure reflected in the passage of racist immigration laws discriminating against Japanese. The weakness of Noguchi's position, however, was one he shared with most Meiji-era intellectuals who had looked forward to eventual

---

110. [Léonie Gilmour], "Regarding Yone Noguchi," *Japan Advertiser*, 7 Oct. 1917, 4, in LG 290.
111. "U.S.A.," "A Poet's Gratitude," *Japan Advertiser*, 9 Oct. 1917, 4.
112. YN, "Analysis of the Americans," *JT*, 21 Oct. 1917, 4.
113. "The Painter on the Human Skin (From the Japanese)," *JT*, 3 June 1917, with the usual byline, "(specially written for the 'Japan Times' by Yone Noguchi)," was a translation of Tanizaki's "Shisei" (The tattoo, 1910); he also published it as "Skin Painter," *English Review* 25 (Dec. 1917): 501-08.

acceptance and equal treatment when the Japanese proved themselves worthy. Rather than working to undermine racial ideologies Japanese intellectuals typically chose to work within them, arguing that Japan should be counted among the superior races. Noguchi's own ethnic biases reflected this tendency: as, for example, his backhanded anti-Semitic jab at the editor of the *Advertiser*, Benjamin Fleisher, a prominent member of Yokohama's small Jewish community whose recent efforts to obtain transit visas for Russian Jewish refugees fleeing the revolution had drawn attention to his Jewishness. Committed to such racial ideologies and unable to break the hold of white supremacy by peaceful means, it appeared that the Japanese would only gain recognition by aggressively demonstrating the power of the Japanese empire. That the United States had no intention of upholding its principles of liberty and equality for all was again illustrated at the Paris Peace Conference when Woodrow Wilson, along with the leaders of Australia, New Zealand, and South Africa, voted down the Japanese proposal to include a clause in the League of Nations charter opposing racial discrimination, which would have delegitimized race-based immigration systems. Instead, Japan received recognition of most of its wartime Chinese territorial gains.

Noguchi eventually published a reworked American version of his "Analysis of the Americans" in the July 1918 *Bookman*, under the title, "To the Americans"—in a convenient second-person format. The essay did have its memorable moments. "Your country is floating comfortably on the ocean all by itself, as if a well-fed seal or lazy iceberg," he wrote, in a comment picked up by influential American critic Van Wyck Brooks, who agreed with the characterization and praised Noguchi as "the spokesman of contemporary humanity." "Those who have an interest in America, its true life, its true historic rôle, are aware that such a posture is a perilous posture," Brooks wrote.[114] Noguchi explained that his more controversial argument about America's "feminized culture" had been borrowed, for the most part, from recent essays by Michael Monahan and Anna Rogers.[115] While following Tagore in his critique of American materialism, he disparaged what poet Joyce Kilmer was calling the Tagore craze, for which Noguchi thought women primarily responsible. "They might be to-day cringing round Tagore of India and Chinese vases of jade. So long as things look and sound exotic and mysterious, your women are content with them." However shallow American women might be, Noguchi conceded, they were still far better informed, culturally and spiritually, than American men (to whom the article was ostensibly directed).

Léonie continued her plans to make an American boy out of Isamu.

---

114. Van Wyck Brooks, *Sketches in Criticism* (New York: Dutton, 1932), 20-21.
115. Michael Monahan: "Mannahatta," *The Phoenix* 5:2 (July 1916): 44-64; Anna A. Rogers, "Some Faults of American Men," *Atlantic Monthly* 103 (June 1909): 732-38.

By June 1918, she had received approval from the school and prepared Isamu for a hasty departure on June 27th. Yone's opposition continued. "At this crucial moment," Isamu recalled, "I was again made aware of my father, whom I had not seen in many years. He came to the boat to try to stop my going." Isamu steamed off on the *America Maru* (Léonie thought a Japanese ship would be a less likely target for German U-boats), and Yone returned home evidently weary and embittered.[116]

"To the Americans" was followed by the first American appearances (again in *The Bookman*) of two earlier American critiques. "The Failure of American Optimism," a revision of his February 1917 *Egoist* essay, "The Future of American Humour"),[117] was now rather belated in its criticism of American insularity, with the United States having joined the war and taken a prominent role in the peace process. The critique of American democratic principles in "Whitmanism and Its Failure" (slightly revised from his 1916 *Japan Times* essay) still remained relevant, for those concerned about such matters.[118]

"There is a great anti-American drive on now," John Dewey observed when he came to Japan in 1919 for a series of lectures at Tokyo University.[119] Dewey suspected it was "stimulated artificially somewhat" by the militaristic government because "criticism of the United States is the easiest way to arrest the spread of liberal sentiments and strengthen the arguments for a big militaristic party." There was some truth in this assessment, but the anti-American sentiment had been building for some years; Americans were simply unaware of it. Dewey also noted that "discussion about race discrimination is very active and largely directed against the United States in spite of Australia and Canada, and also in spite of the fact that Chinese and Korean immigration here is practically forbidden, and they discriminate more against the Chinese than we do against them."

In April 1918, as Noguchi busied himself with his American criticism, he received an inquiry from an American editor and publisher interested in his work, by the name of Edmund Randolph Brown. The Harvard-educated Brown owned a small bookshop and publishing operation in Boston, the Four Seas Company, from which he had been publishing *The Poetry Journal*, with the help of a wealthy but not very talented New York poet, Blanche Shoemaker Wagstaff.

Brown wrote Noguchi to solicit a contribution for the *Poetry Journal*, and offering to exchange Four Seas publications for autographed copies of books by Noguchi and other Japanese poets. Noguchi obliged, sending a Nō play and two signed books, with a promise of signed books

---

116. ASW, 13.
117. "The Failure of American Optimism," *Bookman* 48 (Dec. 1918): 501-03.
118. "Whitmanism and Its Failure," *Bookman* 49 (Mar. 1919): 95-97.
119. John Dewey and Alice Dewey, *Letters from China and Japan* (New York: Dutton, 1920): 74-75.

from five or six Japanese poet friends if Brown would send books to give them in exchange. "When you brought out my Noh play in the Poet Journal," Noguchi added, "I hope that you will let me have some two or three copies containing it." He requested copies of the books by Aldington, Fletcher and Williams: "particularly I like to see 'Japanese Prints,'" Fletcher's forthcoming volume of ukiyoe-inspired verse.[120]

88. John Gould Fletcher.

Between the Four Seas

Noguchi was excited by Fletcher's *Japanese Prints* volume, which arrived at the end of the summer. Perhaps it was the echoes of his own work that he found so enthralling, for Fletcher later acknowledged *The Pilgrimage* as an early influence.[121] Noguchi must have been moved by the spirited but humble preface in which Fletcher argued that it was "necessary, if poetry in the English tongue is ever to attain again to the strength and vitality of its beginnings, that we sit once more at the feet of the Orient, and learn from it how little words can express, how sparingly they should be used, and how much is contained in the meanest natural object . . . If we do not want art to disappear under the froth of shallow egoism we must learn the lesson Basho can teach us."[122] Then there were the poems themselves, as well as the printing: little vignettes inspired by Japanese prints, printed one to a page, surrounded by plenty of white space and illustrations by talented illustrator Dorothy Lathrop. Noguchi was so impressed by Fletcher's book he made a complete translation of the poems, which he included as a chapter in his book *Roku-dai-ukiyoe-shi* (six masters of ukiyoe) the following June.[123]

120. YN to Edmund Brown, 5 Apr. 1918, FSL.
121. John Gould Fletcher, "The Orient in Contemporary Poetry," in *The Asian Legacy and American Life*, ed. Arthur E. Christy (New York: John Day, 1945), 159.
122. John Gould Fletcher, *Japanese Prints* (Boston: Four Seas, 1918), 15.
123. "Ukiyoe ni daisu John Gould Fletcher no saku" (John Gould Fletcher's Ukiyoe collection), in *Roku-dai-ukiyoe-shi* (Six masters of ukiyoe) (Tokyo: Iwanami shoten, 1919), 240-65.

"I was hoping for some time to publish such a book myself," he told Brown, thanking him for the book in September. "Perhaps you might be able to bring out my Hokkus in America."[124] Brown had been in dire straits when he had written Noguchi, and by the time he received Noguchi's reply, the *Poetry Journal* was no longer of this world, having vanished after the March issue, with Brown having no chance to include the Nō plays Noguchi had sent him. But Brown was continuing his book-publishing operations, and responded favorably on October 11, not only for a volume of Hokkus, but also a collection of Nō plays, and perhaps more. Noguchi was delighted and immediately assembled *Ten Noh Plays* out of translations he had on hand.[125] He included his recently published *Egoist* Noh essay as preface, two woodblock prints from Kōgyo Sakamaki as illustrations, and a dedication to Robert Bridges.[126] Although he included only plays in dramatic form, he admitted in a prefatory note that the plays were "rewriting rather than translation." He sent the manuscript under separate cover with a November 15 letter promising, "I hope that my Hokku poems will follow soon after it."[127] "My other books which I like to bring out in America are as follows," he added: "From the Eastern Sea and other Earlier Poems," "The Pilgrimage," "The Summer Clouds [*sic*] (a Book of Poems in Prose)," "'New Poems' (I do not settle my mind yet with its title)," "Japanese Essays," and "More Japanese Essays." Brown might, he said, "arrange with any London publisher for 'Ten Noh Plays.' But there is little hope in Japan, because it is difficult to sell a book dearer than fifty cents." Two weeks later, he sent the manuscript of *Japanese Hokkus*, reiterating his wish to give *Ten Noh Plays* precedence, "—but if you think 'Japanese Hokkus' should come out first, I have nothing to oppose you."[128]

Noguchi's excitement over the prospect of restarting his American book publications was soon brought down by the realities of Edmund Brown's dodgy operation. Brown, a publishing enthusiast since his teens, had started *The Four Seas* magazine in 1910 after his graduation from Harvard, naming it out of a Confucian saying, "all men between the four seas are brothers." In 1912 he had started *The Poetry Journal*, which *Boston Evening Transcript* poetry editor William Stanley Braithwaite edited for the first two or three years. In 1914 Brown moved the business into a "rather unattractive" second hand bookshop at 67 Cornhill, "small, with rather a dingy and unpossessing front," that had been vacated after the previous owner's sudden death. The company's finances were precarious, barely propped up by Blanche Wagstaff's family wealth, and the

124. YN to Brown, 16 Sept. 1918, FSL.
125. "Ten [^Japanese] Noh Plays," *Collection of letters and papers from Yoné Noguchi*, Bancroft.
126. "The Japanese Noh Play," *Egoist* 5 (Aug. 1918): 99.
127. YN to Brown, 15 Nov. 1918, FSL.
128. YN to Brown, 15 Nov. 1918, FSL.

ongoing financial problems had reduced Four Seas—which had begun its poetry journal promising that "pay is to be granted for whatever is accepted"—into little more than a vanity press, with Brown quietly persuading authors to subsidize or cover publishing costs. The young poets who gravitated to his shop—many of them quite talented—tended to see him as struggling to keep a profitable business afloat, and rarely blamed him. Brown negotiated 25-year-old Harvard graduate Conrad Aiken's first book with Macmillan in 1914, with Aiken guaranteeing all costs; "To pay for the printing of *The Jig of Forslin*" (his second book), Aiken was forced to sell the family car."[129] In 1915 John Gould Fletcher had spoken to Aiken about his own difficulties in obtaining and keeping his publishers and been introduced to Brown, "a dark-haired, pale-complexioned individual" Fletcher found "amusing—an equal compound of adventurous daring, Yankee resourcefulness, and complete irresponsibility."[130] Brown had published his *Japanese Prints* in the *Poetry Review*, and then, after a two-year wait, in book form. William Carlos Williams was another willing victim: after Ezra Pound helped him publish his first two books of verse to little effect, he went to Brown for the next three, *Al Que Quiere* (1917), *Kora in Hell* (1920), and *Sour Grapes* (1921). "For each of these three books I paid the Four Seas Company of Boston something in the neighborhood of two hundred and fifty dollars," Williams later recalled. "To get a book published! What a marvelous thing it was to me."[131]

With Noguchi, Brown did not discuss financial questions at the outset, but simply delayed publication. Delays were common in publishing, but could also be used to encourage authors to contribute to printing costs. Amy Lowell sent Richard Aldington to Brown, but then "had to endure his frustration—often misdirected at her—at the publisher's tardiness, first in bringing the book out and then in promoting it and paying the royalties."[132] Noguchi was not offering to pay, and it took considerable effort on his part to get Brown to finally produce a shoddily-made edition of *Japanese Hokkus*. Getting Brown to sell two Japan-printed editions under the Four Seas imprint was easier, but collecting royalties proved difficult. But there were few other American publishers willing to take a risk, and likely loss, on modernist writers.

Little Poems

Japanese Hokkus was not simply Noguchi imitating Fletcher: he really had been working on a collection of short poems—in both English and Japanese—for at least two years. It was a bilingual project that came out

---

129. Edward Butscher, *Conrad Aiken: Poet of White Horse Vale* (Athens, Ga: U of Georgia P, 1988), 248.
130. John Gould Fletcher, *Life Is My Song* (New York: Farrar and Rinehart, 1937).
131. *The Autobiography of William Carlos Williams* (New York: Random House, 1951), 158.
132. Vivien Whelpton, *Richard Aldington: Poet, Soldier and Lover 1911-1929* (Cambridge, UK: James Clarke, 2014), 118.

of the debates over his Japanese poetry lectures after he published them in Japanese translation. *Nihon Shiika Ron* (On Japanese Poetry), the book in which they appeared, marked a new beginning for Noguchi as a writer in Japanese.[133] Thus far, despite the two half-Japanese books published a decade earlier, and the occasional periodical essay since, he had remained a predominantly English-language writer. Now, with new foreign adventures to write about, and an Oxford lecture success to publicize, it was time for Yonejirō Noguchi's second coming. At least, this was the view of Waseda-educated translator Asadori Katō, who was willing to do most of the translation.[134] The chosen publisher was, surprisingly, Hakujitsusha, a coterie of mainly tanka-writing poets led by tanka modernizer Yūgure Maeda. Despite the focus on tanka, the group maintained wide-ranging interests in poetry, and its inclusive journal, *Shiika* (poetry), included many of Noguchi's friends. Hakujitsusha's newly formed book-publishing sideline, begun in 1914 as a vehicle for Yūgure's own poetry and essays, was expanding in 1915 to include several Rofū Miki verse collections and Ryūkō Kawaji's translations of Verlaine.[135]

For Japanese readers, "The Japanese Hokku Poetry" lecture was really (as Noguchi retitled it) "On Haiku in Relation to English Poetry."[136] In the new preface he wrote for the Japanese edition, Noguchi characterized it as an attack.[137] "My poetry discourse in England was like the battle cry of an assault meant to breach the ancient ramparts of English poetry. I may not have achieved complete triumph in breaking through those defenses, but I am confident that I was not merely the defeated general of a routed army." The English defenses were typified by Lascelles Abercrombie, in the *Manchester Guardian*.[138] Though an admirer of Noguchi,[139] Abercrombie recoiled at Noguchi's attack on English poetry's "words, words, words": "Poetry is utterance; and when there is no utterance there is no poetry," he argued. Japanese poetry had "a wistfulness and delicacy not to be met with in the general run of English poetry," but "a literature composed entirely of 'wistfulness and delicacy,' admitting nothing but exquisite moods and exquisite senses, seems to us an extraordinarily truncated literature." "Europe is unable to sum up the essentials of life in sensuous beauty and emotional beauty: we must have intellectual beauty

---

133. NY, *Nihon shiika ron* (On Japanese poetry) (Tokyo: Hakujitsusha, 1915) included the main chapters of *SJP* and selected essays from *TT*.
134. NY, "Nihon hanashi jōshi ni saishite" (On publishing my talks about Japan), *Nihon shiika ron*, 15.
135. It was no doubt a point in Noguchi's favor that he had mentioned Rofū as one of the leading poets of the last few years "to whose work special attention should be called" (*SJP* 111); the Japanese version of the essay had additional comments about him (*Nihon shiika ron*, 207).
136. "Haiku tai Eishi-ron," *Nihon shika ron*, 39-82.
137. NY, "Nihon hanashi jōshi ni saishite," 8-15.
138. Lascelles Abercrombie, "New Books: Japanese Ideals," *Manchester Guardian*, 6 July 1914, 6.
139. See Abercrombie, "A Marriage of East and West," rpt. *Pilg.* 10-15, and Abercrombie to YN, 22 Feb. [1910], *CEL* 394.

as well, and this it is that escapes Mr. Noguchi, and, as far as we can make out, is ignored by Japanese poetry at large." Noguchi might be wonderful at "making us feel Japanese poetry in a series of hints, similes, and symbols; but it all seems flimsy when he tries to philosophise it into a manner of life . . . as a foundation for aesthetics (which means art as a department of life) it is disastrous, because, it is a muddle. It mixes up poetic feeling with poetry." But that was not how Noguchi saw it: "I value the poetic feeling more than poetry itself," he explained. "Breaking through the intellectualism of English poetry is a very difficult task, but to accomplish it even to some extent is, for a literary scholar, a matchless pleasure, I think."

A few weeks after the book's publication, he attempted to explain in a *Yomiuri* essay what he had tried to do in his Oxford haiku lecture, namely, to point out the commonalities between haiku and Western lyric poetry.[140] "Certain poems by Wordsworth, for example, could easily be transformed into a series of haiku," while his friend John Tabb, whose poems were nearly all less than twelve lines, could be considered a "Western haiku poet." "My poetic theories, which are distilled from both Western literature and the Seven Anthologies of the Genroku period," he explained, "have provided Western poets with valuable insights and served as a form of spiritual resistance for the general public. I take great pleasure in this achievement."

Not everyone shared his joy. Some criticisms were mild, like that of his youthful admirer, Makoto Sangū, who wondered whether "his eagerness to link the virtues of haiku with the flaws of English verse . . . may have needlessly provoked some English critics."[141] Others were more serious, like that of Tokyo-University-trained poet-critic Kensaku Aoki. "I concede that Mr. Noguchi understands haiku to some extent," Aoki had written, "but I cannot help doubting he has truly and thoroughly grasped the subjective state of mind of the haiku poet."[142] Noguchi responded in a *Mita Hyōron* essay a year after the book's publication. He was unclear what the phrase "understands haiku up to a certain point" was supposed to mean, but in any case, "the subjective state of mind of the haiku poet," whatever that was, and whether or not he understood it, had not been central to his argument. "Although the original title refers to hokku poetry," he explained, "it was not a particular study of haiku or haiku poets; my aim was rather to explain the special qualities of Japanese haiku as opposed to English poetry, and show how those qualities

---

140. "Watashi no haiku-tai eishi ron" (My discussion of haiku in relation to English poetry), *Yomiuri Shimbun*, 9 Jan. 1916, 7, revised as "Shigaku no itadaki" (Climbing Parnassus), *Shi no honshitsu* (Tokyo: Daiichi Shobō, 1927), 37-45.

141. Sangū Makoto, "'Nihon shiika-ron' o hyōsu," (Nov. 1915), rpt. *Shibun kenkyū* (Tokyo: Sekibundō, 1918): 144-52.

142. NY, "Watashi no haikuron" (My haiku essay), *Mita Hyōron* 231 (15 Oct. 1916): 35-38. Aoki's criticism is quoted by Noguchi from an unidentified *Jiji Shimpō* article.

might open up new realms of poetic expression." He had, he admitted, used haiku to discuss his own poetic ideals, emphasizing those aspects he found useful for his purposes.

It was after reading Noguchi's defense in *Mita Hyōron* that Seisensui Ogiwara, the leading representative of Japan's radical haiku faction, took the opportunity to publicly express support for Noguchi's ideas in the *Yomiuri*.[143] Seisensui was evidently anxious to claim Noguchi as an ally as he prepared to publish his own controversial manifesto, *Haiku Teisho* (haiku proposal) in October 1917, in which he would lay out his rationale for dispensing with the more rigid strictures of traditional haiku.

By this time, Shiki Masaoka, reformer and modernizer of Japanese haiku, had been dead for more than a decade, but his influence remained strong. His followers had split into two broad camps, the conservative school led by Kyoshi Takahama, who edited the *Hototogisu* magazine founded by Shiki, and the more radical New Trend (Shinkeikō) faction, led by Hekigotō Kawahigashi, who had taken over Shiki's haiku column in the *Nihon* newspaper. Kyoshi and Hekigotō had been classmates at the Matsuyama Middle School that Shiki had earlier attended, but their views on haiku had diverged. Hekigotō was attracted to the more experimental elements of Shiki's haiku renovation project, championing the abolition of seasonal words and even the traditional 5-7-5 metrical pattern.

After Shiki's death in 1902, Hekigotō was "universally acknowledged as the leading figure in the world of haiku."[144] While Kyoshi turned his attention to *shasei* (sketch-from-life) prose, popularized by Sōseki Natsume, whose first novel had been serialized in *Hototogisu* in 1905, Hekigotō drew other talented haiku poets into his Shinkeikō camp, most importantly Seisensui, with whom he founded *Sōun* in 1911. Hekigotō was then beginning to retreat from his radicalism, and had withdrawn from *Sōun* by the time Seisensui officially declared the magazine's abolition of seasonal words in 1914. Seisensui saw the haiku as a poem of impressions that "should evoke great nature itself and one's whole being" based on feelings that "may be described as a response that can be felt flashing like lightning."[145]

In *The Spirit of Japanese Art*, Noguchi argued for the superiority of hokku over uta, saying that his attention was "never held by the harmony of language": he preferred to "go straightforward to the writer's inner soul," and his poetical taste desired "far more intensity than the *Uta* poems, whose artificial execution often proves ... to be their weakness rather than strength." He also criticized English poetry for being

---

143. Ogiwara Seisensui, "'Watashi no haiku ron' no Noguchi Yonejirō shi ni" (To Mr. Yonejirō Noguchi who wrote 'My view of haiku'), *Yomiuri*, 31 Jan., 1, 2, Feb. 1917, 7.
144. Donald Keene, *Dawn to the West*, 2:109.
145. Ogiwara Seisensui, *Shizen no Tobira* (The Portals of Nature, 1914), tr. in Keene, *Dawn to the West*, 2:119.

"governed too greatly by old history and too-respectable prosody." Seisensui found in these comments proof that Noguchi was a kindred supporter of haiku "who really understands haiku."[146] He then summarized his own views: the haiku world was at present "irrecoverably corrupted" because the poets were obsessed with the restrictions of the form. "On the contrary, I insist that we must find haiku rhythm within ourselves. First, we should catch ephemeral, intense emotions within us, and then consider how we can express them with intense, rhythmic words." Noguchi's similar views particularly pleased Seisensui because he believed Noguchi had "arrived at the haiku spirit without starting from the haiku form."

In the second part of his letter, Ogiwara gently prodded Noguchi to become more involved in the reform of Japanese poetry. "Rather than trying to redeem Western poets with your theory, I think it would be much more significant, both to yourself and to us, for you to put your poetic theory into practice in your own poems, as you are now trying to do." In doing so, Noguchi might "find a much higher ideal than previously seen in haiku poetry—an ideal you can immediately put into practice and which can be set as a new ideal for the Japanese poetic world." Seisensui made the prospect sound thrilling, but the realities of the Japanese haiku world, with its endless society meetings and factional disputes, were considerably less so; what little fame, glory, or money was to be had was unlikely to be given to a writer of little Western-style poems, especially one who, as Seisensui felt obliged to point out in the third part of his article, believed that everything he needed to know about haiku could be found in Bashō's seven haiku anthologies. "You cannot really talk about haiku without looking at haiku after Bashō, which are not only brilliantly beautiful but also have a depth of genuineness approaching Symbolism."

Noguchi had likely read Seisensui's letter before its publication, because three weeks before it even appeared, he had already published his first group of five bilingual *Sankōshi* (three-line poems) in *Mita Bungaku*.[147] The three-line poems began with apologies and explanations:

> Full of faults, you say.
> What beauty in repentance!
> Tears, songs ... thus life flows.

And:

> Bits of song ... what else?
> I, a rider of the stream,
> Lone between the clouds.

The English versions all scanned as 5-7-5 syllables. But the Japanese

---

146. Ogiwara Seisensui, "'Watashi no haiku ron' no Noguchi Yonejirō shi ni" (To Mr. Yonejirō Noguchi who wrote 'My view of haiku'), *Yomiuri Shimbun*, 31 Jan., 1, 2, Feb. 1917, 7.
147. "Sankōshi," *Mita Bungaku* 8:1 (1 Jan. 1917): 52-54.

versions were quite long—12-10-15 and 14-17-11 metric units—and were written with little attention to rhythm.[148] That was true as well of a second, similar group of six three-line poems he published in a collection issued later in the month by Ryūkō Kawaji.[149]

Noguchi had accommodated Seisensui's wishes by writing his "hokkus" in Japanese as well as English, but for even the most radical Japanese haiku poet, the results had to be disappointing. Even Noguchi could never bring himself to call his Japanese versions hokku, or haiku, nor was anyone else likely to do so. Aside from their excessive length and rhythmical awkwardness, their subject matter and style bore little if any resemblance to what Japanese poets—even Seisensui—wrote as haiku. Since Noguchi knew well enough how haiku were supposed to look and sound, the failure must have been deliberate. His youthful wish to be a haiku poet had evidently changed.

Noguchi refrained from further bilingual poetry demonstrations until two years later, when, after sending off his *Japanese Hokkus* manuscript to Boston, he published two longer sets of Japanese-only short poems in two magazines: a group of thirty-four "*Shōkyoku*" (little lyrics) in the Shinchōsha magazine *Shinchō* in January 1919, followed by a different selection of thirty-five "*Chīsai shi*" (little poems) in the *Bunshō Sekai*. From February to December the *Eigo Bungaku* magazine which he coedited included groups of the "Little Poems" / "*Chīsai shi*," sometimes in bilingual form, sometimes only in English.[150]

In these poems Noguchi generally dispensed with the 5-7-5 syllabic pattern in English, including poems of two, four, and even more lines; the Japanese versions invariably weighing in at over thirty syllables, Noguchi evidently being unwilling to reduce his "words, words, words" in Japanese even to the length of a tanka. He called the poems, in Japanese, *shōkyoku* or *chīsai shi*—small lyrics or little poems—*kyoku* being used mainly for song lyrics—though none of the poems seemed designed for musical accompaniment—and *shi* being the usual word for poems in a foreign style. Regardless of what he called them, none ever appeared in any of Japan's many haiku magazines. Nor did he make any public response to Ogiwara's letter. He could not, finally, offer much inspiration to Japanese haiku poets, other than a demonstration of other uses to which one might put short poems. Any influence his little poems had, would have been, as he presumably intended, on modern Western-style poets who also wrote short poems. Introducing *Japanese Hokkus* in one of his own collections many years later, he explained, "I took the word *hokku* to simply mean

148. "'Ketten-darake' to kimi wa iu. / Kōkai no nantaru bi! / Namida, uta, kakute sei wa nagareru." "Uta no kiregire—sono hoka nan da? / Watashi wa nagare ni notte hashiru otoko, / kumo no aida de sabishiku."

149. "Sankōshi rokuhen" (Six three-line poems), *Bansō* 2, ed Kawaji Ryūkō (Tokyo: Shokōshisha, 1917), 26-29, published on January 26.

150. "Shōkyoku sanjūshi-hen" (34 little songs), *Shinchō*, 1 Jan. 1919, 37-43.

a small poem (*chīsai shi*), but used a long essay on haiku as a preface."[151]

The radical haiku movement was not destined to gain a very strong following in Japan. Over the following decades there would be a few notable successes like the free-verse haiku of Santōka Taneda, a Waseda graduate who divorced his wife and adopted the life of a mendicant priest in the style of haikai poets of old. But the radical movement proved difficult to sustain. Meanwhile the haiku traditionalists regained popularity, in part, by becoming more slightly more inclusive with regard to subject matter. Kyoshi returned to prominence, with his conservative, sketching style, advocating traditional forms and seasonal words, and advocacy of "flowers and birds" as ideal subject matter. He and his disciples went on excursions in order to "catch something of the new life of nature." "Japanese poets are not a race apart," Noguchi would say; they did not "claim special regard" as poets did in the West. The appeal of Kyoshi's style was its simplicity. Noguchi might have been thinking of Kyoshi's simple approach when he wrote: "we in Japan treat the poet as a natural phenomenon, as natural as a flower or bird."[152] "Kyoshi made of haiku a national avocation," in the view of Donald Keene. "He encouraged poets even of minor talent, provided he could detect something fresh in the poems they submitted to *Hototogisu*. Haiku became the literary art of the common man."[153]

Noguchi summed up the Kyoshi style nicely in one hokku:

> Is there anything new under the sun?
> Certainly there is.
> See how a bird flies, how flowers smile!

Of course, this was not a sketch-style haiku, but, rather, a short poem about sketch-style haiku. Though he was not critical of such poems, he could not actually write them himself, being unable to easily cast off the voice and poetic perspective he had developed through two decades as an English poet. He was still trying, too hard, perhaps, to load his little poems with the qualities critics like Aston and Abercrombie said Japanese poets lacked: profundity, passion, sublimity or intellect. Perhaps he should have refrained from offering his little poems to Western readers as "Japanese Hokkus." But if that helped to overcome prejudices against the triviality of Japanese poetry, was it really a mistake?

---

151. *Shikaden* (Tokyo: Shunyōdō, 1943), 215.
152. "Japanese Poets and Poetry," J&A 92.
153. Keene, *Dawn to the West*, 4:116, 118.

7

LET THE EAST GREET THE WEST

1918-1921

In August 1918, the Noguchis traveled to the hot spring town of Ikaho for a holiday, intending to stay at the Hōraikan, managed by an old San Francisco acquaintance who had married into one of the town's prominent innkeeper families. But Ikaho turned out to be overrun by summer bathers, and the friend could only hastily arrange for them to stay in an attic of another inn, with assurances of finding them something better soon. In the tiny pair of rooms, whose soot-blackened cedar pillars looked to be hundreds of years old, they endured raucous shouts of drunken revelers, a translator in the next room spewing lewd English and loudly mocking "Yone Noguchi next door," and relentless fleas that occupied his wife, a skilled flea-catcher, through the nights. Evidently unable to focus on much else, Noguchi wrote up the scene with a mixture of frustration and fascination in a letter entitled "Ikaho News," for his friend "H-kun" and the *Yomiuri*.[1]

British Japanese Effects

With the war moving in 1918 towards a conclusion, Noguchi returned to his former role as Japanese commentator for the London *Graphic*. In "The Effect of the War on Japan," he described how the Japanese, though "often impassioned and sometimes too proud when national characteristics are in question," had become critical of "mistaken patriotism, a foolhardy bias built on an enlarged vulgar self-interest, or a misguided national

---

1. "Ikaho shōsoku" (Ikaho news), *Yomiuri*, 18 Aug 1918, 7, rpt. *Yonejirō zuihitsu* (Tokyo: Daiichi Shobō, 1926), 44-54.

instinct, emphasised by a barbarous sense of monopoly," suggesting that even in Japan, "the day of narrow-minded, wild, cruel, avaricious patriotism" had passed.[2]

In an essay the following week on "The Effect of Britain on Japan," Noguchi offered a more optimistic reconsideration of Japan's appreciation of British morality he had treated with some cynicism in the New York *Nation* two years earlier. "The vital question," he now concluded, "is to make the Anglo-Japanese Treaty a real living force not only in Japan, but also in England; that is to say, to perfect the mutual understanding of Japanese and Englishmen."[3]

Shoring up the Anglo-Japanese Alliance, Prince Arthur of Connaught had visited Japan in June. Noguchi offered a Kiplingesque welcome poem, making it clear that he saw Japan as an equal member in a protective, masculine, military partnership. "There's no south, there's no north, / When the brave men meet together." "We two guard the world in the East and the West," he concluded; "Pour the red friendship-wine, / Let the East greet the West!"[4]

In return, Prince Yorihito visited Britain in late October, to present a ceremonial sword to King George V. "The presence of Prince Yorihito in Europe lends a renewed interest to the part being played by Japan in the War," *The Graphic* observed the following week, introducing Noguchi's essay on the "Spiritual Effect of the War on Japan."[5] Noguchi put on his best English literary moralism for the essay, beginning with the somewhat exaggerated claim that the "Japanese—at least the intellectual class, who ride joyfully into the 'Woods of Westermain'" were now "becoming faithful believers of [George] Meredith, this wonderful Englishman," particularly in Meredith's asceticism and belief "that nothing noble can be achieved except by suffering pain." [6] Sacrifice had long been a keynote of patriotism for the Japanese, but patriotism had been "a kind of seven-headed Fetish whose command, wise or unwise, reasonable or unreasonable, true or untrue," one "had only to obey in blind unquestioning silence . . . not with an intelligent initiation of mind, but with mysterious fear." The belief that the "Japanese alone were capable of the silent unquestioning sacrifice of life for the nation's destiny" had been shattered by the war, as the Japanese found Westerners to be also possessed of "an unmistakable patriotic fire." The Western interpretation of patriotism "as guarding the liberties or democratism of the country"

2. "The Effect of the War on Japan," *Graphic* 97 (9 Mar. 1918): 296.
3. "The Effect of Britain on Japan," *Graphic* 97 (16 Mar. 1918): 12.
4. "A Japanese Welcome to Prince Arthur," *Graphic* 98 (17 Aug. 1918): 18.
5. "Spiritual Effect of the War on Japan," *Graphic* 98 (9 Nov. 1918): 10.
6. Noguchi had recently published "Meredesu no shisō" (Meredith's thought), *Yūben* 9:5 (10 Apr. 1918): 82-94, an early version of "Meredesu e ike" [Go to Meredith], *Suwaru ningen no hyōron* (1925), 49-65. Noguchi's reading of Meredith owed an unacknowledged debt to Shiran Wakatsuki's "Merejisu no shisō" in *Tōa no Hikari*, 4:9-11 (Sept.-Nov. 1909).

had provoked first wonder, then, admiration, and finally, understanding. "Individual intellectuality" had come to be seen as "a vital force" to lead the country into "organic harmony," the war serving as "an inspiration to complete the unity of the nation's soul." As a result, Noguchi felt the "literary atmosphere" had much improved since the start of the war, with even "democracy" and "people's literature" becoming "meaningful catchwords," and readers turning to Whitman, Edward Carpenter, and Horace Traubel. This so-called Taishō Democracy would scarcely outlast the Anglo-Japanese Alliance (which lapsed in 1923). But Noguchi, even as he followed the turn toward national unity, would remain firmly attached to the idea of patriotic individualism: "Where there is no true individualism there will be no real democracy, just as you may say that there is no perfect obedience without a true sense of freedom."

Theosophical Cousins

Noguchi's approach to teaching students consisted mainly (he later explained) in the belief that he "should free their tired brains from the spirit of studies" and that what he needed was "an idea not to teach them."[7] The task of instilling this tiresome "spirit of studies" therefore fell to other faculty members, especially the foreign faculty, who remained crucial to maintaining Keio's collegiate atmosphere, even if students like Noguchi often excused themselves from their difficult classes.

A year after Noguchi's appointment, Keio had hired Alfred William Playfair, a Canadian of Scottish ancestry with a master's degree, to round out the English literature department. Although he never published any work of his own, students and colleagues thought him "a great authority on English literature" and appreciated his "warm kindliness and earnest devotedness." Playfair divided his time between Keio and the First Higher School, adding Tokyo University when the English professor there, John Lawrence, died of influenza-related pneumonia in the spring of 1916. In addition, Playfair had, two years earlier, agreed to serve as editor for the *Transactions of the Asiatic Society*. It is a fair guess that overwork contributed to Playfair's declining health—on his winter holiday of 1917, he sought to alleviate his rheumatism and pleurisy at a Hakone hot-spring, where he suffered a fatal heart attack at the age of 48.[8]

Keio had two other foreign English instructors: David T. Weed, "well known in both Yokohama and Kobe sporting circles as an unusually clever all-round athlete," whose junior black belt rank in judo had been his most notable credential at the time of his 1910 appointment,[9] and

---

7. "Kara ni shirizoita katatsumuri" (A snail withdrawn into its shell), *Tsuyoi chikara yowai chikara* (Tokyo: Daiichi Shobō 1939), 40.
8. "Dr Lawrence's Successor," *JT*, 13 Apr. 1916, 8; "Sudden Death of Prof. Playfair at Kowakudani," *JT*, 29 Dec. 1917, 1.
9. "Local and General," *Japan Chronicle*, 3 Nov. 1910, 784; H.J. Bird, "David T. Weed: An Appreciation," *JT*, 9 Mar 1940, 8.

Stanley Hughes, who worked in the preparatory department. Hughes organized Keio's English Speaking Society, and was a noted member (along with his wife) of the Yokohama Amateur Dramatic Club. Neither was qualified to replace Playfair, so his courses were temporarily handed over to undistinguished instructor H.J. Bird, and a search for a more suitable replacement began.

With recruitment in Britain and America obstructed by the war, Noguchi called on friends in other places, including Sarojini Naidu in India. James Cousins, the Irish poet she recommended, knew only "the piece of good karma that has come to me through the collusion of two poets, Sarojini Naidu and Yone Naguchi."[10] James and his wife Margaret (known as Gretta), enthusiastic members of the Theosophical Society, had offered their services to its president, Annie Besant, who had sent them money for their passage to India in 1915. James had offered his services as a journalist but had been invited, on arrival, to take up a teaching post at the new Theosophical College opening at Madanapalle, of which he became principal in 1918.

Annie Besant's power in India had grown, at least among Indians, with her creation of an All India Home Rule League in 1916 and her subsequent arrest by British authorities the following summer; after her release she had been elected the Indian National Congress's first female president at its December 1917 meeting (preceding Sarojini Naidu's presidency by eight years). Despite Besant's vocal opposition to British rule, the Theosophical schools had managed to gain government acceptance, and were in the process of being merged into a new national university system. This involved a good deal of academic politics, in which James Cousins's Japan trip could serve some useful purposes. It would strengthen Cousins's lackluster night-school credentials (especially after Keio awarded him an honorary doctorate in 1923). But equally important, it would allow Besant to address staffing problems at several Theosophical colleges.[11] For Margaret Cousins, in her husband's absence, there was a job as Head Mistress of the new National Girls' School at Mangalore.

On the morning of May 29, 1919, an overnight train brought James Cousins from Kobe, where he had arrived the previous day, to Yokohama Station, where he looked in vain for Yone Noguchi.[12] "I figured to myself a little man in an artistic *kimono*, his feet in *geta*," he recalled in

10. James H. Cousins and Margaret E. Cousins, *We Two Together* (Madras: Ganesh, 1950), 342.
11. F. L. Woodward, a noted scholar of Pali Buddhist literature, had announced his departure in 1917 from Mahinda College in Ceylon, one of the oldest Theosophical colleges, where he had served as principal since 1903. Rather than promoting the 26-year-old university graduate, Frederick Gordon Pearce, recently hired as vice-principal, Besant wanted to move Pearce temporarily into Cousins's Madanapalle position, and offer the Mahinda position to another 26-year-old, Kalidas Nag, a promising graduate of Calcutta University then teaching at Calcutta's Scottish Churches College.
12. James H. Cousins, *The New Japan* (Madras: Ganesh, 1923), 12.

his interesting and detailed memoir of his Japanese year, *The New Japan*. "There were very few people on the platform, none resembling my idea of Noguchi. After some time my protruding head caught the attention of a young man who came towards me evidently with intent to be of service. He wore a suit of rather rough English clothing and a bowler hat."

"Are you Cousins?" the stranger asked.

"I am," Cousins replied.

"I am Noguchi," the stranger replied, and boarded the train. An hour later they arrived at Tokyo station, where they took an electric street car to the University. Cousins continued to adjust his expectations.

"Where is Tokyo?" he asked, evidently expecting something different.

"*This* is Tokyo," Noguchi replied. But surely it wasn't the center of the city, Cousins insisted.

"This is the center," Noguchi calmly informed him. "This is the heart of the Empire of Japan." Further questioning elicited the explanation that the station building was built in the French Renaissance style.

"But why French? This is Japan," Cousins protested.

"There are several Japans," Noguchi informed him.

Cousins told himself he would have to observe in silence; in any case, no conversation was possible in the crowded street car that went at appalling speed between stops which felt "as if a sword had suddenly severed the strained neck of speed." Cousins contented himself with observing the artful motions of the ticket collector and a woman's elaborate coiffure which, though beautiful, reeked of fish oil. After exiting the car, they passed through streets of shops, curious to Cousins's eyes, before coming into sight of the large brick building which was Keio's library. Noguchi took him to a smaller building where he was introduced to the University's president and had tea before meeting some of the faculty, who mainly impressed him with their horn-rimmed spectacles and gold-crowned teeth.

Cousins was baffled by the question of where he was going to reside, having "assumed that Universities which called professors from the ends of the earth had arrangements for their storage." That evidently not being the case, it was suggested to convert for his use an old teahouse in the middle of campus, next to the Banraisha ("Hall of a Thousand Welcomes") which served as the faculty lunchroom. The tearoom, formerly used by the president, delighted Cousins. "Here was *Japan*, the Japan of aesthetic sensibility expressed in sliding doors to hidden presses decorated with floral designs, a thickly matted floor, and little white-paper panes through which the light came as a silver radiance with here and there a shadow cast by a tree." There was a goldfish pond of story-book exquisiteness, and in the clear air of autumn, he was told, he should see the white peak of Fuji from the second stepping-stone from his door. Around the other three sides were faculty buildings, one of which was "the Club, called by the hearty name of the Hall of a Thousand Welcomes (*Banraisha*)" where Cousins was invited to luncheon with the teaching staff. "The meal was, to my surprise and disappointment, entirely western save for green tea as the wash-down. Another of Noguchi's Japans stared me in the mouth, the Japan that had turned its back upon the gentle teaching of the Buddha and had adopted carnivorism in its food. I felt myself, when I declined the flesh-foods, to be the only true Buddhist at the table."[13]

Noguchi had invited Cousins to stay at his home for a few days. After taking the train to Higashi-Nakano, "several turns through quiet byways brought us to a wooden wall and gate." Sliding aside a small portion of the larger gate they passed into the stone pathway of the garden and the entrance to the house. Mrs. Noguchi was in the hall to meet them, called by the tinkle of a bell on the outer gate. She sat on the polished floor while the two men took off their shoes, and bowed several times to the floor. Cousins got up onto the floor and bowed back. With Matsuko were a young woman servant and a girl and boy who seemed about ten and eight (actually Hifumi was eleven and Masao nearly six) who also joined in the salutations. Two-year-old Shimako, in the background, postponed her acceptance of the visitor pending further examination.

Noguchi took Cousins into his study where, after Cousins admired Noguchi's library, they sat facing the garden and drank tea brought in by Mrs. Noguchi. Afterwards, Cousins had a bath, emerging to find a kimono awaiting him: "the vestment of the first stage of my initiation into the mystery of that gentle thing, the home life of Japan." Noguchi, too, had transformed himself into the kimono-clad Noguchi of Cousins's imagination. Little Shimako could now be persuaded to present the guest with a small cake and cherry, accompanied by three bows.

89. James Cousins and Yone Noguchi, May 29, 1919.

13. Cousins, *The New Japan*, 25-26.

After dinner, Cousins was introduced to the guest room, which was, in fact, the finely-appointed reception room. His reveries on his new life in Japan were interrupted, however, by the arrival of three journalists, come to record his first impressions of Japan. They were "almost childishly delighted" at finding Cousins in a Japanese garment, being prepared, in any case, to record the moment on film. "The photograph will stand as a perpetual denial of the allegation that Noguchi cannot smile," Cousins noted.

Cousins spent three nights at the Noguchi house before moving into his new residence and beginning his lectures. In addition to his main lecture on modern English poetry, he had been asked to give a lecture course on Irish political history, for which he was quite unprepared.

Cousins had written several volumes of tepidly-received poetry and a book entitled *The Renaissance in India* documenting the new literary and social movements there; before the Indian pilgrimage, he had been a fringe member of the Irish literary movement, serving a year on the Irish Literary Theatre committee at the invitation of W.B. Yeats. In their Dublin days, James and Margaret had been friendly with the young James Joyce, who memorialized "Gretta" in his famous *Dubliners* story, "The Dead."

The students, most of whom wore "dismal and formal" uniforms that reminded Cousins of railway servants', were quiet and undemonstrative. He soon became uneasily aware that his lectures were not understood; the spoken English of the students was very elementary and anything more than a rudimentary knowledge of the English language was apparently considered unnecessary to the study of English literature. He found the students almost incapable of abstraction, in contrast to his Indian students, "heirs of long ages of metaphysical disquisition," who tended to overemphasize the abstract.[14]

Cousins made regular weekend visits to the Noguchi home, staying over Saturday nights and even entering into a sort of language-exchange arrangement with Hifumi. "Part of my diversion was the teaching of rudimentary English to the kind and earnest little lady in return for a similar service to me as to Japanese." Cousins often saw Noguchi at the university and entered into his intellectual world accompanying him to a Nō play and the Autumn art exhibition at Ueno park, among other adventures, but "it was in his home life, where he was the pure Japanese poet and head of a family . . . that the essential being blossomed."[15]

It was Cousins's habit during his week-end visits to take a rest in the afternoon on a couch in the poet's study, but there was a leering stage-mask hanging on the wall above the foot of the couch which disturbed his rest. Cousins had recently discovered that another mask, hanging in

14. Cousins, *The New Japan*, 48-51.
15. Cousins, *The New Japan*, 54.

the entrance hall of the house, was none other than the death-mask of the English poet Francis Thompson.[16] (Noguchi had explained that he "had been given this copy of the mask by Francis Meynell in London with strict injunctions that he was not to let it out of his possession or to allow it to be copied.") Cousins proposed exchanging the places of the two masks. "My suggestion was accepted, and the family (maid-servant included) and myself formed a quaint procession as Noguchi carefully took the mask of the immortal English poet from the hall to the studio and hung it up amongst its affinities."[17]

90. *Life Mask of Francis Thompson* by Everard Meynell.

The mask "became a living thing to my imagination," Cousins wrote, and two years later, after he had returned to India the memory of it remained so strong he could only lay the ghost by writing a long poem, which he entitled "Installation Ode: For the placing of the death-mask of Francis Thompson in the home of Yone Noguchi in Japan." Noguchi published his own poem, "Shijin Tomuson" (The poet Thompson) in 1923, in which he explained that he had once encountered Thompson's poetry in a San Francisco library and afterward had no desire to read or understand it. But "perhaps if I had understood him," he concluded, "I wouldn't keep his mask hanging in my study."[18]

Transcontinental Lecture Tour

A few days after storing Cousins in his campus teahouse, Noguchi received a long-anticipated letter inviting him to return to America, expenses paid, as a lecturer for the J.B. Pond Lyceum Bureau. Noguchi

16. This was evidently one of Everard Meynell's life masks of Thompson. There was "a curious likeness between the death-mask of Keats and the life-masks of Francis Thompson, taken in the last years of his life" observed a writer in *The American Review of Reviews*, June 1913, 508.
17. Cousins, *The New Japan*, 108-09.
18. "Installation Ode: For the placing of the death-mask of Francis Thompson in the home of Yone Noguchi in Japan" *Surya Gita* (Madras: Ganesh, 1922), 136-44; NY, "Shijin Tomuson," *Saigo no butō*, 1923, 116.

had been actively imagining the prospect for several years, at least far back as the summer of 1916, when Tagore visited Japan on his way to a Pond-financed American lecture tour, and Noguchi sought advice from Charles Keeler, who had visited in Japan a few years earlier at the beginning of his around-the-world lecture and reading tour. Informing Keeler of his own experience of being "called to Oxford and London" where "at the special invitation of Robert Bridges of Oxford (the Poet Laureate)" he had "delivered a series of Japanese lectures," with the result appearing "in the 'Spirit of Japanese Poetry' published by John Murray of London," he came to the point:

> I am thinking at present that I might come to America through San Francisco perhaps in next year; but I like to cover my own American expense with my lecturing. I want to deliver (as I did at Magdalen College) a series of Japanese lectures at the Stanford University; don't you know somebody in authority there personally? Of course the University of California will answer very well for my purpose. I was told by somebody that the University of California was going to have a Japanese chair; who will become the professor for that chair? If you are able, I wish you will make some arrangement for my lectures in California. Perhaps you can introduce me to some agent who would like to handle my Californian business; I shall be glad to give my lectures at any big cities of California. If I come to America, I hope I will stay for some three months in your club. I believe that you have much experience about lecturing yourself; so I am sure that you will give some suggestion for this matter.[19]

Keeler had made inquiries, and there had been—after nearly three years—a favorable outcome. "I must thank you for your kindness in writing to Mr Pond about my American lectures a few years ago," Noguchi now wrote. "James B. Pond gave me a satisfactory offer, —so I am going to America under his management."[20]

Harriet Monroe, editor of *Poetry* magazine in Chicago, had also been instrumental in promoting him to Pond. "Now I understand that you acted as a true ambassador who brought Mr James B. Pond and myself together," he wrote her on July 9. "I thank you so much for your kind service,—perhaps I thank God too."[21]

God was no longer a decisive factor in the selection of Lyceum lecturers; even the affiliated Chautauqua movement retained little of the religious flavor of its origins as a Sunday school teacher training camp. The Chautauqua and Lyceum movements had become hugely popular, with annual attendance estimated at over thirty million—around a third of the American population. Enthusiastic organizers were still driven

19. YN to Charles Keeler, 4 Aug. 1916, Keeler Collection, Box 4, Huntington.
20. YN to Charles Keeler, 20 June 1919, Keeler Collection, Box 4, Huntington.
21. YN to Harriet Monroe, 9 July 1919, Poetry Magazine Papers, University of Chicago.

by populist idealism and sometimes feared they were "beginning to think of it too much as a business and too little of it as a movement."²² But business was a crucial element, and over a century, the Chautauqua and Lyceum circuits had evolved efficient management strategies to insure their survival. Bringing the world's lecturing talent to small-town America and keeping audiences interested enough to buy tickets in the necessary quantities required business savvy and a willingness to cater to popular tastes, even when the results were barely distinguishable from vaudeville. Local managers selected from ever-changing lists of available lecturers, musicians, and entertainers, and were financially responsible for meeting sales targets. Pond faced continual competition from other agencies: Redpath, with offices in nine cities, Affiliated Management, a closely organized group of bureaus in ten cities, the Coit Lyceum Bureau, and Ellison White, among others. Some were doing a better job than Pond at bringing cosmopolitanism to small town America. That winter Affiliated Management's roster boasted Yale- and Oberlin-educated Congregational minister, Rev. Yutaka Minakuchi (billed as "the ablest representative of the Christian Japanese in America"), two Chinese lecturers—San Francisco editor Ng Poon Chew and American-trained botanist Woon Young Chun—and a Syrian woman, Sumayeh Attiyeh. Affiliated's list of talent also included entertainers and musicians, some imported from Hawaii, New Zealand, and the Philippines. Pond's offerings, in contrast, were almost exclusively literary. Pond himself had spent the summer in Europe recruiting talent, landing what he thought was a prize catch in popular Belgian writer Maurice Maeterlinck.

Pond had also secured the services of several Irish writers anxious to escape the turmoil of the ongoing War of Independence: W.B. Yeats and Lord Dunsany among them. In England he had signed up war poet Siegfried Sassoon and prolific novelist Hugh Walpole. In Chicago, where Pond's second office was located, he recruited *Poetry Magazine* poets Carl Sandburg, Lew Sarett, and Eunice Tietjens, and announced the opening of the Court Lecture Room for Sunday afternoon recitals and lectures through the winter, in what had lately been the home of the Chicago Little Theatre in the Fine Arts Building.²³

Yeats had often expressed a wish to visit Asia. The prospect that he might continue eastward when his American tour ended set in motion a flurry of inquiries. In addition to his position as arguably the greatest living English-language poet, Yeats had also secured permanent respect in Japan by publishing and introducing Ernest Fenollosa's Noh translations and writing and staging his own Noh-inspired Irish plays. Noguchi must have received strong support from his collaborators at *Eigo Bungaku*, Kenzō Wadagaki and Tokuboku Hirata, both of whom had been

---

22. "Platform Prospect and Retrospect," *Lyceum Magazine* 29 (Feb. 1920): 23.
23. "Pond Opens Court Lecture Room," *Lyceum Magazine* 29 (Nov. 1919): 38.

deeply involved with Fenollosa and the Noh. Wadagaki with his position at Tokyo University could surely arrange a joint appointment with Keio that would be sufficient for Yeats's needs. James Cousins could smooth out any difficulties with the elder poet, having been connected with him since 1901, when Yeats had thought him a promising young playwright and appointed him to the committee of the Irish Literary Theatre, then planning its third season. Yeats had publicly applauded Cousins at his first curtain-call ("Splendid, my boy. Splendid. Beautiful verse beautifully spoken by native actors. Just what we wanted.")[24] True, Cousins's subsequent effort, an Irish farce, had been privately dismissed by Yeats as "rubbish and vulgar rubbish" when up for discussion, and Yeats had admitted to his sister the following year that Cousins was "one man we did snuff out."[25] But Cousins, mild-mannered and respectful of his superiors, was not one to hold a grudge.

By the second week of July, Yeats was consulting his American lawyer friend John Quinn about the Japan proposal. "I have just been invited to lecture for two years in Japan at a university there but have not had time to decide anything," he told Quinn. "It would be pleasant to go away until the tumult of war had died down, and perhaps Home Rule established, and even the price of coal settled on. But would one ever come back?—would one find some grass-grown city, scarce inhabited since the tenth century, where one seemed surpassing rich on a few hundred a year?"[26] The "few hundred a year" on which Yeats might continue nurturing his dreams of escape was already in question the following week with the sudden death of Kenzō Wadagaki on July 18. But there was still hope that Tokyo University would support the plan.

If anything about James Cousins's one-room on-campus teahouse-office-lodging ever made him feel surpassing rich, it was likely the "fish-pond with goldfish" which, he wrote, "gave a touch of I know not what story-book exquisiteness." Noguchi made frequent visits through September and into October as he prepared for his tour. "As he put each lecture into typescript," Cousins recalled, "he brought it to my room at leisure hours or after lunch in order that I might criticise his delivery of it." The poet's English elocution still left something to be desired: "he had never got beyond the mechanical limitations that the Japanese language has put upon the Japanese mouth." So Cousins drilled him on distinguishing his l's from his r's and his b's from his v's, trying vainly to make his beloved sound less "berubbed."[27]

On October 10, a few weeks after Matsuko gave birth to a third

24. James H. Cousins and Margaret E. Cousins, *We Two Together* (Madras: Ganesh, 1950), 76.
25. W. B. Yeats to Lily Yeats, 25 Dec. 1903, in *The Letters of W.B. Yeats*, ed. Allan Wade (London: Rupert Hart-Davis, 1954), 417.
26. Yeats to Quinn, 11 July 1919, in W.B. Yeats, *The Letters of W. B. Yeats*, 659.
27. Cousins, *The New Japan*, 24, 203-05.

daughter, Yapako, Cousins joined "a small farewell dinner to Noguchi in a city restaurant." On the 11th Hōmei Iwano arranged a farewell party at Tokyo's new Inokashira Park.[28] On the 14th, amid considerable fanfare, Noguchi embarked on his second voyage to America. James Cousins canceled his classes and went with his students to the railway station to join the "large crowd of friends, including many men and women of high distinction, assembled to give a hearty *sayonara* (good-bye) to the poet."[29] This time he was crossing the Pacific in comfort on the *Tenyo Maru*, a ship more than three times the size of the *Belgic*, in a first-class cabin paid for by the J.B. Pond Lyceum Bureau.

91. The *Tenyo Maru*.

Noguchi's lectures were to officially begin after his arrival in San Francisco, but Honolulu offered too attractive a lecturing opportunity for Noguchi and his island friends to pass up. At 6 a.m on the 23rd, as the ship was waiting to dock, a *Nippu Jiji* reporter "searched the ship for a person matching his description. We found a man with a poet's keen sensitivity and asked directly, 'You aren't Mr. Noguchi?' to which he replied, 'I am.'"[30] By the time the ship docked for its one-day stopover, he had a busy schedule lined up, in which he lectured on Japanese poetry at noon at the Nuuanu YMCA, took in several sights, including the statue of Kamehameha, the Bishop Museum, and the Moanalua Garden, dined with a small group that included an old friend from his San Francisco newspaper days, Tomizo Katsunuma, and then gave a second lecture on Japanese poetry at 7:30 p.m. capped by a poetry reading, at the home of minister and local historian William Westervelt, whose house, one of the first in Waikiki, had become a gathering place for literati.[31]

In the morning the *Tenyo Maru* embarked on its six-day final leg to San Francisco.

On the morning of Friday, October 30, Noguchi was back in the remnants of his old stomping grounds. With the Pond Bureau taking

28. Iwano, *Hōmei zenshū* 12, 543.
29. YN to Harriet Monroe, 9 July 1919, *Poetry* Magazine Papers, U of Chicago Library; Cousins, *The New Japan*, 204-05.
30. "Shijin no Hawai daiichi inshō" (Poet's first impressions of Hawaii), *Nippu Jiji*, 23 Nov. 1919, 2.
31. "Wafuku sugata nite eishi rōdoku" (In Japanese attire: English poetry reading), *Nippu Jiji*, 24 Oct. 1919, 4. Noguchi read from his now famous *From the Eastern Sea*: "O Hana San" and "a poem about the seashore," presumably "By the Sea."

care of most of his travel and hotel arrangements, he checked into the Hotel St. Francis on Union Square. He had a week to get organized and reacquainted, before his first scheduled lecture in Los Angeles on November 7. "I might give a lecture here too,—that is not still settled at this moment," he told his publisher.[32]

Pond was not having a great year, with profit margins reduced by competition, overbooking, and the ongoing influenza pandemic. But it was still early in what Pond must have hoped would be a successful season, anchored by outstanding overseas writers. It would prove a disastrous one, mainly due to his misguided recruitment of Maurice Maeterlinck, who, it turned out, was not being modest when he said he could not lecture in English. Noguchi had been wise to practice his elocution, and lucky to arrive more than two months ahead of Maeterlinck.[33] Arrangements for Noguchi probably resembled those Pond made with Siegfried Sassoon, who had the misfortune to arrive in late January. For Sassoon, Pond had "guaranteed to pay $100 each for a minimum of twenty-five lectures. Yet by the time Sassoon was due to leave for America, he had managed to book only two paid engagements." Pond had even "cabled the bad news to Sassoon in England, urging him to cancel his trip. By catching an earlier boat, however, Sassoon had missed the cable." When Sassoon arrived at the New York office, Pond seemed "a bit blue" as he informed Sassoon "that the market was glutted by Walpole, Dunsany . . . Yeats, Cannan, Drinkwater, Housman—not to mention Sir Oliver Lodge and Coningsby Dawson!"[34] Noguchi's schedule, too, had been, on the eve of his departure, "completely uncertain." Writing from England in August, Pond had simply advised him to go first to San Francisco where everything could be arranged.[35] Noguchi had nothing more helpful to tell a Japanese reporter on arrival. "This trip," he explained, "was arranged by telegram, so the plans are still to be decided, and even the lecture topics have not been settled."[36] He had told reporters in Hawaii he was expecting to give around fifty lectures, but by the end he would give only twenty-five.

The Japanese community had changed considerably since Noguchi's departure in 1904. It had grown in size and moved after the great quake from the Chinatown area to a more distant one north of Geary Street called *Nihonjinmachi* ("Japanese people's town") and then simply *Nihonmachi* or "Japantown."

---

32. YN to Edmund Brown, 1 Nov. 1919, FSL.
33. "Maeterlinck Tries in Vain to Lecture in Phonetic English," New York *Sun*, 3 Jan. 1920, 1.
34. Jean Moorcroft Wilson, *Siegfried Sassoon: The Journey from the Trenches: A Biography (1918-1967)* (London: Duckworth, 2003), 75-6.
35. "Honjitsu chaku-Sō no Yone Noguchi" (Yone Noguchi arriving at San Francisco today), *Shin Sekai*, 30 Oct. 1919, 3.
36. "Gun'yūkakkyo no bundan" (powerful rivals of the literary world), *Shin Sekai*, 1 Nov. 1919, 3.

92. "Distinguished Visitors to America," Maeterlinck, Yeats, Sassoon, Noguchi, and St. John Ervine.

Two newspapers had survived: the *Shin Sekai* (New World), and the *Nichibei Shimbun* (Japanese American News). The *Shin Sekai* was now neither the Christian paper it had been under Hachirō Soejima, nor the businesslike paper of Frank T. Kuranaga.[37] Its young editor,

37. After the earthquake, the *Shin Sekai* was "the first newspaper to resume printing at San Francisco with its own type," and Frank Kuranaga's Japanese art store on Van Ness, having escaped the fire, was doing a booming business, as was his Great Japan Mercantile Company in Pasadena. But in March 1907 Kuranaga's fortunes came crashing down when he was arrested on charges of borrowing large sums of money from banks under false pretenses. His white wife suffered a nervous breakdown, and weeks later, what remained of "the beautiful dragon tea room of the Frank Kuranaga Japanese art curio store, famed throughout the west, was partially destroyed by fire" due to an employee burning trash after the closeout sale. In August, $74,000 in debt, Kuranaga filed for bankruptcy. In Reno the following month a lucky roulette bet netted him $3,500 with which he moved his family to Seattle and tried to live on a smaller scale, but the marriage fared poorly under the straitened circumstances. "Lately he has required that I work to support myself and our child," his wife told a reporter in 1914, "and after that had continued for six months without any financial assistance from him, submission to his ideas of the woman's position in the family became more than ever unbearable and I determined to ask for divorce." Kuranaga, she explained, "regarded her as a slave" and demanded "strict obedience, silence and entire self-abnegation in the care of our child." Kuranaga refused to criticize his wife, attributing her behavior to economic strain; he also thought "the discussions in the newspapers of the possibility of war with Japan and the prejudice among Americans against inter-marriage with our people exerted a constant mental pressure on her which finally produced this crisis." The divorce petition was granted the following year: a sad outcome for the once "Wealthy Japanese Proud of His Fair American Spouse." See "F. T. Kuranaga Arrested by Detectives After Hunt of Several Days," San Francisco *Call*, 9 Mar. 1907, 14; and "Flees Japanese Hubby," *Oakland Tribune*, 22 Mar. 1914, 20.

Goroku Ikeda, had emerged as the most articulate spokesman during the recent, hard-fought battle over Japanese student segregation in the public schools. Ikeda had recently returned to San Francisco with a degree from Teachers College in New York, where he had set up his own newspaper, the New York *Japanese Weekly* (*Nyū Yōku Shūho*) but had failed to wrest significant market share from rival Columbia graduate Hajime Hoshi's *Japanese America Commercial Weekly* (the *Nichibei Jiho*). Appointed secretary of the new Japanese Association of America, Ikeda had served as spokesman for San Francisco consul, Kisaburō Ueno, during the school controversy.

The rival *Nichibei Shimbun* (*Japanese American News*) was still owned by Kyūtarō Abiko, although Abiko, now a pillar of the Japanese-American community, had little involvement with the day-to-day running of the paper, and was likely off, during Noguchi's stay, on one or more of his many enterprising projects, which ranged from railroad labor contracting to farming and even banking, and politics, including the Yamato Colony he had established on a large parcel of land in Merced County, one of the first and most successful large-scale Japanese agricultural communities in the United States, which, by 1920, comprised 2,450 acres.[38] Abiko had been president of the Japanese Association of America at the time of the clamor leading up to the Gentlemen's Agreement, and had been vocal in criticizing the Japanese consul in Washington, Viscount Aoki, for failing to represent Japanese immigrant interests in the matter. Abiko's advocacy of permanent settlement aligned him with the interests of Japanese immigrants and probably accounted for the *Nichibei*'s 43% higher circulation in 1920 (12,568 vs. 8,750).[39] Still serving as editor and writer was at least one survivor from the early days, Bunzō "Shakuma" Washizu. Sadly gone, however, was Kosen Takahashi, who had settled in St. Louis and passed away there of an unspecified illness in 1914, at the age of 37.[40]

It was the *Nichibei* that organized a welcome party for Noguchi on his first night in the city. "Our company will hold a dinner meeting this Saturday at 7 PM at the St. Francis Hotel, inviting Mr. Yonejirō Noguchi, who is currently in the United States for a lecture tour and staying in the area. At the same time, we will also invite Consul General Ōta, prominent local figures, and Mr. Noguchi's old acquaintances."[41]

38. Valerie J. Matsumoto, *Farming the Home Place: A Japanese American Community in California, 1919-1982* (Ithaca: Cornell UP, 1982), 30.
39. Circulation statistics are from *N.W. Ayer and Son's American Newspaper Annual and Directory* (Philadelphia: Ayer, 1920), 99.
40. Takahashi, having "led an adventurous and varied life as a newspaper reporter, painter, architect, speculator, English writer, entertainment manager, and China traveler," had died "after an illness of several months" ("Takahashi Kosen no kakushi" (Kosen Takahashi dies abroad), *Nyū Yōku Shimpō*, 12 Dec. 1914, 3; "Japanese Artist Dead," *Oakland Tribune*, 5 Dec. 1914, 20.
41. "Noguchi shi shōtaikai" (Mr Noguchi's welcome party), *Nichibei Shimbun*, 1 Nov. 1919, 3.

93. Tamekichi Ōta in 1926.

Tamekichi Ōta, appointed Consul General a year earlier and already at odds with Abiko, the *Nichibei*, and the local Japanese immigrant community, declined the invitation; he would arrange his own reception for Noguchi before the poet's departure from the West Coast. Ōta had taken over the position during the last months of the war, when Japanese-American relations were at their most cordial, but within a few months the situation had deteriorated dramatically. Much of the trouble was again the work of long-time senator James Phelan, who had kicked off his reelection campaign with a renewed attack on Japanese immigration. Having for the most part succeeded in his earlier campaigns to prevent Japanese labor immigration and land ownership, Phelan turned his focus toward the largest remaining obstacle to total Japanese exclusion: picture brides. It was not a new issue—the loophole in the immigration law had been troubling exclusionists since the passage of the Gentleman's Agreement of 1907. Phelan, aided by V.S. McClatchy, an editor at the *Sacramento Bee*, had been collecting statistics and developing arguments and strategies, and in the summer of 1919 they had conducted hearings aimed at introducing congressional legislation abolishing the practice.

94. Reelection campaign advertisement for James Phelan in *Sunset*, July 1920.

The Japanese community was divided on the picture bride question. The Japanese government had never been interested in encouraging Japanese emigration, and tended to accept immigration restrictions as long as they did not overtly discriminate against Japanese. The exclusionists' fear-mongering escalated through the summer, and on October 5, Ōta cabled the Foreign Ministry to cease issuing passports to picture-brides, believing this would have the effect of "taking away the most effective source of agitation from the exclusionists."[42] Ōta had then persuaded the executive board of the Japanese Association of America to issue a statement, on October 31, stating the practice "should be abolished because it is not only in contravention of the accepted American conception of marriage, but is also out of harmony with the growing ideals of the Japanese themselves." But picture brides were for most Japanese immigrants their only realistic hope for establishing families, and children their only remaining hope for legally purchasing land. Moreover, local Japanese community leaders were offended that Ōta had not consulted them before issuing his request. Leading the attack was Kyūtaro Abiko's *Nichibei*. On November 19 Ōta had told the foreign minister that Abiko was "playing on the ignorance of the masses." But with the exception of the *Shin Sekai*, all the West Coast Japanese papers were lined up against him.

95. Kyūin Okina.

The *Nichibei* now had an Oakland office, headed by a talented thirty-year-old journalist named Kyūin Okina. Okina had come to the West Coast at the age of eighteen in 1907 and spent his first decade among Japanese immigrants in places like Seattle and Stockton. A prolific writer since his arrival, he had founded a Seattle Japanese immigrant literary society, and had established something of a reputation in Japan, his work having appeared in *Teikoku Bungaku* and the *Asahi Shimbun*. His first novel, about the struggles of four Japanese immigrants, had been serialized in the *Nichibei* in 1915. In the preface to his first short story collection published in Tokyo, he explained, "From now on the Japanese people in

---

42. Yuji Ichioka, "Japanese Associations and the Japanese Government: A Special Relationship," *Pacific Historical Review* 46 (1977): 431-32.

America will stop living as overseas migrant workers [*imin*] and begin the life of permanent settlers [*ijūmin*]. And, after the mid-twentieth century, we will have writers who write their stories in English—the world language—among our own descendants. Until their time arrives, we, as an intermediary generation and in the tradition of the Japanese race, must give expression to the emotional pain we suffer in an alien land."[43] Okina had moved to Oakland in 1917 to work for the Oakland Japanese Association (*Nihonjinkai*) but after a falling out with its president, had accepted Abiko's offer to head the *Nichibei*'s Oakland office.

The emotional pain felt by Okina's generation of Japanese immigrants was hard to avoid. Noguchi's generation had maintained their optimism by shrugging off the angry glares of passersby with the thought that they were being mistaken for Chinese and when properly recognized would be welcomed as equals. Now they knew the angry looks were for them. The hatred, spread by politicians, labor unions, the press, and groups like the Native Sons of the Golden West, was growing stronger, not abating. It took a profound act of will to cling to the belief that they would eventually be accepted, and yet many still did, including Noguchi.

Making his long-anticipated pilgrimage to the Oakland Hights, Noguchi was joined by Okina, Washizu, and enough *Nichibei* associates to fill two cars. After stopping for flowers at the Domoto Brothers' nursery, they began the uphill drive, while Yone talked of his California days. He had never been Miller's disciple, as everyone supposed, he told them, but he was yearning to return to the cabin where he had inscribed his poems by candle-light.

They found Miller's widow, Abigail, and daughter, Juanita, both at home. Okina correctly surmised they had not met Yone before (they had moved to the Hights a few years after Noguchi's departure, when Joaquin fell seriously ill) "but they both knew his name as a poet and delightedly welcomed him like a near relative returned home." Coffee and sandwiches were brought out and Juanita played the piano and sang like a bird, accompanied by actual birds which flew in from the woods outside, and then talked with Yone for a while. Okina "was filled with rare delight, but Yone, driven to stronger emotions, was wiping his tears with a handkerchief."[44]

The little group of houses on the hillside were now surrounded by a

43. Okina Kyūin, preface to *Ishokuju* (Transplanted Tree) (1923), trans. Teruko Kumei, quoted in Orm Øverland, "The American Novel Beyond English," in *The American Novel 1870-1940*, ed. Priscilla Wald and Michael A. Elliott (Oxford: Oxford UP, 2014), 223. See also Ikuko Torimoto, *Okina Kyūin and the Politics of Early Japanese Immigration to the United States, 1868-1924* (Jefferson, N.C.: McFarland, 2016).

44. Okina Kyūin, "Mirā no sanso o tazuneru Yone Noguchi shi Ōkurando nite" (Mr. Yone Noguchi visiting Miller's mountain villa in Oakland), *Yomiuri*, 1 Feb. 1920, 7; Okina Kyūin, "Yone Noguchi no omoide" (Memories of Yone Noguchi), *Kenkyū*, v. 2, 188-89, my translation. Okina, in the *Yomiuri* article, gives October 31, as the date of the visit, but Noguchi told Helen Bonnet he had visited the Heights on Sunday, i.e., November 2, which seems more likely.

lush forest of trees that Noguchi had helped Miller plant. Miller had died in 1913, intending to treat his remains to an Indian-style cremation on the funeral pyre he had built overlooking the San Francisco Bay. But the plan had been stopped by city authorities, and it was only possible to scatter the late poet's ashes on the pyre. A year or two before he died, Miller had made arrangements to donate his property to the City of Oakland as a public park, with the provision that his wife and daughter, who had come to take care of him in his final years, be allowed to live there during their lives.[45]

96. Miller's Hights in *The Overland Monthly*, February 1920.

Noguchi's return to the birthplace of his muse inspired a new poem drawing on his memories of Miller.[46]

> Thou wert a prophet, or a god, in top-boots, with a bearskin on shoulders.
> How in day we climbed up the mists furrowed by the hills,
> Where we buried words and dug God's silence!
> What a mighty silence there sailed in from the San Francisco Bay's silvery room!
> Again what a silence, when the king-like sun sank down through the gate!

---

45. Henry Meade Bland, "California's Olympus Becomes a Public Park," San Francisco *Call*, 10 Sept. 1911, 3.
46. "At Joaquin Miller's Heights After Twenty Years," *Dial* 69 (July 1920): 33-34.

He imagined Joaquin's spirit riding on the mists, as in his poem "Columbus," singing "Sail on! Sail on! and on!"

> I cannot think thou art dead quite many years now,
> I feel I hear a voice saying: "Joaquin has gone to town for a leg of mutton,
> Or a bottle of claret; wait, Noguchi, he will soon come home."

But Miller would not be coming home any time soon.

Nor were most of the other writers Noguchi had known in his California days. The great writers of the first generation—Bret Harte, Mark Twain, Stoddard, and Ambrose Bierce—had all passed on except Ina Coolbrith (now nearly eighty), the state's poet laureate since the post was created in 1915. Ambrose Bierce had vanished in Mexico in 1914. Many of the important writers of the succeeding generation had also passed on: Jack London, Frank Norris, and Adeline Knapp; the survivors had moved away—Edwin Markham had remained in Staten Island, Gelett Burgess and his wife, Estelle, preferred Paris and New York. Blanche Partington's job as the *Call*'s music and drama critic had gone up in smoke in the great earthquake, and she now lived in semi-retirement assisting her talented siblings and pursuing her interest in Christian Science.

Only a few survivors remained active: among them Porter Garnett and George Sterling. Garnett and Sterling had long been among the most enthusiastic members of San Francisco's famously exclusive Bohemian Club, where creativity mixed with wealth and power. A decade earlier Garnett had authored and published *The Bohemian Jinks: A Treatise*, a forty-year history of the club's annual midsummer retreat at a redwood grove seventy-five miles northwest of San Francisco, where an elaborate pageant called the High Jinks, culminating in a ritualistic Cremation of Care, and a counterbalancing humorous revel called the Low Jinks, comprised the main events.[47]

White men made up the membership of the Bohemian Club, a tinge of color being provided, on occasion, by the unofficial participation of Mexican American artist Xavier Martinez and German-Japanese poet Sadakichi Hartmann. There is no record of Noguchi ever attending a Bohemian Club event during his years in California, and for all his close connections with key members during the glory days of the 1890s, the

---

47. Porter Garnett, *The Bohemian Jinks: A Treatise* (San Francisco: Bohemian Club, 1908) lists Garnett as Sire (club parlance for author or organizer) of two jinks, the 1903 Low Jinks, *Mazuma*, and the 1906 Christmas Jinks, *The Conquest of the Philistines*. George Sterling sired the 1907 Summer Jinks, *The Triumph of Bohemia*, while Gelett Burgess was credited with two Christmas Jinks, *The Christmas Nightmare* of 1896 and his 1902 *Christmas in Hell*. Sires were not always litterateurs: local politician James Phelan sired the 1888 High Jinks, *The Convention*, as well as Christmas Jinks of 1903 and 1904; local architect Newton Tharp sired the 1906 High Jinks, *The Quest of the Gorgon*, among many others. Local lawyer Joseph D. Redding, sire of the 1893 High Jinx, *The Sacrifice in the Forest*, was credited with shaping the Cremation of Care ceremony (a feature introduced in 1881 by local journalist and poet, James F. Bowman).

proposal for a gesture of recognition would hardly have been raised had Noguchi not—with his usual skill at creating invitations for himself—floated the idea to Keeler: "I must meet with your artistic people in such a limited time. Is there any way to meet them somewhere? I believe that you are connected with the Bohemian Club,—perhaps that club might be the best place to see your poets and writers."[48]

And so "On Monday" (November 3) as the weekly *Town Talk* reported, "Mr. Richard M. Tobin entertained at the Bohemian Club at luncheon, in honor of Yone Noguchi, the Japanese poet. George Sterling and Joseph D. Redding were the other guests."[49] The luncheon, held at the club's city quarters at the corner of Post and Taylor, gave Noguchi an opportunity to become reacquainted with San Francisco's leading men. But as those men included leaders of the Japanese exclusion movement like Senator James Phelan, it is unlikely that he felt entirely comfortable.

Helen Bonnet, who assisted her husband as editor of the local magazine, *Town Talk*, was interested in interviewing the Japanese poet. "Mr. Noguchi, when I met him last week at the St. Francis, had just returned from a luncheon given in his honor by Richard M. Tobin," she explained in her article.[50] The Bonnets had not known Noguchi personally during his California days—though Theodore Bonnet had written a few notes in the *Town Talk* expressing his view that Noguchi was probably a real person, and his poetry was "quite as good as Stephen Crane's—or for that matter, much of Walt Whitman's." What Helen Bonnet recalled was Noguchi's little piece about the local revival of the musical comedy, *The Geisha*, in the San Francisco *Call*:

> "I asked him if he remembered writing about a performance of 'The Geisha,' at the Tivoli, about nineteen years ago. He did, but couldn't recall what he had written. So I told him, as I had only a few months ago quoted his words, when I interviewed Mme. Tamaki Miura, the Japanese prima donna. The poet, when he heard the American at the Tivoli sing in 'The Geisha,' likened her voice to 'the music of spring rain, the whispering of mountain winds, the fine, clear, high voices of birds,' and visualized the passing of ten centuries before Japanese vocalists could emulate it. He had exclaimed at the time: 'O, my countrymen, come to America and fight a thousand years to free the captive song-angel from Japanese throat prisons!'

It must have been somewhat galling for Noguchi to be remembered for these lines, for the most part written by Blanche Partington, expressing a condescending sense of Western musical superiority that was not his own. But Helen Bonnet's interest in these comments was quite understandable. In 1900, she, as Helen Merrill, had been the very actress playing the

48. YN to Charles Keeler, 20 June 1919, Keeler Collection, Box 4, Huntington.
49. Tantalus, "Social Prattle," *Town Talk* 35 (8 Nov. 1919): 10.
50. Helen M. Bonnet, "Yone Noguchi, Poet of Japan," *Town Talk* 35 (15 Nov. 1919): 3.

lead role of O Mimosa San in the San Francisco production of *The Geisha*. The warm praise of her performance by a real Japanese poet had been a source of pride she had carried with her through the years, having left the stage soon afterward to marry Theodore Bonnet. She saw Noguchi as "the exponent of the lofty philosophy of Japanese thought" that might "take us along strange paths of beauty and solace."

Noguchi told her that, at first, San Francisco's buildings had seemed to him strange and different, but soon the spirit of localities easily revived in his memory. At Miller's house, "his emotions had overwhelmed him, he said, and he had cried. 'There were so many memories of Joaquin about the place and of our happiness there,' he said. 'I saw the trees which we had planted, now grown into a forest. Everything there spoke to me of him. I was very young, the world was all so new to me twenty years ago, and the charm of his personality made a profound impression upon me.'"

"Mr. Miller's wife and daughter, whom you saw yesterday, are not literary are they?," Bonnet asked.

"I do not know," Noguchi replied. "They were lovely to me and as they live there where Joaquin lived, in the place he loved so well, they must be in sympathy with his ideals." He told her about the poem he had written, which she understood was to be published "in one of the dailies." (It was, in fact, published in the *Nichibei Shimbun* two days later, and in the prestigious Chicago monthly, *The Dial*, the following July. [51])

When Bonnet tried to steer the conversation toward more political matters, "Noguchi expressed it to be his own opinion that a feeling of great cordiality exists in his country for the United States. 'Why should we wish to fight?' he asked with an unanswerable gleam of sadness in his poet's dreamy eyes."

Bonnet had better luck getting Noguchi to talk about the San Francisco fog. Correcting her, "he called it mist." "Some other Japanese gentleman had just advised, in the Chronicle, the planting of many trees in gardens, on streets and roofs, to absorb the moisture. Noguchi said: 'Do not try to get rid of it. Your mist is beautiful, under the reflection of the moon or the street lights. It does no harm to the human body—it is not penetrating like the damp of Japan and other countries.'" Bonnet thought it a picturesque comment.

Two days later, Bonnet phoned George Sterling to ask his opinion on Noguchi. Roused at 11 a.m. from slumber after the previous night's wedding at the Bohemian Club, Sterling said: "It is very hard for me to give tangible expression to what I think of Noguchi." But he quickly warmed to the occasion. "He is absolutely subjective and makes the rest of us feel coarse and objective. He weaves his visions from the finest textures, but which have an everlasting durability." Asked whether

---

51. "At Miller's Heights After Twenty Years," *Nichibei Shimbun*, 5 Nov. 1919, 1; "At Joaquin Miller's Heights After Twenty Years," *Dial* 69 (July 1920): 33-34.

"lectures or readings by a Japanese author would be frowned upon in San Francisco owing to the antipathy to Japanese," Sterling scoffed at the idea. Though there was undoubtedly opposition to the Japanese, it had "nothing to do with individuals or their intellectual or commercial productions," he said. "There is absolutely no reason why we should object to Japanese poetry."[52]

97. George Sterling with Joaquin Miller and Charles Warren Stoddard.

Sterling wrote to his friend Henry Louis Mencken on November 8, "I've had Yone Noguchi with me a bit—he's here for the Pond Lyceum. But he's as sad as Masefield was. Why don't poets save their melancholy for their poems, like commendable me?"[53]

The Pond Lyceum Bureau prepared a flyer for the *Transcontinental Lecture Tour* listing lectures on four subjects—*Japan Today, East and West in Literature and Life, The Noh Play of Japan*, and *Japanese Poetry*—plus an additional offering of *Readings—Hokku Poems*. In spite of the fanfare and grand title, Noguchi had a hard road ahead. His efforts to publish several books in advance of the tour having run into delays, it was now four years since his last book publication, a full decade since his last book of poems. In contrast to Nobel laureate Tagore, or well-known writers like Yeats and Maeterlinck who could expect to be greeted by legions of adoring fans, Noguchi could only hope for audiences motivated by curiosity, or interest in the anti-Japanese movement. Decades earlier he had been told to approach America with a determination "as if entering among enemies." Now that enmity was a daily topic of discussion in the California papers.

52. Helen M. Bonnet, "Yone Noguchi, Poet of Japan," *Oakland Tribune*, 23 Nov. 1919, 9.
53. Sterling to Mencken, 8 Nov. 1919, in S.T. Joshi, ed., *From Baltimore to Bohemia: The Letters of H.L. Mencken and George Sterling* (Teaneck, NJ: Fairleigh Dickinson UP, 2001), 70. Sterling's own melancholy was undoubtedly a factor in his 1926 suicide.

98. Flyer for Noguchi's Transcontinental Lecture Tour, 1919-20.

Noguchi took a train to Los Angeles on the 6th and headed to Pasadena, where he checked into the posh Hotel Maryland, formerly the residence of Theo Lowe in the days of *The Raven*. The lecture was to take place at Pasadena's YMCA auditorium under the auspices of the Throop Institute. Founded as a vocational school by Amos Throop in 1891, the Institute had been trying to rebrand itself—Throop Polytechnic Institute and Throop College of Technology had been tried and rejected—and was on the verge of dropping its founder's name to become in 1920 the California Institute of Technology.[54] James Scherer, its president for more than a decade, had been a missionary and teacher in Kyushu, and in 1904, at the height of the Russo-Japanese War, had published a book entitled *Japan Today*, which likely explains Noguchi's choice of "Japan Today" as his lecture title.[55]

The Los Angeles Japanese community was eager to welcome Noguchi, and it fell to an old newspaper world acquaintance, Ginnosuke Yuasa, and a business associate named Itō, to arrange a luncheon in his honor at the Kawafuku Cafe. Among the local Japanese of importance attending was Ujirō Ōyama, appointed in 1915 as Los Angeles's first Japanese Consul General, who was still on good terms with the local immigrant community. "During the meal, they discussed the matter of a lecture for the local Japanese community. As a result, it was decided that

---

54. Judith Goodstein, *Millikan's School* (New York: Norton, 1991).
55. "Japanese Poet to Speak on Nippon," *Tulare Advance-Register*, 7 Nov 1919, 2.

the Student Association and various newspapers would host a lecture titled 'The Pacific as Seen from a Literary Perspective' on the 11th at 7 p.m. at the Honganji Buddhist Hall. The admission fee will be 50 cents, and tickets will be sold."[56] Afterwards, a second lecturer was added to the program, Kaiichirō Suematsu, a high-ranking colonial administrator in Taiwan for the past two years, who "spoke about his observations during his inspection of the South Seas and the Pacific." Noguchi's lecture on "the Pacific from a literary perspective" rehearsed some of the points of his English lecture on "Literary co-operation between America and Japan," in which he discussed the movement of American culture towards the Pacific Coast.[57] Noguchi also spent time with Los Angeles' best known Japanese celebrity: actor Sessue Hayakawa. "With his guidance, I toured the countless movie studios in Hollywood, and I was thoroughly impressed by the grand scale of each."[58]

Noguchi's first Bay Area lecture was scheduled for November 12 at Stanford University. The San Jose *Evening News* praised it enthusiastically: "Yone Noguchi, Japanese poet and professor, spoke at the university assembly hall yesterday on the subject of 'Japan Today.' He presented a sketch of the conditions as they now exist in Japan. His talk proved especially interesting, as he spoke of the relations of California with the incoming Japanese people."[59] This was, unfortunately, "fake news": there had in fact been no lecture. "On account of Professor Yone Noguchi being unable to arrive at the University this afternoon, the assembly scheduled for 2:15 was postponed until November 19," the *Stanford Daily* reported.[60]

That left Noguchi with several days before beginning a grueling series of Bay Area readings and lectures. First up was a reading of his poems at the Paul Elder Gallery on the 17th.[61] David Paul Elder had been a clerk in William Doxey's bookstore during the *Lark* years, but had left in late 1897, around the time Doxey was publishing *The Voice of the Valley*, to start a new printing and bookselling venture. Since 1909 Elder had leased an eight-story building on Grant Avenue near Union Square. The main book room on the ground floor had an arched ceiling and hand-carved screens which created an atmosphere reminiscent of a gothic cathedral. The second floor had an art room and a room of children's books. Elder's publishing operation, dubbed the Tomoyé Press (after the Japanese *tomoe* emblems that fascinated Elder) occupied the third floor. The lecture room occupied one of the upper floors. When Noguchi arrived, he signed the guest book: "Yone Noguchi. Nakano. Happy to return to California."

56. "Noguchi shi no raira" (Mr. Noguchi's LA arrival), *Shin Sekai*, 12 Nov. 1919, 7.
57. "Noguchi Suematsu ryōshi kōen" (Noguchi and Suematsu lectures), *Nichibei*, 14 Nov. 1919, 6.
58. "Minami Ka-shū zatsuroku" (Southern California miscellaneous notes), *Asahi Shimbun*, 15 Dec. 1919, 3.
59. "Stanford Notes," San Jose *Evening News*, 13 Nov. 1919, 7.
60. "Assembly Postponed Until November 19," *Stanford Daily*, 12 Nov. 1919, 2.
61. "Yone Noguchi to Read his Japanese Poems Here," *San Francisco Chronicle*, 13 Nov. 1919, 2.

Elder was "plump, affable," with a neat mustache and round face; like his shop, a visitor noted, "everything in excellent taste, nothing eccentric."[62] In the evening, Noguchi lectured at the San Francisco Y.M.C.A. on "California's Place in English Literature."[63] "Yone Noguchi has a right to talk about California's place in English literature. He knows. He is a part of California literature himself," a local journalist commented.[64]

Advance publicity for Noguchi's November 18 "Japanese Poetry" lecture at Berkeley's Wheeler Hall dwelled on his humble local beginnings. "Oriental Poet Once Eastbay Kitchen Boy," the *Oakland Tribune* announced. "From the humble peeler of potatoes in Oakland restaurants Noguchi has risen with the guiding hand of the late Joaquin Miller to a recognized place in the literary world." The Berkeley student paper, *The Daily Californian*, noted that "Mr. Naguchi [sic] is a famous Japanese poet and has lectured on American poetry at the University of Kaio [sic], at Tokio" but "will probably be remembered in Oakland as the young Japanese student who, twenty years ago, became the protege of Joaquin Miller, making his living by working in restaurant kitchens around the bay as other Japanese youths of lesser fame have done." On the subject of Miller, the writer cited the "recent biography" [sic] in which "Naguchi speaks affectionately of how the venerable California poet used to address him as 'Mr. Naguchi.' 'It was the first occasion,' he writes, 'to hear myself so addressed in California; hitherto, I had been a 'Charlie' or a 'Frank,' according to the employer's fancy.'" That Noguchi's name was now being merely misspelled instead of disregarded could be taken to represent some advance in the status of the Japanese in California.[65]

Prior to the lecture, which was scheduled for the evening, Consul-General Ōta had arranged a reception in Noguchi's honor. "Three hundred invitations have been issued by Tamekichi Ohte [sic] consul-general of Japan and Mrs. Ohte, to a reception to be given this afternoon at the Fairmont Hotel in honor of Yone Noguchi the distinguished Japanese poet," noted a *Chronicle* columnist.[66] But the now alarmingly-unpopular Ōta did not attend this event either; instead his wife presided over it. The *Shin Sekai* estimated attendance at around a hundred at the reception's end. The *Nichibei*, three days later, gave a front-page summary of Noguchi's speech, but about the event, mentioned only that Mrs. Ōta had hosted it. Readers missing the implied criticism of the Consul-General's absence could find it in a page three article with the headline: "Hiding in the Mist: The True Nature of Consul General Ōta: The Man

---

62. Robert Cortes Holliday, *Men and Books and Cities* (New York: George H. Doran, 1920), 226.
63. "Japanese Poet Will Lecture Before YMCA," *San Francisco Chronicle*, 17 Nov 1919, 9.
64. "On the Rialto," *The Wasp*, 22 Nov. 1919, 5
65. "Oriental Poet Once Eastbay Kitchen Boy," *Oakland Tribune*, 16 Nov. 1919, B-3; "'The Spirit of Japanese Poetry' To Be Discussed By Native Poet," *Daily Californian*, 18 Nov. 1919.
66. Lady Teazle [Mrs. Marshall Darrach], "Society and News of Interest to Women," *San Francisco Chronicle*, 18 Nov 1919, 9.

Behind the Blunders: Look at the Various Failures Since His Appointment: Japan's Puppet or Mastermind?"[67]

The crisis would culminate a week later in a three-day representative assembly of the local Japanese associations. When Ōta spoke there on the first day, stating his expectation that the Foreign Office would concur with his and the executive board's views, and was roundly booed by the members and spectators present, he "accused them of being 'ruffians' sent by Abiko to disrupt the proceedings," which did little to help matters; at the end of the session, the officers and staff members all resigned. Over were the days of friendly cooperation between the consul and the Japanese Association, which was now in the hands of *nisei*: second-generation Japanese who were often culturally Americanized and held citizens' rights by virtue of their American birth. Fortunately for Noguchi, by the time this quarrel played out, he would be safely in Chicago.

99. Wheeler Hall, University of California, circa 1917.

If Noguchi read the papers as he rode the train down to Palo Alto for his rescheduled Stanford lecture on the morning after his Berkeley lecture, he would have been dismayed to find no mention of it. Even the university's own *Daily Californian* had not deemed the former kitchen-boy's thoughts on "The Spirit of Japanese Poetry" worthy of comment. The papers were, however, full of coverage of the Japanese exclusion movement, with the front page of the *San Francisco Call* announcing that the "S.F. NATIVE SONS DEMAND JAPANESE EXCLUSION." The latest labor resolutions being promoted by Senator Phelan were

67. "Notable Reception," *San Francisco Chronicle*, 23 Nov. 1919, S3. "Nichibei kōkakai: seiso narishi shumi no kaigō" (Japan-US diplomatic meeting: Neat and clean hobby meeting), *Shin Sekai*, 19 Nov. 1919, 3; "Nihon shikaron" (On Japanese poetry), *Nichibei Shimbun*, 23 Nov. 1919, 1. "Usugiri naka ni kakuren to suru Ōta sōryōji no shōtai," *Nichibei*, 23 Nov. 1919, 3.

calling for "the rigorous exclusion of Japanese and other Asiatics from the United States, with legislation to forever bar Asiatics from American citizenship." There was also substantial coverage of another Japan-related event, a debate at the St. Francis Hotel pitting American-educated Japanese journalist Kiyoshi Karl Kawakami against a Chinese spokesman, Ng Poon Chew.

With, or despite, Noguchi actually showing up this time, the Stanford lecture was apparently successful. According to the *Nichibei*, "there were over 200 attendees, and notably, Dr. [David Starr] Jordan, the honorary president, chaired the event." Noguchi "discussed the recent rapid changes in Japanese thought, moving away from bureaucracy towards democratic tendencies," a description that accords with the "Japan Today" chapter published in *Japan and America*.[68] He returned to San Francisco to spend the night before leaving on the 9 a.m. train for Chicago.[69]

Fountain of Youth

In Chicago, Noguchi planned to stay for three or four weeks before continuing on to Cleveland, Buffalo, and perhaps Toronto. But Chicago turned out to be more attractive than he had anticipated, with a thriving poetry scene and an outstanding art museum with a world-class collection of Japanese prints. The warm welcome he received persuaded him to stay longer.

100. Harriet Monroe, circa 1925.

The center of Chicago's new poetry scene was Harriet Monroe, the sixty-year-old poet-critic who had founded *Poetry: A Magazine of Verse* in 1912. Monroe had raised the magazine and by extension the city of

---

68. "Su-shi daigaku no Noguchi shi kōen" (Mr. Noguchi's Stanford University lecture), *Nichibei*, 20 Nov. 1919, 3. "Japan Today," *J&A* 1-34.
69. "Noguchi shi ippaku" (Mr. Noguchi stays over), *Nichibei*, 28 Nov. 1919, 7.

Chicago into an international center of modernism through her extraordinary acuity in discovering new poetical developments locally, nationally, and around the world, her skillful fund-raising, and her ability to maintain friendly relations with modern poets who were difficult almost by definition. Two talented assistant editors, Alice Corbin Henderson and Eunice Tietjens, to whom Monroe delegated considerable authority, also did much to promote the intelligent but generally benevolent tone of the magazine, and Ezra Pound, who served as international editor during the early years, had brought in writers like Yeats, Fenollosa, and Tagore. Noguchi had been first adopted by Henderson in 1915 (against Pound's advice) and his poems had been subsequently included in the influential Monroe-Henderson *New Poetry* anthology of 1917. In the November 1919 issue of *Poetry*, appearing at the time of Noguchi's arrival in Chicago, Noguchi's early poems were acclaimed by Eunice Tietjens as neglected modernist precursors:

> Looking back on them now one can see how directly they forecast the modern movement. They were in free verse—in the nineties—they were condensed, suggestive, full of rhythmical variations. In matters of technic they might have been written today, and, though few people understood them then, time has proven Mr. Noguchi a forerunner.[70]

Noguchi was now "the most important link between the poetry of America and the poetry of Japan," Tietjens explained. She promoted Noguchi's books, his "delicate lyrics, full of that strange blend of old Japan and the West of today which makes the poetry of contemporary Japan so intriguing," and his essays, "a door through which the western reader can take the first steps towards understanding, and therefore loving, the sharp, condensed, almost aching beauty of classical Japanese poetry."

This time around, Chicago offered no William Denslow, Frank Putnam or Onoto Watanna. Denslow, having squandered his *Wizard of Oz* fortune and three marriages, had died of alcoholism-induced pneumonia in 1915. Onoto no longer existed; the woman who once went by the name had quietly discarded her Japanese identity and taken up ranching in Calgary with a second husband, and was now known as Winnifred Eaton Reeve. Frank Putnam had left Texas a few years earlier to take a job in Milwaukee, where Noguchi had planned to visit him. But Putnam was out of town in November and sent Noguchi a telegram inviting him to come to St. Louis. "Many thanks for your telegram," Noguchi replied on November 26, "but you know that St Louis is quite far away from Chicago. I wanted to see you at Milwaukee and spend some ten days, if possible, with you there, because Milwaukee is quite near here." Now he thought he would stay in Chicago for four more weeks and then go on to New York.[71]

---

70. Eunice Tietjens, "Yone Noguchi," *Poetry* 15 (Nov. 1919): 97-8.
71. YN to FP, 26 Nov. 1919, FPL 58.

On November 29 he wrote Zona Gale in Portage, Wisconsin: "if it is possible for me to get an engagement of lecture for the University of Wisconsin, I may have a chance for seeing you." Returning to Chicago after an engagement in Lincoln, Nebraska, he found Zona's reply. There was a prospect of a lecture, but it was not certain the fee would meet Pond's standard.[72]

Gale also put Noguchi in contact with Chicago's unofficial patron of poetry and the arts, Harriet Moody, the wealthy widow of the famous poet William Vaughn Moody. Harriet Moody had made her home (on Groveland Avenue, the same street where Onoto Watanna once lived) into a kind of literary salon, and visiting poets were usually invited to stay. Tagore had done so on several occasions, as had Padraic Colum, Vachel Lindsay, and a host of others.

Noguchi had a day to recuperate in Lincoln before his December 6 lecture. The lecture, promoted by University of Nebraska faculty as part of a new Lincoln Lecture League series, was set for a local church but then moved to the Lincoln Hotel. "Those who love the poetry of Joaquin Miller will be especially interested in hearing his distinguished disciple and friend," urged chancellor Samuel Avery. "The coming of the distinguished Japanese poet to Lincoln will be an event in our civic life," affirmed Frederick A. Stuff, an English professor whose only publication was a study guide for a Tennyson poem; "No citizen who prides himself on being alive to progress should fail to hear Yone Noguchi, one of the great poets of modern times." Philosophy professor Hartley Burr Alexander went further: "Yone Noguchi is the most distinguished poet now in the United States. He is more than an Oriental. If any oriental poet is worth hearing, he ought to be." The advertisement closed with an appeal to civic pride: "The Lincoln Lecture league is bringing to this city authors of international importance, men of world fame, who heretofore have been available only in the larger cities. It should be a matter of Lincoln pride as well as personal pleasure that men of such character and reputation as Maeterlinck, Yeats, Noguchi, Ibanez and Ellsworth should be received here as generously as elsewhere."[73] The report in the *Lincoln Star*, entitled "Compares Verse of East and West," suggests that this was "The East and West in Literature and Life." (There is no publication with this title, but from quotations in the *Star* and in Salt Lake, where he repeated it, it seems to have consisted of "Japanese Poets and Poetry" plus a part of his Oxford hokku lecture.[74]) The reviewer for the *Star* noted the "small sized audience, composed

---

72. YN to Zona Gale, 29 Nov. 1919, ZGP.
73. "Amusement Notices," *Lincoln Evening Journal*, 5 Dec. 1919, 4. The series barely made it through the season, hobbled by cancellations by Maeterlinck and Ibanez.
74. "Japanese Poets and Poetry," J&A 90-100, also used as the Foreword to *Selected Poems* (1921), first appeared in *The Outlook* 125 (16 June 1920): 325-27, with an additional section at the end derived from "The Japanese Hokku Poetry," SJP 34-37.

largely of university people, listened attentively" and was interested in Noguchi's claims that "poets of the west are of a race apart from the common people" while it is "not so in Japan," and that "the Japanese mind can enjoy things which the western mind finds unsatisfactory," because "sounds which may seem primitive to the western people have music for the Japanese."[75]

While Noguchi, back in Chicago, enjoyed Harriet Moody's hospitality, the Pond bureau arranged for a lecture in Milwaukee on December 16. By the time Noguchi arrived there, Frank Putnam was back in town. On the day of the lecture, the *Milwaukee Journal* reported that Noguchi was "visiting Milwaukee as guest of Mr and Mrs Frank Putnam of the Stratford Arms" and would speak that evening at the City Club.[76]

The *Milwaukee Journal* also quoted Noguchi making an uncharacteristically forthright denunciation of American immigration policy: "One important thing stands in the way of true friendship between our countries. It is your law which will not permit an Asiatic to become a citizen of the United States by naturalization. That is really an affront to pride. Japanese feel they have much to offer and that America has much to offer us, and we should like to be taken into America on a like basis with other peoples of the earth." This was considerably farther than Noguchi usually went in his advocacy of Japanese immigrant rights. Addressing the topic six years earlier in *The Nation*, he had said that allowing Japanese to become naturalized citizens would likely be "a damaging affair equally for America and Japan." His lectures touched on issues like friendship and equality but sidestepped the controversial topic of immigration.

The immigration comments were probably the work of Putnam, who was, unlike Noguchi, a strong advocate of Japanese immigration. For some years, Putnam had been collaborating with another Japanese writer, the journalist Kiyoshi Karl Kawakami, a passionate advocate of naturalization for Japanese immigrants. K. K. Kawakami was a Japanese Christian with Socialist sympathies who had studied at a number of American and Japanese universities, married an American woman, and taken up journalism with a focus on international issues. Before meeting Putnam, Kawakami had published his Iowa Master's thesis, *Political Ideas of Modern Japan*, as well as articles on Japan-related topics in a number of respectable periodicals. Putnam helped him with his first important book, *American-Japanese Relations* (1912), and its sequels, *Asia at the Door* (1914), and *Japan in World Politics* (1917).[77] Putnam also expressed his sup-

75. "Compares Verse of East and West," Lincoln Star, 7 Dec 1919, 6.
76. "Noted Japanese Poet Guest in Milwaukee," Milwaukee Journal, 16 Dec. 1919, 2.
77. K.K. Kawakami, Political Ideas of Modern Japan, (Iowa City: U. of Iowa P, 1903); in American-Japanese Relations: An Inside View of Japan's Policies and Purposes, (New York: Fleming H. Revell, 1912), Kawakami wrote, "without [Putnam's] cooperation, sympathy, and encouragement, the book might never have seen the light"; Asia at the Door (New York: Fleming H. Revell,

port of Japanese-American naturalization in a 1915 essay, "America's Issue with Japan," arguing forcefully that the Alien Land Law of California had been "an economic blunder as well as a violation of treaty obligations" and that naturalization laws should be amended to allow limited Japanese immigration.[78] It is therefore not surprising to find Noguchi supposedly voicing the same sentiments in an article Putnam had presumably arranged, if not actually written.

From the *Milwaukee Journal*'s account of Noguchi's "Japan Today" lecture at the City Club, it seems that his lecture was not in the rather literary style of its later published version,[79] but more like that of his recent political essays in *The Graphic* and *The Nation*, from which he seems to have adapted the lecture. From "The Spiritual Effect of the War on Japan" came his discussion of Japanese patriotism changing, through the war, from "a kind of fetish, that we had only to obey in blind questioning silence" to something more reflective. And his essay on "The Future of Japanese Shintoism" was likely the basis of his discussion of "unmistakable agitation today in the ancient ancestor worship or Shintoism of Japan."

At 8:45 on the morning after the lecture, Noguchi was at the station telegraphing Zona Gale: "I AM TAKING 1150 TRAIN TO PORTAGE AND GOING TO SEE YOU." Since breaking off her engagement to Ridgely Torrence in 1904, Zona had been spending more and more time in Portage, mainly writing short stories of life in "Friendship Village," a fictional small town modeled on it. Her first novel, *Romance Island*, published in 1906, had been a more whimsical story, a romantic fantasy-adventure.[80] Its commercial success netted her sufficient profits to build an extravagant Greek Revival house on the bank of the Wisconsin River for her parents and herself. She had, however, remained single. Her steady stream of novels and stories continued to sell well, and gained critical respect as she turned to more serious topics. She had become involved in civic affairs and politics, advocating for women's labor rights, suffrage, and pacifism during the war. She was on the verge of publishing the most successful book of her career: *Miss Lulu Bett*. The novel, about a woman's failed attempt to escape the drudgery of her small-town life, would be published in March to rave reviews, and her stage adaptation of the novel in December would earn her the Pulitzer Prize in drama.

1914) mentioned "the encouragement and co-operation of my friend, Mr. Frank Putnam, of the *St. Louis Post-Dispatch*"; and *Japan in World Politics* (New York: Macmillan, 1917) again acknowledged "my loyal friend Frank Putnam, of Milwaukee, Wisconsin, to whom I owe a debt of gratitude." For a brief overview of Kawakami's career, see William D. Hoover, "Kiyoshi Karl Kawakami: A prewar Liberal Journalist's Struggle to Give Japan International Respectability," *Transactions of the Asiatic Society of Japan* (1996): 117-19.

78. Frank Putnam, "America's Issue with Japan," *National Magazine* 41:4 (January 1915): 599-607.
79. "Japan is Truer Because of War," *Milwaukee Journal*, 17 Dec. 1919, 8.
80. Noguchi later translated Gale's *Romance Island* as *Gentō romansu* (Tokyo: Kaizōsha, 1929).

101. Zona Gale's house, Portage, Wisconsin.

Noguchi later turned his reunion with Zona into a Japanese poem entitled "*Yuki no hi*" (Snowy day).

> Outside, snowflakes were falling on the ground like peonies,
> while in the room a fire was going, gently throwing silvery shadows on the ceiling.
> Sitting alone on the hardwood floor, I took my hostess's novels from the shelf, one by one, and flipped through the pages . . .
> In my mind I think, 'since we last met, fifteen, sixteen, books, always promising to send the next book, and never actually sending.'
> After some time the novelist-hostess is standing at my side (she is a woman who walks without the slightest sound).
> She says, 'you shouldn't be reading those novels: you wouldn't enjoy any of them!'
> And when I look up at her face, she is making a face as though she had shuddered seeing some distasteful thing . . .
> I thought to myself, 'aha, she was surprised to see the top of my head, wasn't she?
> But as for that, how was Zona's hair: it had gone half grey.'[81]

102. Zona Gale, circa 1920.

81. "Yuki no hi," *Shisei* (March 1923): 36-37, rpt. *Waga te o miyo* (Tokyo: Ars, 1923), 16.

One person Noguchi did not see during his stay in the Midwest was his son Isamu Gilmour, then in La Porte, Indiana, a two-hour train ride from Chicago. The Interlaken school in Silverlake where Isamu had been sent had been closed due to the war, and, with no money and nowhere else to go, the school's founder had arranged for him to live in the home of a Swedenborgian minister, Dr. Samuel Mack. "It was under this protection that I lived for the next three years and managed to get through high school, while at the same time I earned my keep, or part of it, by tending furnaces, mowing lawns, delivering newspapers. I constantly worried about my mother in Japan and developed a moral loathing for my father." A fragment of a letter from Yone to Léonie, dated September 7, 1919, gives some indication of Yone's feelings. The top half—perhaps three or four lines—of the brief letter has been torn off. The remainder reads: " . . . Since then I lost my interest in you and even in Isamu. So I did not put the matter of insurance into practice." The remainder deals with matters evidently connected to Léonie and Ailes's passport application: the Tokyo address of "Mr. Kataoka" (the former Genjirō Yeto, now Genjirō Kataoka, witness to their relationship in both New York and Koishikawa) and "the picture Mitsukoshi had taken."[82] At the American consulate in Yokohama Léonie applied for an emergency passport for herself and Ailes on January 16, and the two departed Japan on January 25, arriving in San Francisco on February 11. It made sense for Léonie to reenter the United States while Yone was still there, so that if immigration officials considered her an illegal Japanese alien, she might at least be able to enter the country as a visiting lecturer's wife. But there was not, apparently, any trouble. By March she and Ailes had moved into a small apartment at the corner of Golden Gate Park. There is no indication that Yone and Léonie saw each other when he passed through the city on his way back to Japan.[83]

Around Christmas, Noguchi returned to New York, where he stayed at the National Arts Club, thanks to an introduction from Padraic Colum, and saw Ridgely Torrence. After his breakup with Zona, Ridgely had remained single for a decade, but in 1914 he married Olivia Howard Dunbar, a Smith College graduate who wrote in various genres. Torrence had been writing poetry and plays, most notably his *Three Plays for a Negro Theatre* (1917), the first non-musical Broadway productions to feature an all-African-American cast. His literary successes were sporadic, and in 1920 he would take a job as poetry editor for the *New Republic*.

Interviewed by John Walker Harrington for an article in the *New York Times Magazine*, Noguchi had again become unrelentingly cheerful

82. YN to LG, 7 Sept. 1919, INF.
83. Atsumi Ikuko, "The Newly Discovered Letters of Yone Noguchi During His Stay in America," *KBS Bulletin On Japanese Culture* 107 (April-May 1971): 2; Isamu Noguchi, *A Sculptor's World*, 13; YN to LG, 7 Sept. 1919, INF.

about the United States, focusing almost exclusively on the positive influence America was exerting upon Japan. The article began with the declaration that "they of Japan who would their youth renew come to America." His Japanese friends supposed he had undertaken the journey "to be made young again," Noguchi told Harrington. They had perhaps meant this in a merely personal sense, but Noguchi took it in a more general way: America was still a new country, not steeped in constraining traditions like Japan, and American optimism and initiative might regenerate Oriental pessimism and fatalism. Noguchi talked about the Japanese admiration for Emerson and the current vogue for Whitman, whose "vigor" and "exalted sentiment" were now much admired.[84]

New York had by this time its own pair of competing Japanese newspapers, the weekly *Nichibei Jihō* (*Japanese American Commercial Weekly*), run by the president of the Japanese-American Trade Bureau, Joske Komori, and the twice-weekly *Nyū Yōku Shimpō* (*The Japanese Times*) edited by Shōzō Midzutani, who, in addition to his newspaper work, was completing an 870-page history of the New York Japanese community.[85]

The *Nyū Yōku Shimpō* had announced Noguchi's inclusion in the upcoming Pond lecture season back in September, and the *Nichibei Jihō* reported on November 15 that he had left California toward New York, and, on December 13, that he had passed through Chicago, Lincoln and Milwaukee.[86] But his arrival in New York went quietly unmentioned by either paper. On December 31st, however, a young writer by the name of Shigetaka Naganuma started off a lengthy diatribe about the sorry state of American literary culture by taking issue with Noguchi's idea that American culture had been moving westward, a claim Naganuma found "neither historically accurate nor meaningful." Naganuma could find nothing in contemporary American literature to compare with the greatness of Whitman or Poe; and where there was greatness, it went unappreciated. "Horace Traubel, who was called one of the three great democratic poets of the world alongside Whitman and Carpenter, recently died in extreme poverty."[87]

Naganuma was, in fact, one of those vigorous Whitman admirers. He had come to America a decade earlier at nineteen with a letter of introduction to Bunzō Washizu, with whom he worked for three years on the *Nichibei Shimbun*. A more proletarian version of Noguchi, he had

---

84. Yone Noguchi to Harriet Moody, 30 Dec. 1919, Univ. of Chicago Library; John Walker Harrington, "America as a Fountain of Youth to the Japanese," *New York Times Magazine*, 18 Jan. 1920, 7.

85. Mizutani Shōzō, *Nyūyōku Nihonjin hattenshi* (History of the Japanese in New York), 2 vol. (New York: Japanese Association of New York, 1921). See Mitziko Sawada, *Tokyo Life, New York Dreams* (Berkeley: U of California P, 1996), 18-19.

86. "Sekai shisō-kai no kyojin-tachi" (Intellectual giants), *Nyū Yōku Shimpō*, 24 Sept. 1919, 2.

87. Naganuma Shigetaka, "Santō geijutsu kuni no Beikoku" (America a country of third-rate art), *Nyū Yōku Shimpō*, 31 Dec. 1919, 9.

worked as a laborer to earn money to travel to the east coast with the aim of meeting Horace Traubel. "At present, I'm working on a farm to save enough money that enable me to go to the East," he had written Traubel the previous April. "I want to see many interesting things there, but above all, it is my dream to call on the author of 'Chants Communal' in the editor's room of 'The Conservater.'"[88] He had spent the fall and winter working in a copper smelting plant in Utah, sleeping in a tent with five other laborers. He made it to New York for the May 31st Whitman Centenary celebration, where he read a speech on "Whitman's influence in the Orient" which appeared in the final issue of *The Conservator*,[89] and spent much of June and July with Traubel and his family. Sadly, Traubel was already in poor health after a series of strokes and heart attacks, and soon after leaving in August with his family for a vacation in Canada he died there in September of another heart attack.

As Naganuma recalled, his first meeting with Noguchi took place in January, during a chance encounter with another literary adventurer.[90] Torao (Sōfū) Taketomo was, like Naganuma, in his late twenties, but from a more privileged background. After studying at Doshisha and Kyoto Universities, he had come to America to study Greek at Yale Divinity School, but finding the curriculum not to his taste, changed to Columbia University. An academic prodigy, witty and "wickedly charming" according to one of his professors,[91] he had supported his studies by publishing a collection of Japanese short story translations, *Paulownia*, in 1917, and working for the Brooklyn Museum's Oriental Prints department, and was now about to return to Japan. "Taketomo and I knew each other only by name," Naganuma recalled, "but we talked like old friends when we met. That night, as a farewell gesture, we dined together at a Japanese restaurant in New York. During our conversation, the topic of Mr. Noguchi came up, and we decided spontaneously to visit him together. At that time, Mr. Noguchi was staying at the Arts Club in Gramercy Park, so I immediately telephoned to see if he was available. Although he had not met either of us, he warmly replied, "Come right over, I'll be waiting." On another occasion Noguchi took Naganuma on a snowy Madison Avenue walk to lunch at his old boarding house. Noguchi continued to take a warm interest in both men, helping Naganuma with his Traubel book, and encouraging Taketomo to submit his work to *Eigo Bungaku*.

An even more youthful admirer was 11-year-old Shōji Kimura. "When I first met him in New York in the winter of 1919," Noguchi later recalled,

---

88. Shigetaka Naganuma to Horace Traubel, 7 Apr. 1918, Traubel Papers, Library of Congress.
89. "Whitman's influence in the Orient," *Conservator* 30 (June 1919), 55-58.
90. Naganuma Shigetaka, "Noguchi-san no koto" (Something of Mr. Noguchi), *Nippon Shijin* 6:5 (May 1926), rpt. *Kenkyū* 2: 162-66.
91. John Erskine, *My Life as a Teacher* (Philadelphia: Lippincott, 1948), 120.

"I thought: 'Dear me, what a precocious boy this is!'"[92] The Kimuras were an unusual family, to say the least. After his mother Komako's acceptance at Sadayakko Kawakami's new Imperial Actress Training School was revoked because of her out-of-wedlock pregnancy, she and her husband Hideo had started two theaters of their own, a new religion, and a feminist association and magazine. In 1917 they came to the United States, where Komako gave theatrical performances and became prominent in the suffrage movement, using the pages of the *Nichibei Jihō* to advise the new Japanese prime minister on women's rights. Of late the Kimuras had opened a free clinic and were promoting their mystic healing powers with sensationalistic body piercing demonstrations.[93] Shōji afterward remembered a visit with Yone to Staten Island to see Edwin Markham.[94] Yone remembered Shōji, always bursting with energy, devouring book after book, each more surprising for his age than the last.

And then there was the extraordinary love triangle of Takeshi Kanno, Gertrude Boyle, and Eitarō Ishigaki: a long-running melodrama now in its second decade. It had begun on Joaquin Miller's Oakland Heights, where the lapsed Doshisha-trained missionary Kanno claimed Yone's old room and poetic vocation in 1905.[95] Free-spirited local artist Gertrude Boyle arrived to sculpt Miller and his late mother in 1907 and the two were soon seeking a marriage license: denied in California, but granted in Seattle. For seven years they lived at the Hights as the Bay Area's token bohemian interracial couple—Boyle increasingly successful as a sculptor, Kanno rather less so as author-performer-director of a mystical lyric pageant, *Creation Dawn*. Kanno also ran a small English school for Japanese immigrants, where he befriended Eitarō Ishigaki, a young art student (Ishigaki was twenty, Boyle and Kanno both in their mid-thirties). In 1915 Boyle announced that she was in love with Ishigaki and intended to divorce Kanno, provoking her sister to have her arrested on grounds of insanity. The charges were dropped but her petitions for divorce were denied. Frustrated, she moved to New York, where Ishigaki followed her, and they lived together in Greenwich Village. Kanno followed them and moved in with Edwin Markham on Staten Island, but it was not until May 1919 that he sued for divorce, freeing the couple to marry.

Shōji Kimura, a few years later, noticing Gertrude Boyle's drawing

92. YN, "Introduction" to Shoji Kimura, *A Japanese Scrapbook* (Tokyo: Japan Press, 1940), xi.
93. "A needle through the flesh of her arm neither draws blood nor causes any pain to Mme. Komako Kimura, teacher of a philosophical Japanese religion based on concentrated will power by which she hopes and knows that she can cure any disease," *New York Tribune*, 28 Sept. 1919, 6:3.
94. Shoji Kimura, "My Song Of Nature Begins With Mount Fuji And Ends With It Says Yone Noguchi," *JT*, 4 Oct. 1925, 18.
95. Shinoda Sataye, "Uōkin Mirā no deshi Kanno Isen no shōgai (1)" (The life of Joaquin Miller's protégé Isen Kano), *Historical English Studies in Japan* 27 (1995), 151-64. Kanno usually used his birth name, Takeshi, in English, but preferred his later name Isen in Japanese.

hanging outside Noguchi's Nakano parlor, supposed it reminded Noguchi "of the unforgettable nights in the Quartier Latin of New York."[96] The unforgettable nights are now forgotten, but Noguchi said, when he organized Boyle's Tokyo exhibition in 1935, that he had visited Boyle's Greenwich Village studio, and knew her well.[97]

Asked to write something for the *Nyū Yōku Shimpō*, Noguchi produced a brief but thoughtful essay outlining the need for Japanese propaganda, based on his experiences on the Pacific Coast.

> "The development of the Japanese community there is truly extraordinary, with various businesses becoming firmly established. The difference since I was in California twenty years ago is like night and day, and I couldn't help wishing my compatriots well. However, at the same time, Americans' anti-Japanese sentiments seem to be rising in proportion to our compatriots' development. Newspapers, especially, are stirring up anti-Japanese fervor, which has been on the rise of late, making travel along the Pacific coast extremely unpleasant. That said, I was mainly going around giving lectures, and no one expressed direct hostility toward me personally, so I was able to travel comfortably. But certainly the general attitude of American society towards the Japanese community is worsening."

Intelligent people in America were all concerned about the problem, and the conclusion was that "Japan must somehow engage in activities to make the American public correctly perceive and truly understand Japan." This was an era of populism, not only in America; "Britain and France are also engaging in propaganda with great vigor." He added that "Japan must relinquish militaristic-nation thinking and must resolve all Japan-U.S. issues through mutual understanding between the peoples. With this in mind, during my stay here, I intend to give as many lectures as possible and write for magazines as well."[98]

On January 5 Noguchi was in Buffalo to give a "Japan Today" lecture. Sub-freezing temperatures and Prohibition-mandated sobriety may have contributed to reviewers' displeasure with the lecture, which he "read with more or less difficulty in pronouncing his very excellent English," according to the *Buffalo Evening News*, the *Buffalo Morning Express* concurring that "in construction the lecture showed remarkable command of English, but its delivery was extremely poor, entire sentences being unintelligible."[99] Such criticisms were, fortunately, rare. While Noguchi's English lecture performance could not compare with the mellifluous delivery of Yeats or Tagore, neither could it be compared to what

---

96. Shōji Kimura, "My Song Of Nature," 18.
97. Introductory pamphlet to Takashimaya exhibition, Sept. 1935.
98. "Tai-Bei puropaganda wa saikyūmu" (Propaganda toward America most urgent task), *Nyū Yōku Shimpō*, 3 Jan 1920, 4.
99. "The Social Chronicle," *Buffalo Evening News*, 6 Jan. 1920; "Old Faiths in Japan Sure to Die, Says Yone Noguchi," *Buffalo Morning Express*, 6 Jan. 1920, 11.

Maeterlinck had done, three days earlier, at his Carnegie Hall debut. Unable to comprehend or speak English, Maeterlinck had "evolved a thought that for sheer brilliance and originality did even him credit. He hired a polylingual stenographer and dictated in French a lecture that would set forth the author's ideas upon Spiritualism and mysticism. Then he had this secretary read it off to him in English. As the secretary read in English, Maeterlinck wrote it down in English. It was English as Maeterlinck heard it. He wrote phonetically. The word 'Indeed' became, beneath Maeterlinck's pen, 'ainedide.' 'Issues' became 'ichiouse' and 'transcendent' was written 'traincaindint,' and so on." The results, needless to say, were unintelligible. Maeterlinck next tried to read the lecture in French with his translator translating. "That lasted just two sentences. Maeterlinck flung his hands into the air and gave up." His translator then simply read the English translation of the lecture. The audience, full of diehard Maeterlinck fans, were deeply disappointed. Afterward, Maeterlinck announced his intention to give his remaining lectures in French, prompting cancellations and a breach-of-contract lawsuit from Pond.[100] In comparison, Noguchi, with his poor delivery and occasionally unintelligible sentences, was doing quite well.

On January 8, he was in Cleveland for two lectures at Case Western Reserve University.[101] On January 15, he was in a rustic town in upstate New York called Wyoming, staying with some friends of Zona Gale, visiting Niagara Falls and stopping over in Rochester *en route* to Toronto, where he made what was probably his only Canadian lecture, on the 17th "to a large audience on the 'Noh Play of Japan'" in the University of Toronto's Saturday lecture series.[102] On the 18th he stopped in Waterbury, Connecticut to speak at a school for girls.[103]

On January 19, Noguchi returned to New York City where he would spend about three weeks. In New York he would have the opportunity to see W.B. Yeats, who checked into the National Arts Club on January 22 to begin his lecture tour.

According to the *Nyū Yōku Shimpō*, Noguchi's January 24 "Japanese Poetry" lecture to the Japan Society at the Hotel Astor drew, despite severe weather, about 150 attentive Japanese and American attendees.[104] Immediately after, he departed for Boston, *en route* to a lecture at Exeter, New Hampshire on the 28th.

100. "Maeterlinck Tries in Vain to Lecture in Phonetic English," New York *Sun*, 3 Jan. 1920, 1; "Pond to Ask $35,000 From Maeterlinck," New York *Tribune*, 15 Jan. 1920, 20.
101. YN to Edmund Brown, 8 Jan 1920, FSL.
102. *University of Toronto Monthly* 20:5 (Feb. 1920): 185.
103. "Jogakkō ni kōen Noguchi Yonejirō" (Lecture at a girls' school), *Nichibei*, 28 Jan. 1920, 2, likely St. Margaret's School, offering a college preparatory course including "broad and liberal training for girls from 12 to 20 years."
104. "Shizen kanki no jō" (Enjoyment of nature), *Nyū Yōku Shimpō*, 28 Jan. 1920, 4.

103. Yone Noguchi, photographed by Arnold Genthe.

The visit to Boston would give Noguchi a much-needed opportunity to visit the Four Seas Company's bookshop and find out why publisher Edmund Brown had made no progress on the four books he had offered to publish more than a year earlier. The delay had been a major disappointment of the tour. Brown had seemed interested in bringing out the *Ten Noh Plays* and *Japanese Hokkus* for which Noguchi had sent manuscripts the previous November, and perhaps some of the other six titles Noguchi had suggested. Noguchi had insisted "you must bring the [*Ten Noh Plays*] book out before I make my appearance before American audiences," and Brown had included it in his list of forthcoming books for the fall at a price of $1.50. But neither book was ready on Noguchi's arrival and he had been sending off increasingly aggravated notes from around the country. Noguchi's Boston visit prodded Brown into delivering the set of *Japanese Hokkus* proofs in late January that Noguchi hastily returned in the first week of February, believing the book might be ready by mid-March.[105]

On the 29th he returned to New York City in time for the event that was for him the most meaningful event of the tour, the Poetry Society of America's annual dinner, at which he would be a guest of honor, along with W.B. Yeats and Siegfried Sassoon. Among the seventeen poets seated at the long table in the Hotel Astor's large banquet hall were Edwin Markham, W.B. Yeats and Laurence Housman, and among the over two hundred guests seated at the tables below, his old friends Witter Bynner, Percy MacKaye, Cale Young Rice, and Ridgely Torrance. It was a long event—four and a half hours, sans alcohol—far too long for the newly-arrived Siegfried Sassoon, who grumbled in his autobiography about the "long-winded and diffuse" speakers, including "the Japanese writer Noguchi, who read an elaborate lecture in colourless tones, thereby

---

105. YN to Edmund Brown, 8 Feb. 1920, FSL.

producing an inevitably flat effect."¹⁰⁶ Yeats had arrived only a few days earlier, escaping his castle in a revolution-torn Ireland which, he told the *New York Times*, had "gone mad over politics." It was "now a country of oppression," and little would be accomplished there "until some form of self-government is determined upon to the satisfaction of the people."¹⁰⁷

It was probably Yeats who introduced Noguchi to Michio Itō, the dancer who had assisted Pound with his Fenollosa Nō plays and performed in Yeats's Nō-inspired play, *At the Hawk's Well*. Itō now ran a dance school in New York. Noguchi sent two letters on the school's stationery on February 7, his last day in New York.¹⁰⁸

104. Michio Itō in samurai warrior costume, photographed by A.L. Coburn, October 22, 1915.

Noguchi's last letter to Edmund Brown from America was one of them, an ironic reminder that the Japanese name connected with Yeats, Pound and the Nō would be Itō's rather than Noguchi's.¹⁰⁹ But the meeting with Itō was a fruitful one in other ways. According to Fujio Fujita, when Yeats visited New York, Itō and Noguchi took Yeats to a Japanese restaurant, and Itō told Yeats his dream of establishing an artists' colony on a small island in the Inland Sea of Japan. In later years Itō would be

---

106. Siegfried Sassoon, *Siegfried's Journey 1916-1920* (London: Faber & Faber, 1945), 177. Helen Bullitt Lowry, in "Another 'Contemptible Little Army': Minor Poets," *New York Times Magazine*, 15 Feb. 1920, 7, also complained of being "tired, because the welcoming speeches have been so long."
107. "Irish Poet Tells of Storms at Home," *New York Times*, 25 Jan. 1920, 27.
108. The letters were to Edmund Brown, 7 Feb. 1920, FSL; and to Frank [Gelett Burgess], 7 Feb. 1920, Gelett Burgess papers, Bancroft.
109. Noguchi's *Ten Noh Plays* and Catherine Dupont's *What is the Noh?* were listed in *Bookseller, Newsdealer and Stationer* 51 (15 Sept. 1919): 281; *Dial* 67 (Nov. 1919), 454, and *Publishers' Weekly*, 13 Mar. 1920, 862. On Catharine Dupont's Nō performances see "To Revive An Ancient Dance, *El Paso Herald*, 22 Feb. 1919, 11; "Shakespeare and Japanese Dances," *New York Sun*, 15 Feb. 1919, 8 and "Happenings on Stage and Screen," *Washington Times*, 8 April 1919, 15.

an important mentor to Isamu Noguchi, giving the young artist his first theatrical commission and introducing him to Martha Graham. Yone in turn introduced Itō to the Japanese public with a collaborative dance-lecture in 1931.[110]

By mid-February Noguchi was back in Chicago at the home of Harriet Moody. This time he was slated to lecture on February 16 at the University of Chicago on "Japanese Poetry" as part of the university's monthly William Vaughn Moody Lecture series.[111]

One of Harriet Moody's artist friends was the Italian-born sculptor Alfeo Faggi, who had emigrated to the U.S. in 1913. Moody had introduced him to Tagore during the Indian poet's visit, and Tagore, "quite bowled over by Faggi's work," allowed him to sculpt a bust. Noguchi sat for Faggi during his visit, and the resulting head, depicting Noguchi in a meditative pose with closed eyes, was to have an interesting life.

105. Alfeo Faggi, *Head of Noguchi*, 1923.

Several castings were made. One was prominently displayed in the Moody drawing room, where it was frequently admired by visitors, among them Moody's friend Robert Frost, who wrote her in late 1921, "Surely it is a beautiful thing Faggi has made of Yone Noguchi. I have the picture of it in Noguchi's book." A presumably different casting was

110. On the Yeats lunch, see Fujita Fujio, *Itō Michio sekai o mau: Taiyō no gekijō o mezashite* (Tokyo: Musashino Shoin, 1992), 80-81, cited in Norimasa Morita, "Itō Michio (1892–1961): Dancer and Producer," *Britain and Japan: Biographical Portraits*, Vol. X, ed. Hugh Cortazzi (Folkstone, Kent: Renaissance, 2016), 700. On Itō's introduction of Isamu to Graham, see Duus, *Life*, 179. On the 1931 dance-lecture at the *Asahi Shimbun*'s lecture hall in Tokyo, see "Dai 77-kai Asahi minshū kōza Itō Michio buyō kōen-kai" (Number 77 Asahi public lecture Michio Itō dance lecture meeting), *Asahi Shimbun*, 10 Apr. 1931, 10.

111. "Events: Past and Future," *The University Record* 6:1 (Jan 1920): 63. Yeats gave the next Moody Lecture two weeks later on "The Friends of My Youth." 6:2 (Apr. 1920): 145.

included in a show of Faggi's work at the Art Institute of Chicago in the spring of 1923. Noguchi also had a copy, and wrote two poems about it: "*Faggi-saku 'Yone Noguchi no kao' o mite*" (Looking at Faggi's *Face of Yone Noguchi*, 1922) and "*Jibun no kamen ni muitte*" (1922) the latter of which he published in English as "Looking At My Own Mask" (1924). "What are you thinking about, / What are you looking at from under your heavy eyelids?" he wondered. Though the mask seemed to "die many times a day," the brow seemed "a volcano ready for bursting out, / Something quite dangerous,— / What a thought and passion struggling there!"[112] He used a photograph of the mask as a frontispiece to his *Selected Poems* and in some of his later Japanese books. Copies were later acquired by the Minneapolis Art Institute and the Addison Gallery of American Art in Andover. Harriet Moody was also impressed by Noguchi himself. "We have liked him well," she declared after his departure. "He is an inspiration to me."[113]

Noguchi, in return, liked Chicago well, and when he gave his account of the present state of American literature, wrote of it glowingly. "Who can doubt to-day that Chicago once only famous for hog-killing machines, now proud of the Chicago University and the city library and of course 'Poetry: a Magazine of Verse,' an oracle with many prophets and prophetesses rising from the middle-west, is dictating the American poetry."[114] The basis of the New Poetry, Noguchi explained, was that poetry should be situated in its home and in harmony with real American lives. Poets should coin new phrases and idioms appropriate to their usage, as a matter of course. The New Poetry was to embody a native and regional tone, and its poets were to incorporate real situations of life: railways, newspapers, photographs, popular novels and songs, regional festival, expositions, and all the noise of the city." The best example of the new style was Edgar Lee Masters, who had constructed in his *Spoon River Anthology* (1914) a fictional Midwestern anytown based on tombstone inscriptions. Each buried person emerges to frankly confess what he or she has experienced in life, revealing the heartrending realities of Midwestern small-town life. Carl Sandburg had managed to transform the city of Chicago itself into poetry: "Hog Butcher, Tool Maker, Stacker of Wheat, Player with Railroads and Freight Handler to the Nation." "If a poem like this had been written more than 20 years before," Noguchi observed, "no one could have answered immediately what it was," but time had changed, or rather, it was continually changing.[115]

---

112. "Faggi-saku 'Yone Noguchi no kao' o mite" (Looking at Faggi's Face of Yone Noguchi), *Taiyō* 28:12 (Oct. 1922): 150-51; "Jibun no kamen ni muitte" (Looking At My Own Mask), *Shisei*, 1 Apr. 1922; "Looking At My Own Mask," *Double Dealer* 6 (Aug.-Sept. 1924): 182.

113. Olivia Howard Dunbar, *A House in Chicago* (Chicago: U of Chicago P, 1947), 8, 172-73, 187.

114. J&A 38-41.

115. *Beikoku bungaku ron* (Essays on American Literature) (Tokyo: Daiichi Shobō, 1925), 5-16.

Before returning to California, Noguchi had a final major stop in Salt Lake City. Greeted by the press upon his arrival, he informed them that this would be his final appearance on the lecture platform before returning to Japan (since coming to this country four months ago, he said, he had spoken in twenty-four cities). And he made wide-ranging comments about Japan's economy, educational system, and international politics.[116] In the morning before his lecture (on February 25), Noguchi spoke to the poetry class of University of Utah professor Benjamin Roland Lewis.[117] He was then "shown about the city" by Elbert Thomas, the professor of Oriental Life and Culture who had organized the lecture: Thomas had a strong relationship with the local Japanese community, after serving five years as one of the first LDS Church missionaries to Japan. A fluent speaker of Japanese, he had appealed to the Japanese for support, explaining that the extracurricular lecture program was running at a substantial deficit due to the influenza pandemic "and because highbrow literary tastes are not yet widespread in the area."[118] Noguchi's lecture, delivered in the evening at the Assembly Hall on the Temple Square, was on "The East and West in Literature and Life." Rather than simply reading from his forthcoming text, he was adjusting his wording, improvising, and adding specific examples: "In the west, poets are a race apart, a Swinburne or a Keats could not be compared to a shoemaker; but in the east, it is different. There the arts are considered a most necessary factor of our development. A shoemaker or a street beggar may be a poet or an artist."[119] The *Nichibei*'s Salt Lake correspondent reported that "the audience consisted largely of professors, students, and university affiliates, totaling about five hundred men and women, with around fifty to sixty Japanese also in attendance."[120] According to the *Deseret News*, Noguchi thought an open breach between Japan and the United States would never happen. "In my opinion there is not as much anti-Japanese feeling in America as some sources would have us believe." He thought that Chinese anti-Japanese feelings had been overstated, and that "Japan and China must one day be one." "Old Asiatic countries, must, it seems to me, remain friends, not to the extent of combining against occidental countries but rather because friends close to home can be of the greatest help."

On February 27, the day before Noguchi's return to San Francisco, the

---

116. "Japan Uneasy, Author States," *Salt Lake Tribune*, 25 Feb 1920, 7.
117. "Japanese Poet Sees No Danger of War," *Salt Lake Herald-Republican*, 26 Feb 1920, 14.
118. "Noguchi-shi saru" (Mr. Noguchi will leave), *Nichibei*, 1 Mar. 1920, 6.
119. "West is West, Noguchi Says," *Salt Lake Tribune*, 26 Feb 1920, 9. The simpler passage in J&A 92, omits the examples of specific poets and occupations: "It is said in the West that the poets are a race apart. The fact that our Japanese poets are not a race apart should be the very focus for a discussion of Japanese poets."
120. "Japanese Poet Sees No Danger of War," *Salt Lake Herald-Republican*, 26 Feb 1920, 14; "Noguchi shi saru" (Mr. Noguchi will leave), *Nichibei*, 1 Mar. 1920, 6; "Eminent Japanese Speaks of East and West," *Deseret News*, 25 Feb. 1920, 2:8.

Nichibei printed the first of two detailed reports on Yeats's planned visit to Japan: "Irish Poet Said to be Japan-Bound." It was a rumor, the article said, but there was plenty of substance to it. Yeats had "communicated his desire to lecture to Cousins, a literary friend currently teaching English literature at Keio University. Consequently, the authorities at Keio and Tokyo Universities had proposed inviting Yeats, and reached an agreement. A decision on the expenses for the invitation was made, and an official invitation letter was sent, but whether Yeats has accepted or not is yet unknown, although it is likely that he has accepted."[121]

The second report, appearing three days later, corrected some of the assertions of the first, based on Noguchi's statements to the editors. "The Truth About the Irish Poet's Japan Visit Problems" was that a formal invitation had not yet been sent.[122] "Yeats," Noguchi explained, "had expressed his desire to visit Japan to Keio professor Cousins, and it was from this wish that the plan for his visit began. Before I left for America, I proposed that Keio and Tokyo universities jointly invite him, but shortly thereafter I had to go to America, so I left the matter to Cousins." Cousins had subsequently written him saying that "Keio was very pleased with the visit of the poet and gladly agreed to cover half of the invitation expenses. However, the so-called Imperial University, considered Japan's highest academic institution, did not agree to bear their share, so unfortunately, the invitation could not proceed." However, "somehow they would manage." "When I explained this to Yeats, he said, 'I really wish to go to Japan in the fall, but I cannot afford to go at my own expense, and since I must bring along my wife, the expenses will be considerable. Is there no good way?'" Noguchi said that on his return to Japan, he would consult about the money and then issue a formal invitation.

From Salt Lake, Noguchi had told the *Nichibei* he would stay in the San Francisco bay area for about a month before leaving by steamer at the end of March.[123] But upon his arrival in San Francisco, he received devastating news about a death in his family. It was not his infant daughter, as he had initially been led to believe. A month after Noguchi's departure, James Cousins had learned that it had been Shimako, "she who had accepted me into her friendship with a cherry and a cake and a bow on the floor. I knew his fondness for the bright little creature and grieved for him; but his wife (with typical Japanese restraint of feeling) bound me not to tell him anything of the death in my letters for fear it would do him harm in his lecture-work."[124] Noguchi wrote to Harriet Moody on

---

121. "To-Nichi-setsu aru Airurando no shijin" (Irish poet headed for Japan), *Nichibei*, 27 Feb. 1920, 2.
122. "Airurando shijin tonichi mondai shinsō" (The truth about the Irish Poet's Japan visit problems), *Nichibei*, 1 Mar. 1920, 2.
123. "Noguchi shi saru," *Nichibei*, 1 Mar. 1920, 6.
124. Cousins, *The New Japan*, 205.

March 7th: "I was meaning to write you before, —but I was quite upset, when I came to knowledge that the one who died at home was my four-year-old girl. Not the baby girl! So I have to leave San Francisco on the 11th, taking the steamer Persia."[125] Now he was left with only a week and a half to conclude his visit.

Noguchi had returned to San Francisco to find the Japanese American community still under siege, and more deeply divided than ever from Consul-General Ōta's faction. Faced with lack of support, Ōta withdrew the advisory role on passport applications the local associations had been granted at the time of the Gentleman's Agreement. This resulted in the resignation of the president of the Association and calls for Ōta's removal, but to no avail. When the Japanese government announced it would stop issuing passports to picture brides as of February 25, the announcement was scarcely even mentioned in the press, and was greeted with considerable skepticism: brides continued arriving through August on earlier passports, and after that, could still be imported if immigrant men returned home to marry them.

106. An article in the *Washington Times*, January 4, 1920, wondered "what new device will be arranged to get these brides in?"

The *Nichibei* ran three days of interviews with Noguchi, giving a more optimistic picture of hopes for cultural exchange. The first part recounted highlights of his lecture tour: "everywhere I went, I was warmly welcomed, and the audiences were very enthusiastic, and many old friends from various places, hearing of my visit, came specifically to meet me, and it was quite delightful to reconnect after sixteen or

125. YN to Harriet Moody, 7 Feb. [in error for March] 1920, Harriet Moody collection, U of Chicago Library.

seventeen years.... Particularly enjoyable was the visit to Milwaukee, ... when my old acquaintance of twenty years, Frank Putnam, came all the way from St. Louis to see me. And the most interesting and memorable for me was the New York Poetry Society where I was a guest of honor along with the Irish poet Yeats and the English poet Sassoon, who gained fame as a war poet." In the second part Noguchi expressed his belief that "Americans are fundamentally the same as they were twenty years ago." They were "entirely self-centered and without exception, deeply satisfied with their own country's merits, filled with self-confidence, seeing no need to study others or learn from them." He gave his views on postwar political trends and described being hounded out of a Barnard Club lecture for asking whether Americans had forgotten their democratic principles. In the third, he talked about the international relations between Japan and the United States. During his tour he had found Americans in the eastern states to be as ignorant of Japan and the Japanese as they had been two decades earlier, but eager to learn more. Journalists had frequently approached him "to inquire about issues like the Shantung problem and Japan-U.S. relations, sometimes to the point of being bothersome." He believed that "issues like the China problem and the Korean problem caused Japan to be greatly misunderstood at times, with certain classes being constantly misled by propagandists working for China," but this seemed to have lately diminished. "Japan," he felt, "should make great efforts to be understood correctly in the future."[126]

107. Charles Warren Stoddard's grave.

126. "Yo no gan ni eijita" (My impressions), *Nichibei*, 2, 3, 4 Mar. 1920, 2.

On the 3rd, the *Nichibei* reported, Noguchi left for Monterey. After he returned to the Bay Area, it was announced, he would give a final lecture on the 9th at the Japanese Hall in Oakland.[127]

The visit to Monterey was for a final personal pilgrimage Noguchi needed to make, to the grave of Charles Warren Stoddard, who had died there of a heart attack in 1909, and was buried in the Catholic cemetery. Noguchi placed a wreath on the grave, and wrote a poem to Stoddard, which he published in the *Pacific Review* the following year. "Dear old Charley, how I wish with thee to talk on things or nothings," he began; "how I wish again / To sleep with thee in the same bed under the burning font, / Whose golden heart of flame rose to the innocent song of thy snore."[128]

On the evening of the 9th, Noguchi gave his final lecture at Oakland's Japan Hall. For an hour and a quarter, he regaled the audience with reminiscences of his early career leading into a condensed version of his "Literary Cooperation between America and Japan" lecture. Concluding, he said he looked forward to a day when Eastern and Western poets would understand each other without compromise. Kyūin Okina chaired the event, which was written up in both the *Nichibei* and *Shin Sekai*.[129]

108. Sailing calendar for the Tōyō Kisen Kaisha, 1921.

The officers of the Tōyō Kisen Kaisha *Persia Maru* all had "a touch of the 'flu,' but felt well enough to make the voyage," and the ship departed San Francisco on March 11, as scheduled.[130]

During the ship's brief stop in Honolulu, Noguchi spoke to reporters

---

127. "Noguchi shi no kōen" (Mr. Noguchi's lecture), *Nichibei*, 7 Mar. 1920, 6.
128. "To Charles Warren Stoddard," *Pacific Review* 1:3 (Dec. 1920): 309.
129. "Bunmei wa higashi kara nishi e" (Civilization goes from East to West), *Nichibei*, 11 Mar. 1920, 6; "Noguchi shijin no kōen" (Poet Noguchi's lecture), *Shin Sekai*, 11, 12, 13 Mar. 1920, 7.
130. "Pacific Coast Shipping Notes," *Morning Oregonian*, 12 Mar. 1920, 17.

from the local Japanese papers. In line with his propaganda message, he told the *Nippu Jiji* he was against Japanese language schools. "Closer contact between the Americans and the Japanese is the only solution of the anti-Japanese problem in the United States." "The reason why anti-Japanese movements exist in America is because the Americans do not understand the good points of the Japanese that are worthy of respect," he said. He acknowledged that "there are some elements of unreasonableness in the anti-Japanese movements in America." But he felt that "Americanization is very necessary to clear away all misunderstanding between the Japanese and Americans." "As to Japanese language schools in Hawaii, Mr. Noguchi said that they should be abolished." If the Japanese of the Islands insisted upon educating their children in Japanese they should send them to Japan, he concluded.[131]

Sword of Consolation

The *Persia Maru* docked at Yokohama on the afternoon of March 30. Noguchi's arrival was met with unexpected new condolences: as reported in the morning *Asahi*, he was returning unaware of a second death in his family.[132] "I think that I told you I lost my three-year-old girl,—and when my steamer reached Japan, I was informed that I lost my old mother also. You can easily imagine how upset I was in my mind," he wrote Harriet Moody a few weeks later.[133] He omitted telling her of the third blow that had followed a few weeks later, when he learned of his dear friend Hōmei Iwano's sudden death.[134] "Hearing of his death left me with an even deeper sense of despair," Noguchi wrote in an obituary essay. "The last time I saw him was at the farewell party held at Inokashira to see me off to America. It was at the beginning of last October, when the autumn at Inokashira was deepening. And since then," he added, "another member of the party has also died, Otsuji Ōsuga." An important member of Hekigotō's modernist haiku faction, Otsuji had been the theorist responsible for developing the modern conception of seasonal words.[135] "Thinking about how seven or eight people around me have died from last autumn to this year, I cannot help but feel the fragility of life," Noguchi wrote.

Another shock was the discovery that James Cousins had suddenly left. Keio had renewed Cousins's contract and even invited his wife

131. "Poet Noguchi is Against Nippon Language School," *Nippu Jiji*, 19 Mar. 1920, 8. On the controversy, see Noriko Asato, *Teaching Mikadoism* (Honolulu: U of Hawai'i P, 2005)
132. "Noguchi-shi kichō: Sanjūnichi Yokohama ni nyūkō: Aiji to bodō no seikyo o shirazu" (Mr. Noguchi returns: At Yokohama on the 30th not knowing the death of his beloved child and mother), *Asahi Shimbun*, 30 Mar. 1920, 12.
133. YN to Harriet Moody, 29 May 1920, Harriet Brainard Moody collection, U of Chicago Library.
134. On May 9 of peritonitis after catching a cold walking home from the theatre. Yoichi Nagashima, *Objective Description of the Self*, 49; YN, "Iwano Hōmei kun o itamu," 175.
135. Kenneth Yasuda, *The Japanese Haiku* (Tokyo: Tuttle, 2002), 55-61.

Margaret to teach. But on March 5, James had received a telegram, and on the 22nd, was aboard a ship bound for India. "Perhaps you know that James Cousins left Japan before I got back," Noguchi wrote Padraic Colum in May. "Even today it is not clear why he hurried back to India so suddenly."[136] Cousins later wrote vaguely in his memoir about the reasons,[137] but Margaret's memoir made clear that the call came from Theosophical Society president Annie Besant.[138] A reshuffling had been set in motion at Mahinda College in Galle, where Kalidas Nag, having anticipated that "it would not be possible or congenial for me to remain as principal of the college for long," had run into trouble.[139] That left Madanapalle with no principal unless James returned. "My feelings went against the recall," Margaret Cousins had concluded; "my judgment saw it was the only solution of problems. I cabled to Jim."

Noguchi's first order of business was to try and salvage the plan for Yeats's visit to Japan. On a visit to Osaka, Noguchi mentioned his predicament to a friend who worked for an Osaka newspaper (perhaps former Ayame-kai member Kyūkin Susukida, now the chief literary editor at the *Mainichi Shimbun*). The newspaper agreed to bear the other half of the expenses. But arrangements between Keio and the newspaper proved to be complicated, and there were other circumstances that prevented a quick realization of the plan. In the meantime, Yeats had already given up on it for the time being.[140]

The spirit world had been militating against the plan through the automatic writing of Yeats's wife, George—a practice she had taken up shortly after their marriage in the fall of 1917. A spirit she had been channeling named "Ameritus" had, in mid-November, expressed firm opposition on the grounds that Yeats was to write a book of philosophy (presumably the book that became *A Vision*). "I said before no Japan

136. YN to Padraic Colum, Sept. 7th 1921, Berg Collection, NYPL.
137. There had been letters, he explained in Cousins and Cousins, *We Two Together*, 365: "I had sensed problems that appeared to need my personal attention... Then came the recall, urgent and final. I had no choice."
138. In Cousins and Cousins, *We Two Together*, 380, Margaret explains that her move had been approved by Besant in January but then retracted in a letter she received on February 28, which "put all [her] machinery, as the motorists say, into reverse." "My dear Margaret," Besant had written, "I would be delighted if your husband came back: then we could continue the College which is otherwise hopeless after Pearce leaves.'"
139. Kalidas Nag, *Memoirs* (Calcutta: Writers Workshop, 1991), 1: 82. Mahinda was as close to a Buddhist college as the Theosophists could manage, and Nag was neither a Buddhist nor a Theosophist, but a cosmopolitan Bengali with a spiritual outlook similar to Tagore's. Nag also "had a dream . . . to fulfil with regard to research training in Europe" which, when it came through, required him to leave in August, at which time the school would be left in the hands of its London-educated Ceylonese Vice-Principal, S. D. S. Jayaratne. Faced with this prospect, "the Buddhists of Galle had an anxious time about the fortunes of the College, till the generous offer by Mrs. Annie Besant to send back Mr. Pearce to be Principal," according to the "Report of the Galle Buddhist Theosophical Society, Ltd. Up to October 31, 1921," in *General Report* (Adyar: Theosophical, 1922): 175.
140. Oshima, *W. B. Yeats and Japan*, 5, note 2.

next year," Ameritus insisted, adding that Yeats should send a telegram rejecting the invitation, a demand he had ignored.[141] With finances now uncertain, Ameritus' warnings must have seemed prescient.

Then in Portland on March 20, resting after the previous day's lecture, a "very distinguished looking Japanese" named Junzō Satō had visited Yeats's hotel room and presented him with an heirloom sword wrapped in silk brocade. Though he later said the gift had been made impulsively, Satō, who was researching canned foods for Japan's Ministry of Agriculture and Commerce, must have been a regular reader of the San Francisco Japanese papers, and would have been aware of the difficulty with Yeats's proposed Japan trip, as well as its cause: the Japanese government's reluctance to provide the necessary funding. Satō had a sufficiently well-developed appreciation of Yeats from his friendship with one of the more enthusiastic younger Yeats scholars, Hōjin Yano, to understand the government's shortsightedness in failing to fund the visit of such an important poet, while instead, sinking money into materialistic projects like his own canned food industry research. Though he was not, of course, personally responsible for such policies, it seems likely he meant the gift as a kind of apology. In Satō's later recollection, Yeats had already accepted the failure of the plan. "When I met him in Portland, he said to me, 'Japan is just across the Pacific. How vexatious it is that, coming so near to Japan, I cannot go there.'"[142] Two days later, Yeats wrote to Edmund Dulac: "We are not going to Japan. At least not for the present. The offer from there grew vaguer and the expense of living is immense. We should be bankrupt before we reached Tokyo."[143] Despite Noguchi's ongoing efforts to secure funding, with Yeats returning to England in May, prospects dimmed.

Noguchi's lecture room was also waiting. "A few weeks ago my college work began, and as a photographer asks one always, I had also to bear a pleasant smile before my students, —oh, that is quite awful," he told Harriet Moody.[144]

When the spring term ended in mid-July, Noguchi took his family for a much needed hot spring holiday. Bypassing Ikaho, they traveled further into Gunma to Shima Onsen. "The place lies more than two thousand feet up in the mountains, the hot spring waters are extremely abundant, the mountains are green, and there is hardly a day without some rainfall—it feels almost like the beginning of autumn," he wrote Kyūin Okina in California, apologizing for taking so long to thank him for his support

141. Brenda Maddox, *Yeats's Ghosts: The Secret Life of W. B. Yeats* (New York: HarperCollins, 1999), 153; Hirata Tokuboku, "Raichō sento suru ieitsu no fūkaku" (Profile of Yeats who is coming to Japan), *Eigo bungaku* 4:1 (Jan. 1920): 2-3. Oshima, *W. B. Yeats and Japan*, 5, 128.
142. Oshima, *W. B. Yeats and Japan*, 127.
143. Yeats to Dulac, 22 Mar. 1920, in Yeats, *Letters*, 622. See also Edward Marx, "No Dancing: Yone Noguchi in Yeats's Japan," 76.
144. YN to Harriet Moody, 29 May 1920, Harriet Brainard Moody collection, U of Chicago Library.

during his lecture tour.¹⁴⁵ The problem of the Japanese immigrants in California remained worrisome. "It seems imaginable that this will end badly for the Japanese." He had been glad to hear from the *Asahi Shimbun*'s international editor, Minoru Maita, that the *Nichibei* was adding an English page. "In truth, the Japanese in California are helpless without even a single English-language newspaper. Even a single page a week is better than nothing." He indicated he would be happy to write something for it and asked to have a sample issue sent.

His summer holiday was already ending, although it was only August 4. "My stay here at Shima ends today," he told Okina. "Upon returning home, with autumn arriving, I have quite a number of studies and obligations to pursue."

Words, Words, Words

After rushing back the proofs of his little book of *Japanese Hokkus* in January, Noguchi waited through the spring and summer until the small, plain book finally arrived in late October, with one poem badly misprinted.¹⁴⁶ He wrote back with a request for Brown to add an errata slip, which seems to have been ignored. A belated, poorly printed book being better than none at all, Noguchi was not ready to give up on Brown. He still expected Brown to publish his Nō book. And he thought Four Seas might do better as the nominal publisher for books he would print in Japan.¹⁴⁷ These, his *Selected Poems of Yone Noguchi* and a *Through the Torii* reprint, Brown handled well enough, at least up to the point of payment. That was better than the fate of the *Ten Noh Plays* manuscript, which Brown, lacking financial incentives to publish, simply left to gather dust.

The response to *Japanese Hokkus*, a book that should have shown the pioneering English haiku poet and "words, words, words" critic at his poetic best, was mixed. The book revealed the Imagist forerunner touted by *Poetry* magazine to be a writer of short poems not only redolent of the 1890s, but also flouting Imagist principles borrowed from Japanese poetry itself. "Use no superfluous word," Pound had insisted in his famous 1913

---

145. NY to Okina, 4 Aug. 1920, Okina Kyūin Foundation.
146. YN to Edmund Brown, 30 Oct. 1920, FSL. The printer had replaced the last line of poem 54 with the last line of poem 50.
147. YN to Edmund Brown, 30 Oct. 1920, 2 Mar. 1921, 3 Apr. 1921, 8 May 1921, 9 Sept. 1921, 11 Dec. 1921, FSL. Noguchi proposed sending Brown "a small American edition (say, 450 or 400) with your imprint" of *Selected Poems* from which Brown would take a thirty percent commission on the proposed $2.50 cover price. Brown preferred to buy the whole edition outright at a lower price. Noguchi was agreeable but could not accept less than a dollar a copy since "manufacturing cost itself is about 75 cents per copy" plus "some ten cents each for postage and other expenses." He would also, with Brown's permission, send out fifty review copies from Japan. In September, Noguchi sent Brown 375 copies, 75 of them autographed, and another 50 (presumably the review copies) to be sent by mail; the cover price had risen to $3.00. A similar arrangement was worked out for *Through the Torii* in December, Noguchi would send Brown 400 copies at $1.50 per copy and "under any circumstances the published price of the book cannot be more than $3.50."

list of Imagist "don'ts." "Go in fear of abstractions." [148] *Japanese Hokkus* had plenty of both.

Poetry magazine now had a local Japanese immigrant poet-journalist, Jun Fujita, who had begun publishing his own English verse, and was happy to explain how Noguchi's use of the hokku form failed to live up to the poet's own critical ideals. Considering the poem,

> Speak not again, Voice;
> The silence washes off sins.
> Come not again, Light.

Fujita wrote,

> This is written in a hokku form, seventeen syllables in three lines. But the form does not make a hokku. . . . Where is that fine and illusive mood, big enough to illuminate the infinity of the universe, which is essential to the hokku? I cannot find it. This verse may be poetic, but perhaps it should have more words, more lines, and stronger expression. The hokku is not condensed milk; condensed milk never becomes cream.

Fujita's critique was in part a foreshadowing of his own work in progress, *Tanka: Poems in Exile* (1923). Fujita's *Tanka* would offer "more words, more lines, and stronger expression," and poems arguably superior, in many respects, to Noguchi's.[149]

Other critics continued to view haiku as too trivial to bear comparison to more serious forms of poetry. "However much suggestiveness of the 'Infinite' a Japanese poet may get into his three-lined 'hokkus,' and Mr. Noguchi shows well what can be done in so tiny a space," wrote Richard Le Gallienne, "it is as idle to compare such poetical butterfly-wings with some of the great English odes, to name but those, as to compare the music of those Japanese 'grass larks' of which Lafcadio Hearn writes so charmingly with the music of Beethoven." As example, Le Gallienne quoted Noguchi's hokku:

> It is too late to hear a nightingale?
> Tut, tut, tut, . . . some bird sings,—
> That's quite enough, my friend.

Such a trivial poem, Le Gallienne implied, could never bear comparison with Keats's "Ode to a Nightingale." But that is a claim worth reconsidering, now that the hokku has been twice anthologized by former poet laureate Dana Gioia.[150] Like several of Noguchi's other "Japanese

---

148. Ezra Pound, "A Few Don'ts by an Imagiste," *Poetry* 1:6 (Mar. 1913): 200-06.
149. Jun Fujita, "A Japanese Cosmopolite," *Poetry* 20:3 (June 1922): 162-64.
150. Richard Le Gallienne, "Two Wise Men From the East," *New York Times Book Review and Magazine*, 11 Dec. 1921, 3. The poem, #48 in *JH*, is anthologized in Dana Gioia, Chryss Yost, and Jack Hicks, eds., *California Poetry:* (Berkeley: Heyday, 2004), 45, and in Dana Gioia, David Mason, and Meg Schoerke, *Twentieth-Century American Poetry* (Boston: McGraw-Hill, 2004), 108.

hokkus," this one began life as a fragment of an unpublished poem from his first trip to England. Disappointed that "it was not that Immortal Bird we hear nowadays at Hampstead"—where Keats heard it as he wrote his poem in 1819—"but the thrush, which might be a better subject for the pages of *Punch*," Noguchi had written "At Hampstead," which began:

> It is too late, dost thou say, to hear a nightingale,
> What I hear is not Keats' immortal bird but the thrush.
> Tut, tut, tut,......speak not it when I have no desire to know;
> What I wish to be assured is this: some bird ever sings . . . [151]

The hokku version is helped by compression, and when one reads it armed with the knowledge that Hampstead Heath, where the songbirds had once been numerous, had hosted the last of its migratory nesting nightingales in 1899, just a few years before Noguchi's visit, the plaintive question, "it is too late to hear a nightingale?" takes on a more profound meaning, turning the hokku into a powerful ecopoetic alternative to Keats's "forlorn" reflections.

Another blow to the *Hokkus* came from *The Freeman*, where Llewellyn Jones's scathing review skewered it from all sides.[152] The whole recent trend for Chinese and Japanese verse forms was, as Jones saw it, "a sign of the debility of our taste," often producing not even an exotic poetry, but "a mere shadow of poetry." He saw no reason for English poets to write in seventeen syllables; Noguchi's poems were "often as not written without regard for that arbitrary limitation," and when Noguchi did observe it, it was often by "desperate devices" such as elision or omission of words, which suggested that "its observance in the first place is not sincere." Noguchi's hokkus "lack that embodiment of the content which the English poet finds in his metres, rhythms, and melodies," and he "frequently indulges in cacophonous lines, often in positively bad grammar," ostensibly for "the sake of the picture." As Jones understood it, the picture was supposed to be suggested by the poem, but Noguchi had evidently moved beyond suggestion, and was now writing lines like "Eternity, rolled in love, / Bids the visible world to sing," incorporating generalizations that even "Keats would have scorned."

Babette Deutsch, a New York poet-critic, reviewing the book alongside Arthur Waley's *Japanese Poetry: The "Uta"* in the *Dial*, was nearly as critical. "Whether it is because he is writing in a foreign language, or because English cannot have packed into it the associations of thousands of years and the treasure of half-forgotten philosophies, the Japanese poet fails to produce the effect achieved by Waley in his translations." Moreover, Deutsch observed with admirable restraint that one poem

---

151. *SYN* 131-32; "Some London Poems," *Tōa no hikari* 7:11 (1 Nov. 1912): 99-100; Andrew Self, *The Birds of London* (London: Bloomsbury, 2014), 343.
152. Llewellyn Jones, "A Japanese Poet," *Freeman* 2 (24 Nov. 1920): 260-61.

"seems like an odd rearrangement" of a nearly-identical poem by Arthur Symons, which for Deutsch was troubling as a sign not of Noguchi's ongoing plagiaristic tendencies, but of his continued wallowing in the aesthetic atmosphere of the 1890s. "Japanese poetry is utterly distinct from the sick languors of the eighteen-nineties," Deutsch observed. "It is crisp and terse, rich and brief."[153]

For all the criticism, Noguchi's hokku continued to exert a powerful influence on practicing poets. The *Japanese Hokkus* volume, culmination of more than two decades of hokku promotion, demonstrated for the first time the possibility of publishing a book consisting entirely of haiku in English. Many poets who found merit in it had already been influenced by Noguchi's earlier writings, or their refractions through Gelett Burgess, Arthur Ransome, Ezra Pound, John Gould Fletcher, and others.

A case in point was that of E.E. Cummings, who, as a Harvard undergraduate, was deeply influenced by *The Spirit of Japanese Poetry*.[154] Drawn to Noguchi's claim that "the real poet in the Japanese understanding is primitive, as primitive are the moon and flowers" and conception of Japanese poetry as "a searchlight or flash of thought or passion cast on a moment of Life and Nature," Cummings, in his senior-year Advanced Composition class essay, pursued what he saw as Noguchi's "main question," namely, "what is the real poetry of action for which silence is the language?" As an answer, Cummings offered Noguchi's reading of Hokushi's "It has burned down; / How serene the flowers in their falling." "With that action as a background, his (Hokushi's) poem, although it is slight in fact, bursts into a sudden light and dignity." The following year, Cummings published three of his own attempts at hokku in the *Harvard Monthly*. One reads,

> I care not greatly
> Should the world remember me
> In some tomorrow.

By the narrower standards of a more recent haiku critic, "these experiments fail" due to their inclusion of opinion, epigram, and abstraction. "They all lack strong images, are too subjective, and do not offer implication, juxtaposition, childlike wonder, or sharply focused now-moments. . . . readers are left at the altar with flat statements packed into rigid external form."[155] While supported by haiku traditions, such lists of complaints also highlight the attractions of Noguchi's more permissive conception of hokku for English language poets making their first explorations of a new form. The extent to which Cummings' early hokku resemble canonical or other

---

153. Babette Deutsch, "The Soul of Wit," *Dial* 70 (Feb. 1921): 204-06.
154. E. E. Cummings, "The Poetry of Silence" [1915], ed. Michael Webster, rpt. *Spring* 23 (Fall 2020), 131-39. See also Michael Webster's helpful "Afterward to 'The Poetry of Silence,'" *Spring* 23 (Fall 2020): 140-59.
155. Michael Dylan Welch, "The Haiku Sensibilities of E. E. Cummings," *Spring* 4 (Oct. 1995): 109.

definitions of haiku matters less than the role his encounter with hokku played in the development of his unique poetic conception and style.

Haiku readers with exacting requirements often have trouble warming to the English language hokku and haikai of the 1910s and 1920s, not only Noguchi's *Japanese Hokkus* but its successors, some well known, like Amy Lowell's "Twenty-Four Hokku on a Modern Theme," others mostly forgotten, like the hokku sequence in Zona Gale's 1921 poetry collection, *The Secret Way*. Some have begun to be reevaluated, like the pioneering work of African-American poet Lewis Alexander, published in prominent Harlem Renaissance publications, who at one point sought out Noguchi's advice, and Rabindranath Tagore, whose short poems, in *Fireflies* and elsewhere, have begun to be read in the context of Tagore's writings on Japanese verse.[156] For better or worse, these, along with the better-appreciated experiments of Pound's Imagist circle, represent the early development of what is now a major global poetic form.

Perhaps the most interesting instance of Noguchi's hokku influence in the 1920s was on Russian film director and theorist Sergei Eisenstein. In "The Cinematographic Principle and the Ideogram" (1929), Eisenstein looked to Fenollosa and Pound's theory of the ideogram—"by the combination of two 'depictables' is achieved the representation of something that is graphically undepictable"—in order to argue for a modernist style of film montage based on an aesthetic of laconism, which he found exemplified by haiku. "From our point of view, these are montage phrases. Shot lists. The simple combination of two or three details of material kind yields a perfectly finished representation of another kind—psychological . . . We should observe that the emotion is directed towards the reader, for, as Yone Noguchi has said, 'it is the readers who make the haiku's imperfection a perfection of art.'"[157]

Help for Noguchi's publishing predicament arrived in Tokyo in August 1920, bearing a letter from Harriet Moody, in the person of Ananda Kentish Coomaraswamy. The formerly British-Ceylonese cultural historian, in exile from the British Commonwealth since 1917 due to his refusal to join the British Army, had taken up residence in the United States and now worked for the Boston Museum of Fine Arts. "We had the most delightful meeting before he left Tokyo for Kyoto a few days ago," Noguchi informed Moody. "And I expect to see him again when he returns to Tokyo in September. Coomaraswamy has many interesting

156. Amy Lowell, "Twenty-Four Hokku on a Modern Theme," *Poetry* 18 (June 1921): 124-27; Zona Gale, "Hokku," *The Secret Way* (New York: Macmillan, 1921), 20-21; Lewis Alexander, "Japanese Hokkus," *Crisis* 27:2 (Dec. 1923): 67; "Japanese Hokku," *Opportunity* 3:33 (Sept. 1925): 278; "A Group of Japanese Hokku," *Palms* 4:1 (Oct. 1926): 15; Gwendolyn Bennett, in "The Ebony Flute," *Opportunity* 4 (Sept. 1926): 292-3 noted that "Yone Noguchi is criticizing the Japanese themes as presented by Lewis Alexander"; Rabindranath Tagore, *Fireflies* (New York: Macmillan, 1928).

157. Sergei Eisenstein, "The Cinematographic Principle and the Ideogram" (1929) in *Film Form*, tr. Jay Leyda (New York: Harcourt, Brace, 1949), 30-33.

things in his mind, with which I am delighted to cooperate."[158] One of these was his Orientalia Bookshop, newly established at 32 West 58th Street in New York: the first American bookshop devoted exclusively to books on the Orient, which would have an attached publishing operation. Noguchi signed on to have Orientalia issue several books under a similar arrangement to his previous collaborations. They would start with a new edition of his very first book, *Seen and Unseen*, followed by *Japan and America*, a selection of essays derived mainly from his American lectures and printed by Keio University Press, and then launch into the first of his illustrated books on ukiyoe, *Hiroshige*, to be co-published by Elkin Mathews in London. Coomaraswamy was also making inquiries about a visiting Japanese lectureship that Harriet Moody hoped to establish at Cornell University, where she served as a trustee. Noguchi told Moody he thought the idea would be "quite easy to carry out" with financial support from the Japanese government, and he himself would be "would be glad to give a course of lectures on the Japanese literature there." He was less optimistic about a plan for an "Asiatic and European Art Museum," which he had discussed with friends who could "hardly see the way at once how to put it in practice."

Noguchi enjoyed discussing these projects during the two months Coomaraswamy spent "keeping himself so busy with the old books and pictures to buy or examine."[159] Within four months of their meeting, the first of the Orientalia books, the *Seen & Unseen* reprint, was available, followed by *Hiroshige* and *Japan and America* in March and May. Of course, the speed came mainly from Noguchi's Japanese printers, and did not apply to payment schedules. "I am tired with Orientalia," he told Léonie in 1925, after the shop had repeatedly failed to meet its payment obligations.[160] Nor had the visiting lectureship or art museum materialized. Noguchi had similar payment problems with Edmund Brown at the Four Seas Company. Noguchi wrote him in April 1923, "it is about the time when you must think about your duty toward my books." He trusted in Brown's sense of honor, but "when you say nothing to me, I must ask my friend to see you in person."[161] His grand plans for Four Seas to publish his books of Nō plays, essays, and new poems had to be shelved.

The first book with Orientalia, the reprinted *Seen & Unseen*, attracted little attention aside from nostalgic Bay Area columnists now eager to hail the proto-Imagist, and a savage review in the London *Bookman*. The reviewer was happy to agree with Noguchi's own description of the book as "wild fugitive words sounding almost like a child's babbles" but scoffed at his claim to have succeeded in making himself "more naked

---

158. YN to Harriet Moody, 26 Aug. 1920, Harriet Brainard Moody Collection, U of Chicago.
159. YN to Harriet Moody, 14 Oct. 1920, Harriet Brainard Moody Collection, U of Chicago.
160. YN to LG, 10 Dec. 1925, in *LG* 314.
161. YN to Edmund Brown, 4 Apr. 1923, FSL.

and true." "If Mr. Noguchi wishes us to understand that in the writing of these verses he succeeded in giving literal expression to the thoughts and fancies which entered his head while musing on the hills behind San Francisco, we are doubly amazed—first at his pretence that the verses give intelligent expression to ideas, and secondly at his complacence in presenting such platitudes and posturings as a serious contribution to English literature."[162]

Selected Poems of Yone Noguchi was on sale from Four Seas and Elkin Mathews in September 1921. "The many admirers in America of Mr. Noguchi's work will gladly welcome this volume," wrote William Stanley Braithwaite in the *Boston Evening Transcript*.[163] Richard Le Gallienne praised it as "a treasure of exquisite poetry" in a lengthy review in the *New York Times Book Review*, but remained unpersuaded by Noguchi's claims for Japanese verse. "Western poetry attempts a far wider and deeper range in the embodiment and interpretation of human life than Japanese poetry, just as European music and painting attempt to do more than the same arts in Japan; and, however much we may admire Japanese poetry, one cannot but feel that the greater includes the less." Padraic Colum reviewed the book in *The Freeman*, but evidently preferred Noguchi's prose, reserving most of his praise for Noguchi's *Hiroshige*.[164] Sending Witter Bynner a copy, Noguchi wrote, "I will be happy if you can say something about my selection publicly. As you know my work is not known enough."[165] But Bynner did not review the book. Nor did it get much attention from modernist publications, which was not really surprising, since the poems were all more than a decade old.

Even *Japan and America*, "a series of rather thin papers . . . written in very imperfect English, made worse by poor proofreading," according to the *Pacific Monthly*, was "quite interesting" for "the picture it gives of Japanese reaction to our American civilization." The *Overland Monthly* appreciated that Noguchi "is invariably genial and he certainly knows our national strength and weakness." Van Wyck Brooks, who delighted in Noguchi's characterization of America as "floating comfortably on the ocean all by itself, as if a well-fed seal or lazy iceberg," wrote an unsigned review in *The Freeman* supporting Noguchi's appeal for literary co-operation between America and Japan. On the whole, the response to *Japan and America* was fairly sympathetic. But there was "something unreal" about Noguchi's genial discourse, Arthur Clutton Brock wrote in London's *Times Literary Supplement*, as was often the case "when literary men

162. D.J.E., "Poesy and Posturing," *Bookman* (London) 60 (Aug. 1921): 218.
163. William Stanley Braithwaite, "Books of the Day: A Japanese Poet," *Boston Evening Transcript*, 3 Dec. 1921, 4:5.
164. Richard Le Gallienne, "Two Wise Men From the East," *New York Times Book Review and Magazine*, 11 Dec. 1921, 3; Padraic Colum, "Japanese Artistry," *Freeman* 5 (22 Mar. 1922): 43-44.
165. YN to Bynner, 7 Sept. 1921, Witter Bynner Additional Papers, bMS Am 1891.28-1891.29, Houghton Library, Harvard University.

give us accounts of the ideals and intentions of their country." There was no getting around the fact that the political aims of Japan and America, particularly with regard to China, had come to seem opposed since the end of the Great War, and "no amount of literary explanation will maintain friendship if the peoples talk one way and act another."[166] A reviewer in G.K. Chesterton's magazine, *The New Witness*, gave this cynical but prescient assessment:

> Almost all who live on the Pacific coast think that a war between Japan and America is only a matter of time. The majority of those who live in the East also think the same. . . . In Japan . . . the military party is determined to conquer China, occupy Northern Manchuria, annex Shantung and Fuchien, and defy the world. The Japanese press supports the military party and is ultra-chauvinistic. But Japan is an oligarchy, and the Mikado and his great nobles see very clearly that a war between Japan and the United States would ultimately end in the total defeat of Japan. Like Germany, she would win everywhere at the beginning, and like Germany, she would collapse in the end. This the elder statesmen know, and they are forever doing all they can to allay the fever that ever and again attacks the Japanese nation. Thus a practiced writer like Yone Noguchi is kept busy smoothing down the waves of the press storms with his oleaginous sentences. In a way, he succeeds.[167]

Noguchi must have been grateful for the admiration of Robert Nichols, the young war poet from Oxford who arrived for a three-year teaching stint at Tokyo University in 1921. Nichols had been an undergraduate at the time of Noguchi's Oxford lecture, and it was he who recalled the comical scene in which "Noguchi, a short-legged tortoise, runs for life after Bridges, a long-legged stork!"

109. Robert Nichols in his office at Tokyo University.

---

166. "New Books on the Far East," *Pacific Review* 2:2 (Sept. 1921): 332-33. "Editor's Notebook," *Overland Monthly* 78 (Aug. 1921): 63. [Van Wyck Brooks], "A Reviewer's Notebook," *Freeman* 3 (22 June 1921): 358. [Arthur Clutton-Brock], "Japan and America," *TLS*, 4 Aug. 1921, 492.
167. "Library List," *The New Witness*, 26 Aug 1921, 115.

Nichols, "brought up in an atmosphere of ancient houses and connoisseurship" and having "imbibed taste and the historic sense as simply as babies imbibe milk," as William Rothenstein wrote in 1923, had grown into a somewhat troubled young poet. Shell-shocked in the war, he had still to find himself, and Rothenstein thought it improbable that he would do so in Japan. He did, however, find Noguchi, and wrote an admiring review of *Through the Torii* for Noguchi's old nemesis, the *Japan Advertiser*, in which he recalled "a charming meeting with Mr. Noguchi" during which his mind had become "more and more distracted (for all the vigorous conversation) as the evening wore on by the softness of Mr. Noguchi's voice and the nihilistic sadness of the continual smile about his lips—beyond a doubt the saddest smile I ever beheld." He thought Noguchi "a rare and subtle humorist" and "an extremely delicate and penetrating critic," and defended him vigorously against "those who have asserted that Mr. Noguchi is not at home in English," a group that, he noted, included the editor of the other major English paper, the *Japan Chronicle*, "the usually acute Robert Young," who "in this case ... blundered badly, showed in fact an extraordinary incapacity for understanding the very rudiments of what the writer's art is."[168] Young obligingly responded the following week by demonstrating the grammatical flimsiness of the sentences whose "fluctuant and subtle beauty" Nichols had praised, affirming that "the same irritating errors are still present."[169] Young was no longer the tireless Noguchi gadfly he had once been. When he died suddenly of a heart attack that November, Noguchi was in the process of publishing *Teki o aise* (Love your enemies), the title essay of which argued the importance of having enemies.[170] Essentially a reworked and expanded translation of Richard Le Gallienne's *Yellow Book* essay, "On Loving One's Enemies," the essay explored an idea dear to Noguchi ever since the days when he had been attacked—and made famous—by Jay William Hudson. Just as Christ "knew that the spiritual fire He strove to kindle would spread but a little unless the four winds of the world blew against it," Le Gallienne had argued, "most of us would never be heard of if it were not for our enemies." As "a negative embodiment of our personalities or ideas," the enemy is "a creature of our making," an "involuntary witness to our vitality," and should be valued: "make your enemies, and your enemies will make you."[171]

The essay was well timed for the arrival of Noguchi's latest and best-armed enemy, the British Orientalist and translator Arthur Waley, a highly proficient linguist who claimed to have learned classical Chinese

---

168. William Rothenstein, *Twenty-Four Portraits* (London: Chatto & Windus, 1923): 62; Robert Nichols, "One Half Japan," *Japan Advertiser*, 5 Mar. 1922, 6; 7 Mar. 1922, 4, 10.
169. "Notes of the Week," *Japan Chronicle*, weekly ed., 16 Mar. 1922, 371.
170. "Teki o aise" (1918), rpt. *Teki o aise* (Tokyo: Genbunsha 1922), 3-10.
171. Richard Le Gallienne, "On Loving One's Enemies," *Yellow Book* 6 (July 1895), 307-10.

and Japanese in a matter of months, and scoffed at anyone who might profess the languages difficult. He had been appointed as Laurence Binyon's assistant in the British Museum's Department of Oriental Prints and Drawings in June of 1913, a few months before Noguchi's arrival (they would likely have met at the time), when he had not yet read a word of either language. By the end of the decade, he had risen to dominate the field of British Japanology. Where Binyon remained a practitioner of what his biographer describes as "belated Romantic poetry," Waley's straightforward translations allied him with the younger modernists.[172] *Japanese Poetry: The "Uta"* was "chiefly intended to facilitate the study of the Japanese text; for Japanese poetry," Waley wrote, "can only be rightly enjoyed in the original. And since the classical language has an easy grammar and limited vocabulary, a few months should suffice for the mastering of it." He even offered seven pages of "notes on grammar" to get readers started.[173]

110. Arthur Waley.

Waley unleashed his scorn for Noguchi in an anonymous review in the *Times Literary Supplement* that revisited Noguchi's critically acclaimed *Through the Torii* in conjunction with Noguchi's first Japanese poetry collection, *Nijū-kokusekisha no shi* (Poems of a dual national). He had no use for the delicate style of the essays that had so attracted earlier reviewers.

> For the writer who decides to use a language which he has not perfectly mastered, the first essential is absolute simplicity. So long as he avoids any attempt at 'fine writing' he has on his side a great natural asset, the reader's hospitable indulgence and chivalry. Provided he has anything to say which is worth hearing he need only strive to say it intelligibly. Obviously neither poetry nor the purer forms of prose literature can be produced in such circumstances. But a story can be told, knowledge can be imparted, impressions recorded.[174]

---

172. John Hatcher, *Laurence Binyon* (Oxford: Clarendon, 1995), 155.
173. Arthur Waley, *Japanese Poetry: The "Uta"* (Oxford: Oxford UP, 1919), 8.
174. [Arthur Waley], "Japanese Essays and Poems," *TLS*, 6 Apr. 1922, 227.

Waley's advice was not actually backed by experience; in fact, the great British Orientalist would spend his entire professional career without publishing any writing in the languages he translated so fluently into English. It was perhaps Waley's own fear of venturing into the language of the "Other," and perhaps even his fear of creative writing itself, that drove him to criticize Noguchi's English efforts so mercilessly. "It is when he is conveying information that he certainly appears at his best," Waley states. "But much of the book suffers from the author's desire to gallop before he can trot, to be decorative and epigrammatic before he is even securely intelligible."

Waley's review appeared in 1922, after Noguchi had published his first collection of poetry in Japanese, offering Waley the opportunity to expose Noguchi's pretentions and flaws as a Japanese poet, the most annoying of which, in his view, was Noguchi's inescapable egoism. "While reading his verses one cannot for an instant be rid of him," Waley complained. "It is 'boku,' 'boku' at every turn." Noguchi's enthusiastic use of personal pronouns ("*boku*" being an informal form of "I" in Japanese) was a habit he had picked up writing English poems. Noguchi's poems suggested to Waley some sobering "general reflections upon modern Japanese as a vehicle for poetry. The language is an amalgam of two metrically irreconcilable elements, Japanese and Chinese," he noted, and "the incursion of Chinese has, it seems to us, absolutely killed Japanese poetry." "The present alternatives," Waley states, "are to write completely in Japanese or completely in Chinese." Writing entirely in Japanese would be as impractical as writing in Anglo-Saxon for an English poet, so he suggested Noguchi try the latter: "an attempt to use the lucid and rigorous forms of Chinese verse would be a salutary exercise for a poet whose *vers-libres* flap and sprawl like wet linen that has torn from its pegs. From the Chinese, too, Mr. Noguchi might borrow a wholesome tradition of objectivity."

A Beautiful Scene

Hiroshige, Noguchi's first illustrated art book in English, received almost universal critical approval. A modest volume consisting of 32 pages of text culled from a decade of Hiroshige writings,[175] to which he added a color-print frontispiece, nineteen monochrome reproductions, and a prefatory poem, the book was printed and bound in Japan for distribution in London through Elkin Mathews and in New York by the Orientalia bookstore. The Western appetite for ukiyoe was still very strong, and all of the books on the subject had been written by non-Japanese art collectors. Writing in the London *Bookman*, R. Ellis Roberts found it

---

175. The *Hiroshige* book was derived from a 1911 *Academy* article reprinted in *SJA*, rewritten as a panegyric for the 1917 Hiroshige Memorial Exhibition (and printed in the exhibition catalog and in *Arts and Decoration*), an essay "Hiroshige, A Great Japanese Artist," *JT*, 22 Oct. 1916, and two Hiroshige poems from Ariake Kanbara's 1915 *Mandala* anthology.

a welcome addition to books on "Things Japanese," placing it ahead of Arthur Waley's new collection of Nō translations in his review article. William Butler Yeats, to whom Noguchi sent a copy, responded with warm gratitude and encouragement in what may be the only survival of the correspondence between the two poets. *Hiroshige* had given him the greatest pleasure, Yeats told Noguchi, explaining,

> I take more and more pleasure from oriental art; find more and more that it accords with what I aim at in my own work. The European painter of the last two or three hundred years grows strange to me as I grow older, begins to speak as with a foreign tongue. When a Japanese, or Mogul, or Chinese painter seems to say, "Have I not drawn a beautiful scene", one agrees at once, but when a modern European painter says so one does not agree so quickly, if at all. All your painters are simple, like the writers of Scottish ballads or the inventors of Irish stories, but one feels that Orpen and John have relatives in the patent office who are conscious of being at the forefront of time.... I would be simple myself but I do not know how. I am always turning over pages like those you have sent me, hoping that in my old age I may discover how.

Yeats was eager to read more about Japanese artists. He told Noguchi,

> I wish some Japanese would tell us all about the lives... their talk, their loves, their religion, their friends.... of these painters. I would like to know these things minutely and to know too what their houses looked like, and if they still stand, to know all those things that are known about Blake, and about Turner, and about Rossetti. It might make it more easy to understand their simplicity. A form of beauty scarcely lasts a generation with us, but it lasts with you for centuries. You no more want to change it than a pious man wants to change the Lord's Prayer, or the Crucifix on the wall—at least not unless we have infected you with our egotism.

With the current unrest in Ireland, Yeats was in temporary exile in Oxford. "I have not seen Galway for a long time now for I am warned that it is no place for wife and child," he told Noguchi. "I wish I had found my way to your country a year ago & were still there."[176]

Other reviews were also appreciative. "Readers who are already familiar with Noguchi's work in prose and verse will be able to foresee what kind of illumination he will have to offer them about Hiroshige," wrote Noguchi's old friend Arthur Davison Ficke, who had recently sold off his own print collection for upwards of $60,000.[177] "They will come expecting neither a technical treatise nor a compilation of facts, but rather a poetic interpretation of the great and poetic spirit of Hiroshige. No one alive is better fitted than Noguchi for such an undertaking."[178] The *New*

---

176. W.B. Yeats to YN, 27 June [1921], *CEL* 414, also in Oshima, *W. B. Yeats and Japan*, 20-21.
177. "Print Sale Nets $62,497," New York Times, 12 Feb. 1920, 10, roughly $1 million 2025 dollars.
178. A.D.F., "Among Our Books," The Arts 1:7 (June 1921): 47.

York Times Book Review devoted a full page to the volume.¹⁷⁹

With such encouragement, Noguchi was able to continue the series of art books for the firm of Elkin Mathews, despite Mathews' death in November of 1921. He heeded, as far as possible, Yeats's advice to explore minutely the lives of the Japanese artists, a subject which Yeats rightly saw as a weakness of Western books on Japanese art. Since his first long article on Hokusai written in 1903 after London, where the Rossettis' Hokusai-covered walls had amazed, and a Sturge-Moore-reception Hokusai Fuji emboldened, him, Noguchi had been steadily accumulating knowledge of ukiyoe. Until the 1920s, however, it had comprised a relatively small part of his art interests, which were more drawn to the contemporary art scene, and to artists more highly valued in Japan, like the Kyoto school artists Kōetsu and Kenzan. The West was still far ahead of Japan in recognizing ukiyoe as an important art form.¹⁸⁰ More significant was the success of the exhibition itself, which had drawn sixteen thousand visitors in three days. Noguchi contributed a panegyric on Hiroshige to the exhibition catalog, which was printed in both Japanese and English editions. When Frank Lloyd Wright, an indefatigable ukiyoe collector, came to Japan the following year, he found Hiroshige prices had skyrocketed. "The Japanese are awake to Hiroshige now," he wrote a fellow collector friend, enclosing a copy of the catalog. "Read M. Yoneguchi's [*sic*] article. It is worth reading. I sold my Hiroshiges to the Metropolitan for half the price I should have."¹⁸¹

Noguchi's first Japanese book exclusively devoted to ukiyoe had been a small volume of essays entitled *Roku dai-ukiyoe-shi*—Six Great Ukiyoe Masters, published in 1919, which actually contained nine essays on seven artists, adding Harunobu, Kiyonaga, and Sharaku to Noguchi's previous subjects, Hokusai, Hiroshige, Utamaro, and Yoshitoshi, along with a translation of John Gould Fletcher's poetry collection, *Japanese Prints*, for good measure.¹⁸² The new book paved the way for several series of print-artist books Noguchi published over the following decades, each a step up in size and production values over the last.¹⁸³

179. Herbert S. Gorman, "Hiroshige, Japan's Landscape Artist," *New York Times Book Review*, 1 May 1921, 44.
180. When Noguchi reviewed the Hiroshige memorial exhibition held at Tokyo's Takashimaya department store in September 1917, he could refer to Japanese Hiroshige studies as "greatly advancing," but aside from a brief biographical entry he translated from Shotarō Umemoto's useful collection of short artist biographies, *Ukiyoe biko* (1898), the only evidence he could point to was a recent study of Hiroshige's landscape paintings by art scholar Usui Kojima.
181. "The Hiroshige Memorial Exhibition," *JT*, 16 Sept. 1917, 6. The book by Kojima was Kojima Usui, *Ukiyoe to fūkeiga* (Ukiyoe and landscape painting) (Tokyo: Maekawa Bun'eikaku, 1914). Julia Meech, *Frank Lloyd Wright and the Art of Japan: The Architect's Other Passion* (New York: Japan Society and Harry N. Abrams, 2001): 134.
182. *Rokudai ukiyoe shi* (Tokyo: Iwanami shoten, 1919).
183. The first was the five-volume English series sold by Elkin Mathews (London) and Orientalia (New York), comprising *Hiroshige* (1921), *Korin* (1922), *Utamaro* (1924), *Hokusai* (1925), and *Harunobu* (1927). This was followed by a six-volume bilingual series, first published privately by

A Face at Which Stones are Sometimes Thrown

Aside from the art books—and articles written as the "Editor of the Department of Oriental Art" for *Arts & Decoration* magazine—Noguchi had, since his return from the United States, virtually ceased writing for the American and British press. A few months earlier he had been stressing the importance of educating Americans about Japan, a necessary measure to improve conditions for the immigrants and Japan's relationship with the United States. He had been writing articles promoting Japan and Japanese culture for two decades, and he had spoken during his lecture tour of his plans to continue doing so. But now that he had returned to Japan, he changed direction, without explanation.

It was a difficult time for Noguchi. He had hurried back to Japan on hearing of his young daughter's death only to discover he had also lost his old mother; then his dear friend Hōmei Iwano had suddenly died. James Cousins had abandoned his post, without explanation, leaving the Keio English department understaffed, while the last hopes of bringing Yeats to Japan crumbled. His publication difficulties had found no help on his American tour. *Japanese Hokkus* had done little to buoy his reputation, and chances of *Ten Noh Plays* ever appearing dwindled with each passing day. Léonie, to whom he had so often resorted for editing and typing, had left for good. Even if he could get his manuscripts corrected and typed, who would publish them? The political climate was against him. The Anglo-Japanese Alliance, strained on both sides, was heading toward expiration, and American-Japanese relations were as poor as they had ever been.

The declining political situation had not fueled his interest in criticizing America and Americans. Having been kindly treated during his American lecture tour, he had no personal grudges to motivate him. Nor was he eager to involve himself in the rancorous immigration debates in which even the Japanese factions were divided.

Having grown, through more than two decades, into a predominantly English-language writer enjoying a unique position abroad, as well as in his home country, the course that now attracted him was that of redirecting his energies toward reinventing himself as a Japanese-language poet and critic. He would limit his English book-publishing efforts to studies of Japanese artists, mainly woodblock print artists popular in the West. From time to time he would write essays about Westerners who loved Japan, like Ernest Fenollosa, or the Japan-trained British potter, Bernard Leach, or report on a Japanese production of John Masefield's

---

Noguchi in 1929-31, then reissued by Seibundō in 1932-33, which replaced *Korin* with *Sharaku* and *Kiyonaga*. Noguchi then started over with larger English volumes: *The Ukiyoye Primitives* (1933), *Hiroshige* (1940) and *Harunobu* (1940). The Second World War effectively ended the series, aside from the shortened *Hiroshige and Japanese Landscapes* in Maruzen's Tourist Library which remained in print from 1934 to 1954.

Japanese play, or the warm reception of Crown Prince Hirohito in Britain. Such articles might draw readers away from the relentless negativity of so much recent writing about Japan, even if it was unlikely to have a major impact on American-Japanese relations. The art books would be a comfortable sideline, welcomed by his Japanophile friends abroad, and providing pleasant research opportunities of meeting and talking with art collectors.

Now he felt it was the Japanese that needed to be shaken out of their complacency. Returning from America had once again sharpened his perceptions of Japan's failings, and he felt compelled to speak his mind, even if his message was not always welcome. It was not simply that he wanted to complain; he was also bothered by the Japanese avoidance of complaints. "The faces of most Japanese people to-day are the faces of people who are eager to compromise, to conciliate, to make concessions: they are faces lacking in spiritual vitality, they seem to know only how to express appreciation of material things: in short they are the faces of street-stallmen on fête day." What was missing, he felt, were obstinate, independent-minded critics, like Thomas Carlyle.[184] A description of Carlyle by G.K. Chesterton especially struck him. "One seeks in vain for a face with a wild eye, with an expression of silent anger, such a face as Mr. Chesterton describes Carlyle's to have been, a face at which stones are sometimes thrown."[185]

Carlyle, unlike many of the modernist writers Noguchi introduced to Japanese readers, was a fairly well-known name in Japan. Carlyle translations and a biography had been already available in Noguchi's student days; he might not have read them at the time, but he certainly became aware of Carlyle's profound influence on Inazō Nitobe, who was promoting both Carlyle and Noguchi in *The Student* in the fall of 1903.[186] Since then, Noguchi had made several Carlyle promotion efforts himself. The first was a (mostly translated) article for the *Keiō Gijuku Gakuhō* in 1907 on Carlyle's birthplace.[187] More recently, he had written an essay for *Gakutō* about his own visit to Carlyle's Chelsea house, and a more

---

184. Of Carlyle, Chesterton had written in *The Victorian Age in Literature* (London: Williams and Norgate, 1913), 49, "If he had laboured obscurely in his village till death, he would have been yet locally a marked man; a man with a wild eye, a man with an air of silent anger; perhaps a man at whom stones were sometimes thrown."

185. A Japanese Professor, "Letter from Abroad: Through Japanese Eyes," *Freeman* 3 (20 Apr. 1921): 133-34.

186. YN, "The Evolution of Modern Japanese Literature," *Critic* 44 (Mar. 1904), rpt. *EE* 67: "And the *Student*, a semi-monthly publication for the study of the English language and literature, issued its Carlyle number last September, and indirectly denounced the present condition of Japan." Nitobe's essay "What Carlyle Taught" is reprinted in his *Thoughts and Essays* (Tokyo: Teibi, 1909): 28-33.

187. "Kārairu no kyūseki" (Relics of Carlyle), *Keiō Gijuku Gakuhō* 121 (Sept. 1907): 29-34; 122 (Oct. 1907): 28-37, rpt. Kārairu no Kyōdo], (Carlyle's birthplace), *Shijin no Kyōdo* (Poets' birthplaces) (1927). The article was mainly derived from Henry C. Shelley, "Gleanings in Carlyle Country," *New England Magazine* 11:17 (Oct. 1894): 194-205.

argumentative essay, "Let a Carlyle be Born in Japan," for *Yūben*.[188]

The latter article was largely based on Frank Harris's memoir of the Scottish writer, as Noguchi acknowledged, but the wish for a Japanese Carlyle was (presumably) his own. It is worth mentioning that this was his first contribution to *Yūben*, the flagship magazine of the newly-prominent publishing company recently renamed Kōdansha, which "gave rise to what has since become known as the 'mass style'—writing that can be appreciated by the masses as distinguished from the educated minority which had hitherto formed the reading public of Japan," as its founder, Seiji Noma, proudly wrote. "It virtually 'democratized' reading, shifting it from the educated few to the mass of the people, literate and illiterate."[189] Noguchi's choice of topic for this first contribution to Noma's growing magazine empire offered a provocative reminder that successful publishing needed more than popular appeal: it also needed critical voices oblivious to it.

How and where Noguchi published the American version of his Carlylean critique of Japan's shopkeeper mentality is also of interest: it was via an anonymous letter for *The Freeman*, a magazine often described as an early libertarian magazine. Noguchi may have been attracted by *The Freeman*'s politics, or he may have been trying to court the editors' sympathies after the magazine's unfavorable review of his *Japanese Hokkus*. But the possibility that Noguchi may have been, in essence, a libertarian ,might go some way toward explaining his frequent vacillations between conservative and liberal positions and publications. It might also explain his continued attachment to Carlyle-esque individualism even as his politics veered to the right in the mid-1920s.

A Giant as Big as the Sky

The international reputation of "Yone Noguchi, the Japanese poet" had persisted for decades despite the Japanese poet having produced little if any Japanese poetry. He had published English poetry as a barely-literate immigrant three years after arriving in the United States, but back in

---

188. "Kārairu" (Carlyle), *Gakutō* 21:22 (20 Nov. 1917): 1-5; "Nihon ni Kārairu o umareshimeyo" (Let a Carlyle be born in Japan), *Yūben* 9:1 (1 Jan. 1918): 168-76.

189. Noma Seiji, *Noma of Japan* (London: Methuen, 1934), 176-77. *Yūben* was the first magazine of the Dai Nippon Yūbenkai (Great Japan Oratorical Society) founded by Noma, a Tokyo University administrator, in 1910. The entrepreneurial Noma had set his sights on the youth magazine market the next year with his second magazine, *Kōdan Kurabu*. "Some of the old kodan (historical romances recited by professional story-tellers known as Kodanshi) were just the kind of stuff which, if printed in readable form, would provide first-rate reading matter useful for popular education" (176). Noma was convinced that the often-retold popular stories, adapted into an easily-readable print style, would sell. Three years later he added *Shōnen Kurabu* (Youth Club) aimed at younger readers, followed, the next year, by *Omoshiro Kurabu* (Interesting Club). "In January, 1917, we printed our customary special New Year numbers," he later recalled; "If I remember rightly, we printed 15,000 copies of *Yuben*, and 40,000 each of the three popular organs... such numbers... were gigantic at the time and were the envy of smaller publishers" (199).

Japan, it took a decade for him to make any attempt to publish poetry in his native language, and several years more for him to take up the idea seriously. He had never discouraged the belief that Japanese was somehow at the root of his English verse; had this been true, he ought to have had no trouble producing poetry in Japanese. Yet "the Japanese poet" had resisted the pressure to demonstrate the authenticity of his title, from his many Japanese poet friends, as well as enemies, eager to see his native poetic capabilities. Noguchi's late friend, Hōmei Iwano, had been among those urging him.

> He says, 'Seeing that you don't write in Japanese, your value is an unknown quantity . . .
> Write us some Japanese poetry, don't be bashful, I'll read it if I can!'
> I make another indifferent reply.[190]

The truth was that he had left Japan a raw seventeen-year-old with a half-completed college education, and had a good deal of catching up to do before he would be in a position to compete in the crowded field of Japanese poetry. While his linguistic deficiencies writing in the foreign language of English might be excusable, writing bad poetry in his native language would certainly damage his credibility. Whatever Japanese poetic thoughts had been rolling around in his mind among the fragments of Poe and Milton and other English poets as he composed his English poems had evidently not been in any sort of finished poetic form. And why should he risk exchanging his exceptional status as Japan's only English-language poet for that of an average, or possibly below-average, Japanese poet?

Postponing his emergence as a Japanese poet gave him time to consider questions of poetic style, and where to place himself in Japan's evolving field of poetic factions. The careers of Japan's early modern poets had been short: those of the first Shintaishi poets had not outlasted the decade of the 1880s in which they appeared. "The Younger Poets of Present Japan" that Noguchi had commended after returning to Japan had all left the field, or at least its forefront. Deferring his debut gave him the possibility of fitting himself into the new generation of poets, born in the late 1880s and early 1890s, who were inventing a new "new style poetry" in a more colloquial language, rejecting the literary airs favored by the earlier Symbolist group from which they were descended.

The new school had its roots in the short-lived Pan Society (*Pan no kai*, 1908-1912), whose name (alternatively taken to refer to the Greek god of music, or to the French-Japanese word for "bread") indicated its generally Western orientation. Originally organized by Hakushū Kitahara and a few other poets and Western-style painters, the group had quickly expanded to around forty members, including Noguchi and his new Keio

---

190. "Iwano Hōmei," *Myōjō* 2:3 (Aug. 1922), rpt. *Sanjō ni tatsu*, 116.

colleague, Kafū Nagai, and the young Junichirō Tanizaki; Bin Ueda, though somewhat distant in Kyoto, had been regarded as the intellectual leader of the group, which generally followed the Symbolist rather than Naturalist path among the competing literary ideologies of the day.[191]

Noguchi had ended his 1914 "Poets of Present Japan" with a glance at "two names, Hakushu Kitahara and Rofu Miki, to whose work special attention should be called." In the Japanese version of the book, he expanded his appreciation of the admirable, idiosyncratic approach of Hakushū, who managed, he said, to combine an "unrestrained and perhaps irresponsible indulgence of his own satisfaction" with a consideration of traditional aims of Japanese poetry, and thereby "discovered a new literary kingdom within the so-called 'old Japan.'" Meanwhile, Rofū had "sought a form of his beloved Western poetics within traditional Japanese art."[192]

Noguchi had made his first experimental appearance as Japanese poet with a group of nine poems, eight of them new, in the November and December 1914 numbers of Keio's literary magazine, *Mita Bungaku* (edited by Kafū Nagai from 1910 to 1916). He followed this, the next October, with a group of eleven Japanese versions of earlier English poems.

Noguchi often cited the first of the new poems, "Chō" (Butterfly), as a breakthrough. It took as its subject an epiphanic moment in his garden-facing room (at Engakuji, he would later say), when a butterfly (or moth in some versions) passed through a stream of light, and "Over the gray of the garden and my breast, suddenly large wings shone, and passed over like a giant in the air."[193] A decade later he called the effect "baptism of the imagination." "Although it is only a small moth in reality, if it received the baptism of the imagination, it taught me that it would be a huge phenomenon bigger than the actual thing."[194] It was, in effect, a rebuttal to Robert Young's dismissal of poetic exaggeration. Aggrandizement was not deception; it was, for a poet, a useful natural phenomenon. Still, enamored though he was with the concept, he was evidently dissatisfied with his expression of it in poetic form. He rewrote it, using different words, in an extended form, as a preface to Hiroko Katayama's tanka collection, *Kawasemi* (Kingfisher), in 1917, with an English version as well, Katayama being a leading translator of Irish literature. "Where is the old song I used to sing with high style and joy?" he wondered. "Oh, to rebuild a new song on the ruins of my heart."[195] He rewrote the poem again in 1921.[196] But he did not make the poem or his epiphany available

---

191. Noguchi recorded an interesting anecdote of the Pan Society's harassment by the police in 1911 in "The Japanese Government and the New Literature," *Academy*, 1 July 1911, 11.
192. SJP 111; *Nihon shikaron*, 206.
193. "Chō" (Butterfly), *Mita Bungaku* 5:11 (Nov. 1914), 123.
194. "Shi ni okeru sōzō no chikara" (Imaginative power of poetry), *Suwaru ningen no hyōron*, 66-67.
195. YN, "Lines," in Katayama Hiroko, *Kawasemi* (Tokyo: Chikuhakukai, 1916), 1-3.
196. "Chō" (Butterfly), *Nijūkokusekisha no shi* (Tokyo: Genbunsha, 1922), 7.

to English readers.

Another of the early Japanese poems took up the modernist "cult of ugliness" being promoted by modernist theorists like Marinetti and Pound, which Noguchi had encountered on his second visit to Britain a few months earlier. Entitled (for no evident reason) "F.O.," and afterwards, "Mudai" (Untitled), and then "Shū" (Ugliness), it begins,

> He is full of faults, I think; did someone say that the age of beauty is passed? Did someone say that in imperfection and ruin is a greater beauty?
> As you know, I wear the uniform of those moved by his ugliness, because there seems something fascinating in his failure.[197]

Two years later, that had become the first of his bilingual three-line poems, in the January 1917 *Mita Bungaku*, as we have seen:

> Full of faults, you say.
> What beauty in repentance!
> Tears, songs . . . thus life flows.

Another of the first group of poems, "Therefore I Am Me," attempted to sort out the question of the poet's connected and yet separated relationship with nature.[198] In his Japan Society "Japanese Poetry" lecture, he had raised the question, saying, "The Japanese poetry is that of the moon, stars, and flowers, . . . to sing the stars and the flowers in Japan means to sing Life, since we human beings are not merely a part of Nature, but Nature itself."[199] In "Therefore I Am Me," he speaks directly to the stars, moon, and trees, telling them, "You are not simply the background of my existence but part of reality." "My poetry and your poetry, can they flow into each other completely?" he wonders. Evidently, they could not: "My poetry is peculiar, independent—therefore I am me, and you are the moon, stars, and trees." Although an instructive exercise, it fell somewhat short of a major metaphysical breakthrough, which may be why he never reprinted it.

Noguchi's other *Mita Bungaku* poems displayed further facets of his developing conception of the modern poet's role, but he was evidently not yet ready for full exposure.

He was probably wise to wait. Amid the ferment of the war years and the influence of European modernism, a new generation of younger poets was emerging out of the bohemian atmosphere of the Pan Society and its aftermath. Hakushū Kitahara wrote prefaces for the debut volumes of two younger poets: Sakutarō Hagiwara's innovative, weirdly-disturbing *Howling at the Moon* (*Tsuki ni hoeru*), which appeared in the spring of

---

197. "F.O.," *Mita Bungaku* 5:11 (Nov. 1914), 114; "Mudai," *Nijūkokusekisha no shi* (1921), 50; "Shū," *Dai-ni hyōshō jojō shi* (1926), 96.
198. "Desu kara watashi wa watashi desu," *Mita Bungaku* 5:11 (Nov. 1914), 115.
199. *SJP* 18-19.

1917, eliciting Noguchi's lengthy, enthusiastic review in *Mita Bungaku*,[200] followed by Saisei Murō's collection of love poems, presented to Noguchi on New Year's day, 1918, which elicited another warm Noguchi review.[201] As in the case of Hiroko Katayama, Noguchi was generally supportive of younger poets who approached him. By supporting their work, he was not only passing on kindnesses he had received from established writers in his younger days, but also paving the way for his eventual acceptance as a respected elder among the younger generation of poets already supplanting his own.

Noguchi's next Japanese verse experiment, the Japanese versions of his "Little Poems," began appearing in 1917. They had been an interesting experiment, though mainly as a demonstration that haiku or tanka, in their traditional, or even new-style forms, were unlikely to emerge from his pen. Any serious hope for his future as a Japanese poet would have to be as a writer of longer, Western-style poems.

The three essays on poetry Noguchi wrote for the tanka magazine *Shiika* in 1918, which he drew on for his overseas "Japanese Poets and Poetry" lecture and essay, gave some indications of where his evolving understanding of Japanese poetry was heading.[202] In the first, he argued that poets in Japan were not "a race apart," or "special beings standing between humans and gods" as the Greeks thought, but simply "people of the same class as you and me" whose existence was treated as "a natural phenomenon, as natural as a flower or bird." Nor was the Japanese poet focused on the goal of "inspiration" as Western poets often were, considering it as something to "strive to attain, like a great piece of luck or a discovery"; instead, "what we value is the journey toward it—in other words, how we walk the 'path of poetry' by riding on the natural rhythms."

In the second essay, he quoted Sarojini Naidu's lines: "And all our Mortal moments are / A session of the infinite," which he felt well expressed the Japanese poet's approach. "To feel the infinite within the moment, and to understand the dynamic significance of the moment within the infinite—this is the true secret of art," Noguchi explained. "True art must embrace both the accidental and the absolute at the same time."

And in the third essay, he considered whether "we, as Japanese poets, might also wish to interpret our psychological state with the word 'madness' as in Western poetic theory, where words like 'poetic madness' or 'divine frenzy' are often used." Noguchi did not name any names, but he was likely thinking of Sakutarō Hagiwara, whose poetic talent was not

---

200. "Hagiwara Sakutarō kun no shi" (Sakutarō Hagiwara's poetry), *Mita Bungaku* 8:5 (May 1917), 79-89. The volume, and its sequel, *Blue Cat*, have been translated by Hiroaki Sato.

201. NY, "'Ai no shishū' o yomu" (Reading *La poésie de l'amour*), *Mita Bungaku* 9:2 (Feb. 1918): 103-08.

202. "Shiron dai ichi soku" (On poetry I), *Shiika* 8:1 (Jan. 1918): 2-4; "Shunkan to mushū" (Moment and eternity), *Shiika* 8:2 (Feb. 1918): 26-27; "Shiron dai san soku" (On poetry III), *Shiika* 8:3 (Mar. 1918): 12-14, rpt. "Shiron," *Nijū kokusekisha no shi*, 225-38.

easily separable from his psychopathology.[203] "But we must not value the turbulence of 'madness,'" Noguchi counseled; "rather, we must respect its stillness. That is to say, it is when 'madness' returns to a normal state that true poetry emerges for Japanese poets." What Japanese poets most wished to cultivate, he argued, was "a realm of purity and clarity" not the "states of confusion and disorder" that Western poets, "when their desire to be creators of passion or reformers of life rises to a peak, are never afraid to throw themselves into."

The *Mita Bungaku* poems, the "little poem" experiments, and his new essays on poetry were a start: a slight opening of a door. This time, though, he could not expect to steal quietly into the realm of poesy. Having deferred his debut so long while subjecting his peers, elders, and juniors to unreserved criticism, he could expect his belated efforts to be carefully scrutinized. It would be good if he did not stumble, but, being a trickster poet still, it might be better if he did. He could disarm his critics with a humorous confession, a self-deprecating, half-serious joke, about how Japanese readers found his Japanese poems quite awful, but excused them by saying his English poems were supposed to be quite good, while English readers made the exact opposite claim. "To tell the truth," he would admit, "I have no confidence in either language." Anxious expectations would evaporate in laughter, tension released, pressure gone. Then he would write as he wished, as he always had.

Fortunately, he had a powerful ally in his Keio colleague, Hiroshi "Tekkan" Yosano, who was preparing the second coming of *Myōjō*, the long-defunct, but fondly-remembered literary star of the early years of the century. For Tekkan, *Myōjō*'s rebirth offered a chance to reassert his importance in the literary world, alongside his now-famous wife, Akiko, whose fame as a tanka poet had long ago eclipsed his. For Yone, it would provide the vehicle he needed for his reentrance onto the poetry stage in a new role, that of a modern poet of the Japanese language.

What, then, would Japanese readers would make of this new Yonejirō Noguchi, reinvented for the 1920s as a semi-serious Japanese poet and unflinching critic?

---

203. As Yoshiro Hayashi states in "The Expressive Psychopathology of the Japanese Poet Hagiwara Sakutarō," *Psychiatry and Clinical Neuroscience* 52 (1998): 621, "the various and characteristic psychotic symptoms exhibited by this poet, such as phobic obsession, anxiety, depersonalization. persecution complex, sexual perversion and so on, have been the subject of much discussion and pathographic description."

Illustrations

1. Pier of Yokohama. Postcard. Private collection.
2. Nihonbashi district. *Tōkyō-shi chōbō no zu fūkei* (Prospective views of Tokyo), 1901.
3. "Mr. Yone Noguchi (From a photograph just taken in Tokio)." *The Critic*, December 1904.
4. Lafcadio Hearn, circa 1900. *The Life and Letters of Lafcadio Hearn*, Volume 1, 1906.
5. Waseda University. *Taiyō*, 1909.
6. Lafcadio Hearn's funeral procession. *The Critic*, January 1905.
7. Lafcadio Hearn's funeral: jinrikisha men outside Hearn's house. *The Critic*, January 1905.
8. Investiture of Yūshin Noguchi. Photograph. Collection of Jōkōji, Fujisawa.
9. *Chō* (Butterflies), 1904. Painting by Takeji Fujishima. Private collection.
10. Noguchi's New Year's greeting card, addressed to Frank Putnam and inscribed to Mrs. Putnam, December 11, 1904. Postcard. FPL, Bancroft Library.
11. Sinking of the *Pallada*, December 8, 1904. Photograph. Library of Congress.
12. Portrait of Yone Noguchi. *Kichō no ki*, December 1904.
13. Article in the *New York Tribune Sunday Magazine*, October 9, 1904.
14. Marchioness Oyama. *National Magazine*, July 1907.
15. "Wealthy Japanese Proud of His Fair American Spouse" (F. T. and Leona Kuranaga). *Los Angeles Herald*, November 27, 1904.
16. "Yone Noguchi's Babe Pride of Hospital." *Los Angeles Herald*, November 27, 1904.
17. The Peers' Club (former Rokumeikan). From a hand-colored photograph. Rijksmuseum, Amsterdam.
18. *Japan of Sword and Love*, 1905.
19. Mutsuhito, Emperor Meiji. Portrait derived from sketch by Eduardo Chiossone, 1888. Fame Portfolio Co., 1904. Library of Congress.
20. Hōmei Iwano. *Taiyō*, 1908.

21. A Los Angeles tent house. *Out West*, March 1904.
22. Sadayakko Kawakami as Oriye (Ophelia). *The Critic*, March 1905.
23. Ethel Armes. Advertisement for *The Story of Coal and Iron in Alabama*, 1910.
24. *The Summer Cloud*, 1906.
25. Bin Ueda, 1911. *Ueda Bin zenshū*, vol. 1 (Tokyo: Kaizōsha, 1929).
26. Kenzō Wadagaki. *Gleanings from Japanese Literature*, 1919.
27. "Pilgrims preparing to ascend Mount Fuji." Stereoview photograph, circa 1905. Private collection.
28. "On the Summit of Fuji." *Fuji San Photographed by Herbert G. Ponting* (Tokyo: Ogawa, 1907).
29. Isamu Noguchi, Léonie Gilmour and Albiana Gilmour at their newly-built house, late 1906. Photograph. Isamu Noguchi Foundation.
30. Léonie Gilmour and Isamu Noguchi in Los Angeles. Photograph (Isamu Noguchi as a child in California, at his home with Leonie Gilmour and his aunt or grandmother). Isamu Noguchi Foundation.
31. Kazutomo Takahashi, 1909. Keio University archives.
32. Ginza from Shinbashi. Photograph, circa 1910. Private collection.
33. Isamu Noguchi with two maids. Photograph by T. Miyauchie, Koishikawa, Tokyo. Isamu Noguchi Foundation.
34. Isamu Noguchi, circa 1907. Photograph. Isamu Noguchi Foundation.
35. Marie Stopes in her laboratory, 1904. Marie Stopes International Australia.
36. Yonejirō Noguchi in a 1909 Keio graduation album. Keio University archives.
37. Noguchi family, neighbors and servant (left), Tsushima, circa 1909. Photograph. Arita family collection.
38. Charles Warren Stoddard at Monterey. *Overland Monthly*, June 1909.
39. Ridgely Torrence. *The Younger American Poets* (Boston: Little, Brown, 1904).
40. Engakuji Naichokushimon (Engakuji Imperial Envoy's Gate). Postcard, circa 1908.
41. Kochō Baba, circa 1912. *Meiji bundan no hitobito* (Tokyo: Mita Bungaku Shuppanbu, 1942).
42. *Sanemori*. Woodblock print by Kōgyō Tsukioka. *Nōgaku hyakuban* (One hundred Nō dramas), 1922.

43. Ogyō no Matsu, Negishi, circa 1910. Postcard.
44. Hirobumi Itō. National Diet Library.
45. *Two Dragons*. Painting by Hōgai Kanō, 1885. Philadelphia Museum of Art.
46. *Ōna* (Old woman). Painting by Eisaku Wada, 1908. National Museum of Modern Art, Tokyo.
47. Isamu Noguchi and Ailes Gilmour, 1912. Isamu Noguchi Foundation.
48. The Chigasaki house. Photograph. Collection of Edward Marx.
49. Pro-immigration advertisement. San Francisco *Call*, May 1, 1913.
50. Edmund Gosse. *The Bookman*, January 1912.
51. Yoshio Markino. *When I Was a Child*, 1913.
52. Alvin Langdon Coburn. Self-portrait, May 19, 1922. *More Men of Mark* (New York: Knopf, 1922).
53. Yone Noguchi. Photograph by Alvin Langdon Coburn, December 14, 1913. *More Men of Mark*, 1922.
54. Georg Brandes. Photograph by Alvin Langdon Coburn, November 29, 1913. *More Men of Mark*, 1922.
55. John Masefield. *The Bookman*, March 1914.
56. John Masefield. Sketch by Max Beerbohm. *Fifty Caricatures* (London: Heinemann, 1913).
57. Robert Bridges. Photograph. Library of Congress.
58. George Bernard Shaw. Photograph, September 1914. Library of Congress.
59. W. B. Yeats. Photograph by G. C. Beresford, 1911. Private collection.
60. Ezra Pound. Photograph by Alvin Langdon Coburn, October 22, 1913. *More Men of Mark*, 1922.
61. Sarojini Naidu. Photograph. Sarojini Naidu Memorial Trust, Hyderabad.
62. Arthur Symons. Photograph by Alvin Langdon Coburn, September 22, 1906. *Men of Mark* (New York: Kennerley, 1913).
63. The Poetry Bookshop. *The Bookman*, February 1913.
64. Magdalen College. Postcard.
65. Dr. Herbert Warren. *The Graphic*, April 20, 1912.
66. Stratford-on-Avon. Postcard, circa 1914, Raphael Tuck & Son.
67. Jacob Epstein. Photograph by Alvin Langdon Coburn, January 24, 1914. *More Men of Mark*, 1922.
68. Roger Fry. Photograph by Alvin Langdon Coburn, February 27,

1913. *Men of Mark*, 1913.
69. *Joaquina*. Painting by Henri Matisse, 1911. National Gallery, Prague.
70. Charles Ricketts and Charles Shannon. Photograph by George C. Beresford, October 13, 1903. National Portrait Gallery.
71. Joseph Pennell's studio. *The Bookman*, February 1917.
72. Savage Club smoking room. *A Savage Club Souvenir* (London: Savage Club, 1916).
73. *Seer of Visions: Yone Noguchi*. Sketch by Edmond Xavier Kapp, 1914. *Personalities: Twenty-Four Drawings* (London: Secker, 1920).
74. *Genji Yūgao no maki* (The Yūgao chapter of Genji). Woodblock print by Yoshitoshi Tsukioka. *One Hundred Views of the Moon*, 1886.
75. Shimazaki Tōson. *Taiyō*, 1908.
76. Lothrop Stoddard, *The Rising Tide of Color Against White World-Supremacy* (New York: Scribner, 1920).
77. Eunice Tietjens. Photograph. The Poetry Foundation.
78. Tagore's arrival at Tokyo. *The Far East*, June 24, 1916.
79. Entrance to Sankeien. Postcard.
80. Manzaburō Umewaka as Yamanba. *Nōgaku Gahō*, July 1916.
81. *Kanojo no subete* (All about her). Painting by Seiji Tōgō, 1917. Kagoshima City Museum of Art.
82. *Ashi o arau onna* (Woman Washing her Feet). Painting by Sōtarō Yasui, 1913. Museum of Modern Art, Gunma.
83. *Murogimi* (Ladies in a Room). Painting by Eikyū Matsuoka, 1916. Kumamoto Prefectural Museum of Art.
84. *Eigo Bungaku*, September 1918.
85. Arthur Ficke, Matsuko Noguchi, Witter Bynner, Yone Noguchi, Hifumi Noguchi, Evelyn Ficke. Photograph. Beinecke Library, Yale.
86. Party for Bynner and the Fickes. *Shinchō*, May 1917.
87. Léonie and Isamu in Chigasaki. From a photograph (Isamu Noguchi as a child in Japan, with his mother Leonie Gilmour and Mr. Paget). Isamu Noguchi Foundation.
88. John Gould Fletcher. *Tendencies in Modern American Poetry* (New York: Macmillan, 1917).
89. James Cousins and Yone Noguchi, May 29, 1919. James Cousins, *The New Japan*, 1923.
90. *Life Mask of Francis Thompson* by Everard Meynell. Photograph by Sherril Schell. *The Life of Francis Thompson* (London: Burns &

Oates, 1913).
91. The *Tenyo Maru*. *The World's Work*, November 1908.
92. "Distinguished Visitors to America." *Shadowland*, January 1920.
93. Tamekichi Ōta. Photograph, 1926. Nippu Jiji Photograph Archive, Densho Digital Repository.
94. Reelection campaign advertisement for James Phelan. *Sunset*, July 1920.
95. Kyūin Okina. Photograph, 1924. Okina Kyūin Foundation.
96. Miller's Hights. *Overland Monthly*, February 1920.
97. George Sterling with Joaquin Miller and Charles Warren Stoddard. Photograph. Bancroft.
98. Flyer for Noguchi's transcontinental lecture tour, 1919-20. James B. Pond Lyceum Bureau, 1919.
99. Wheeler Hall, University of California. Photograph, circa 1917. Bancroft.
100. Harriet Monroe. Photograph, circa 1925. *Poetry* magazine archives.
101. Zona Gale's house, Portage, Wisconsin. Photograph. Private collection.
102. Zona Gale. *The Secret Way* (New York: Macmillan, 1921).
103. Yone Noguchi. Photograph by Arnold Genthe, 1919. Library of Congress.
104. Michio Itō. Photograph by Alvin Langdon Coburn, October 22, 1915. *More Men of Mark*, 1922.
105. *Head of Noguchi*. Sculpture portrait by Alfeo Faggi, 1923. Phillips Collection, Washington, D.C.
106. "Jap Picture Brides Are Japanizing California," *Washington Times*, January 4, 1920.
107. Stoddard's grave. Photograph by Edward Marx, August 2012.
108. Sailing calendar. Tōyō Kisen Kaisha, 1921.
109. Robert Nichols in his Tokyo University office. *The Bookman*, May 1923.
110. Arthur Waley. Photograph. Private collection.